Fighting Jim Crow in the County of Kings

FIGHTING JIM CROW
IN THE
COUNTY OF KINGS

The
Congress of Racial Equality
in Brooklyn

BRIAN PURNELL

UNIVERSITY PRESS OF KENTUCKY

The University Press of Kentucky,
scholarly publisher for the Commonwealth,
serving Bellarmine University, Berea College, Centre College of Kentucky, Eastern
Kentucky University, The Filson Historical Society, Georgetown College, Kentucky
Historical Society, Kentucky State University, Morehead State University, Murray
State University, Northern Kentucky University, Transylvania University, University
of Kentucky, University of Louisville, and Western Kentucky University.
All rights reserved.

Editorial and Sales Offices: The University Press of Kentucky
663 South Limestone Street, Lexington, Kentucky 40508-4008
www.kentuckypress.com

Maps by Bill Nelson.

The Library of Congress has catalogued the hardcover edition as follows:

Purnell, Brian, 1978–
  Fighting Jim Crow in the County of Kings : the Congress of Racial Equality in
Brooklyn / Brian Purnell.
      pages cm. — (Civil rights and the struggle for black equality in the twentieth
century)
  Includes bibliographical references and index.
  ISBN 978-0-8131-4182-4 (hardcover : alk. paper) —
  ISBN 978-0-8131-4183-1 (epub) — ISBN 978-0-8131-4184-8 (pdf)
  1. Brooklyn (New York, N.Y.)—Race relations—History—20th century.
2. Congress of Racial Equality. Brooklyn Chapter. 3. African Americans—Civil
rights—New York (State)—New York—History—20th century. 4. Civil rights
movements—New York (State)—New York—History—20th century. 5. New York
(N.Y.)—Race relations—History—20th century. I. Title.
  F129.B7P87 2013
  323.1196'0730747—dc23   2013001707
ISBN 978-0-8131-6558-5 (pbk. : alk. paper)

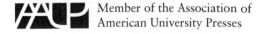 Member of the Association of
American University Presses

For Leana, and our children

CONTENTS

Maps and Tables

Maps

Tables

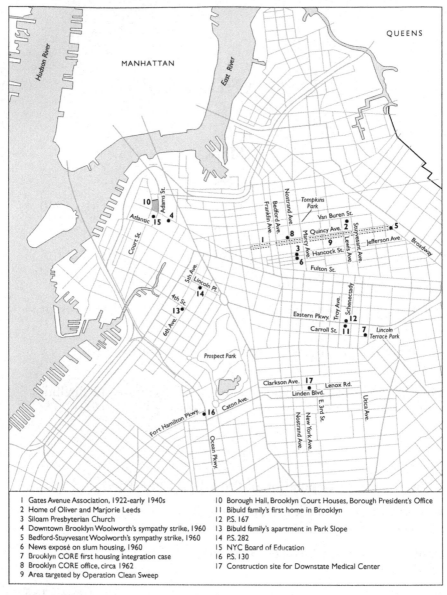

1 Gates Avenue Association, 1922–early 1940s	10 Borough Hall, Brooklyn Court Houses, Borough President's Office
2 Home of Oliver and Marjorie Leeds	11 Bibuld family's first home in Brooklyn
3 Siloam Presbyterian Church	12 P.S. 167
4 Downtown Brooklyn Woolworth's sympathy strike, 1960	13 Bibuld family's apartment in Park Slope
5 Bedford-Stuyvesant Woolworth's sympathy strike, 1960	14 P.S. 282
6 News exposé on slum housing, 1960	15 NYC Board of Education
7 Brooklyn CORE first housing integration case	16 P.S. 130
8 Brooklyn CORE office, circa 1962	17 Construction site for Downstate Medical Center
9 Area targeted by Operation Clean Sweep	

Locations of key persons and places mentioned in the text.

Nostalgia, Narrative, and Northern Civil Rights Movement History

> What was that place called Brooklyn really like back then, when you were growing up?
> —Elliot Willensky, *When Brooklyn Was the World,*
> *1920–1957*

> Only two things have remained constant in the history of race in Brooklyn: the social symbolism of color and the extraordinary maldistribution of power. The former has faithfully followed the career of the latter.
> —Craig Steven Wilder, *A Covenant with Color:*
> *Race and Social Power in Brooklyn*

On February 3, 1964, one of the largest civil rights demonstrations in U.S. history occurred. Nearly half a million students boycotted a racially segregated municipal public school system as parents and activists demanded a plan for comprehensive desegregation. Ten years after the Supreme Court's *Brown v. Board of Education* decision had declared racially segregated public schools unconstitutional, this city's government had failed to desegregate the school system. The integration movement rallied behind a Christian minister, a man known for his eloquent, trenchant sermons against racial discrimination and poverty. He transformed his church into a movement headquarters, which organized racially integrated "freedom schools" throughout the city. The man and the movement made history.

But this minister's name was Milton, not Martin; and his church was in Brooklyn, New York, not Birmingham, Alabama.[1]

Fighting Jim Crow in the County of Kings narrates the history of the early 1960s civil rights movement in Brooklyn, New York, through an analysis of the Brooklyn chapter of the Congress of Racial Equality (CORE). This book highlights the ways northern civil rights activists worked diligently for roughly five years to make forms of racial discrimination in New York City visible to the public and matters of political debate. The chapters that follow also examine how Brooklyn CORE developed a culture of interracial camaraderie through creative direct-action protest campaigns, and how it formed alliances with numerous community-based organizations and local civil rights activists, such as the Reverend Milton Galamison, referred to above. The demonstrations that clearly dramatized the everyday ways racial discrimination circumscribed black citizens' social lives and economic opportunities won Brooklyn CORE a seat at negotiation tables, and in some cases the chapter secured jobs, housing, and improved city services for black Brooklynites. Mostly, though, an assortment of power brokers—union leaders, elected officials, real estate tycoons, business managers, and school board officials—ignored Brooklyn CORE's protests, made limited concessions on certain demands, or used investigations and empty promises to delay dealing with widespread forms of racial discrimination. This book therefore pays close attention to Brooklyn CORE's shortcomings and failures. Its narrative invites readers to question how any band of activists could eliminate systematic forms of racial discrimination, especially without strong, clear, consistent government support, at both the local and national levels.

Most readers will come to this book familiar with what the civil rights movement veteran Julian Bond calls the "master" narrative of the movement. This version of the civil rights movement's history covers the mid-1950s through mid-1960s, when national leaders and nonviolent activists eradicated Jim Crow policies in the South. The movement achieved major legislative victories in the form of the Civil Rights and Voting Rights Acts and moved the country closer to true democracy, but it declined when activists brought nonviolent protest tactics north. There the civil rights movement encountered riotous African Americans, black power activists, and white backlash. This master narrative is essentially built on a series of dichotomies: North versus South; racial integration versus black power; nonviolent pacifism versus self-defense and violence; the "good early 1960s" versus the "bad late 1960s." Like many heroic histories, the civil rights movement's master narrative and its accompanying dichotomies overlook a far more complex, wide-ranging story. They limit civil rights movement history to roughly one decade of events that took place almost entirely in the South and in Washington, D.C. The rest of the country, and events leading up to and following the 1954–65 period, become background props in what is mostly a story of the nation's triumph over its long history of racial discrimination.[2]

Academic historians have developed three frameworks that challenge this master narrative's interpretations. The "freedom North" paradigm expands the geographic scope of the civil rights movement. These studies show that activists fought against local forms of racial discrimination outside the South before, during, and after civil rights movements emerged in southern cities and towns. Northern, urban activists created struggles for black economic and social justice that demanded employment opportunities, desegregated education systems, open housing, and increased political power. This scholarship has proven that the movement did not move from the South to the North; it was already there, and in some places it predated the more familiar southern movement. The history of the civil rights movement outside the South also shows that the national struggle against racism did not end when states or Congress passed antidiscrimination laws and enshrined voting equality; nor did northern civil rights movements fall apart because black power movements emerged. Black power, in many cities outside the South, represented continuations of earlier civil rights movement struggles, albeit with different philosophies, organizations, leaders, and strategies.[3]

The second framework, the "long civil rights movement" paradigm, expands civil rights movement history to before 1954 and beyond 1965. This expanded chronology locates the civil rights movement's origins in earlier periods, and it includes radical and conservative forms of activism. Black southerners fought against Jim Crow discrimination in the early twentieth century. They pushed for what the historian Tomiko Brown-Nagin has called "pragmatic civil rights": a protest agenda that challenged racial discrimination but protected the power and influence that black business owners and political figures wielded within the racially segregated system. The long civil rights movement paradigm also includes antidiscrimination activism spearheaded by the Old Left, particularly through studies of the Congress of Industrial Organizations and its efforts to unionize African American workers, and the antiracist activism of the Communist Party, U.S.A. The long civil rights movement framework reveals a history of struggle against American racism that unfolded over several decades, not merely one, and was marked by moments of continuity and change. It seeks to reveal how the wave of national activism that flourished in the late 1950s and the 1960s was an extension of earlier phases of antiracist activism. It also extends the chronology of the civil rights movement beyond the 1960s and examines the similarities and differences between the civil rights and black power movements.[4]

Last, a "black power studies" paradigm challenges a dichotomous separation of civil rights movement history from black power movement history. New histories of the black power movement have rejected representations that frame it solely as a denunciation of interracial organizations and nonviolence. They also go beyond chronologies that orient the black power movement's origins in the mid- to late 1960s and geographical frameworks that situate the black power movement only in cities outside the South. The black power movement was southern and northern, cultural, political, and economic, revolutionary and conservative, local, national, and international, feminist, and intergenerational. Postwar black power movement organizing, these studies have begun to demonstrate, took many different economic, intellectual, cultural, artistic, gendered, and political forms.[5]

In addition to these three paradigms, roughly three decades of revisionist work has produced numerous new vantage points from which to study civil rights movement history. In 1980 William Chafe's *Civilities and Civil Rights* paved the way for local studies of the long black freedom movement that offered new interpretations of the movement's leadership, political and economic effects, and long-term legacies. Civil rights and black power movement histories have also expanded to include histories of the post–World War II welfare rights movements. Studies of black women in the civil rights and black power movements have forced historians to analyze how competing leadership styles, social movement philosophies, and gender ideologies influenced the modern black freedom movement. Studies of memory and the civil rights movement have analyzed how, over time, modern politics has influenced which stories about the civil rights movement people have preserved. Histories of the black freedom movement in the Southwest and transnational studies have expanded even further civil rights movement history's geographic scope. Histories of the civil rights movement in parts of the country where Asian, Mexican, and Latin American activists fought alongside, and against, blacks and whites have pushed this field beyond a strictly black-white paradigm. All these revisionist approaches have placed the civil rights movement within much broader understandings of post–World War II U.S. and even global history.[6]

These revisionist interpretations have important critics, who raise questions about losing sight of a national synthesis narrative in favor of countless local studies; the dangers of blurring ideological lines between civil rights and black power; and stretching the chronological and spatial boundaries of the postwar black freedom movement to the point where the period loses its historical specificity. *Fighting Jim Crow in the County of Kings* does not argue against or attempt to disprove legitimate criticisms of the new paradigms. Over time, new branches of historical research, and the debates they generate, will inevitably foster new syntheses of postwar U.S. history. This book contributes to that new, emerging synthesis with a narrative analysis of interracial civil rights activism in one of the largest, most iconic postwar cities.[7]

This book's analysis draws from and contributes to several of the paradigms mentioned. Brooklyn CORE's early 1960s history shows that members of the Old Left did not disappear completely from political organizing with the onset of post–World War II anti-Communist McCarthyism but instead resurfaced and contributed to local civil rights movement campaigns. *Fighting Jim Crow in the County of Kings* highlights the Brooklyn movement's connection to the national movement, but at the same time it furthers the argument that the national movement was essentially a collection of many different local variations and activists. Unlike many other histories of the northern civil rights movement, this book takes up the interracial, nonviolent phase of activism as its main subject. Who those interracial activists were, how they formed a cohesive social movement culture, how they tackled racial discrimination in their city, what they achieved, where they failed, and what happened to them are the main subjects of this book.

Set in a city that had a growing Puerto Rican population, the history of Brooklyn CORE touches briefly on the ways African Americans and whites included Puerto Ricans in the early 1960s civil rights movement. Occasionally in its campaigns, Brooklyn CORE lumped together Puerto Ricans and African Americans, claiming that both groups experienced similar forms of racial discrimination. As migrants from largely agricultural societies subject to housing discrimination, underserved neighborhoods, inferior public schools, and racially segmented job markets, Puerto Ricans and African Americans shared similar social experiences in postwar New York City. But Puerto Ricans were also multiracial Spanish speakers from a Caribbean Island who carried their own diverse ideologies about race and politics. Brooklyn CORE activists may have assumed that Puerto Ricans and African Americans experienced the same racially discriminatory system in identical ways, but political coalitions between blacks and Puerto Ricans were never natural or inevitable. In fact, the history of Brooklyn CORE reveals that many times during the early 1960s interracial civil rights activists may have spoken for

Puerto Ricans in ways that Puerto Ricans might not have spoken for themselves.[8]

Forging strong African American–Puerto Rican ties was one challenge Brooklyn CORE faced, but maintaining members' political focus in the face of frustrating campaigns was the most significant factor that influenced Brooklyn CORE's rise and fall. Though most early histories of the civil rights movement posit that nonviolent, interracial protest failed in the North because northern blacks turned quickly to identity politics and violence, the history of Brooklyn CORE shows that the interracial northern civil rights movement declined slowly and several years before African Americans organized around black power, because direct-action protest could not produce tangible results quickly. Local power brokers in government, labor unions, and real estate never fully embraced the civil rights movement's agenda in such a way that reversed decades of racial discrimination in housing and employment, and activists grew disillusioned with these power brokers' penchant for delaying comprehensive desegregation plans. Some members of Brooklyn CORE became unfocused and traded direct-action protest targeting everyday forms of racial discrimination for massive symbolic demonstrations. The World's Fair "stall-in" demonstration in the spring of 1964 was effectively the last major campaign that Brooklyn CORE's interracial membership initiated. It generated a massive media response, but it showed that Brooklyn CORE activists no longer influenced public discourse in such a way that forced power brokers to negotiate, as it had done in previous years. A combination of internal and external factors led to the decline of the interracial civil rights movement in Brooklyn, but none of them really stemmed from the emergence of black power or black nationalism, which became prominent two years after the interracial, nonviolent, direct-action phase of Brooklyn CORE ended.

Not until Americans are able to see how the interracial phase of the northern, urban civil rights movement developed—not as some transplanted southern social movement being tested on foreign streets, but as a social movement that grew out of northern activists' specific needs to fight northern forms and systems of racial discrimination—will they be able to expand their notions of how the post–World War II black freedom movement unfolded on national terms, and the ways racism is truly an American dilemma, not merely a southern one.

Part of Brooklyn CORE's raison d'être was to make the effects of racial discrimination in the New York City visible and recognizable to ordinary citizens and municipal power brokers. Many post–World War II

New Yorkers simply ignored local forms of racial discrimination. They differentiated the supposedly benign forms of segregation in their city from the pernicious racism in the South. New York State had passed the nation's first law banning racial discrimination in employment in 1945. And no public signs designated some spaces in Brooklyn "Whites Only" and others "Colored Only." New Yorkers, therefore, used the term *de facto* to describe their racially segregated social and economic worlds. De facto implied that racially segregated neighborhoods and employment patterns resulted from chance, or they reflected natural choices. Either way, de facto differentiated the North's forms of racial difference from the South's de jure system of racial segregation, which was enforced by law. But this distinction was only superficially accurate: the absence of racist laws in the North was never tantamount to the absence of racism. The term *de facto* provided convenient cover for northerners' racial prejudices and for discriminatory policies that shaped the North. It allowed northerners to believe that, with respect to residential segregation and employment discrimination, they were not as bad as southerners, and that whatever racism existed in the North was simply unfortunate, but nonetheless uncontrollable. Or, as the novelist and essayist James Baldwin summarized, labeling New York City's segregation system de facto meant that "Negroes are segregated but nobody did it."[9]

As James Wolfinger and Jeanne Theoharis have argued, activists in northern cities struggled to address local forms of racial discrimination because "at times it hid in plain sight." Gunnar Myrdal put it this way when he surveyed American racism in the 1940s: "It is convenient for Northerners' good conscious to forget about the Negro." In the North, Myrdal concluded, a social paradox existed in which "almost everybody is against discrimination in general but, at the same time, almost everybody practices discrimination in his own personal affairs." Robert Self has correctly argued that the North and West were places where civil rights activists "confronted not a de facto racial segregation that was de jure Jim Crow's weak cousin but a complex and embedded structure of laws, social practices, public policy, municipal political machines and spatial history that produced ferocious racial and class inequality." Brooklyn CORE activists therefore had a two-part mission: to expose the ways racial discrimination and segregation resulted from individuals' specific choices and power brokers' weak enforcement of antidiscrimination laws, and to force bigots and reluctant power brokers to actively desegregate jobs, housing, schools, and unions. In short, Brooklyn CORE's campaigns against housing and employment discrimination, racially segregated public schools, and infrequent municipal services attempted to force New Yorkers to *recognize* and to *reverse* powerful, everyday forms of racial discrimination.[10]

To do this, Brooklyn CORE's civil rights campaigns had to address the borough's particular history of racism, as well as the specific ways postwar citizens developed a cult of nostalgia that conveniently allowed them to forget that history. The paradox of racial discrimination in a place like Brooklyn is that its effects were clear and visible, but the actions that brought it about were often disguised and difficult to discern. Rarely did white Brooklynites burn crosses on black people's lawns or hang "whites only" signs in public accommodations and vacant residences. The truth is that they did not have to use those methods to discriminate aggressively against African Americans.[11]

A case study of one homeowners' organization in Brooklyn, the Gates Avenue Association (GAA), details the ways white residents in north-central Brooklyn actively discriminated against black newcomers and, at the same time, worked hard to mask their bigotry behind color-blind language and surreptitious machinations. Members of the GAA would probably never have described their actions and ideas as overtly racist. The GAA's brief twenty-two-year history reveals how citizens contemplated all sorts of allegedly nonracist methods, from overt legislative action, to covert restrictive covenants, to veiled intimidation for the sake of "social order" when they planned and discussed ways to keep their neighborhoods all-white. As much as Brooklyn was known as a place where people of all colors and creeds came together to live and work, it was also a place where whites worked very hard to keep black people out of white communities. In mid-November 1922 roughly 120 white people who lived on Gates Avenue between Grand and Franklin Avenues formed the GAA to, in the words of its president, Frederick H. Paine, keep "the neighborhood free from encroachments by businesses, nuisances, etc." During its first meeting, and throughout its twenty-two-year history, GAA members discussed the neighborhood's "Negro question." Though the GAA addressed mostly civic affairs such as subway line expansion, suitable public bus routes, removal of elevated train tracks, playground construction, late postal deliveries, garbage disposal, traffic congestion on Gates Avenue, and new traffic lights, its members were consistently concerned with what one participant called "the widening spread of the black belt all over Brooklyn."[12]

White homeowners in the GAA debated whether public legislation or private practices were the best way to halt black settlement. When

Paine opened the GAA's June 3, 1924, meeting for "discussion of the Negro question," a man named Dr. Kevin suggested that "propaganda be undertaken in cooperation with other neighborhood associations towards some form of zoning or restricting to be done by the alderman." Two weeks later the GAA hosted representatives from the St. James, Monroe Street, and Clinton Avenue Associations. Frederick Paine read a letter from the Grand Avenue Association that stated, "The situation of the colored invasion can best be met by all persons being careful when they dispose of property, to put it in the hands only of reliable dealers." Others thought a legal restriction was best. A participant read excerpts of Atlanta's racial zoning laws. A prolonged, heated discussion ensued, after which the coalition of block associations decided to join the Civil Council of Brooklyn, an organization of more than eighty neighborhood associations that had access to the borough's Chamber of Commerce. Power in numbers, the GAA and its allies decided, would be the best way to thwart north-central Brooklyn's "colored invasion." With an expanded network of business leaders, realtors, and block associations, the participants agreed that "action can be initiated."[13]

The debate over whether to erect legal barriers against black citizens continued. Paine reported back from his meeting with Civic Council leaders that "the only remedy that has been devised" to keep neighborhoods all-white "is found in neighborhood solidarity and care in disposing of property." Dr. Kevin persisted in his argument "that legislation through the Board of Alderman is the only way to accomplish results." The GAA settled on a more passive-aggressive approach. If white residents did not welcome blacks into the area, did not advocate for amenities that would benefit black people, did not sell black people property, and did not extend to black people invitations to their churches, then black people would inevitably settle elsewhere. A real estate dealer, Miss Claxon, who was also a member of the Downing Street Association, attended the GAA's annual meeting in 1924. Her advice was "not to list property with unknown or questionable dealers and not to sell to people one does not know." Restrictive covenants became the most effective weapon white Brooklynites used to maintain racially homogeneous neighborhoods. In 1926 the GAA reviewed the wording of a real estate agreement signed in Washington, D.C., "where by residents of a neighborhood agreed not to sell to colored [people]." Miss Claxon once again encouraged her neighbors to deal only with real estate agents who had unofficial "whites only" policies. In addition to agreeing to work with realtors who discriminated against black people, GAA members undertook several civic campaigns whose sole purpose was to dissuade black settlement. Color-blind in language and in principle, these schemes served the GAA's racially discriminatory goals.[14]

For years the GAA petitioned the city to complete construction of the Fulton Avenue subway line and to raze the Fulton Avenue elevated subway trestle. GAA members hoped these initiatives would improve property values and "drive out less desirables." They reasoned that if home insurance premiums and mortgage interest rates increased, poor residents would have to move. "The colored element," warned Irving Hughes, a Fulton Street realtor, "is not likely to be able to hold their property very long with the increase in values." Debates over construction of a local playground also indicate the GAA's methods of discouraging blacks from moving into the area. In 1922 the GAA opposed building a neighborhood playground because the project required increased property taxes. By 1928, after the city fully underwrote the playground's construction expenses, the GAA changed its rationale for rejecting the project. Some argued that "heavy traffic" around the proposed play area made the project dangerous. Others claimed the playground would be built on unsafe terrain. Still others called the playground a needless expense. Coincidentally, by the late 1920s more black people had settled in the areas that surrounded the new playground's proposed construction site. In their meetings GAA members discussed how they feared "the race riot which a playground will invite" if it was located on the border between black and white neighborhoods. Black Brooklynites, on the other hand, fought vigorously for the new playground. They wrote articles that attacked white homeowners' opposition to the playground as reflections of their racial prejudice.[15]

As threatening as a new playground was to the area's racial demography, black churches were even more dangerous and foreboding. The GAA first addressed this issue in 1925 when it received word that the Washington Avenue Baptist Church and another church on the corner of Irving Place and Gates Avenue were "in danger to be sold to Negroes." By May 1927 two other black churches had opened in the vicinity: one on Grand and Lefferts and one on Irving and Gates. The GAA invited Amos Lamphere, a Manhattan realtor who lived on Cambridge Place in Brooklyn, to give an honest assessment of the area's future. Lamphere told GAA members they had nothing to fear, that in five years, with the expansion of the Fulton Street subway and the removal of the elevated train tracks, their community's property values would increase. Lamphere said that "the Washington Avenue church and one other church property are both now assured," but he gave no further detail. In the case of the Washington Avenue Baptist Church, white residents may have dissuaded blacks from purchasing that property when they invited speakers from the Ku Klux Klan to address the congregation. A Klansman, dressed in his hooded uniform, preached a Sunday sermon from the church's pulpit in the mid-1920s. Washington Avenue Baptist's pastor, the Reverend Robert McCaul, even claimed publicly that the Klan was necessary to preserve right and order. If crosses had not yet burned on black people's doorsteps, the message was clear that they soon might.[16]

As more black people from the South, Harlem, and West Indian islands moved to Brooklyn, the handful of blocks to which they were confined burst at the seams, and the GAA's plots to keep out black migrants eventually failed. But though it failed to ban blacks from north-central Brooklyn, the GAA's actions during the 1920s, 1930s, and 1940s, along with government and banking policies, indirectly turned the area into a black ghetto. The GAA's racial fears invited price gouging and rampant real estate speculation in the hopes of avoiding living alongside working- or middle-class black homeowners in racially integrated neighborhoods. Blockbusting realtors and real estate speculators who played on white homeowners' fears that black neighbors caused property values to plummet convinced GAA members to sell their properties for a song. They then resold the brownstone and limestone homes to black newcomers for large profits. To afford the high interest rates and exorbitant mortgages, black homeowners cannibalized properties to accommodate multiple rental units. Before 1930 Bedford-Stuyvesant was overwhelmingly white and fairly affluent. In 1920 Brooklyn's 31,912 black residents were scattered throughout different neighborhoods in the north-central area of the borough. But in 1935 the racial geography of the borough began to shift. North-central Brooklyn slowly turned solidly black. Housing in Bedford-Stuyvesant, Brownsville, and East New York decayed as redlining policies ensured that banks denied home improvement loans to property owners, and as more black residents doubled and tripled up in aging brownstones and tenements.[17]

The Home Owners' Loan Corporation (HOLC), a New Deal agency created in 1933 to prevent foreclosures and bank repossessions of property, made conditions in north-central Brooklyn worse. The HOLC functioned in the interest of lenders and housing developers by determining which areas in Brooklyn were "desirable" places for investments. HOLC agents created maps that coded an area's "desirability" with letters and colors. An area marked "A" and colored green was "well-planned" and "not yet fully developed." An area marked "D" and colored red had poor housing stock, "undesirable" residents, poverty,

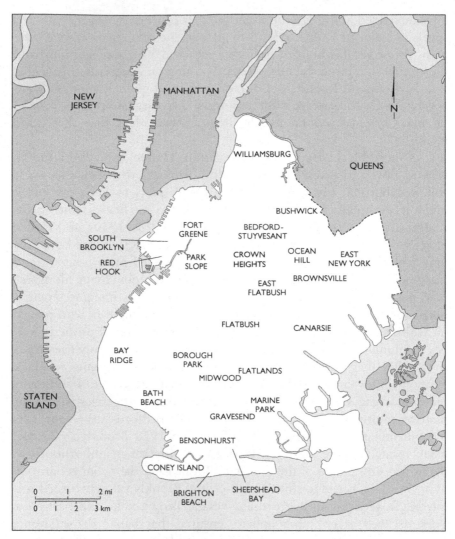

Major neighborhoods in Brooklyn, New York, since circa 1940 (based on Harold X. Connolly, *A Ghetto Grows in Brooklyn* [New York: New York University Press, 1977], 57).

and crime. The HOLC considered these redlined areas unsafe for mortgage investments.

To determine these grades HOLC agents surveyed an area's housing, with special attention to its age, condition, and occupancy rates. Surveys noted market demands for housing, transportation infrastructure, residents' occupations, and median income levels. The survey also noted a community's number of foreign-born people, its percentage of black

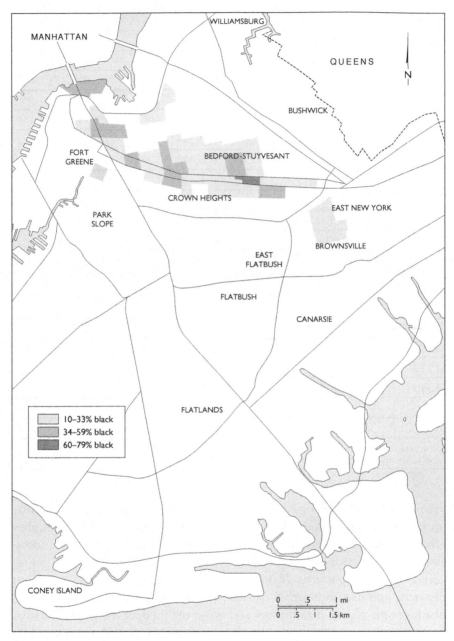

Black population in Brooklyn, 1930 (based on Harold X. Connolly, *A Ghetto Grows in Brooklyn* [New York: New York University Press, 1977], 56).

Table 1. White and Black Population of Brooklyn, 1900–1990			
Year	White	Black	Brooklyn's total[a]
1900	1,146,909	18,367	1,166,582
1910	1,610,487	22,708	1,634,351
1920	1,984,953	31,912	2,018,356
1930	2,488,815	68,921	2,560,401
1940	2,587,951	107,263	2,698,285
1950	2,525,118	208,478	2,738,175
1960	2,245,859	371,405	2,627,319
1970	1,905,788	656,194	2,602,012
1980	1,265,769	723,748	2,230,936
1990	1,079,762	873,620	2,300,644

[a] Includes Chinese after 1900 and Latinos separated out from white and black after 1970.
Source: Craig Steven Wilder, *A Covenant with Color: Race and Social Power in Brooklyn* (New York: Columbia University Press, 2000), 178.

Table 2. Concentration of Black Population in Bedford-Stuyvesant, 1930–1957			
Year	Blacks in Bed-Stuy	% of all Bed-Stuy	% of all blacks in Brooklyn
1930	31,215	12	45
1940	65,166	25	61
1950	136,834	51	66
1957	166,213	66	—

Source: Craig Steven Wilder, *A Covenant with Color: Race and Social Power in Brooklyn* (New York: Columbia University Press, 2000), 206.

people, and whether one of these groups was "infiltrating." A white, middle-class community, with low population density and high-quality housing stock, received the higher rating. Such standards, and the accessibility to government loans they granted, encouraged racially segregated residential patterns. Brooklyn's manufacturing areas, its waterfront districts, and its neighborhoods that were teeming with immigrants and black people received D ratings and were redlined as risky investments. Over time these redlined areas became more impoverished, overcrowded, and segregated by race and class.[18]

When property owners in north-central Brooklyn could not attain home improvement loans or sell for a profit, they held on to their homes, carved them into smaller units, raised rents, and crammed them with black people seeking residences. Bigots refused to rent apartments or sell homes to black families in other parts of Brooklyn, which would have relieved north-central Brooklyn's overcrowding and placed less strain on its housing stock. In 1940 Brooklyn's black population was 107,263. From the 1950s through 1960s its black population tripled, and Bedford-Stuyvesant became the epicenter of Brooklyn's black community. By 1970 Brooklyn's black population had mushroomed to well over 656,000, which made it one of the most densely populated urban areas in the country. Tens of thousands of incoming black people, many of them poor and working-class, who could not live in other sections of the borough, occupied decaying buildings in north-central Brooklyn and paid exorbitant rents. In effect, government policies, banking regulations, and the discrimination schemes of white homeowners' associations turned Bedford-Stuyvesant into a racially segregated, socially isolated, overcrowded, increasingly poor community.[19]

And yet many white and black people who came of age in Brooklyn during the postwar period did not see their borough as a place shaped by a history of racial discrimination. Many who lived in Brooklyn from the late 1940s through the early 1960s considered their borough an exemplar of the golden age of American cities. When Brooklynites looked back during the postwar decades, they saw a place of cohesive communities where functional families lived. They saw how the neighborhoods of their childhood formed around parishes, synagogues, and public schools. They remembered pictures of Franklin Roosevelt that hung on apartment walls, and that neither race nor religion barred individuals from full participation in democratic institutions or from social opportunity. Memory, and its nuanced re-creations of past events, can be a rich source for historical analysis, but nostalgia, with its fixation on how all that was good has been lost, distorts and bends the past around static figments of imagination. Nostalgia, when passed off as history, becomes an exercise in mythmaking. It is a product of forgetting the past as much as it is a result of selective memory. Nostalgia for Brooklyn's pre-1960s golden age was the product of amnesias regarding the ways racial discrimination powerfully shaped the borough's everyday life and socioeconomic history. Popular understandings of postwar Brooklyn's racial past, dominated by nostalgic, romantic views of the borough during the "good ol' days" of the 1940s and 1950s, became substitutes for its history.[20]

During and after the war, nostalgic Brooklynites lived in what Jack Newfield, a self-described "working-class journalist," remembered as a "magical" place of "open fire hydrants, the spaldeens [rubber balls], the double-bill movie theaters, the comic books in candy stores, the egg

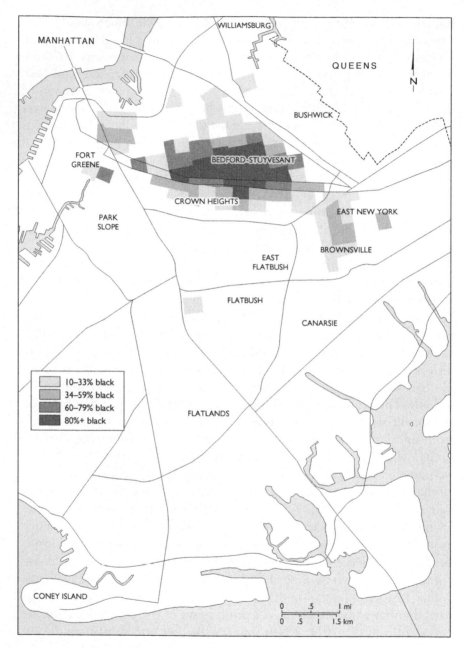

Black population in Brooklyn, 1950 (based on Harold X. Connolly, *A Ghetto Grows in Brooklyn* [New York: New York University Press, 1977], 131).

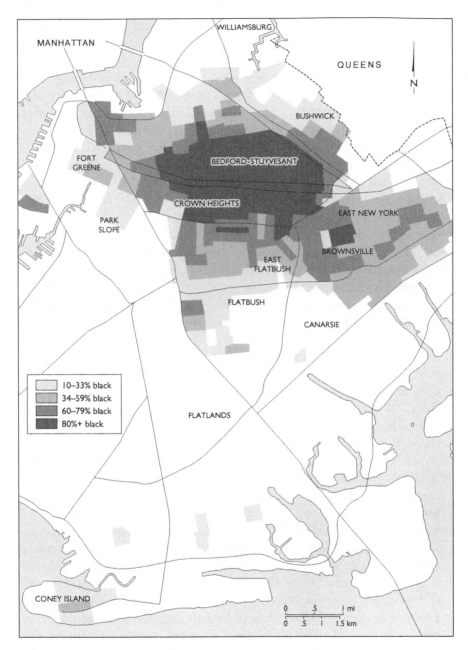

Black population in Brooklyn, 1970 (based on Harold X. Connolly, *A Ghetto Grows in Brooklyn* [New York: New York University Press, 1977], 133).

creams, the stickball games with a broomstick handle." Jim Sleeper, another journalist who pined for Brooklyn during the war years, was convinced that "countless people who left Brooklyn" shared a "grieving for a lost home." He waxed nostalgic: "The borough is haunted by ghosts for me"—not by specters of dead people, but of a dead place and a dead mood. "The whole density and intensity and diversity" of what Brooklyn was "just seizes me by the throat," he reminisced. Brooklyn at midcentury, Sleeper summarized, "was like a vast empire with beaches and hills and woods in Prospect Park, with tenements and rows and rows of infrastructure." Sleeper, who became one of the leading journalistic voices decrying the social unrest that beset Brooklyn and New York City after the 1960s, said that his "greatest dream is to be able to get into a time machine and make it 1952 and just roam across the borough." For Sleeper that was the time when, as the title for Elliot Willensky's popular history described, "Brooklyn was the world."[21]

Some African Americans who grew up in Brooklyn during those midcentury years also believed those were Brooklyn's golden years, and they looked at their past through rose-colored glasses. A committed Bedford-Stuyvesant-born community activist, local historian, and preservationist, Joan Maynard remembered that "with all the world upheaval" of the Depression and war years, "people had come into Brooklyn by the bushel, and there was hope and a spirit of optimism, a feeling we had made it." When the weather was warm, she left open the iron gate that protected her family's brownstone, went out "to dances and parties and came back at three in the morning, and there'd be singing in the street." She even remembered that during those raucous, joyous moments, "the milkman would wave to us" as he made his morning deliveries.[22]

For postwar Brooklynites, black and white, perhaps nothing better symbolized the belief that their borough represented the epitome of American democracy during the decade after World War II than the Brooklyn Dodgers. When the Dodgers were at the bottom, Brooklynites affectionately referred to the team as "bums," and much of the nostalgia that surrounds memories of the borough at midcentury is tied to the fabled baseball franchise considered "the team of the ordinary man" and its rise to national glory. A hapless ball club for much of the early twentieth century, Brooklyn's "bums" became a sensation during the postwar years, winning multiple consecutive pennants, forging an intense rivalry with the titans of baseball, their uptown neighbors, the New York Yankees, and developing a legendary roster of players: "Pee Wee" Reese, Gil Hodges, Duke Snider, Carl Furillo, Sandy Koufax, Roy Campanella, Don Newcombe, and, of course, Jackie Robinson, the first

African American player to break into the major leagues. With a southerner, a midwesterner from coal country, a Californian, a Jew, and African Americans on its all-star roster, the Dodgers seemed to embody the type of interracial, interfaith, democratic community that America promoted as its domestic identity during the wartime fight against fascism and the postwar struggle against global Communism. This melting-pot team became all-stars, and they did it by exuding an admirable work ethic and sense of team solidarity that epitomized both Brooklyn and the nation's spirit and culture. "You could be an Irishman, an Italian, and a Jew," Pete Hamill recalled, "and you could all be in Ebbets Field, sitting together, rooting for the Dodgers." Hamill, a Brooklyn-born, Irish-American journalist and writer, remembered how in June 1947, when he was just shy of his twelfth birthday, he saw Jackie Robinson get hit by a pitch, steal second, and score on a single, which evoked a "gigantic roar from all the Brooklyn tribes. Bed-Stuy was joined at last with Bensonhurst and Park Slope, Flatbush and Bay Ridge." According to Hamill, the Brooklyn Dodgers "had done more than simply integrate baseball. They had integrated the stands." Even if people did not live together, work together, or pray together, they all "were consumed by love of the Dodgers." The Dodgers—and by extension Brooklyn—appeared, as Marc Eliot wrote, to be a reflection of what America had supposedly fought for and won in World War II: "the right to live, work, and play alongside fellow Americans regardless of race, color, or creed."[23]

Thanks to the successful interracial, interethnic, interfaith Dodgers, postwar Brooklyn's identity grew beyond its status as bedroom community for the city's working classes. The borough became known for more than Coney Island, its onetime thriving breweries, its bustling port and shipping industry, its majestic bridge, and its ethnic ghettos of Jews and Italians. Brooklyn became a symbol of postwar American hope, liberalism, and democracy. "In the years after the war," recalled the Brooklyn-born novelist Alan Lelchuk, "nothing symbolized the feeling of hope and optimism more than the Brooklyn Dodgers." Racial integration made the team "truly representative of the borough, which at that time flourished as a unique place." Not only had Brooklynites survived the Depression and the war, but, Lelchuk remembered, Robinson and the Dodgers made residents feel they "were on the way up. . . . There was a feeling that merit would be recognized. It was like coming into a bright light." A future New York State Assembly representative, Roger Green, who grew up in Bedford-Stuyvesant, recalled, "Jackie Robinson breaking through the color line in the years following the war gave folks the perception that there was something different about Brooklyn, that it was a special kind of place." Bill Feigenbaum attended Dodgers games with "local synagogue groups, left-wing groups," and remembered how "all the left-wingers, who were mostly Jews, were great champions of liberal causes at that time." For Feigenbaum and others with progressive politics, "it was a big victory when Robinson got into the major leagues. We'd sit in the bleachers and watch Jackie Robinson and cheer more for him than anyone else."[24]

By the late 1940s this sentiment about Brooklyn had indeed become national. In 1949 Count Basie's rendition of Buddy Johnson's jazz standard, "Did You See Jackie Robinson Hit That Ball," which celebrated the era's greatest black major league players, especially Robinson for his tremendous skill and appeal to all fans, became one of the country's most popular songs. When the Dodgers won the 1955 World Series, many Brooklynites exulted, as they had when Japan surrendered and World War II ended. The Dodgers, who had been for so long a punch line, were now World Champions. "A team that had been one of comedy and futility," Lelchuk recalled, "now, suddenly, with the introduction and acceptance of Robinson and then other black players, became one of the two great teams of the postwar era." The team's victory on the field and in its racial and religious integration became important identity symbols for Brooklyn and Brooklynites. In the minds of residents and fans, the Dodgers and all the ways the team represented grit, pride, and democracy *were* Brooklyn. "Dodger fans were the salt of the earth, the common folk who believed in social progress, the American way, the underdog," said Joel Berger, a Brooklynite who went on to become a professor of science education. "Where did Jackie Robinson come to if not to Brooklyn?"[25]

As the borough seemed to develop a common multicultural identity, epitomized by Robinson and the Dodgers, a generation of black people came of age. Robert Law, who joined Brooklyn CORE in the 1960s, had memories of Brooklyn that were similar to those of many other blacks of his generation. Born in 1940, Law grew up in the Kingsborough housing projects on Bergen Street and Buffalo Avenue in the Crown Heights section of Brooklyn. At that time, before the borough's black population exploded in the 1950s and 1960s and was practically confined to the north-central sections of Brooklyn, Law's neighborhood was predominantly Italian and Jewish. Law recalls how "most of the black people lived in the projects." The Kingsborough Houses were some of the earliest large-scale housing projects built in Brooklyn in the postwar period, and during the 1950s they were predominantly working-class, interracial, and harmonious places to live and raise a family. "It was a very cohesive community," Law remembers. "Every adult in Kingsborough had dominion over me. Everybody's parent was a parent. They could yell at you. They could tell you to go home, it's dinnertime. They could tell you you're not supposed to be playing ball on that wall, and we were compelled to honor and respect them."[26]

For southern, working-class, black migrants like Law's parents, this was an ideal place to live. They took steps to shield their children from the racism they had known living in the Jim Crow South. Growing up, Robert Law was not made aware of the politics of racism: "Our parents never said anything," he recalled. When he traveled to the South, his family always drove. They never flew or took a train, and they never told the children why. As Law tells it, "They never told us that they couldn't eat in the dining car of the train. They never told us they couldn't stop in restaurants along the way. They made accommodations for racism but they never told the children." Boys who grew up in the Kingsborough Houses with Robert Law socialized in integrated groups. Blacks, whites, and Puerto Ricans played together with few interracial altercations. "When we played," Law recalls, "we did everything together. We never had a fight among ourselves, we fought other people, but it was a very innocent time."[27]

Looking back, however, Law recalled some instances when whites discriminated against him. A junior high school teacher discouraged Robert Law and other black students from taking the tests for New York City's specialized high schools, and she was angry when Law took and passed the entrance exam for the High School of Art and Design. According to Law, "She said that had she known we were taking the test she never would have let that happen." As a young teen, Law also tried to get a job cleaning the kitchen of a popular local diner. He and his Italian American friend Junior Mercochio would go every summer and ask for employment: "Whenever we went they would say, 'No, the job's already taken. Come back Easter.' We'd come back . . . and they'd say, 'Oh you're too late, the job's already taken.' It never occurred to us that those jobs were set aside for white kids only, and because Junior Mercochio was with me, they wouldn't hire him either."[28]

For the most part, however, Law does not remember racial discrimination shaping his or others' childhood experiences. In the mid- to late 1950s black and white kids from Kingsborough Houses went to movies together, fished together in Prospect Park, and sat together at Ebbets Field to watch the Brooklyn Dodgers. In his memories, black children never let racial discrimination discourage them from achieving their goals or befriending whites. Law said his interracial cohort of playmates "just assumed that everything was fair and if we'd run into resistance we thought they were just mean people."[29]

Perhaps the title of the 1950 book by the *Brooklyn Eagle* reporter Ralph Foster Weld summarized best the popular perception of Brooklyn's new position in local and national identity. By the postwar years, people in Kings County who had long been known for their peculiar accents and for living in Manhattan's shadow could say with confidence, "Brooklyn is America." Brooklyn's working-class whites and blacks, Jews and Christians, and people with left-leaning politics may have fond memories of their borough, but neither Brooklyn nor New York City, with its unique brand of political and social liberalism and cultural cosmopolitanism, was ever immune to the racial, religious, and political prejudices that shaped postwar America. Despite the powerful hold nostalgia has on many people's memories of postwar Brooklyn, some black and white Brooklynites, both ordinary people and well-known public figures, could never forget how much racial discrimination shaped everyday life in their postwar neighborhoods and schools.

After the famed historian John Hope Franklin accepted a full professorship at Brooklyn College and chairmanship of its all-white History Department, an event publicized on the front page of the *New York Times*, he came in contact with the full force of Jim Crow racism in Brooklyn. Whenever Franklin attempted to purchase one of the stately homes in a neighborhood that surrounded the college, every single private seller and realtor told him the homes listed for sale were no longer available. After they met Franklin in person, realtors who had made appointments with him over the phone or by letter suddenly had no properties for sale.[30]

Racial barriers did not end after Franklin found an owner of a house near Brooklyn College willing to sell to him. They extended into his ability to secure a mortgage. Franklin learned that, since he had a policy with New York Life Insurance Company, he could access the company's home mortgage pool. But when the insurance company called Franklin to discuss the details of his loan, the agent started the conversation cryptically. "I don't want you to misunderstand this," the New York Life Insurance home mortgage representative told Professor Franklin, "but we've done a lot for you people." He then told Franklin that the insurance company "can't lend you the money to buy the house you want because it's fifteen blocks away from where blacks live, and you will be jumping blocks, and therefore we can't do that. If you want to buy a house in a black neighborhood we can let you have the money." Seething with rage, Franklin contemplated saying "to hell" with Brooklyn's racism.[31]

Eventually, Franklin was able to purchase a home in the all-white area that surrounded Brooklyn College with a white intermediary's help. Franklin likened his situation to that of a black sharecropper who could secure a bank loan only through the assistance of his white landowner. Franklin's lawyer's father negotiated with a realtor on the celebrity professor's behalf. But even on the day his family moved in, Franklin's new next-door neighbor refused to move his car, which had blocked access to the driveway that led to Franklin's home. In Franklin's eyes, even after World War II, racial discrimination in America, North and South, was still bad. "The war hadn't changed things," he recalled. "And what little that had happened after the war had not changed things by 1957, or not enough, so that I was not free to buy a house in Brooklyn."[32]

Some whites also recall how separation and segregation were powerful parts of social life in Brooklyn after World War II. John Karlen, an actor in television and movies since the 1960s, was born in Brooklyn in the early 1930s and grew up there. He recalled how neighborhoods were strictly divided by race, religion, and ethnicity. "You had your own little piece of turf," Karlen remembered. And despite the rosy memories of postwar unity, Karlen remembered how "everyone in Brooklyn was always separated by all this supposed 'togetherness.'" Jerry Della Femina, who grew up in the postwar Italian neighborhood of Gravesend, echoed this sense of provincial isolation and prejudice against outsiders, no matter what their color or creed. If people were not Italian from Avenue U, Della Femina recalled, he and his neighbors shunned them, either mentally or through violence: "The Italians in my neighborhood were consistent: they were as bigoted about 'the Jews' as they were about Protestants and anything or anybody who wasn't Italian Catholic. About the Irish, they were violent. Not so the blacks. For the Italians of my youth the blacks simply didn't exist. We had no maids coming into our neighborhood in the morning and then leaving at night. We had no black laboring class working for the store owners on Avenue U. We didn't see blacks. They were from a foreign country." That foreign country was only a few miles away in the north-central sections of Brooklyn that included Bedford-Stuyvesant, but for Della Femina and his neighbors, it might as well have been across the Atlantic Ocean.[33]

Black people living in Bedford-Stuyvesant could never see whites as living in a foreign country. Because black Brooklynites interacted with white police officers, teachers, sanitation workers, businesses owners, bus drivers, and politicians all the time, black people did not have the freedom to imagine a social world where they did not see whites or where whites did not exist. As residential segregation patterns hardened, and Brooklyn's black population grew, Bedford-Stuyvesant increasingly suffered from poor city services, crime, under-resourced public schools, joblessness, overcrowding, drugs, serious housing deficiencies, and general neglect by landlords and residents. Residents of Bedford-Stuyvesant, such as Rita Heinegg, who grew up on Nostrand Avenue near Fulton Street, experienced these issues as a part of their everyday lives.

Shortly after Heinegg's birth in October 1944, her parents, who had left school after the third grade, quit farming in Seaboard, North Carolina, a small town near the Virginia border, for work in New York City. Barred from the longshoremen's industry by discriminatory unions, Rita Heinegg's father found similar work loading and unloading cargo with the Pennsylvania Railroad. Work in the "steamer doors," as Rita Heinegg remembers, was reserved for blacks, and "they did the same job" as longshoremen, "just for less money." Rita Heinegg's mother found work in Brooklyn as a domestic, in a local sweater factory, and as a babysitter. The family moved to Bedford-Stuyvesant in 1945, where they lived on the top floor of a three-floor walk-up for fourteen years. Excessive trash was only one of the things Rita Heinegg remembered about the neighborhood in the late 1950s and early 1960s. "It wasn't a very nice neighborhood," she recalled. "You would wake up in the morning and we were seeing needles in the stairwell." To avoid embarrassment about where the family lived and to enroll the children in a better public school, Rita Heinegg's mother would lie about their address. "We used to use our aunt's address so that we didn't go to P.S. 3, which was only two blocks away. She lived right outside Gates Avenue. It wasn't much better. It was still only a few blocks away but my mother felt that there was a little bit better school."[34]

Finding quality public education was a growing challenge for black Brooklynites. As a child attending P.S. 44 on Madison Street in Bedford-Stuyvesant, Roger Green remembered that he "always felt, from the first grade on, very oppressed and repressed in the public school system. . . . All the kids were black, but the whole power structure was white except for one African-American teacher." Grade groupings by intelligence seemed to follow color-coded patterns. "We had 1-A, which might have been the smartest, and those children were the lightest-skinned." When he attended the "integrated" schools in Crown Heights, "it was the same kind of thing: the white students were always in the smarter classes and the black students in the so-called slower classes." Such stark divides "really implanted in the minds of some of the children" a message that they were "just not as bright." Green remembered that people in Crown Heights were "very civil." Only once did he remember a white boy calling him and another black student "nigger," but no student or teacher came to their defense. When Green attended Winthrop Junior High school, which was an integrated school located near a predominantly Italian American section of Brooklyn commonly called Pigtown ("because people used to raise pigs in their backyards"), he and other black teenagers "made sure not to wear our better clothes on Fridays, because we knew we would have to fight our way home. The white kids from Pigtown . . . would waylay us." Judy Berger, who worked in Franklin Delano Roosevelt High School when it opened in 1965, remembered how, at that time, the school was located in a lower-middle-class Italian neighborhood. Black students who traveled there by subway from other parts of Brooklyn were greeted by the words "Niggers go home" scrawled on the front of the school building. The ten-block walk between the school and the black students' subway stop "became a gauntlet," and black students were "frequently beaten up." In the school, however, Berger remembered that "tensions were less pronounced." Black students from other neighborhoods became leaders in the high school student government and performed well in their classes.[35]

Not surprisingly, tensions cut both ways. Over time, as black majorities developed, young blacks bullied and harassed whites who seemed vulnerable or who transgressed the invisible social lines that demarcated black neighborhoods from white ones. Distrust and anxiety festered. When postwar politicians, journalists, academics, and citizens attempted to analyze the effects of decades of discriminatory practices—in housing, jobs, school systems, and politics—and urban interracial tensions, they often explained away patterns of racism with arguments about destructive "cultures of poverty." Black people's bad behavior and poor choices, many argued, not whites' conscious discriminatory practices and policies, had created the widespread poverty, racially segregated neighborhoods, stressed housing stock, and substandard schools that came to characterize black urban communities. According to these theories, the solution to the problems of the black ghetto was for black people to get a handle on their community's crime, education, family structure, and work ethic.[36]

But what these arguments failed to recognize is that the levels of poverty and the inequality in housing stock, job options, educational systems, and municipal services, as well as the social alienation that fostered crime, stressed community organizations, and fractured families, all of which metastasized during the postwar period, could never have been born from people's culture and behavior alone. The urban crisis that tore through American cities like a tornado after World War II was a product of decades of policies, bigotries, and fears directed against hundreds of thousands of black residents. Many Brooklynites, white and black, developed nostalgic amnesia and viewed their borough's postwar years as a time only of cohesion and unity. They blamed black Brooklynites' poverty and struggling neighborhoods solely on black people's behavior, and they forgot about organizations like the GAA, about redlining and blockbusting, and about realtors, lenders, and neighbors like those John Hope Franklin encountered. Part of the way Jim Crow racism worked in the North as it did in the South was to make black people completely responsible for the social and economic effects of white racism.

In the early 1960s the interracial membership of Brooklyn CORE chose to deal directly with their borough's history of racism and discrimination. Because of Brooklyn CORE's dynamic activism during the first half of that momentous decade, try as they might, New Yorkers could not totally ignore the realities of racism and segregation in their liberal, cosmopolitan city.

From 1960 to 1964 Brooklyn CORE's interracial, nonviolent, direct-action protest campaigns, its audacious and dynamic demonstrations, and its masterful manipulation of the media forced average citizens and municipal power brokers to recognize the racial discrimination that shaped their society. Brooklyn CORE possessed a unique ability to create dramatic direct-action protest campaigns that seized on the everydayness of racial discrimination in the lives of black Brooklynites and made that inequality visible and palpable. But the problems that Brooklyn CORE tried to correct proved far too difficult for any one local protest group to redress through direct-action protest campaigns and without massive assistance from the state. Racial discrimination was too ingrained in the city's banking industries, real estate and housing practices, machine politics, public education, craft unions' apprenticeship programs, unions' seniority rules, religious institutions, policing practices, and individuals' ideologies concerning community composition and public safety. To reverse the racially discriminatory patterns that determined most black Brooklynites' employment opportunities, housing options, the quality of their neighborhood's public schools, and the level of municipal services their neighborhood received required a greater exercise of political and social power than one protest group, even one as dynamic and creative as Brooklyn CORE, and its local allies could attain.[37]

Activists in Brooklyn CORE drew inspiration for protest campaigns from their local, everyday context, and they used the quotidian nature of racial discrimination in Brooklyn to fashion dramatic demonstrations that made supposedly invisible forms of racial discrimination visible for others to witness. Brooklyn CORE was able to do this because of its blend of seasoned community organizers, movement veterans, many of whom learned about interracial direct-action social movements from their involvement in the Communist Party, and committed and energized newcomers (see chapter 2). During the early 1960s, but especially from 1961 through the end of 1963, Brooklyn CORE's campaigns drew attention to patterns of racial discrimination in housing (see chapter 3), employment (see chapter 4), municipal services (see chapter 5), and public education (see chapter 6). Like grassroots activists in the South, especially those in the Student Nonviolent Coordinating Committee, members of Brooklyn CORE often debated whether their movement's main strategy should be direct-action protest or community organizing that fostered black people's empowerment. The chapter also weathered internal storms that brewed when more politically influential power brokers, such as a coalition of powerful black ministers, jockeyed with Brooklyn CORE for leadership of a popular protest campaign, or when outsiders sought to spread violence on a Brooklyn CORE picket line, both of which happened during Brooklyn CORE's campaign against discrimination in the building trades industry (see chapter 7). Brooklyn CORE's interracial membership was able to exist and thrive even as it debated the role of whites in the black freedom movement, the effect of violence on a nonviolent movement, and the best ways to fight for black political, social, and economic empowerment.

When Brooklyn CORE targeted the opening day of the 1964 World's Fair with a traffic snarling "stall-in" (see chapter 8), its internal culture began to crack. Members not only were frustrated with and exhausted by several years of partial victories, but also lost sight of the power of orchestrating campaigns with clearly defined targets and goals. Brooklyn CORE, like the larger northern civil rights movement of which it was a part, developed a political movement and a discursive attack against the racism that shaped black citizens' everyday experiences. Brooklyn CORE's demonstrations attempted to strip the "culture of poverty" discourse of its explanatory power by revealing racially discriminatory policies and practices that shaped social and economic life in the city. But with the stall-in Brooklyn CORE's tactics and discourse had become less connected to tangible, specific instances in which systematic racism socially and economically disadvantaged black people. When that happened, Brooklyn CORE's direct-action protest lost its power to uncover the ways racism in the North was both hidden in plain sight and maintained by specific practices that perpetuated social and economic structures of white privilege.

After the stall-in, Brooklyn CORE's veteran members were ready to move on to other forms of activism. Because, in the minds of many citizens, the stall-in had made Brooklyn CORE synonymous with unfocused militancy, the chapter ceased to be a dynamic, productive social movement organization. Its interracial direct-action phase was effectively over. A new Brooklyn CORE, with different tactics and a leadership cadre shaped by black nationalist ideology, emerged in the late 1960s, along with the national movement's shift toward black power. These turns toward a black power movement and black nationalists' rejection of interracial civil rights activism did not overlap, or replace, the interracial action-oriented membership of Brooklyn CORE. That culture and movement had already faded away slowly over the course of nearly two years before black nationalists and black power emerged in Brooklyn CORE. Black power did not forcefully replace the civil rights movement in Brooklyn so much as it filled in the ideological and political vacuum left by the inability of interracial activists and liberal power brokers to alter significantly the structures of racial discrimination that shaped social and economic life in the city.

Because the black power movement was such a diverse and dynamic part of urban politics and black people's political, cultural, and economic lives, black power in Brooklyn deserves its own study. This book's conclusion only hints at the ways black nationalists and black power activists emerged in Kings County. This book's main purpose is to uncover the early 1960s interracial civil rights movement that arose in Brooklyn, New York. Brooklyn CORE was a dynamic and audacious force in New York City protest politics. Its successes and shortcomings reveal a great deal about the history of racial discrimination, and local attempts to change that history, in the urban North. Brooklyn CORE also shows that the post-1960s history of urban crisis was not predestined. Black urban communities did not have to suffer such traumatic social and economic decline during the decades when fiscal austerity, deindustrialization and automation, and conservative politics eviscerated urban social safety nets and exacerbated ghettoization of poor black people. Northern urban interracial nonviolent civil rights movement activists attempted to use direct-action protest to bring systematic racism to the attention of liberal northerners, and to alter those patterns by attacking racial discrimination in housing, schools, jobs, and municipal services. They faced great opposition in the form of willful ignorance and half-hearted reform attempts. That Brooklyn CORE tried to eradicate racism, and the reasons it did not fully succeed, provides some much-needed insight into why racism and racial and class segregation persisted in American urban life during the latter half of the twentieth century.

2

"PASS THEM BY! SUPPORT YOUR BROTHERS AND SISTERS IN THE SOUTH!"

The Origins of Brooklyn CORE

We were the first to picket in the North. We were the first to call for a nationwide boycott. We were the first to enter into negotiations with the managements of the chains.
—James Robinson, national director of CORE, 1960, on CORE's support of the student sit-in movement

I was impressed with the militancy of their demeanor. They were clean. They were neat. They were forceful in what they had to say.
—Maurice Fredericks, speaking in 2001 about the first time he saw Brooklyn CORE members picketing Woolworth's

CORE's Early History, 1942–1960

The Congress of Racial Equality (CORE) formed in Chicago in 1942. Initially, CORE was a spin-off group of an interfaith, pacifist organization called the Fellowship of Reconciliation (FOR). In the early 1940s a handful of FOR members formed CORE as an organization committed solely to attacking racial segregation in America. Like FOR, CORE was committed to philosophies of nonviolence promoted by the Indian anti-colonial nationalist and pacifist leader Gandhi. The other pillar of CORE's principles was its strict devotion to interracial membership. CORE hoped to create an interracial, nonviolent army that would end racial segregation in America with campaigns that employed what Gandhi called *satyagraha,* which translates as "soul force" or "truth force."

CORE founders believed that local chapters' public displays of interracial solidarity and disciplined use of nonviolence would transform America into a truly color-blind democratic society.[1]

During CORE's first five years local chapters formed in nineteen cities, but in that time six of the groups disbanded. All these chapters were outside the South, and most were located in the Midwest. CORE also created a central committee, called the National Action Council (NAC), which was headquartered in New York City. In 1947 the NAC sponsored the Journey of Reconciliation, which sent interracial teams into the South to test local compliance with the Supreme Court's ruling in *Morgan v. Virginia* (1946). In *Morgan* the Court declared that racially segregated accommodations on interstate buses and trains and in depot waiting rooms were unconstitutional. CORE hoped the Journey of Reconciliation would bring national attention to racial segregation in the South, but other than a handful of arrests and one violent showdown in Chapel Hill, North Carolina, the campaign did not attract much notice. CORE limited the journey to the upper-South states of Virginia, North Carolina, and Kentucky, where few whites knew about the *Morgan* decision and local law enforcement paid the CORE activists little attention. Significantly, CORE did not repeat this strategy in 1961, when it initiated the Freedom Rides and sent those interracial teams to the Deep South, where they encountered bombings and beatings and focused the entire country's attention on CORE's nonviolence and the brutality of Southern segregation.[2]

But CORE almost did not survive the 1950s. From New York City the NAC struggled a great deal to create and support vibrant, active chapters. In the early 1940s CORE chapters in Columbus, Chicago, Cleveland, Denver, Detroit, Los Angeles, and New York, among other places, addressed local forms of racial discrimination in housing, restaurants, barber shops, amusement parks, beaches and other public places, and employment. Their victories were often limited in scope. CORE chapters might successfully desegregate a downtown roller-skating rink or open up housing for a handful of black people, but the process CORE chapters had to follow was prolonged and laborious. First, members thoroughly investigated potential racial discrimination. Then CORE members attempted to use moral suasion tactics, such as appeals to democratic and Christian ideals, to change bigots' hearts and minds. If that failed, CORE members threatened to wage a direct-action protest campaign. At first, this was only a threat that CORE hoped would leverage a negotiated settlement. If negotiation efforts stalled without any progress on CORE's demands, CORE members finally initiated nonviolent direct-action protest in the form of pickets, sit-ins, and boycotts. Such drawn-out procedures made attracting new members, keeping existing members, and actually completing campaigns difficult. If a local CORE chapter met with stiff resistance from a landlord or restaurant owner, the NAC gave little assistance. Mostly, throughout the late 1940s and the 1950s, the NAC was plagued by infighting about how much executive control it should have over local chapters' affairs. Aside from collecting modest dues and publishing a periodical called the *COREspondent,* the NAC had very little power over the everyday affairs of local chapters. Some chapters ended almost as soon as they began. By the close of 1954 many CORE chapters around the country had fallen apart because of low membership, financial insolvency, unimaginative protest campaigns, and National CORE's failure to provide guidance and leadership to struggling local chapters. Brief accounts of CORE chapters in Brooklyn during this time illustrate the organization's early problems at both national and local levels.[3]

In November 1946, as part of a wider campaign to integrate YMCA swimming pools, CORE sent an interracial group of fifteen members to test whether the pool at the St. George Hotel in Brooklyn Heights admitted black patrons. CORE called this action a "winter swim." The January 1947 issue of the *COREspondent* reported that the Brooklyn group "splashed and dunked without discrimination." The article called for volunteers to join in a citywide investigation to uncover pools that discriminated against black people. "Let's all get in CORE's winter swims and freeze out pool discrimination," the piece advertised. But after this winter swim, CORE's activities in Brooklyn seem to have ceased. No other Brooklyn CORE group sponsored activities featured in the *COREspondent.* The winter swim actions did not attract large numbers of participants, perhaps because the idea was ill-conceived—swimming in the winter was probably not the best way to recruit members—and because desegregating hotel pools may not have been the most pressing civil rights issue of the day. At a time when the Brooklyn branch of the NAACP was engaged in massive campaigns against police brutality, and the Brooklyn chapter of the National Urban League was working diligently to preserve the employment gains that blacks had attained during World War II, CORE's efforts to desegregate swimming pools may have seemed trivial.[4]

But CORE still attracted people who favored its nonviolent philosophy, commitment to investigation and activism, and promotion of interracial memberships. A CORE chapter existed at Brooklyn College for a short time in the late 1940s and early 1950s, but it was constantly beset with problems. On its application for affiliation with National CORE, the college chapter highlighted thirty-five active members and one hundred names on its mailing list. Its participants called for the college to include Jewish and Negro history courses, and they held several social gatherings. They also tested eating places, a hotel pool, and bowling alleys for signs of racial discrimination. The application stated that the group would develop future projects that investigated whether racial discrimination occurred at the Bedford Avenue YMCA and the Bensonhurst Jewish Community House. Apparently, though, Brooklyn College CORE had an overwhelmingly white membership. It listed on the application that its main handicap was "too few active Negroes in the group."[5]

Regardless of this shortcoming, National CORE approved the Brooklyn College group's application and granted it status as a CORE affiliate. In May 1950 Brooklyn College CORE held a workshop on racial prejudice and race relations, and the chapter introduced CORE's methods of nonviolence, moral suasion, negotiation, and, when all else failed, direct-action protest. But by November the chapter was defunct. The chapter struggled to attract students to attend meetings and volunteer in investigations. The best it hoped to become was an educational group, which one member, in a letter to National CORE's executive director, George Houser, pointed out would make Brooklyn College CORE a duplication of the campus's NAACP chapter. "I don't know for sure," Barbara Pollack wrote, "that I'd want to see CORE become the kind of group that has a big meeting that passes a resolution condemning segregation and then lets everyone go home feeling as if he'd done his share." She wrote to Houser for advice on how to proceed, but in the early 1950s CORE was focused on larger internal issues related to its finances and the NAC's role governing local chapters. National CORE could not harness the energy or the leadership to deal with the types of mundane issues Pollack described. Pollack probably never received a response.[6]

In the 1950s National CORE struggled for its life. CORE's national leadership experienced several moments of heated debate about how much authority the NAC should have over budgets and fund-raising. Local leaders wanted desperately to maintain their autonomy and feared that a powerful NAC would undercut local chapters' independence. While chapter leaders squabbled with National CORE, they failed to invest time and energy in building their own organizations. And as National CORE leaders became mired in debates over how much power the central office should have, local chapters like the one at Brooklyn College dissolved. To make matters worse, the NAC was powerless to help local chapters because it had little authority to raise money or hire a permanent staff that could travel around the country to help chapters with membership recruitment and campaign organizing.[7]

The first major steps toward restructuring CORE came in November 1957, when James R. Robinson took over as CORE's executive secretary and the organization began to increase the size and authority of its national staff. Robinson, a white Catholic pacifist, had been one of the original founders of CORE in 1942. Over the years he had been insistent that if CORE hoped to become a significant force in the fight against racial discrimination, it needed to find new ways of attracting more diverse participants. Otherwise, Robinson believed, CORE would remain a fringe organization that appealed to a handful of pacifists.

After Robinson took the helm, he spent the next three years leading CORE through a period of resurgence. He aggressively expanded National CORE's powers to raise and control funds, hired several veteran activists as field secretaries, and created a liaison to oversee the affairs of local chapters. For the first time in CORE's fifteen-year history, the organization actively sought out black field secretaries to recruit members and organize chapters in the Deep South. Robinson also fortified CORE's long-standing chapters in major cities by dispatching field secretaries to Chicago, St. Louis, Los Angeles, New York, and Washington, D.C., to advise on ongoing campaigns, membership recruitment, and administrative duties. These rebuilding efforts put CORE in an ideal position when the student sit-ins erupted and grabbed the attention of every major civil rights organization. CORE was actually the first organization that local leaders in Greensboro, North Carolina, called when they sought advice on their campaign, and Robinson and other national leaders successfully used the student sit-in movement to strengthen CORE's reputation around the country.

A nationwide wave of "sympathy strikes" against the F. W. Woolworth Company and other national five-and-dime chains whose restaurants racially segregated African Americans was the impetus for the creation of new CORE chapters. CORE saw this campaign as an opportunity to support the southern student sit-ins, but its national leaders also capitalized on the southern students' momentum to build its organization. CORE's new field secretaries worked with local activists on education programs in CORE's philosophy, membership recruitment, and chapter development. Thus, 1960 proved a key year for CORE to rebuild many of its defunct chapters and to organize new ones. Throughout the summer of 1960, as CORE mobilized national boycotts of five-and-dime chains and support throughout the country for the student-led sit-ins in the South, a new chapter emerged in Brooklyn. Its membership pool reflected an array of racial, religious, class, and political backgrounds. One influential group to emerge in Brooklyn CORE's membership was people who, during the 1930s and 1940s, were active in New York City's Communist Party and Popular Front organizations. They were not sectarian ideologues or dogmatic Marxists, but skilled organizers and experienced protest tacticians. Old Leftists who gravitated toward Brooklyn CORE were veteran activists whose experiences in interracial antidiscrimination and labor union activism helped Brooklyn CORE design and implement some of its most significant protest campaigns in the 1960s. Anti-Communists in the chapter clashed and debated with these former Communists and Communist sympathizers, but the disagreements never completely tore apart the group. The participation of so many diverse people actually strengthened the new chapter and helped Brooklyn CORE become one of the most significant CORE chapters of the 1960s.[8]

"The Best Opportunity CORE Has Ever Had for Developing Additional Groups": Woolworth's Boycotts outside the South

On February 1, 1960, four freshmen from North Carolina Agricultural and Technical College, Joseph McNeil, Franklin McCain, David Richmond, and Ezell Blair, ignited one of the country's most dramatic assaults against racial discrimination during the twentieth century. In Greensboro, North Carolina, and throughout the South (as well as in some parts of the North), managers and employees in retail stores and restaurants treated African American customers as second-class citizens. They enforced odious customs of white supremacy that whites designed to keep black people in their "place" as political and social subordinates. Jim Crow politics and mores barred blacks from trying on clothing in stores and banned them from ordering and eating food at front counters in restaurants. For over eighty years a racial caste system that publicly marked African Americans as social inferiors had shaped the contours of everyday life in the South. The four young men resented this way of life and were restless for change. They went to the Greensboro Woolworth's, purchased a few items, and "sat-in" at the lunch counter, refusing to move until the waitstaff served them. Within a week the sit-in movement had spread like wildfire to more than fifteen cities. By the end of February students had initiated demonstrations against racial segregation in every major southern state. The sit-in tactic also traveled to other parts of the country where people were in solidarity with the black students' struggle, which made this one of the most significant nationwide protests during the modern civil rights movement.[9]

CORE played an early and influential role in shaping the character of this movement. At first the college students asked the president of their local NAACP chapter, Dr. George Simkins, for help with the campaign, but he lacked experience in organizing nonviolent direct-action protests. Since the early twentieth century, the NAACP's national office had used the courts and the legal system to fight against racial segregation, so the organization was not known for its leadership of direct-action protest. Simkins told the students that he admired National CORE's commitment to Gandhi's philosophy of nonviolence and tactics of passive resistance. CORE's leaders, Simkins said, would be the best people to advise the students on how to conduct their movement. On February 4 he telephoned the National CORE office on behalf of the students and asked them to send field secretaries to Greensboro.[10]

National CORE's New York City–based officers sprang into action. Marvin Rich, CORE's community relations director since 1959, whose job it was to handle publicity, press releases, and fund-raising projects, and Gordon Carey, who had become a field secretary for CORE in 1958, outlined a plan to attack Woolworth's Jim Crow policies. Carey and James T. McCain, CORE's main southern field secretary, went to North Carolina and organized training programs for the students on the philosophy of nonviolence and correct uses of passive resistance. In New York City, Marvin Rich and James Peck held a conference with executives from the Woolworth Company. Peck was one of CORE's most notable national leaders. He had participated in CORE's 1947 Journey of Reconciliation, was a member of its national governing body, the National Action Council, and would go on to be a major force behind CORE's Freedom Rides in 1961. He and Rich tried to persuade Woolworth's to discontinue discriminating against blacks in their southern stores, but the leaders of the company were not moved to alter their policies. They insisted that a shift toward immediate desegregation would kill their business in the South because southern whites would refuse to eat at the same counter as African Americans. Once negotiations failed, CORE's national leaders decided to intensify direct-action protests by organizing sympathy strikes around the country. They envisioned that these demonstrations would raise people's consciousness about the injustices black people faced in the Jim Crow South and hurt Woolworth's sales to the point where the national corporation would be forced to change its discriminatory practices.[11]

On February 12 Rich called on all local CORE chapters to organize picket lines in front of Woolworth's five-and-dime stores. The very next day Columbia University CORE and New York CORE, which was based in Harlem, organized a demonstration outside the Woolworth's at 125th Street and Lenox Avenue, the heart of the busiest shopping district in the city's most famous black neighborhood. That first day of picketing attracted mostly young white students who paraded with placards that denounced segregation and declared their solidarity with black students in the South. Many black pedestrians looked askance at the overwhelmingly white group, and whites criticized the picketers for becoming involved in what they felt was strictly a southern problem. Martin Smolin, a student at Columbia University who helped organize the demonstration, remembered that people asked him why whites should "take an active part in an issue which doesn't concern them," and Smolin responded that "injustice anywhere is everybody's concern."[12]

Harlem's Congressman Adam Clayton Powell was an ardent supporter of civil rights activism and had led past boycotts against discriminatory hiring policies in retail stores along 125th Street. He agreed that the movement against Woolworth's was not a response to a merely "southern" concern or an issue that pertained only to the "Negro problem." Powell declared that it was not the responsibility of blacks alone to take a stand against racial injustice, but rather that all "America citizens interested in democracy [should] stay out of these stores." New York CORE reached out to local churches and prominent politicians, and eventually an even number of blacks and whites walked the picket lines. By early spring CORE's picket line in Harlem had become one of the most active sympathy strikes outside the South.[13]

The sympathy strikes grew so fast and attracted so much local attention that they prompted CORE's national director, James Robinson, to boast in a letter to local chapters that CORE was the first "to give assistance in North Carolina when the sit-ins began. We were the first to picket in the North. We were the first to call for a nationwide boycott. We were the first to enter into negotiations with the managements of the chains." Indeed, CORE seemed poised to emerge from this spate of activity with an even stronger national reputation as the militant wing of the intensifying black freedom struggle.[14]

But in Greensboro CORE had competition from other civil rights organizations over which of them would become the main adviser to the college students. CORE, the Southern Christian Leadership Conference (SCLC), which had grown out of the passive resistance movement against racially segregated buses in Montgomery, Alabama, and was led by Martin Luther King, and the NAACP each wanted to incorporate the young activists into its ranks, and although the three groups presented a public image of unity and cooperation, beneath the surface there was tension and competition over who could best serve the movement's needs. Regardless of these organizational squabbles, the southern youth had taken the initiative, captured the headlines, and eventually bypassed the older organizations in favor of creating their own, the Student Non-violent Coordinating Committee (SNCC). CORE leaders respected the southern students' desire to remain independent, and Robinson summed up CORE's relationship to their movement in a letter that stated, "CORE is proud of you. . . . If there is *anything* we can do to help, please feel free to call on us."[15]

CORE did not absorb the students into its organization because it did not need them to capitalize on the momentum of the sit-in movement. The sympathy strikes gave floundering CORE chapters a much-needed jolt of enthusiasm, and they also inspired new chapters to form. Throughout the South, in places such as Rock Hill and Sumter, South Carolina, Tallahassee, Baton Rouge, Norfolk, and Nashville, CORE's local chapters quickly organized demonstrations in front of local five-and-dimes. On February 20 St. Louis CORE followed New York CORE as the second area outside the South to participate in these actions when it stationed picket lines outside two separate Woolworth's stores in the downtown district. These sympathy demonstrations immediately stimulated activity in CORE chapters that were nearly defunct, such as those in Lexington, Kentucky; Charleston, West Virginia; and Miami, Florida.

National CORE leaders also recognized that the student sit-ins were the perfect campaign to use in organizing new chapters. Carey wrote to Los Angeles CORE's leader, Henry Hodge, that the action in North Carolina "provides the best opportunity CORE has ever had for developing additional groups," and Robinson echoed that sentiment in a memo to the local chapters in which he admonished members that this was "your opportunity to build your own group on a live issue of national importance. DON'T MISS IT." Chapters emerged in Philadelphia and Ann Arbor, and activists resurrected the chapter in Chicago after months of inactivity. On the West Coast CORE's local activities increased so much that National CORE sent McCain there in March to assist in organizing new chapters in Portland, Berkeley, San Jose, and Los Angeles. McCain bragged to newspaper reporters that "if CORE were not known on the West Coast before my trip, I am sure that it is now."[16]

Outside the South the most elaborate campaigns in support of the student sit-ins took place in New York City, where, with the full weight of CORE's national office, members distributed thousands of flyers that listed locations and times of local picket lines. CORE members went to churches, union halls, and crowded transportation hubs during rush hour to drum up participants for the sympathy demonstrations. The National CORE leaders believed that if the demonstrations could have a significant effect on Woolworth's sales in New York, that could pressure the chain's executives to force changes in southern stores' policies. Starting in mid-February, CORE representatives from Harlem, the Lower East Side, Queens, Long Island, and the various local college chapters assembled each week at large "picket line coordinating meetings." National CORE publicized these gatherings in local newspapers with the hope that they would attract people from areas that did not have active CORE chapters and that these newcomers would be inspired to form new CORE branches throughout the metropolitan area.[17]

In mid-February two veteran community organizers from Brooklyn, Marjorie Leeds and Robert Palmer, attended one of CORE's strategy sessions. Records do not indicate if they knew each other before this meeting. They may have worked together in various political activities or community organizations in Brooklyn. Whatever the case, Leeds and Palmer agreed to work together and organize picket lines in front of Brooklyn's largest Woolworth's store in the downtown section of the borough. Those picket lines attracted a small interracial group of people from diverse class, religious, and political backgrounds. By the end of the fall of 1960, the group had formed a new CORE chapter in Brooklyn, and during Brooklyn CORE's first year and a half of existence, Leeds and Palmer were two of its most influential leaders.

Experienced Local Activists in Brooklyn Gravitate toward CORE

Born on October 3, 1925, Marjorie Leeds (née Marjorie Rothschild Ansorge) was the middle daughter in a nonreligious, upper-middle-class Jewish family. The premature death of her father and her mother's mental illness forced Ansorge to become independent at an early age. She worked part-time while she finished high school, and after graduation she labored in several garment factories and department stores. Although her mother's relatives—the Rothschilds—were wealthy southern Jews, Marjorie Ansorge's experiences working and participating in union organizing led her to develop a strong identity as a working-class woman and a harsh critic of class inequality. Her various jobs and union activities also introduced her to working-class African Americans. Edith Jefferson Diamond, an African American woman, worked with Marjorie Ansorge on the sales floor in different department stores during the 1940s. The two women became close friends and political comrades. For the first time in her life, Marjorie Ansorge socialized with African Americans at union meetings, dances, and parties, which deeply affected her belief that the solution to America's "race problem" was the formation of strong interracial political and social coalitions.[18]

During the immediate postwar years, Ansorge greatly appreciated the interracial communities and camaraderie in those organizations that attracted New York City's Communists, labor organizers, and progressive intellectuals, artists, and musicians. Some of her first experiences as a community organizer were with the Labor Youth League (LYL), a Marxist-oriented, direct-action group, which led demonstrations in the late 1940s against New York City restaurants that did not hire black workers. In addition to working full-time, attending union meetings, and caring for her sick mother, Marjorie Ansorge canvassed on corners in Harlem, Hell's Kitchen, the Lower East Side, and other working-poor neighborhoods in Manhattan. She passed out flyers that announced LYL meetings, rallies, and dances, which were always interracial, and she also went door-to-door collecting signatures on petitions for various local progressive issues, such as increased spending on low-income housing and the creation of a civilian review board to monitor complaints of police brutality against African Americans. Her warm, affable personality made her a successful community organizer, and she spent over five years developing these skills on a variety of different campaigns.[19]

In late 1949 Marjorie Ansorge helped form an LYL branch in the Bronx. As a part-time college student enrolled at City College, she became president of that school's chapter of the Young Progressives of America (YPA), which was one of many Communist-inspired Popular Front organizations that shaped liberal democratic activism during the immediate postwar years. Involvement in leftist politics also brought her under the scrutiny of the New York City Police Department's Bureau of Special Services (BSS), popularly known as the "Red Squad" for its surveillance of groups that city and federal anti-Communist watchdogs tagged as "subversive." The BSS and FBI recorded the many different campaigns in which Ansorge was a participant or organizer. Her activities during this period, which ranged from volunteering on the election campaigns of progressive candidates to demonstrating against capital punishment, greatly influenced her ideas on civil rights activism and social movement building.[20]

During the postwar period Ansorge worked on several political campaigns. She volunteered for Henry Wallace's presidential campaign in 1948 and worked numerous times on City Council election campaigns for the famed Harlem Communist Ben Davis. In January 1950 she traveled to Martinsville, Virginia, with her union local (Distributive Processing and Office Workers of America Local 5) to join the Civil Rights Congress's protest against the incarceration and death sentence of seven black men charged with raping a white woman. "Three cheers for the CRC!" she wrote in her union newsletter, but her enthusiasm deflated when she learned that the Martinsville Seven had been executed in February 1951. The disappointing defeat, however, strengthened her commitment to participating in community-organizing efforts against racial discrimination.[21]

Some time in the early 1950s, probably when they were both students at City College, Ansorge met Oliver Leeds, who was a member of the Communist Party and active in its Harlem branch. They married in 1954 and moved into a small apartment in a Bedford-Stuyvesant brownstone owned by Leeds's mother. They quickly began a family, and Marjorie Leeds attended Parent-Teacher Association meetings and became involved in block associations. She became an avid community organizer and worked constantly with Brooklyn's progressive black civic organizations, churches, and neighborhood associations. At that time the two most active groups in north-central Brooklyn were the Unity Democratic Club, an all-black political organization that sought to break the Brooklyn Democratic Party machine's tight control of Bedford-Stuyvesant's elected officials, and the political action committees at Siloam Presbyterian Church, whose activist pastor, the Reverend Milton Galamison, also had a background in radical politics. When National CORE issued its call for volunteers to stage demonstrations at northern Woolworth's stores, Marjorie Leeds recognized it as an opportunity to connect local efforts to a national movement against racial discrimination. She immediately signed up and, along with another community activist, Robert Palmer, began organizing the first Woolworth's picket line in Brooklyn.[22]

Palmer, an African American chiropractor, lived on Eastern Parkway in Crown Heights. In the 1940s Eastern Parkway was a prestigious residential boulevard, noted by boosters as a "fine middle-class residential area." In 1940 Crown Heights's population was only 5 percent black, and by 1950 it was 11 percent black, but the community was racially segregated: 85 percent of all the black people who lived in the neighborhood were concentrated in Palmer's section of Eastern Parkway. Palmer's status as a middle-class black professional attracted him to community service. Palmer was on the executive board of the Bedford-Stuyvesant Neighborhood Council (BSNC), a coalition of various block associations and community groups that organized campaigns to improve the neighborhood's quality of life. The BSNC also negotiated with city officials for improved government services in the community, especially in the areas of sanitation and transportation. The activities of the BSNC and its approach to political activism serve as the best barometer for his thoughts regarding community organizing, activism, and political leadership.[23]

Palmer probably participated in the BSNC's neighborhood cleanup program in late 1959. Excessive garbage in Bedford-Stuyvesant's streets, alleyways, and empty lots had been a political concern since the early 1950s, when the neighborhood's population exploded and its sanitation services, which the city had cut during World War II, remained unchanged. On many residential blocks in the neighborhood, household trash overflowed from cans that stood in front of brownstones and tenements. Abandoned cars, which people stripped of their used parts and scrap metal for sale at junkyards, sat rusting on streets for weeks and months at a time. Discarded refuse littered abandoned lots. Aside from being an eyesore, the excessive garbage was a magnet for vermin that invaded people's homes and posed a significant threat to public health.[24]

Toward the end of 1959, the BSNC began a campaign to organize neighborhood block associations to clean up Bedford-Stuyvesant's streets. During this push the BSNC emphasized the responsibility of all citizens to care for the conditions of their streets. It purposefully did not petition the New York City Department of Sanitation for assistance because the goal of the campaign was twofold: to create a cleaner community and to empower local residents to take charge of their neighborhood themselves. The BSNC believed that community-wide cleanup actions, not appeals to city agencies, were the main solution for controlling the neighborhood's excessive garbage. Only one group of residents, who organized a cleanup on Decatur Street from Ralph to Howard Avenues, responded in any significant way to the BSNC's call. The Decatur Street block association received accolades from editors of the city's premier black newspaper, the *New York Amsterdam News,* which covered the BSNC's cleanup campaign. *Amsterdam News* editors noted that residents of Decatur Street "have a right to feel proud of their accomplishment," but the article expressed disappointment with other blocks of

Bedford-Stuyvesant that "manifested neither the inclination nor the will to cooperate in this clean-up." Despite the BSNC's efforts and coverage in the *Amsterdam News,* this campaign did not grab the attention of many residents, nor did it affect the neighborhood's garbage problem, which worsened over time. Robert Palmer probably gleaned important ideas regarding methods of community organizing and strategies for bringing about political change from the BSNC's neighborhood cleanup drive. The campaign emphasized that people, not politicians or power brokers, bore the ultimate responsibility for improving their conditions. Such improvement resulted from the slow work of community organizing rather than political agitation and protest.[25]

But the BSNC was not completely opposed to petitioning city government for much-needed community improvements, and when the neighborhood council took its grievances about transportation issues to city hall, it actually achieved some tangible results. During the late 1950s and early 1960s the BSNC petitioned elected officials and government appointees in the Transit Authority (TA), which oversaw the city's transportation system, for improved bus and subway services in Bedford-Stuyvesant. Black residents did not see infrequent, overcrowded service in predominantly white neighborhoods, so they argued that their neighborhood's poor transit services and facilities reflected an undercurrent of racial discrimination in the TA. When the BSNC raised these concerns with the TA, the agency ignored it. The BSNC organized a local meeting and invited a TA official to attend and hear for himself how angry and resentful people were about these issues. The BSNC also used its relationship with the *Amsterdam News* to gain front-page coverage of the meeting.

On January 21, 1960, over 250 residents gathered in the auditorium of a junior high school in Bedford-Stuyvesant. Many of the participants relied on public transportation to commute to and from work, and their daily rides took them to other parts of the borough or to places in Manhattan where people had substantially better transit service and facilities. Bus and subway service in their community, they argued, was not on par with the service in neighborhoods that were predominantly white. People at the meeting pointed out that there was no Sunday bus service on Fulton Street, which forced many residents to walk long distances or to take two or three buses to get to the Fulton Street subway line. They also complained that buses traveled so infrequently on Gates and Putnam Avenues that when one finally arrived, it was often already filled to capacity. Once on board, riders were forced to stand in stairwells, which was clearly a safety hazard. Moreover, TA transfer policies discriminated against people traveling throughout Bedford-Stuyvesant. Those travelers, who were mostly neighborhood residents, did not receive a free transfer to another bus or the subway, but passengers going south into other sections of Brooklyn did.

The conditions of Bedford-Stuyvesant's subway stations were not much better, especially at its busiest station, located at the intersection of Franklin Avenue and Fulton Street. There were no escalators at this station, which forced thousands of riders each day to climb several long flights of stairs. But, as several residents pointed out, there *was* an escalator at a much quieter subway station along the same line in the predominantly Italian neighborhood of East New York. In addition to these problems with Bedford-Stuyvesant's transit system, residents had to deal with everyday slights from bus drivers. Participants in the meeting charged that most bus drivers in Bedford-Stuyvesant were downright discourteous to black passengers and often indifferent to their safety. Many drivers, they argued, refused to pull alongside the curb to let passengers off and instead passengers had to exit onto the street.[26]

At the end of this meeting, the TA official in attendance claimed that his hands were tied and there was nothing he could do to alleviate these problems. Members of the BSNC Executive Committee agreed to form a delegation that would pressure higher-ranking TA leaders to make changes. Some of the more activist-minded participants in attendance, led by Thomas Russell Jones, a prominent Brooklyn Democrat and member of the Unity Democratic Club, wanted to skip negotiating with the TA and begin an immediate grassroots organizing campaign. Jones's plan was for people in Bedford-Stuyvesant to circulate 100,000 handbills in the neighborhood that listed the area's major transit problems and showed how these were issues that affected only Brooklyn's largest black neighborhood. BSNC leaders tabled that motion, and they went ahead with their planned negotiations with the TA.

In this case, persistent and patient negotiations produced favorable results. In early April the TA announced that it had placed 150 new buses in service in Bedford-Stuyvesant's most crowded areas. Still, many upset commuters saw this as only half a victory. Bus service on the Fulton Avenue line remained suspended on Sundays, and TA officials gave evasive answers about when residents could expect its return. The TA also ignored the transfer complaints and the requests for improvements to the Fulton Avenue subway station. Still, the BSNC and its supporters in the *Amsterdam News* praised the new buses as a sign of progress. BSNC leaders promised to continue their negotiations with the TA until the agency addressed all the community's complaints.[27]

As a member of the BSNC's Executive Committee, Palmer played a significant role in these various campaigns and took from them a firm belief in the power of negotiation and compromise. His reputation as a notable local leader earned him the respect of key African American leaders in Brooklyn's Republican Party, who then encouraged Palmer to run for State Assembly in the 1960 primary election. A Democrat had long occupied the seat for the Seventeenth Assembly District, and the GOP felt that Palmer's involvement with the BSNC's recent transit victories would give him a fighting chance against the incumbent, Samuel Berman. When he announced his candidacy, Palmer, characterizing himself as the reform candidate, criticized the way, "year after year, these same forces are elected and re-elected . . . thus they imagine their leadership to be a birthright, with the end result of stagnation, stench and struggle in a community which would otherwise be among the best that New York City could offer." Berman trounced Palmer in the fall election. Still, Palmer emerged from his time as a leader in the BSNC and a candidate for elected office with solid experience as a community organizer and political activist. He was comfortable navigating his way through the complex, convoluted bureaucracies of New York City government and negotiating for political change. These approaches to political organizing heavily influenced Palmer's leadership style in the local Woolworth's campaigns and his stewardship of Brooklyn CORE.[28]

Local People Join Brooklyn CORE

Organizing the sympathy demonstrations against Woolworth's was difficult. Marjorie Leeds was in charge of setting up the picket lines and creating an atmosphere that attracted participants. Palmer used his contacts with local civic leaders to publicize the actions and generate support. They also worked with Tom Roberts, a black attorney from Harlem who was the chairman of New York CORE. Along with the other local area CORE chapters—Lower East Side CORE, Queens CORE, Long Island CORE, Bronx CORE, and the college CORE chapters—they planned a citywide demonstration against the five-and-dime chain on February 27, 1960. Palmer immediately drummed up support for the campaign through Brooklyn's black churches.[29]

Among Brooklyn's black clergy, no minister was more supportive of local civil rights efforts than the Reverend Milton A. Galamison. In 1948 Galamison became pastor of Siloam Presbyterian Church, which freed blacks in Brooklyn had founded in 1849. He quickly earned a reputation as an orator and political activist, especially regarding public education issues, and from 1956 until 1959 he served as president of the Brooklyn chapter of the NAACP. Throughout his career Milton Galamison joined many progressive organizations and causes that fought for racial integration and equality. The FBI labeled him a Communist for these activities, even though he was never a member of the party.[30]

When CORE began picketing Woolworth's in Brooklyn, Galamison quickly endorsed the protest. He wrote to the company's director of public relations and mentioned northern blacks' strong national support for the southern protestors. He argued in his typical blunt style that Woolworth's discriminatory treatment of blacks was both un-American and an example of poor business sense: "We are greatly distressed by the difficulties encountered by Negroes in the South in obtaining impartial service at Woolworth lunch counters. Unless this kind of undemocratic treatment is remedied, surely the economic interests of Woolworth stores throughout the country will suffer. I hope that your Company, which has become an American institution, will direct its attention to the redress of this practice about which the whole of our nation is concerned."[31] Galamison encouraged his parishioners to support the local boycott and allowed its planners to use his church as a meeting space, but other local ministers were more reluctant to offer their support. Many probably saw the boycott as being too small to warrant time away from their parish duties. Others criticized the southern students' militancy and impatience. The college student sit-ins were not controlled by black ministers, at least not in the way that the Montgomery, Alabama, bus boycott had been in 1955–56. So rather than rely solely on the ministers, Marjorie Leeds, Robert Palmer, and Tom Roberts also worked with secular grassroots organizations to create an interracial mass movement in support of the Woolworth's demonstrations. They sent letters regarding the picketing to the chairman of the Brooklyn chapter of the NAACP, the president of the Laundry Workers Union, the president of the Business and Professional Women's Club, the executive secretary for the Community Association of School Districts 25 and 27, the executive secretary of Better Bushwick Community League, the president of the Bedford-Stuyvesant Neighborhood Council, the president of the Interdenominational Ministerial Alliance, and the director of the Bedford Avenue YMCA.[32]

Demonstrations began in front of the Woolworth's at 408 Fulton Street, near the corner of Jay Street in the heart of Brooklyn's downtown district. That afternoon passersby in the bustling shopping area and pedestrians on their way to government offices and the courts on Adams Street saw CORE's large, orderly, interracial picket lines for the first time in Brooklyn. Each weekly protest on Fulton Street drew large crowds. Spectators watched the picketers with interest and some even joined in the demonstration. Marjorie Leeds sensed the protest might catch on, so she organized another picket line at the Woolworth's in Bedford-Stuyvesant, on Broadway near Gates Avenue. When the Broadway picket line did not immediately attract participants, Leeds turned to her husband for help. Oliver Leeds was a self-described "old hand at street-corner speaking" from his days as a member of the Communist Party, and she felt he could bring the exact mix of energy and experience that the picket line needed to become successful.[33]

Born on June 5, 1920, to immigrant parents from Grenada, Oliver Leeds was introduced to political organizing at the age of eighteen when he joined the Young Communist League in Harlem. After that, as Leeds put it, "my eyes began to open up . . . and I became aware of the millions of things which had never even touched me." Leeds participated in Harlem's vibrant Communist-led political activities, including organizing drives for the Congress of Industrial Organizations and political rallies to free the so-called Scottsboro boys, nine young men convicted of raping two white women, eight of whom were awaiting execution in a Scottsboro, Alabama, prison. He worked as a laborer for a Venetian blind company and participated in the party's Popular Front movement by helping push his union local toward the Communist Party's political agenda. For example, in 1941 Leeds represented Local 45-B of the Curtain, Drapery and Venetian Blind Workers at the annual convention of the American Youth Congress, which was another organization anti-Communists characterized as a "Communist front." And in October of that year he joined with a group of workers and labor organizers who demanded a mayoral investigation into charges of rampant police brutality against African Americans. An article on their petition for an end to what they referred to as state-sponsored terrorism against blacks appeared in the *Daily Worker*. Indeed, most of Oliver Leeds's ideas about political organizing, demonstration tactics, and leadership stemmed from the intellectual training, activist work, and political culture he found in the Communist Party.[34]

Leeds supported the party's opposition to fascism, and he enlisted in the U.S. Army on May 11, 1942, with plans to learn a skilled trade, gain clerical experience as an accountant or bookkeeper, or possibly see combat while serving on the front lines in an infantry unit. Like most black men during the war, he was placed in a racially segregated unit that performed manual labor. Oliver spent most of his time overseas in the Pacific theater, stationed in France's South Pacific colony of New Caledonia, where he worked as a stevedore. The backbreaking, dangerous work of loading and unloading cargo did not suit his bookish personality, and the stigma of serving in a racially segregated unit tempered most of the initial enthusiasm he had felt when he signed up to fight a war against racism. Over the course of the three and a half years Leeds served overseas, he slowly became more disenchanted with the United States' and Western Europe's claims that this was a war for democracy and freedom. He remained a committed Communist, but he became increasingly critical of imperialism.

Aside from the U.S. Army's policies of racial segregation, nothing seemed to dramatize more the contradictions of the war's professed mission than the discrimination and disenfranchisement Leeds witnessed in New Caledonia itself. French government officials, landholders, and mine owners there exploited migrant laborers who had come to the Pacific colonies in search of work, subjected migrant laborers to pass laws, and forced them to live on reservations. Only Europeans could vote in New Caledonia's general elections, and colonial magistrates had outlawed the indigenous language in the official school system. Witnessing this discrimination while participating in a war that was supposed to be against injustice and tyranny caused Leeds to become more acerbic in his criticism of Western countries, including the United States, which he saw as nothing more than governments that fostered imperialism, racism, and capitalist-driven wars.[35]

Still, that did not stop him from exercising leadership, demonstrating initiative, and building esprit de corps within his unit, characteristics he had developed as a political organizer in the Communist Party and later brought to Brooklyn CORE. He even exited military service with an award for heroism. On April 7, 1943, a fellow stevedore who could not swim fell off the pier and almost drowned between the docked ship and an approaching boat. Oliver Leeds dived into the water and saved the man's life. Years later Leeds scoffed at the idea that he had done something heroic. He rejected the army's accolade and dismissively claimed that he had jumped in the water with the hope that his actions would earn him a day off from laboring in the sun. The army looked at his actions differently and awarded him a Soldier's Medal, a commendation for noncombat acts of valor. In the official citation, the army lauded Leeds for "unhesitatingly" plunging into the water and "voluntarily risking his life to save another soldier from drowning."[36]

Despite this recognition, Leeds felt no love for the army. He left the service extremely critical of the war effort and even more conscious of Western governments' hypocrisy when it came to the treatment of black people and colonial subjects. He received an honorable discharge in December 1945, and when he returned to New York City, Leeds completely immersed himself in the social and political worlds of the Communist Party and the American Left. He worked as a proofreader for a publishing company and also began taking classes toward an undergraduate degree at City College, which exposed him to the milieu of campus radicalism and is where he met his future wife. Leeds became an avid participant in various leftist discussion groups and organizing committees on campus. But as anti-Communism took hold of American political and cultural life, affiliation with the Communist Party brought serious consequences. During the 1940s and 1950s politicians, bureaucrats, and other activists organized the Cold War Red Scare movement against Communism, which became one of the most repressive and far-reaching crusades against political dissidents in the country's history. Thousands of Communists, fellow travelers (people who sympathized with the Communist Party but were not official members of the party), and leftists, along with people who held critical views of Washington's Cold War policies, lost their jobs and passport privileges and were even imprisoned for their political views or organizational affiliations. For Oliver Leeds the reactionary fears of McCarthyism terminated his undergraduate career. While enrolled part-time at City College, Leeds organized a campus protest to support a professor fired for his suspected membership in the Communist Party. Shortly after that rally, Leeds was expelled from the college. The official reason was improper conduct and inciting campus violence, but Leeds always felt he was a victim of the country's witch hunts against suspected political subversives. His dismissal from City College, he argued, was for his political beliefs and affiliation with the Communist Party.[37]

The experience pushed Leeds further into the intellectual and political world of the American Left. Although he finished college much later in life, Oliver Leeds always fashioned himself as an autodidact. He was a voracious reader, especially of history books on U.S. slavery, the Civil War, and Marxist political and economic theory. Despite a slight speech impediment, Leeds quickly gained a reputation as a gifted orator. Years later, friends, family members and political comrades spoke about how his sharp intellect and practical organizing experience made him a captivating lecturer. During the late 1940s party leaders invited Leeds to address labor union meetings and street-corner rallies throughout the city. Later he became a Negro History Week lecturer for the Brooklyn branch of the Association for the Study of Negro Life and History (ASNLH). Leeds even ran for political office, but as successful as he was as a speaker and a community organizer, he was a lackluster candidate. When he ran for Congress on the American Labor Party ticket in November 1954, he won a meager 1,930 votes. After that crushing defeat, Leeds retired not only from electoral politics, but from public activism as well. Ten years of continuous activism had worn him down. Moreover, he had other pressing responsibilities and commitments after marrying another City College radical, Marjorie Ansorge, in 1954. They quickly had two daughters, and Oliver Leeds had less time for political work. He limited his activism to the ASNLH, and he also turned his love of chess into a community organizing effort when he formed a chess club for black men in Brooklyn called the Kingsmen Chess Club.[38]

When CORE leaders called for northerners to organize picket lines at Woolworth's in February 1960, Leeds tried his hardest to ignore them. "I wasn't looking to get into anything, and certainly I wasn't looking to get involved with anything in CORE!" he exclaimed. "I regarded CORE at the time as nothing but a front for the Social Democrats," and to Leeds that signaled that its members were "violently anti-Communist" and uncommitted socialists. "If they ever saw socialism staring them in the face," Leeds said of CORE's leaders, "they'd climb straight up rather than go into it." To a diehard Communist like Oliver Leeds, Social Democrats were antirevolutionary reformists, and he did not want any part of an organization like CORE.[39]

Oliver Leeds reluctantly acquiesced to his wife's requests for him to man the Bedford-Stuyvesant picket line on the weekends, but only after he had checked the scene for Social Democrats. "Fortunately," he recalled, "the picketing that began at both places had no signs of Social Demos anywhere in sight." Leeds brought all the protest theatrics, intellectual arguments against racism and capitalism, and oratory skill he had acquired as a Communist to the demonstration. Memories of the "Don't Buy Where You Can't Work" campaigns in Harlem during the 1930s were fresh in his mind when he stood on the corner of Broadway and Gates and screamed, "Pass them by, pass them by! Don't put your money where you can't eat! Support your brothers and sisters in the South!" His enthusiasm was noticeable, and it helped maintain the second Brooklyn picket line for the duration of the campaign.[40]

Street-level activists like Oliver Leeds made the New York City Woolworth's picket lines last until the end of the summer of 1960. The efforts of community organizers like Marjorie Leeds, Robert Palmer, Milton Galamison, and Tom Roberts expanded the protest to over twenty locations throughout Manhattan, the Bronx, Brooklyn, and

Queens. In late June National CORE called for a massive demonstration at all the protest sites scheduled for July 2. CORE's letter noted that in the future most stories about the sit-in movement and the Woolworth's boycott "will relate the experiences of the courageous southern students," yet it also emphasized that New Yorkers were instrumental participants in this national movement. CORE shared some of the stories of these local northern people as a way to encourage others to join the demonstrations:

> Some will draw inspiration from the Fox family of the Bronx. This family of three pickets almost every weekend as a family unit; the parents have joined their daughter because they felt they must support their daughter in doing what she feels is her moral duty: to actively support her fellow citizens' demand for human dignity. There is the story of Huldah Blamoville of St. Albans [Queens], who recruited her entire family to form a picket line and who spurred other supporting action in St. Albans. There are many other inspiring stories of supporters in the North. But perhaps the most inspiring of all is the story of 6000 people in New York City who picketed from February on in support of the southern students.

The point of the sympathy strikes was to show solidarity with southern activists, but at the same time these local people were also laying the foundation for their own movement against northern forms of racial discrimination.[41]

The effort to build a strong local movement was a slow process. The number of picketers on the Broadway line remained small and never amounted to more than ten people. Oliver Leeds remembered that some people supported it, but "perhaps one-third to a quarter of the people patronized the store in spite of the picket line." Even in an area that was overwhelmingly black, it was Leeds's opinion that "most people were not terribly aware of the civil rights struggle in the 1960s." Southern blacks experienced different forms of racial discrimination from those undergone by African Americans in Bedford-Stuyvesant, who had no problems eating at a lunch counter in their local five-and-dime. On top of that, Woolworth's stores in New York City did not have discriminatory hiring policies that barred blacks from working on its sales floors and in its restaurants, although some outlets probably restricted managerial positions to white men. When black people in Bedford-Stuyvesant entered their local Woolworth's stores, they probably saw African Americans working as cooks and servers in the restaurants, stocking the shelves, or working the cash registers, and many local people thought twice about supporting a boycott against a place that employed black workers.[42]

Despite these difficulties in generating widespread support for the movement, the national boycott had a significant effect on Woolworth's total sales. According to Gordon Carey, CORE had organized five hundred picket lines around the country, and the movement had caused an 8.9 percent drop in the company's sales during March. The president of Woolworth's, Robert Kirkwood, had predicted that the company would increase sales by 9 percent for the entire year, but during the first quarter sales increased by only 3.1 percent. Carey stressed that CORE's objective "is not to hurt their business. Our objective is to put justice into their business." By late April more community leaders, especially from the clergy, had joined the movement in New York City. CORE had organized New York City's leading black and white ministers into the Church Committee on Woolworth Policies, which included Brooklyn's leading black Democrat, the Reverend Gardner Taylor, pastor of Cornerstone Baptist Church and a mayoral appointee to the Board of Education. On April 18 and 21 Taylor and other prominent members of the Church Committee paraded in front of a Woolworth's at 5th Avenue and 39th Street in Manhattan with signs that read, "Segregation Is Morally Wrong," and "Southern Woolworth Segregates." That spring the Woolworth's demonstrations also played an important role in recruiting a handful of local people who eventually became members of Brooklyn CORE.[43]

Maurice and Winnie Fredericks, an African American couple in their early thirties, were inspired by the Woolworth's picket lines and impressed with the confidence and boldness of its organizers. "They were boisterous," Maurice remembered. "I was impressed with their militancy [and] their demeanor. They were clean. They were neat. They were forceful in what they had to say." He and his wife stood around and watched the demonstration until someone on the line invited them to join. Oliver Leeds was present that day, and he talked with the couple about CORE, its mission, and his wife's and Palmer's plans to submit a formal application to National CORE for a Brooklyn chapter. Throughout the Woolworth's sympathy strikes, Marjorie Leeds and Robert Palmer operated an unofficial CORE chapter. As more people like Maurice and Winnie Fredericks attended meetings and became involved, Leeds and Palmer saw the potential to form a powerful interracial activist group.[44]

Maurice and Winnie Fredericks were typical of the types of men and women who were attracted to Brooklyn CORE. Maurice Fredericks worked full-time as a postal carrier, and Winnie Fredericks was a full-time housewife; they attended church and raised their young children. Having grown up in Harlem during the Great Depression, they both had experienced enough racial discrimination from police officers, landlords, and white New Yorkers in general to know that it was not a problem only in the South. Their motivation to participate in civil rights activism, especially for Maurice, stemmed from personal experiences with racial prejudice. Like Oliver Leeds, Maurice Fredericks had served in a segregated unit during World War II. He was a steward's mate in the U.S. Navy, and his job was to be the officers' personal butler. In the navy "a black guy could only be a steward's mate," Fredericks recalled, "and a steward's mate is a flunky." As Fredericks learned, whites in the navy relegated African Americans to the same servile positions and expected them to observe the same racial etiquette that they followed in civilian life. In spite of this treatment, Fredericks, like many black servicemen of that generation, returned with a stronger sense of entitlement to his rights as a U.S. citizen and a new mission to participate in efforts that opposed racial discrimination.[45]

It took Maurice Fredericks many years before he found the right organization and cohort of people with whom to press for increased rights. Until he met Oliver Leeds and attended the early Brooklyn CORE meetings, organizations such as the NAACP and the Urban League had never given Fredericks a sense of community or excitement. He and his wife joined Siloam Presbyterian Church and supported Galamison's activism, but besides their involvement in the church, the Frederickses spent most of their time working and caring for their home and family. Like most of the other early participants in Brooklyn CORE, they were joining an activist organization for the first time.[46]

The Woolworth demonstrations lasted in New York City until September 1960. In pockets of the South, managers of local restaurants and Woolworth's stores had slowly begun desegregating their eating spaces in late spring. On May 10 six lunch counters in Nashville, which had been the prime targets of local sit-ins, began serving blacks. By August eateries in at least twenty-seven southern cities and counties had allowed African American customers to sit and eat at front counters and receive the same service as whites. And on March 10, 1961, CORE reported that 138 communities had integrated at least some facilities since the movement began. By the fall of 1960 national interest in the Woolworth's boycott had waned and Robert Palmer, Marjorie Leeds, and

Maurice Fredericks turned their attention toward more local issues of racial discrimination. After the national sympathy strikes, National CORE and its local CORE chapters developed different priorities, and northern CORE groups began to differ from those in the South. National CORE began preparations for its Freedom Rides in 1961, and local CORE groups in the South turned their attention to voter registration. In Brooklyn, and in many northern cities, housing discrimination was one of the most pressing issues that CORE groups tackled. Brooklyn CORE received some favorable publicity in local newspapers after it successfully challenged two landlords who discriminated against blacks. These small victories helped build a sense of camaraderie in the young CORE chapter, and, over time, these growing friendships gave members confidence to organize even more elaborate campaigns.[47]

During this time, the active membership of Brooklyn CORE was ready to move on to other action projects. The group was small, evenly divided between whites and blacks, and composed of mostly middle- and working-class people, but despite its low numbers it was able to find inventive ways to sustain two picket lines for over six months and recruit some active members to CORE. Jews accounted for a majority of the white members in the fledgling chapter. A young Brooklyn College student, Arnold Goldwag, who came from an Orthodox Jewish family, joined, as did an Orthodox rabbi named Kurt Flascher. But not all the people who supported the Woolworth's campaign and CORE's overall mission became "active" members in the nascent Brooklyn chapter. Some contributed to Brooklyn CORE as "affiliate" members, which was a status that CORE groups throughout the country used to designate women and men who did not play a role in the chapter's day-to-day affairs but sporadically participated in chapter meetings and programs. Active members, on the other hand, paid dues, regularly attended meetings, planned protest campaigns, served as negotiators, and overall gave a great deal of time and energy to the local chapter's campaigns and projects. Affiliate members could not invest as much time in the organization as active participants, but they served the chapter and the movement in many important ways. Some affiliate members who could not attend regular meetings could always be counted on to make some other contribution to Brooklyn CORE's efforts, such as donating money, performing pro bono legal services, or hosting fund-raisers in their homes. Since the active members rarely numbered more than fifteen or twenty people, organizing the affiliate members was an important part of the work that went into building Brooklyn CORE. The chapter's leaders formed personal relationships with these people, learned about the different contributions they were willing and able to make to the Brooklyn CORE's work, and pressed them for help when they needed it.[48]

Some affiliate members were wives and husbands of active CORE members. Winnie Fredericks was one of Brooklyn CORE's first affiliate members. Her work as a mother of three children prevented her from walking on the Woolworth's picket line each week and attending strategy meetings, but she contributed to the movement in other ways that were equally significant. As she became friendly with the Leeds family, she and Marjorie would take turns babysitting each other's children, and Winnie's home-cooked meals became a staple of early fund-raising parties that she and Maurice regularly hosted. Throughout the 1960s she was a quintessential affiliate member of Brooklyn CORE. Paul Kirchner, whose wife, Rioghan Kirchner, became very much involved in Brooklyn CORE's campaigns against housing discrimination, was also an affiliate member of Brooklyn CORE. He helped his wife host CORE meetings in their apartment, took care of their two children while his wife worked on open housing campaigns, and occasionally marched on a picket line or wrote articles for the chapter's newsletter. Together, the affiliate and the active members, even in the beginning stages of the chapter's growth, worked to make Brooklyn CORE a significant force in local activism.

Brooklyn CORE's early organization and leadership had their fair share of problems. Internally, the group suffered from competing ideas about protest tactics and approaches to combating racial discrimination. Robert Palmer's preference for negotiation and compromise put him at odds with members such as Marjorie Leeds, Arnold Goldwag, and Maurice Fredericks, who favored using dramatic, nonviolent protest to fight racial discrimination. These differences of opinion would climax during one of Brooklyn CORE's most elaborate housing campaigns against the Lefrak Organization. But despite intense infighting over tactics and protest ideology, members worked through the heated debates, social blunders, and awkward misunderstandings that were a part of an interracial organization that also crossed lines of class, religion, politics, and gender. Brooklyn CORE members socialized a great deal with one another, and, over time, the chapter's active membership developed a supportive culture of mutual dependency and camaraderie that took on the characteristics of an extended family.

After they applied for affiliation with National CORE on October 7, 1960, Brooklyn CORE's small group of active members—the chapter's application listed nine—set up committees on housing and education, public relations, social functions, and membership. The Social Committee wasted no time in scheduling a cocktail fund-raiser, Christmas party, debutante ball, and spring dance. The few new members the chapter did attract were eager and enthusiastic and had begun to feel a strong sense of camaraderie. The chapter's first major campaign, which showed its early attempts to reverse widespread practices of racial discrimination, was against housing discrimination.[49]

3

WHY NOT NEXT DOOR?

Battling Housing Discrimination, Case by Case

By 1960 black residential occupancy had not only engulfed Bedford-Stuyvesant but had expanded into the contiguous parts of
Crown Heights and Brownsville. Relatively few blacks lived beyond
the invisible but real boundaries of the ghetto in Brooklyn or
elsewhere in the North. The essential characteristic of black demo-
graphic distribution was segregation.
    —Harold X. Connolly, *A Ghetto Grows in Brooklyn,* 1977

Despite all the housing laws on the books today, discrimination
and exploitation still run rampant. The machinery set up for
enforcement is self-defeating. It is cumbersome, time-consuming,
and often fails because all that is left to adjudicate is an academic
question, once the apartment has been rented. . . . The only answer
we have found is direct action—public pressure achieves the
desired result. Slumlords, blockbusters, and discriminators believe
in the morality of the almighty dollar—if they fear their dollar
power might be hurt they will yield to the pressure of a picket line
or a rent strike.
    —Brooklyn CORE memo, circa 1962

Those niggers are the marauders of Brownsville. They ruined
Brownsville, but I won't let them ruin Canarsie. I'll join a terror
squad to keep them out. The liberals and the press look down on
hardhats like me, but we've invested everything we have in this
house and this neighborhood.
    —Canarsie resident speaking circa 1970,
    quoted in Jonathan Rieder, *Canarsie:*
The Jews and Italians of Brooklyn against Liberalism

A Ghetto Grows in Brooklyn

"How Long Can This Go On?"

Housing discrimination was one of the most rampant forms of prejudice African Americans experienced in Brooklyn and in many other northern cities throughout the twentieth century. By the 1960s residential patterns in Brooklyn had taken on clearly visible racial borders, and nearly all the blacks in the borough lived in a racially segregated residential community whose epicenter was the neighborhood of Bedford-Stuyvesant. Many Brooklynites, but especially whites who had at one point lived in Bedford-Stuyvesant or in neighborhoods surrounding it, such as Crown Heights, Brownsville, and East New York, blamed north-central Brooklyn's postwar decline on black newcomers. Black Brooklynites' identity became inextricably linked with neighborhoods that were fast becoming decayed, dangerous, and dirty. Whites used these conditions and perceptions to explain why they did not want to rent or sell homes to blacks or have them as neighbors in predominantly white communities. Three main arguments became accepted truths that explained why most white Brooklynites—realtors, landlords, and ordinary citizens—did not welcome African Americans as neighbors or tenants. First, black people were innately inferior to whites. Second, the presence of black people lowered property values and turned thriving residential areas into slums. Third, antidiscrimination laws that made it illegal to reject tenants on the basis of their race or religion interfered with an individual's right to manage his private property without government interference. Indeed, at the moment when the black population in Brooklyn was increasing exponentially, nothing seemed to upset whites more than having to live next to blacks or send their children to schools with African Americans. In the minds of many whites in Brooklyn, the arrival of black people was equivalent to a biblical plague of locusts: as soon as one appeared, more were sure to follow, and before long they would completely destroy a stable residential community by driving down its property values with crime, noise, and trash. For the most part, white property owners duplicitously hid their prejudices. Rather than saying outright, "Negroes need not apply," landlords and realtors quietly discriminated against African Americans, telling them that the apartment they wanted was "just rented," or that their credit was inadequate to qualify them for a mortgage on a new home. In one rare case, however, racial bigotry became front-page news, at least in the black press.[1]

On January 2, 1960, the *Amsterdam News* featured a piece on a sixty-one-year-old Brooklyn-born real estate owner and rental agent named Edmond Martin who said publicly what many others usually kept to themselves or spoke about only in private. In bold, capital letters, the newspaper screamed Martin's declaration that he would "bar Negroes," and "spend every cent to fight Negroes" rather than allow them to rent one of his 250 furnished rooms or apartments.[2]

The New York State Supreme Court found Edmond Martin guilty of violating the state's Fair Housing Practices Law (also known as Local Law 80, the Sharkey-Brown-Isaacs Law), which went into effect in 1958 and was the first law in the nation to bar racial discrimination in private housing. The U.S. Supreme Court had mandated ten years earlier, in *Shelley v. Kraemer,* that landlords, neighborhood improvement associations, property owners, and realtors could not enforce race-specific restrictive covenants. But in spite of these laws, whites continued to segregate blacks into certain neighborhoods through ownership agreements that blocked property holders from taking in boarders or carving houses into apartments. Postwar federal and state urban renewal, redevelopment, and public housing policies also spurred ghettoization in American cities just at the moment when black migration to northeastern and midwestern cities exploded. Black urban communities burst at the seams, and housing conditions quickly deteriorated.[3]

Edmond Martin cited his experience living in Bedford-Stuyvesant before blacks had moved there and "began making a mess of the neighborhood" as justification for arguing that African Americans were "more primitive and the worst classification of tenants." Martin recognized that there "are some who have improved," but he refused to incur expenses or waste time choosing "among the classification of Negroes." Martin could imagine having African Americans as neighbors, but he drew the line at having black tenants. Martin described Puerto Ricans as "the most excitable people in the world," and he declared that he never wanted to live near them or have them as tenants. "I could be like other landlords," he declared, "and say we have no vacancies today, or one was just rented." Instead, Edmond Martin took pride in being "honest about it" and letting blacks and Puerto Ricans know that they were not welcome as tenants in any of his rooms or apartments.[4]

Martin also defended keeping his buildings all-white on the grounds that they were his property and he should be able to do with it as he pleased. He argued that if people blindly followed Local Law 80, then eventually "there would be no private rights at all." Neither the city nor the state could browbeat him into racially integrating his rental units. Sitting in the living room of his home in Breezy Point, Queens, a solidly white community composed of second- and third-generation Irish immigrants who worked as police officers, firefighters, and construction workers, Martin foretold of the "white flight" that would occur throughout the city over the course of the 1960s. He predicted that if people like him were stripped of their property rights and their racially homogeneous communities, they "will leave New York City."[5]

These positions, which were widely held, helped deteriorate conditions in black communities. African Americans in Brooklyn needed decent places to live, and at the start of the 1960s tenants in Bedford-Stuyvesant suffered some of the worst housing stock in the entire city. Another *Amsterdam News* exposé reported on residents of a building at 226 Hancock Street in Bedford-Stuyvesant who had repeatedly complained to their landlord that "rats as big as cats run around the apartment as if they were paying rent." That was merely the first of the tenants' many problems. The building had been without hot water for over four months and many apartments had large holes in the walls, which was how the rats and other vermin entered and exited the bedrooms and kitchens. Water leaked from the bathrooms into the kitchens. In one first-floor four-room apartment where Dlorina Bibbins lived with her husband and two other persons, a gaping hole in the kitchen ceiling gave a clear view into the apartment upstairs. She complained that she had repeatedly called city agencies to report the landlord's violations, but had received no help. Elizabeth Murray and her husband lived in the same building in a two-room basement apartment that had no windows, was constantly damp, and was infested with mice and roaches. Her complaints to the landlord also fell on deaf ears. Conditions similar to those that Murray and Bibbins described existed in apartments all across north-central Brooklyn where African Americans were settling as they spread east from Bedford-Stuyvesant into the neighboring communities of Brownsville and East New York. Dlorina Bibbins spoke for many when she asked, in a fit of despair, "How long can this go on? How long can a human being live with these conditions?"[6]

For African Americans who could afford to move out of these buildings and into better living conditions, their rays of hope were often quickly extinguished when they ran into someone who believed, as Edmond Martin did, that black people themselves were the cause of such dilapidated, inhuman living conditions. Moving out of Bedford-Stuyvesant to another community in Brooklyn was almost impossible for most working- and middle-class blacks. And if they were able to save enough money to do so, where outside the black ghetto could they actually move?

Housing Segregation: "The Initial Stride of Domination"

Racial discrimination in housing was the root cause of black people's ghettoization in postwar American cities, and it entailed both physical segregation and social demonization. Ghettoization was a complicated process that individual human agency (from people like Edmond Martin) and structural forces (such as banking, government, and real estate policies) perpetuated. But the outcomes were very clear. With the rise of the postwar racial ghetto, urban blacks became known as an "underclass," infected with a seemingly incurable "culture of poverty" that laid waste to once stable, thriving communities. Urban residential segregation determined that the social meaning of "blackness," indeed the very social identity of black people, was defined by the negative characteristics of the postwar black ghetto: crime, decay, joblessness. In the minds of those who lived outside the ghetto black people brought these social ills on themselves. "The ghetto," writes Craig Wilder, "gave color an unmistakable, undeniable, and unavoidable daily reality, a reality that black people were accused of creating." Housing segregation, Wilder summarizes, was "the initial stride of domination," in the very process that "allowed white people to hoard social benefits"—the best schools, the best housing, the best municipal services, such as trash collection; the clearest access to credit; vibrant social networks that led to employment—"while people of color became the primary consumers of social ills."[7]

Brooklyn CORE's campaigns to rid the borough of racial discrimination in housing, then, were direct assaults against the powerful white privilege that shaped social life in Brooklyn. Dozens of black Brooklynites, who desperately wanted better living conditions and were tired of hearing that the space they were looking at had just been rented, began asking members of the chapter for help attaining apartments. The chapter's interracial membership and its members' willingness to engage in direct-action protest became powerful tools in breaking through the walls of racial discrimination that kept many of Brooklyn's buildings and neighborhoods all-white.

Brooklyn CORE's effort to combat both the ideological aspects of ghettoization and the actual practices and processes that kept black people physically stuck in north-central Brooklyn evolved over time. Brooklyn CORE members learned that to fight residential segregation, they needed to make people who discriminated against blacks recognize that their actions were morally wrong, illegal, and financially costly; that black applicants for apartments in white areas were good, desirable tenants; and that it was in the landlord's or the realtor's best interest to allow black applicants to move into their building, if for no other reason than to stop Brooklyn CORE's direct-action protest campaign. Brooklyn CORE became masterful at using direct-action pressure tactics to make private sentiments and fears of individual property owners and building managers subject to public scrutiny and matters of public record. They also honed protest skills that illuminated the ways institutions, such as banks and realtor groups, perpetuated residential segregation through more structural, policy-driven methods. Many of those institutions' policies and practices, Brooklyn CORE found, were based on outright lies that individual citizens, in the face of weak enforcement of state laws, were powerless to combat on their own. Blacks who wanted to integrate white neighborhoods needed help from an activist organization like Brooklyn CORE.

As these housing campaigns became more frequent and intense, an action-oriented culture came to dominate Brooklyn CORE's internal dynamics. Strong camaraderie also developed within Brooklyn CORE's small inner circle. Though such bonds brought people closer and helped bridge racial, class, and cultural differences, they also revealed rifts as two opposing camps developed within the chapter. One side favored widening Brooklyn CORE's attacks against systematic practices of racial discrimination; the other preferred a more gradual, cautious approach that addressed discrimination on a case-by-case basis. Housing campaigns attracted a great deal of press coverage. The publicity made Brooklyn CORE a well-known civil rights group and placed its networks of activists in high demand. As Brooklyn CORE struggled to keep up with the necessary day-to-day administrative work of building an activist organization, internal divisions between action-oriented members and more cautious, conservative members paved the way for a new cadre of leadership.

Fighting Residential Segregation on a Case-by-Case Basis

CORE's first major housing case in Brooklyn took place in August 1960. It involved David Patterson, a black World War II veteran, who worked as an assistant manager for a sporting goods firm in Manhattan. He and his wife had a one-year-old daughter, and they were looking to move out of Bedford-Stuyvesant to a quieter, cleaner section of Brooklyn. Patterson read the *New York Times* and found an advertisement for an apartment in the Crown Heights section of Brooklyn. The apartment building's address was 1740 Carroll Street, which was an ideal location for a couple raising a young child. It was within walking distance of mass transit and wedged between Utica Avenue, a major shopping thoroughfare, and Lincoln Terrace Park, five square blocks of playgrounds, benches, and athletic recreation space. Patterson viewed the apartment on August 6, the same day he saw the ad for it in the *Times,* and told the building superintendent, Mr. P. Hughes, he wanted to rent it. Hughes abruptly informed Patterson that the apartment was already rented.

Sensing this was a clear case of racial discrimination, Patterson quickly walked across Lincoln Terrace Park to the offices of Howard Silver, the rental agent who managed the building, and inquired if the apartment was indeed already rented. Hughes probably expected Patterson would do this and may have phoned ahead to Silver, who corroborated the story that someone had "just rented" the space. Patterson then contacted National CORE and asked for assistance. Since Brooklyn CORE was not yet an official CORE chapter, New York CORE, which was located in Harlem, handled Patterson's case. New York CORE's chairperson, Gladys Harrington, an African American social worker, was very much involved in CORE's national leadership as the northeast regional representative. Harrington and two white members of New York CORE assisted Patterson with his case. The Brooklyn community organizer Robert Palmer and other newcomers to Brooklyn CORE, such as Marjorie Leeds and Maurice Fredericks, probably watched the New York CORE members and learned about CORE's methods for battling housing discrimination. The string of events that followed would become a template for Brooklyn CORE in its local battles against housing discrimination.[8]

White members of New York CORE called Howard Silver's office five days in a row and each day he told them the apartment was still available. When Patterson and other African Americans called, Silver told them the apartment was rented after he learned they were black. On August 13 the same ad appeared in the *Times* and Patterson went to Silver's office to ask to rent the apartment. Silver told him "the apartment was definitely taken" that morning, but in the afternoon a white member of CORE visited the building, and Hughes was only too happy to show him the space. They repeated this process one more time on August 14, and on the following day they commenced a sit-in at Silver's office. Four CORE members, two black and two white, sat in the rental office for several hours, holding placards that stated Silver discriminated against African Americans. They left peacefully when Silver closed his office.[9]

The *Amsterdam News* did not report whether Patterson eventually attained the apartment, nor did it state whether members from the fledgling Brooklyn CORE chapter had assisted Harrington and the CORE activists from Harlem in their investigation and sit-in. Still, Brooklyn CORE members subsequently used this basic method of interracial testing in its fight to open housing for African Americans throughout the borough. Over the next year and a half, the chapters' housing activists also improved on this basic model and incorporated even more militant and aggressive tactics that helped scores of African Americans move into apartments and homes in mostly white areas of Brooklyn.

In November 1960 Brooklyn CORE interceded in two cases of housing discrimination and received supportive publicity in the *Amsterdam News*. The first case involved Wesley Tann, a single black man who worked as a mathematician at City College. According to the newspaper article, Tann had been "trying to secure a decent apartment for three years" when he saw an advertisement for a four-room apartment on a quiet, tree-lined block in the predominantly white Brooklyn neighborhood called Midwood. When he visited the building, the superintendent told Tann he would call him the following day, but no call came that day or night. The newspaper reported that Tann "had a friend with an English accent call and the friend was informed the apartment was still available." Tann explained his case to Brooklyn CORE, and Robert Palmer arranged for a series of tests. CORE sent a black couple to apply for the apartment, and the building superintendent told them it was no longer available. A white couple from CORE immediately followed them, and when they inquired about renting the space, the superintendent told them the apartment was available and allowed them to take an application form. Marjorie Leeds then went to the office of the realtor, Arthur Brown, who was managing the rental of the apartment. She asked about the Midwood apartment and Brown gave her an application. Wesley Tann then immediately arrived with other Brooklyn CORE members and explained the findings of their investigation. Both Brown and the building superintendent were blatantly discriminating against blacks. The *Amsterdam News* reporter noted that they had "a brief discussion" of unspecified content with Brown, who quickly agreed to lease the apartment to Tann, who closed the deal by leaving one month's rent and a security deposit. A blaring headline that read "APARTMENT BIAS SMASHED BY CORE" accompanied the article in the *Amsterdam News*, which was apparently proud of Brooklyn CORE's efforts.[10]

In Tann's case, the CORE representatives probably threatened to report Arthur Brown's discriminatory actions to New York City's Commission on Intergroup Relations (COIR). The commission's mandate was to "eliminate prejudice, intolerance, bigotry, discrimination . . . and give effect to the guarantee of equal rights for all assured by the Constitution." Its main duties were to receive and investigate complaints, but it also had the power to initiate its own investigations of discriminatory practices against racial, religious, or ethnic groups. By 1960, after the City Council passed the Sharkey-Brown-Isaacs Law, COIR had powers to investigate and hold hearings on allegations of discrimination in private housing. Rather than face the possibility of a lengthy litigation process or negative publicity, the agent rented the apartment to Tann. A similar case involved a black married couple named Jones, who applied for an apartment on Eastern Parkway, not far from where Robert Palmer lived. When the owner refused to rent them the apartment after speaking to Mrs. Jones on the phone, she and her husband reported the incident to Brooklyn CORE. CORE's testers established a pattern of racial discrimination at the building. Just as a white tester was about to sign the lease, Mrs. Jones arrived with Brooklyn CORE members; after a "polite but firm" discussion with the building owner's attorney, she signed the lease to her new apartment.[11]

These situations demonstrated Brooklyn CORE's method for opening up housing for African Americans in predominantly white areas. Two resources were crucial: CORE's white testers and COIR, or at least the threat of forcing landlords to have to answer to COIR, or the state version, the Commission on Human Rights. Repeatedly, after black people experienced racial discrimination from a landlord and reported the incident to the Brooklyn CORE, white CORE members went to the same apartment and expressed interest in renting it. If the owner or realtor offered to rent them the space, they returned with the original black applicants who had been rejected. Having caught the landlord in a blatant act of racial discrimination, which was against the law in New York City, the CORE members were in a powerful position to demand that the landlord rent the apartment to the African American applicants.

If the landlord or realtor still refused to rent to blacks, CORE's white testers threatened to file a complaint with the city's COIR and to picket in front of the building. For landlords or homeowners accused of racial discrimination, hearings before the commission could turn into drawn-out and embarrassing ordeals, and for real estate brokers, they could result in fines or the suspension of their license. After CORE's testers witnessed a landlord discriminating against blacks, threats to report the case to the city or state commissions were often enough to help African Americans attain an apartment.

Intimidation Tactics: Whites Use Violence against Black Neighbors

Problems with racial discrimination did not end after black people became the first to rent an apartment or purchase a home among whites. When African Americans first moved to a predominantly white neighborhood in New York, they could experience ostracism, persecution, or intimidation. In the community called South Brooklyn, a section situated near the Red Hook piers and waterfront that was composed of mostly working-class Italian American families whose husbands and sons worked as longshoremen and dockworkers, bigots twice smashed the windows of a home that a black family had purchased. In early November 1960 fifty-five-year-old Irene Willins moved her family of eight children out of a crowded Bedford-Stuyvesant apartment on Pulaski Street and into their own three-family home on De Graw Street in South Brooklyn, for which she paid $14,500. "Ever since we moved in the house there has been trouble," she told Les Matthews of the *Amsterdam News*. On two separate occasions someone threw rocks through the front windows of the Willinses' home, and arsonists in another two episodes ignited large piles of debris in a lot adjoining the house. During one of the fires, the bigots also tampered with the fire hydrants, which made it almost impossible for firefighters to extinguish the blaze. During the time the firefighters connected hoses to an operable hydrant down the block, the Willins home could have been destroyed. One other black couple, John and Ruby Allen, lived in an apartment building on the same block as the Willins family. When they first moved to De Graw Street, they reported constant abuse from their white neighbors. The Allen family did not experience any trouble after a few months, but they were very familiar with the Willins family's trials. Despite these scare tactics, Irene Willins was determined not to let this violence intimidate her. She let "the vicious trouble makers who need the dark of night to cover them while they attempt to raise havoc on me and my family" know that they "will not force me out of my home."[12]

Such tactics were not uncommon when African Americans integrated previously all-white residential areas of New York City. The Durham family experienced a similar spate of intimidation when they became the first blacks to move onto a quiet block in the Cambria Heights section of Queens. When the Durhams first arrived in the fall of 1960, they received scores of hateful letters telling them they were not welcome. Then, on Halloween, someone set fire to their lawn and defaced their home by slapping green paint on its sides. For a year nothing else happened, until November 1961, when people claiming to be a part of the KKK stuck a four-foot wooden cross in the Durham's front lawn with a note attached that read, "Your last chance—Go home Negra!" Still, Sadie Durham noted that some of the neighbors had become "a little friendly" over the year. The people who lived next door "speak to us," she said, but when reporters asked if they visit each other's homes, Mrs. Durham coolly responded, "That is not done."[13]

Most white people's response to the arrival of African American or Puerto Rican neighbors was to move away. Douglass Bibuld, whose parents became active in Brooklyn CORE, remembered that when his family moved to Union Street in the Crown Heights section of Brooklyn in October 1960, "the neighborhood was integrated, but poor white people were moving out and black people were moving in." When Douglass first arrived, he was eight years old, and he remembered having Irish, Italian, and Jewish playmates, but by the time he and his family moved again in the fall of 1962, he recalled, there were no longer any whites living on the block.[14]

Whether overt or covert, violent or passive, racial discrimination in Brooklyn's housing market had a palpable influence on social life in the borough. Many of Brooklyn CORE's struggles to open housing for African Americans during the early 1960s were uphill battles. In addition to those initial struggles to attain housing for blacks in white areas, African Americans' fight for acceptance and peaceful living conditions often continued long after they moved into a predominantly white area. The chapter's limited resources prevented it from being able to combat the everyday bigotry blacks experienced after they integrated a residential area. Nevertheless, Brooklyn CORE made an extraordinary effort to combat racial prejudice in housing, and, starting in the fall of 1960, it took on as many investigations into racial discrimination as its small, inexperienced staff could handle. Over time Brooklyn CORE members became more sophisticated in the different ways landlords and realtors discriminated against blacks, and they used knowledge gained from these experiences to develop well-organized, aggressive demonstrations.

Confessions of a White Tester

Early successes in housing cases gave Brooklyn CORE publicity and attracted new members. One of the chapter's first white testers, Rioghan Kirchner, joined after reading about its housing campaigns in local newspapers. Born Rioghan Hughes on April 24, 1930, in Liverpool, England, Kirchner grew up in the midst of World War II and experienced the worst of the German air raids. Her family immigrated to Canada when she was sixteen. She finished school, married Paul Kirchner, and started a family. Paul went to New York City in hopes of finding work, and Rioghan joined him with their two children in 1955. They settled in a dingy apartment above a bar in the Sheepshead Bay section of Brooklyn and moved into a local public housing complex once an apartment became available.[15]

Rioghan Kirchner eventually found part-time work at a local public library, where she began reading about civil rights demonstrations occurring throughout the South. During the spring and summer of 1961, CORE's Freedom Rides captured headlines. Interracial groups rode interstate buses throughout the South and attempted to integrate bathrooms and waiting areas at bus stations along the routes. Pictures of fire-bombed buses, beaten Freedom Riders, and angry white mobs shocked and enraged Kirchner. She remembered that she was "brought up to believe that every one was equal and should be treated equally." Images in the newspapers and stories of the injustice blacks in America experienced jarred her sense of justice and motivated her to participate in the movement. After seeing several newspaper articles about Brooklyn CORE's housing work, she called the fledgling chapter's main representative, Robert Palmer, and he invited her to the next meeting. Kirchner was a sprightly, friendly, and outgoing person, if soft-spoken and a bit shy by nature. She thought that she would not have much of an active role in the organization and that most of the work she would do would be "addressing envelopes, or putting stamps on them, or answering a telephone for a couple of hours a week."[16]

But Brooklyn CORE was not yet large enough to have a mailing list, nor could it afford a telephone for Kirchner to answer. Since the chapter needed white people to work as testers in housing discrimination cases, Palmer called Kirchner and convinced her to investigate a Crown Heights landlord suspected of discriminating against African Americans. She felt inexperienced and timid, but also excited by the idea of preventing a bigot from discriminating against others. Kirchner mustered her courage and agreed to investigate the case.[17]

Her first experience as a white tester was a disaster. Street map confidently in hand, Kirchner stepped off the bus that hot afternoon "dressed neatly in a cotton dress, high heels, and white gloves." She walked in the wrong direction for more than five blocks, turned around, and wandered another half hour before arriving at her destination "hot, rumpled, and panicky . . . and feeling slightly ill." During her walk Kirchner realized that she "really didn't know what to do" when she arrived at the building. Climbing the stairs to the apartment's entrance, Kirchner was greeted abruptly by the landlady, who called to her from the basement window and asked her to state her business. She explained that she was interested in the apartment that was for rent. "How do you know about it?" the woman demanded to know. Kirchner stammered that she had read an advertisement in the newspaper. Truthfully, she did not have the slightest idea how the black woman who wanted the apartment had heard about it. "Well we ain't got no apartments for rent!" the landlady shouted as she slammed the window shut. Feeling very discouraged, Kirchner left to go meet Robert Palmer at a nearby diner and discussed with him what had happened. They concluded that all the mistakes could be attributed to their failure to obtain specific background information, such as whether the rental was advertised in a newspaper, in a church or synagogue bulletin, or by word of mouth.[18]

Over the next year Kirchner had many opportunities to become a successful tester as more people sought the chapter's help in cases of housing discrimination. She and other members of Brooklyn CORE's Housing Committee learned how to investigate cases of racial discrimination and to prove that landlords and realtors were clearly in breach of the city's housing laws. They took immense pride in being able to catch people flagrantly discriminating against an African American individual or family. And, when it was necessary, Brooklyn CORE members relished the opportunity to stage a lively demonstration against stubborn individuals who refused to rent or sell a home to blacks. The housing campaigns built esprit de corps in the young chapter and also integrated many blocks and buildings that had previously been closed to African Americans.

A Bigot Sees the Light

Eva McGuire had been looking for an apartment for over a month. A young, single black woman, McGuire found that each time she inquired about an advertised apartment it had been "just rented" when she arrived. She saw an apartment listed in a popular newspaper, the *New York Journal-American*, that seemed perfect: three large rooms in a "pleasant neighborhood" within walking distance of the hospital where she worked as a nurse. Since she was on duty, she asked her friend, a black man named Leroy McLean, to look into it for her.[19]

McLean phoned the owner, Mr. Weiner, who hesitated to show him the apartment after hearing his name. Perhaps Weiner, who was Jewish, suspected McLean was not, and he did not want to rent the space to any person, white or black, who was a gentile. Whatever his reason, Weiner dissuaded McLean by reminding him the residential area was predominantly Jewish, but McLean assured Weiner that he had no problems with Jews. Then Weiner made McLean answer a barrage of questions about his marital status and occupation. Upon hearing that he worked for the Board of Education, Weiner agreed to show him the apartment. When McLean arrived, the building superintendent, Mr. Harcy, told him the apartment was rented. Harcy ignored McLean's protests and told him that three people had visited the apartment in the last hour and one had rented it.

Sensing he was the victim of racial discrimination, McLean immediately phoned Brooklyn CORE, told them the situation, and planned to meet CORE's white testers Rioghan Kirchner and Kurt Flascher, along with Eva McGuire, the next morning a few blocks away from the apartment building. Before leaving home, Kirchner phoned Weiner and told him she was interested in the apartment. He asked her a battery of questions, she presumed, "to ascertain if I were white or Negro." After Weiner's fears were sufficiently allayed, he told Kirchner that she could see the apartment anytime that day.[20]

Kirchner, Flascher, Eva McGuire, and Leroy McLean sat in McLean's car and formulated a plan: McGuire would try to see the apartment even if the superintendent denied her access. If rejected, Kirchner and Flascher would act as white testers and see if they could rent the apartment. When Eva McGuire returned to the meeting spot she told the group that Harcy had not told her the apartment was rented. Instead, he said that the owner would not rent an apartment to a single woman. Kirchner decided to pose as a widow and Flascher would be her brother-in-law. If Harcy allowed her to see and rent the apartment, they would know that this owner and super were discriminating against black applicants.

Harcy conversed with Kirchner about his difficulties renting the apartment. "I hope you like the apartment," he said. "You don't know the trouble I've been having with it." Kirchner inquired if there was something wrong with the space. "Oh no, it's really a nice apartment, and that's the way I want to keep it. But colored people have been trying to rent it. . . . In fact one just left. I didn't like the looks of her at all. They get into a place and they don't take care of it—dirty, you know." Flascher and Kirchner tried to lead Harcy into admitting that the owner instructed him not to show the apartment to African Americans, but he never did. While inspecting the apartment, Kirchner informed the super that she was a widow and asked if that would prevent her from living there. Harcy assured her that she had nothing to worry about. "I can tell that you are a very nice lady. The owner won't object to you," he said.[21]

Kirchner agreed to take the apartment. Harcy went to phone the owner and Kirchner signaled for McGuire and McLean to come upstairs. While Flascher distracted Harcy, McGuire was able to inspect the apartment; it was the nicest she had seen, the price was right, and it was convenient for her commute to work. Just as they were making plans on how to confront the owner, Harcy returned. "I told you that the owner wouldn't rent to you, didn't I?" he said to McGuire, but she stood her ground and accused him of racial discrimination. Kirchner and Flascher revealed that they were investigators from CORE and that their tests proved Harcy discriminated against both Eva McGuire and Leroy McLean. "Well, she can't have the apartment," he protested. "The owner will not let her have it. He told me not to show the apartment to Negroes."[22]

When Weiner arrived, Kirchner and Flascher explained that McGuire and McLean had been denied a chance to look at the apartment because of their race. The owner explained that "he personally had nothing against Negroes," but the building was an investment for his retirement and that if he rented an apartment to a black person it would cause all the other tenants to move out. He was not being prejudiced, he argued, just using "good business sense." Southern business owners relied on the same arguments when they refused to allow blacks and whites to sit together at lunch counters or to allow black customers to try on shoes and clothes before purchasing them. Whether Weiner was a bigot was irrelevant because, according to both state and federal law, his practices were illegal. Still, unless an individual could prove Weiner was racially discriminating against applicants, there was no way to prosecute him through COIR. Brooklyn CORE's pressure tactics were the only way to build a strong case against landlords like him who circumvented government regulations against racial discrimination.

Kirchner and Flascher followed CORE's philosophy and attempted to educate Weiner on the illegalities of racial discrimination. They gave him a COIR pamphlet that outlined the laws against racial discrimination and explained all the inconveniences that went along with a hearing before the commission, but Weiner refused to listen. Flascher and Kirchner then threatened Weiner: unless he changed his mind, CORE would file a complaint against him with COIR and stage a sit-in in the apartment to prevent him from renting it to someone else. Weiner remained resolute. The price of renting to a black woman was too high if it meant losing other tenants or lowering the value of his property.

While Flascher went to call for reinforcements from CORE and organize a picket line outside the building, Kirchner and McGuire found a cardboard box and cut one of its sides into a placard. With lipstick they made a sign that declared, "MR. WEINER DISCRIMINATES!" and hung it in the front window of the apartment, which was located on the third floor. Passersby stopped and read the sign and before long a small crowd had gathered. Weiner returned within minutes, demanding that they remove the sign and protesting that it would ruin his reputation. "I have lived in this neighborhood for twenty-five years and I'm a respected member of the community!" he declared. When Flascher returned, he saw how distraught Weiner had become and began to speak quietly with the older man in Yiddish. He reminded Weiner about the discriminatory treatment Jews faced in America. They spoke for over half an hour, and Weiner shared the fact that he had been refused a cabin in a motel because he was Jewish. Appealing to Weiner's Jewish identity and common experiences with discrimination, Flascher pressed him to rent the apartment to McGuire. These appeals to his conscience helped influence Weiner's change of heart, but they were probably not the deciding factor that made him offer McGuire the apartment.

Many have come to see solidarity between African Americans and Jews as a natural relationship stemming from shared experiences of discrimination and social ostracism in the United States. But the historical presence of Black-Jewish political and social alliances also developed alongside rancorous and contentious relationships between the groups. African Americans vied with Jews for control of businesses in predominantly black neighborhoods. The two groups sometimes struggled for power in interracial organizations. Jews and African Americans adopted prejudices against each other that were no different from what they each experienced from non-Jewish whites. So even though Flascher appealed to Weiner's experiences with prejudice, the threat of an embarrassing picket line in front of his building and long hearings before COIR more than likely were the factors that convinced Weiner to shake Eva McGuire's hand while telling her she could have the apartment and that he hoped she would be happy living there.[23]

The McGuire case was typical of Brooklyn CORE's actions against housing discrimination in 1961. The chapter's most powerful weapon was its aggressive use of interracial testing teams and its willingness to use direct-action protest tactics such as sit-ins, "sleep-ins," and "dwell-ins." Another case that demonstrated its success in this area occurred in the fall of 1961 and involved Margaret Chapman, a medical secretary and widowed mother of three. When the Ira Management Company refused to rent an apartment to Chapman, who was black, Brooklyn CORE staged a twenty-five-hour "sleep-in" at their offices in downtown Brooklyn. Chapman eventually won the apartment, but not the second-floor one she had originally seen advertised in the newspaper. Ira Management gave her the fourth-floor apartment and hiked the rent up 16 percent, from $70 to $81.22 a month. The reason for the increase, the realtor argued, was that brand-new storm windows had recently been installed in the apartment. Chapman preferred not to quibble over the detail and was happy she got the apartment, but the tactic was indicative of the methods landlords and real estate managers used to discourage African Americans from moving into a home even *after* they won the case with Brooklyn CORE's assistance.[24]

Solving the Cases but Not Solving the Problem

Indeed, Brooklyn CORE's record with "open-occupancy" cases, which were instances in which CORE helped an African American individual or family move into an all-white, privately owned building, was impressive. People who came to CORE for help were diverse: working-class black women and men, middle-class professionals, singles, and families. Some sought better schools for their children. Others were fleeing what they perceived to be elements of declining neighborhoods: rising crime rates, deteriorating housing stock, and dirty, trash-filled streets. The chapter did not keep accurate records of exactly how many people it helped attain new homes, but when it targeted an individual landlord or homeowner, Brooklyn CORE's interracial testers, organized strategy, and occasional use of direct-action protest tactics, such as sit-ins and picket lines, had a significant effect on blocks and apartment buildings that had previously had no black residents. On the strength of such victories, Brooklyn CORE decided to take on discrimination cases whose root causes were deeper than the decisions of just one person. Their efforts in these campaigns met with far less success.

Rose Beverly and Brooklyn CORE Attempt to Desegregate the Lefrak Housing Empire

In the early 1960s the Lefrak Organization was, according to one newspaper at the time, "one of New York's largest builders." From his offices in Queens Samuel J. Lefrak oversaw a growing housing empire begun in 1905 by his father. By 1970 the *New York Times* called the Lefrak Organization "one of the nation's leading builders." At the time the housing conglomerate managed a sizable portion of housing in Brooklyn and Queens—over 150 buildings that totaled 21,000 apartments and included the renowned Lefrak City: 20 high-rise buildings in Forest Hills, Queens, which contained 5,000 apartments and housed 25,000 residents. Sparse data exist on the total number of apartments the Lefrak Organization oversaw in 1961, but its large size made it a logical choice for Brooklyn CORE's investigation of widespread racial discrimination in the borough's housing stock.[25]

Toward the end of 1961 Brooklyn CORE examined the progress it had made in its housing program. Rioghan Kirchner wrote that the chapter concluded "that the time had come for expansion. So far, we had helped many people who had come to us with complaints of housing discrimination. Usually we had obtained the apartments for them, . . . [but] we were not making much, if any, impact on 'lily white' areas." Up to that point, CORE's housing program dealt only with open-occupancy cases. Although this program was successful, Brooklyn CORE members were eager to initiate a campaign that would have a larger influence on the borough's residential patterns, which were becoming increasingly segregated by race and class owing to the local real estate industry's unwritten policies that barred blacks from living in white, middle-class neighborhoods. As Oliver Leeds remembered, no matter how many individual cases CORE won, people began to realize "that we really weren't solving anything in a certain sense. . . . There was too much discrimination in Brooklyn. People were solving these cases but they weren't solving the problem."[26]

Some members of Brooklyn CORE decided to change their approach to the housing problem: instead of waiting for complaints of discrimination, they would investigate a large real estate firm for practices of racial discrimination. If CORE members found it to be discriminatory, they would then press for widespread changes throughout all the firm's developments. The Lefrak Organization was the perfect target. In 1961 its size and plans to build Lefrak City in Queens gave the corporation a very high public profile. Brooklyn CORE's investigation teams found Lefrak buildings all over Brooklyn. The company's newspaper advertisements enticed applicants to "live in Lefrak luxury" and "graduate to better living" with such amenities as air-conditioned apartments, free gas, elevators, windows with blinds and screens, and swimming pools. Life Realty, Incorporated, which was the corporation's sales representatives in Brooklyn, also listed these apartments as "Lefrak specials of the week," with low rents of $89 for two and a half rooms, up to $179 for an apartment with five and a half rooms, two bathrooms, and a terrace.[27]

Newspaper advertisements did not mention Lefrak and Life Realty's unofficial "whites-only" housing policy. But CORE members uncovered the reality when they investigated and tested several of the company's buildings in Brooklyn. Teams of blacks and whites went throughout the borough and investigated the company's rental standards. When a building's manager offered an apartment to the white testers, they often said it was too small and turned it down. The strategy often enabled them to see more spacious apartments that were also vacant. CORE's black testers then immediately arrived and asked to see the same apartment. If management told them it was not available, they recorded the incident and left. Testers then followed this procedure at rental offices for Lefrak apartments that were still under construction. Rental agents provided white testers with applications and often encouraged them to apply early, since spaces were limited. When black testers requested an application, they were told that there were no apartments available, that applications were not yet available, or that they had to travel to the main offices in Queens. Often the discriminatory treatment was subtle, but sometimes it was downright blatant. Once, after leaving a rental office, an African American member of CORE recounted to her team how openly some Lefrak employees practiced racial discrimination. "Do they take me for a moron?" she exploded as she got to their car. "They had stacks of applications right on the desk and they had the nerve to tell me to go to Queens."[28]

Neither COIR nor the State Commission initiated housing discrimination investigations. They only followed up on individuals' reports and brought parties before hearings if complaints produced clear and direct evidence that racial or religious discrimination had occurred, which was rare because realtors were so adept at hiding practices of racial discrimination behind numerous other explanations for their behavior. Brooklyn CORE's plan, therefore, was to collect as much data as possible until a pattern of discrimination became clear in several of Lefrak's Brooklyn properties and take those findings to COIR if the Lefrak Organization refused to change its policies. This investigation went on for most of the fall, and testers amassed tangible proof that the Lefrak Organization's property managers consistently discriminated against African Americans at four major developments in the Sheepshead Bay, Brighton Beach, and Flatbush sections of Brooklyn. Rose Beverly, an African American nursing instructor and member of Brooklyn CORE's Housing Committee, worked on the investigation team. She also desperately needed an apartment. The building where Beverly lived was condemned and scheduled for demolition. Most of the other tenants had already moved out, and she felt unsafe traveling home after work late at night. CORE members decided that they had collected enough data and would use Beverly as the test case for forcing the Lefrak Organization to make changes in all its buildings throughout the city. Beverly's case demonstrated not only how difficult it was for black people to get apartments in some parts of Brooklyn, but also the extreme measures the company used to prevent African Americans from living in its buildings.[29]

Beverly answered an advertisement in the *New York Times* for an apartment in College Park, a housing development on the border of Flatbush and Brownsville in Brooklyn. She inquired about two-and-a-half-room apartments but was told that all were rented. The sales agent, Mr. Miller, informed her that the only available apartments were three and a half rooms, which rented for $130 a month, which was more than Beverly hoped to spend. As she left, Kirchner entered the office and requested to see the two-and-a-half-room apartments advertised in the *Times*. Miller gladly gave Kirchner a note that instructed the building's superintendent to show her the vacant apartments. He touted one available space for its separate bedroom, large living room, kitchen, and bathroom that had been rented by a young couple, but they suddenly canceled the lease when the husband was drafted. Kirchner viewed the apartment, reported to Beverly on its size and features, and Beverly agreed that it fit her needs. Their plan was for Kirchner to return to the office, request to leave a deposit for the apartment, and just as Miller was about to accept the money, Beverly would arrive.

Miller left for coffee. His associate, Mr. Johnson, took down Kirchner's information and was about to accept her deposit when Rose Beverly walked into the office. The two women acted like old friends who had not seen each other for a long time. "Rose! I didn't know you lived in this neighborhood," Kirchner exclaimed in mock surprise. "I don't yet," Beverly replied. "I'm looking for an apartment; I thought I might find one here." Just then, Miller returned with two cups of coffee, saw Beverly and Kirchner talking, and tried to duck into a back room before they spotted him. "Mr. Miller," Kirchner called out. "Have you any more nice apartments like the one you showed to me? My friend here is looking for one just like it." Miller evaded the question and passed it off to Johnson while Beverly accused them both of racial discrimination. Johnson stuttered an apology and excused the incident as a simple mix-up, but Kirchner complicated matters further for the realtors when she said that she would like them to show her apartment to Beverly. "If she likes it, she can have it," Kirchner declared. "After all, she was here first." Johnson had no choice but to allow Beverly to see the apartment. Kirchner and other CORE members waited in the rental office to prevent Johnson and Miller from closing early to avoid taking Beverly's application and deposit.[30]

Beverly liked the spacious, well-lit, clean apartment as soon as she saw it. When she returned to the office to fill out the paperwork, Johnson immediately began discouraging her from renting the apartment. He claimed the rent was too expensive even before he asked about her income. Johnson also speculated that her commute to work would be too long, but Beverly suggested he not worry about her travel time, since she had a car. Unable to dissuade her, Johnson gave her an application, accepted her check as a deposit, and wished her luck.[31]

Over the course of the next month, Life Realty and high-ranking officials at Lefrak employed a number of tactics to keep Rose Beverly from renting the apartment and to thwart Brooklyn CORE's attempts to expose systematic patterns of racial discrimination in their Brooklyn properties. First, Reba Gelman, office manager for Life Realty, phoned Beverly and told her that the apartment she had applied for was already rented to a young couple and that there were no other vacant two-and-a-half-room apartments in the entire borough. Gelman reluctantly agreed to keep her application on file.[32]

Robert Palmer, Rose Beverly, and a delegation of CORE members then went to Lefrak's main offices and met with Morton Turner, the corporation's sales manager. Turner confirmed that a young couple had leased the apartment weeks before Beverly arrived and the rejection of her application was not racial discrimination, just a bureaucratic mix-up. The CORE group informed Turner that they knew all about the young couple and how they prematurely terminated their lease when the husband was drafted into the service. Turner hastened to add that the cancellation of their lease had not yet been finalized, which was why the sales reps told Beverly that, even though it was vacant, she could not have the apartment. To prove that the Lefrak Organization did not discriminate against applicants on the basis of their race, Turner took the CORE delegates into Samuel Lefrak's boardroom, in which numerous awards and plaques in recognition of his philanthropy were on display. Turner even made it a point to highlight Lefrak's certificate as a lifetime member of the NAACP, but the CORE members were unimpressed and demanded that he find a suitable apartment for Rose Beverly.[33]

After a few phone calls, Turner happily reported that a similar apartment was vacant in the same building, and if Beverly's references and employment checked out satisfactorily, he would rent it to her. Turner also promised there would be no difference in the monthly rent between this apartment and the original one for which Beverly had applied. After she agreed to this arrangement, Palmer and the delegation revealed that Brooklyn CORE had done a thorough investigation of Lefrak's buildings and that there was a systematic pattern of discrimination against black applicants. Turner listened to the charges and agreed to send all employees a letter that stated Lefrak management did not condone racial discrimination, and anyone found practicing this form of bigotry would be fired.

Two weeks passed without a word or a copy of the letter. A company representative once called Beverly at work, presumably to see if she indeed had a job, and inquired about her salary. Beverly abruptly informed the rental agent that she could obtain that information from the hospital's personnel office, and that the office's number was on the application. This would be the first of several instances in which officials from Lefrak harassed Beverly and searched for reasons not to rent her the apartment in the College Park development.

By early November members of Brooklyn CORE had grown impatient. They decided that unless their next meeting with Lefrak officials brought results, they would commence with a sit-in or a picket line at the corporation's main offices in Queens. On November 16, 1961, twelve CORE members paid the company a visit and demanded to speak with Samuel Lefrak or any of the corporation's vice presidents. When the receptionist told them that all the senior leaders were in a conference, CORE representatives announced that they would hold a sit-in in the lobby and post a picket line outside the office's main doors until they were seen. Within minutes, they had posted a line of picketers holding placards in front of the office building and had telephoned for support from other local CORE chapters and the national office. Arnold Goldwag, the chapter's public relations chairman, called his contacts in the press, and in less than an hour photographers arrived at the scene. Brooklyn CORE was prepared to use all its resources to publicize its research on the Lefrak Organization and force the giant housing developer to cease its practices of racial discrimination.[34]

Within minutes, Arthur Klein, a vice president of the Lefrak Organization, ran into the waiting area and agreed to meet with Brooklyn CORE's representatives. The more reticent Robert Palmer apparently did not attend this demonstration, nor did he lead the negotiations with Lefrak. Indeed, Palmer refused to participate in the planning sessions, investigation tests, and negotiations of the Lefrak campaign if Brooklyn CORE's members prematurely used what he considered to be strong-arm tactics. He thought the best strategy for fighting housing discrimination was on a case-by-case basis, and the chapter's attempt to change policies in the Lefrak Organization struck him as too broad and antagonistic. His position during the Lefrak campaign eventually created an irreparable rift between Palmer and most of the membership, but at that moment the chapter vice chairman, Benjamin Brown, took Palmer's place at the negotiation table, and Brooklyn CORE concentrated on its campaign rather than its internal conflicts over leadership.

With Palmer sitting out this campaign, Brown and Kirchner represented Brooklyn CORE during the first meeting with Klein. Brown was more willing than Palmer to use direct-action protest, especially in situations such as the one Brooklyn CORE faced with Lefrak, but he also modulated the impetuousness of other members such as Goldwag, Maurice Fredericks, Marjorie Leeds, and Kirchner, who were quick to protest before they had exhausted all avenues of negotiation. Brown's leadership, which he had gained from his experiences as a progressive political organizer with the American Labor Party and other leftist groups, filled an important void caused by Palmer's hesitancy. Oliver Leeds recalled that he was "an old, old friend of mine from way back in the Old Lefty days in Harlem, back in the 1930s," when black progressives had to navigate among the many different religious, political, and nationalist tendencies that characterized Harlem's activist circles at that time. This was probably where Brown acquired a special ability to manage different approaches to political action. According to Leeds, he and Brown reconnected during the Woolworth's campaign when Brown was working in National CORE's Park Avenue office and Brown gravitated to the Brooklyn chapter's ranks because it seemed to be the most active and dynamic CORE group in the city.[35]

Brown and Kirchner stressed to Klein that Brooklyn CORE would stage an around-the-clock sit-in if the Lefrak Organization did not meet its demands. They presented him with a statement that showed the housing developments in which CORE found clear patterns of racial discrimination, which included the College Park complex, where Rose Beverly sought an apartment. CORE demanded that Beverly immediately receive a lease and be allowed to move into her apartment by December 1. Brown and Kirchner also insisted that the Lefrak Organization issue a press release that declared members of all races and religions welcome in any Lefrak apartment building and advertise all apartments as "open to all races and religions." Their final two demands repeated Brooklyn CORE's earlier requests that the chapter had issued to Morton Turner: that Lefrak issue a nondiscrimination policy to all its rental agents and that it fire any employee who racially discriminated against a potential applicant.[36]

Klein was in no position to grant any concessions on the demands and seemed ready to call Brooklyn CORE's bluff, but the scene in front of the building and the waiting room quickly changed his mind. Almost twenty people were on the picket line and an equally large group was camped out in the front office's waiting area. Klein quickly called two other senior members of the Lefrak Organization: Arthur Coller, general counsel, and Theodore Kahner, another vice president. They arrived by six o'clock in the evening and reported that Samuel Lefrak would not attend the negotiations. Apparently news of the demonstration exacerbated his heart condition, and his doctors advised that he not risk further stress. Lefrak empowered Klein, Coller, and Kahner with authority to take whatever action was necessary.

Negotiations lasted until close to one o'clock in the morning. Newspaper reporters and photographers remained the entire time, and the sit-in grew to twenty-five people. Throughout the talks, the Lefrak representatives denied that their organization practiced racial discrimination in any way. Rose Beverly's application, which she had filed over three weeks earlier, was held up because of normal bureaucratic procedures and tardiness on the part of the agency that conducted the background check of her financial records. They agreed that a delay of two to three weeks was unusually long, but that it did not indicate racial discrimination. To show they were not biased, they promised Beverly the apartment once her background checks cleared.[37]

Lefrak officials refused to issue to the press the statement that CORE demanded. They also rejected Brooklyn CORE's insistence that the Lefrak Organization add an open-occupancy declaration to advertisements, an action they claimed "would be financial suicide." The Lefrak representatives' rejection of CORE's statement implied that the real estate conglomerate's real fear was white flight and the transformation of Lefrak apartment complexes into black ghettos. Lefrak administrators probably believed that if white tenants read in the newspaper that their buildings were being racially integrated, whites would move away in droves. Furthermore, Lefrak realtors feared that the black people who replaced white tenants would lower the real estate value and eventually turn the entire neighborhood into a slum.[38]

Klein, Coller, and Kahner agreed to issue a nondiscrimination policy to all its rental agents and employees, and they also consented to terminate any Lefrak employee who discriminated against an applicant because of his or her race. Kirchner pointed out that Morton Turner had already agreed to those points two weeks earlier. How, she asked, had Lefrak managed to build so many buildings in such a short time when they took more than two weeks to write a simple memo and send it throughout the corporation? The Lefrak officials had no explanation, but they assured CORE that they would complete the "remaining" paperwork, and that Beverly would also be able to sign her lease on Monday, November 20. Although the Lefrak Organization would not issue its own press release, Coller and Klein signed a joint statement with Brown and Kirchner that outlined the results of the negotiations. Part of the statement declared, "Adherence to the democratic principles of equality of all peoples, regardless of race, color or creed has been and shall always be the policy of [the Lefrak] Organization in its dealings with the public in all matters." Even though Lefrak would not change its advertisements to read "open occupancy," it promised to seek more effective means of reaching African American applicants. At the behest of their editors, reporters from the *Daily News,* the *Post,* the *Mirror,* and the *Amsterdam News* waited for hours to receive the statement and include the story in the morning editions of the papers. Lefrak's concessions on CORE's demands signaled a partial and less-than-satisfying victory. Brooklyn CORE, however, hoped that its ace in the hole, negative publicity, might bring about the desired result.[39]

But stories on the demonstration never appeared in the *News* or in the *Mirror.* The only mainstream paper that ran an article in its early edition was the *Post,* and its headline read, "Queens Sit-in Wins Rental, CORE Reports." The article gave a quick recap of how thirty members of CORE staged an eight-hour sit-in at Lefrak's main offices in Queens, which won Rose Beverly the apartment. The *Amsterdam News* ran a much more detailed story in its next issue, on November 25. Its headline, "CORE Does It Again! Opens Lily-White House," championed Brooklyn CORE's victory, and the article reported that the chapter "had established that a pattern of discrimination existed in Miss Beverly's case and in four other similar test cases."[40] Unlike the other newspapers, which had large advertising accounts with the Lefrak Organization and did not even mention the incident, the *Amsterdam News* never carried advertisements for Lefrak apartments in its real estate section. Later in the week, members of Brooklyn CORE's Housing Committee noticed that newspaper advertisements for Lefrak apartments had changed. Lefrak apartment ads usually proclaimed the property was "built, owned, and managed by the Lefrak Organization," but that information had been suddenly deleted. The "Lefrak specials of the week," became "Life Realty specials of the week." One Lefrak-owned building, the Citadel, located on Prospect Park Southwest and adjacent to the park, had enticed people with an ad that read, "Live in Lefrak Luxury with a view overlooking beautiful Prospect Park" and boasted the building's many amenities—close proximity to subways, minutes away from midtown Manhattan, "best schools and shopping," "apartment suites that achieve an air of elegance, spacious living rooms, tiled bath rooms, abundant closet space"—at "low, low, Lefrak rentals." In an ad for the Citadel printed after the Beverly case, every mention of Lefrak had been deleted. The Lefrak Organization found it easier to disassociate its name from these properties than to advertise apartment buildings as "open occupancy" or to ensure that rental agents discontinued discriminating against black applicants. Racially integrated housing seemed to have a financial cost that the Lefrak Organization was unwilling to pay.[41]

Rose Beverly's meeting to sign the lease with Arthur Coller and Arthur Klein further indicated the company's reluctance to rent apartments to African Americans. Coller received the financial background report two days after the demonstration and called CORE to report that there was a discrepancy in Beverly's reported earnings. If she could account for the missing funds and CORE agreed to sign a guarantee of the rental, Lefrak would proceed with the lease signing. The parties scheduled to meet to review the financial report on Monday, November 20. At that meeting Coller and Klein attempted to reject Beverly's application three different times.

First, Coller pointed out the two discrepancies in the financial statement: one was an unpaid car loan and the other was a lower savings account statement than the one Beverly reported on her application. She provided receipts for the loan payment and showed that the financial report referred to the wrong savings account. Then Coller presented Beverly with a report written by a private investigator whom the Lefrak Organization apparently had hired to find information it could use against her application. Beverly was indignant that they would take such extremely invasive measures to deny her the apartment; she pointed out, however, that the only significant "dirt" uncovered was "an alleged evening spent in her apartment with a man . . . who answered the door in his stocking feet." This was hardly reason for denying her the apartment. Lefrak officials assumed that the report might shame Beverly into dropping her application, but she found it more amusing than embarrassing.[42]

Coller appeared flustered that the report backfired, and he and Klein quickly moved on to their next pretext: Beverly's financial welfare. Klein prepared a budget that included all her expenses and patronizingly suggested that if she rented this apartment, she would have no money left for food and entertainment. The CORE representatives examined the budget and argued that its prices were inflated and the arithmetic was incorrect. Rioghan Kirchner added that it was possible to feed a family of four on the amount that Klein estimated Beverly needed for food. With all their attempts foiled, the Lefrak officials grudgingly handed over the lease, which Beverly signed. After more than six weeks of unnecessary foot-dragging and sinister machinations on the part of Lefrak, Beverly finally signed her lease and prepared to move into her new apartment.

The fight was far from over. Rose Beverly was not greeted with derogatory notes from bigots or rocks thrown through her windows in the dead of night, but the rental agents and landlords for her new building put her through ten more days of frustration that communicated the same sentiment as a blatant act of violence and intimidation: Beverly was not welcome, black people were unwanted as neighbors or tenants, and people would make her life difficult if she decided to move into this apartment. She reported her latest tribulations to members of Brooklyn CORE at the chapter's general meeting that followed their victory in the Lefrak office.

According to her lease, her new apartment was supposed to be freshly painted when she moved into the space. When she made an appointment with the rental agent to choose the paint colors, the agent never showed up. Beverly then knocked on the superintendent's door and asked if she could gain access to her apartment to give it one more look before she made arrangements to move. The superintendent's wife answered the door and "was quite unpleasant" to Beverly. She grudgingly showed Beverly the apartment and afterward telephoned Coller to report that Beverly had "made a fuss" about the floors. All Rose Beverly had said was that she was "surprised that the floors were not wood," but to Coller and the superintendent's wife, these were signs that Beverly was going to be an undesirable tenant. They tried one last tactic to break her spirit and discourage her from moving into the all-white building.[43]

At Beverly's next appointment with the building's rental agent, she discussed the painting schedule for her apartment. The rental agent, Mr. Levine, told her the space would not be ready until December 4 because the painters were behind schedule. Beverly was distraught at this news. She had already hired workers to move her possessions on December 2, a Saturday. If she delayed her move until December 4, which fell on a Monday, she would have to pay a cancellation fee with the moving company and take off more time from her job. Brooklyn CORE's Arnold Goldwag, who had accompanied Beverly, berated Levine, telling him this was just another form of harassment because they wanted to keep the building all-white. They stormed out of the building leaving unresolved when Beverly would move in and when painters would begin and complete their job on her apartment.[44]

Sensing that they might successfully deter Beverly from taking the apartment, the Lefrak Organization sent her a registered letter on November 27, which stated the paint job would not be completed by December 1, but that they still expected her to pay her first month's rent on that date. Frustrated, Beverly went back to CORE for assistance. A member of the Housing Committee telephoned Coller and calmly informed him that Rose Beverly would occupy the apartment as of December 1 and that four days was plenty of time to paint one small apartment. Brooklyn CORE's members also stood ready to stage more protests against Lefrak, whether through another large demonstration at the corporation's office, a picket line at Beverly's new apartment building, or more negative publicity in the newspapers. They informed Coller that "it would be to the advantage of the Lefrak Organization to see the apartment was ready." Lefrak folded. Delaying Beverly's admission was not worth another round of protests. She moved into her new, freshly painted apartment on December 2, just as she had planned. Rioghan Kirchner wrote that the saga ended with a little celebration. As CORE members helped Beverly unpack her possessions and arrange her furniture, they played music, drank a few bottles of wine, and had a victory party.[45]

The level of resolve and determination Rose Beverly exhibited in the face of so much harassment was quite extraordinary. In this case, and in many others, Brooklyn CORE was successful, but, as Rioghan Kirchner wrote in her unpublished memoir, "How many people would show such perseverance and be willingly subjugated to such humiliation in order to try and break the color line?" The Lefrak Organization was willing to bet that its tactics could stave off racial integration in its buildings at least for the near future. Even with the setback caused by Rose Beverly's admission to one of its buildings, Lefrak continued discriminating against black applicants. Lefrak's rental agents continued to lie to African Americans about the availability of apartments, and the corporation's changes in its advertisements made it more difficult for Brooklyn CORE to establish patterns of discrimination in Lefrak properties. In March 1962 Brooklyn CORE began another picket at the offices of Lefrak's rental agent, Life Realty. Employees of Life Realty had informed African Americans that there were no vacant apartments to choose from, even though the Lefrak Organization owned several thousand units throughout the city. Furthermore, ten minutes before the black applicants inquired about available apartments, Brooklyn CORE members had witnessed a Life Realty employee give white applicants a choice of several apartments that were immediately available. Indeed, nothing seemed to have changed after Rose Beverly's case and the apparent agreement by the Lefrak Organization's vice presidents and lead counsel to stop racial discrimination.[46]

In the 1960s federal and state authorities were powerless to intervene directly and sanction a private corporation like Lefrak. Individuals and civil rights organizations shouldered the burden of documenting practices of racial discrimination and proving that they were indeed widespread and systematic within an organization, no small task when challenging a corporation as powerful and well financed as Lefrak. Even after equal access to housing became a federally mandated right under the provisions of the Fair Housing Act of 1968, prosecutors faced an uphill battle trying to prove that Lefrak discriminated against black applicants. In both 1969 and 1970 the New York State Division of Human Rights reported that it had received complaints that the Lefrak Organization had discriminated against blacks, but the office declared it found "no probable cause" for action.[47]

Then, late in the summer of 1970, the U.S. Justice Department filed a suit against the housing giant and its Brooklyn management company, Life Realty, on the grounds that Lefrak had denied the Attorney General's Office access to records that indicated the corporation's voluntary compliance with the Fair Housing Act. U.S. Attorney Edward Neaher declared that the government had "a substantial number of witnesses" who could testify that the Lefrak Organization had made it a widespread practice to offer black applicants the smallest apartments with the fewest amenities located in the most undesirable areas, whereas it saved its choice rentals for whites. Lefrak vehemently denied the charges and argued that his corporation had "thousands of black New Yorkers living in our apartment buildings," and that he had "stood for open and integrated housing throughout my business career." He touted construction projects then under way, which would provide thousands of units of low-cost, low-income housing in Bedford-Stuyvesant, Brownsville, and East New York in Brooklyn and Mott Haven in the Bronx, as examples of the company's willingness to help poor people of color. But by 1970 those neighborhoods had turned into the some of the city's most racially segregated and impoverished neighborhoods—conditions that Lefrak's discriminatory practices during the 1960s helped create.[48]

Samuel Lefrak tempered the bad publicity of the lawsuit by boasting of his goodwill in providing homes for poor blacks and Puerto Ricans, who were the very same people his rental agents had prevented from living in Lefrak's all-white buildings during Brooklyn CORE's campaigns in 1961–62. To avoid dealing with a drawn-out lawsuit and having his company's name vilified in the press, Lefrak brokered a deal with the Department of Justice in late January 1971. The Justice Department agreed to drop its suit in exchange for the Lefrak Organization's agreeing (once again) to prohibit discrimination in all of its 21,000 rental units throughout Brooklyn and Queens, and promising to give the equivalent of one month's free rent to fifty black families to assist them in moving into predominantly white buildings owned and managed by Lefrak. The company agreed without admitting any violation of the 1968 Fair Housing Act.

Lefrak and Neaher praised the agreement as "an historic document, a landmark" that "will make open housing in our city a reality." On the other hand, the New York Urban League, which was the lead civil rights organization in the investigations into Lefrak's bias, called the agreement "a great disappointment to the millions of blacks and Puerto Ricans who for years have been denied an equal chance at Lefrak's housing units all over the city." The Urban League doubted if many black families living in predominantly black Lefrak buildings would accept the free month's rent to integrate an all-white building. It conducted an informal survey and found that only two of a dozen blacks said they would consider Lefrak's offer. Once again, the company avoided responsibility for discriminating against African Americans, and the government's attempt to prosecute an organization that discriminated against racial minorities was rendered moot. Throughout the 1970s the Lefrak Organization continued to reap enormous profits from city contracts to build low-income housing in New York City's black and Puerto Rican neighborhoods.[49]

With Rose Beverly's victory, Brooklyn CORE proved it could win individual cases, albeit with much difficulty. In December 1962 Brooklyn CORE staged a campaign against a construction company and a bank that colluded to bar an African American family, the Whitings, from renting a newly constructed home in the Midwood section of Brooklyn. Brooklyn CORE members held a "dwell-in" and occupied the empty house for nearly two weeks. The property managers tried to break the demonstrators' spirits by turning off the building's heat, which, during the middle of winter, brought the temperature inside the house below freezing. In addition to the dwell-in, CORE members held a sit-in at the bank that financed the construction project and picketed outside its main offices. In the end, neither the construction company nor the bank admitted to racial discrimination, but the Whitings did receive a settlement payment and Brooklyn CORE ended its protest.

As Oliver Leeds summarized, Brooklyn CORE "never won the struggle" against housing discrimination because "the policy never changed." During the first Lefrak campaign and the Beverly case, some members of CORE realized a great deal of action was necessary just to make visible to the public the practices of racial discrimination that occurred in Brooklyn. Even then, as Lefrak's maneuvers with the press and its willingness to hire private investigators to pressure Rose Beverly to drop her application showed, CORE's opponents seemed formidable, if not unbeatable. Still, people like Marjorie Leeds, Maurice Fredericks, Kurt Flascher, Rioghan Kirchner, Benjamin Brown, and Arnold Goldwag held firm that CORE could make a difference in Brooklyn. Some members of Brooklyn CORE concluded, however, that changing policies in housing, employment, and education demanded that the chapter adopt an entirely different leadership style and a more aggressive approach to direct-action protest. Robert Palmer's unwillingness to employ such tactics and the chapter's organizational disarray under his and Brown's stewardship put them both at odds with a majority of Brooklyn CORE's active members and eventually led to Palmer's resignation.[50]

"We'll Get Something Done Here": Oliver Leeds Becomes Chairman

Brooklyn CORE's housing campaigns showed how its membership had begun to outpace Palmer's leadership. Robert Palmer preferred to negotiate rather than demonstrate, and Kirchner, Flascher, Leeds, Goldwag, and other members were committed to using direct-action tactics to fight racial discrimination. They gradually lost confidence in him as their chairman. Rioghan Kirchner recalled that Palmer was a "charming man." According to her, Palmer "had a lot of great schemes, but it was always someone else had to do it. When we had a march or a sit-in, he wasn't there. After a while it began to sink into us that this guy was not a real leader. Unfortunately, when it came to the nitty-gritty, he led from behind." Oliver Leeds described Palmer as "an NAACP type. He didn't mind negotiating, but he certainly looked at direct action with a jaundiced eye. When we found cases of discrimination at Lefrak, he refused to participate in or organize direct action." Indeed, Marjorie Leeds summed up Brooklyn CORE's predicament with Palmer best: "The chapter was in trouble because [under Palmer] there was just going to be meetings and not too much action."[51]

One reason that members of this small group criticized Palmer after the Lefrak campaign was that they had grown close during the months they had worked together testing for discrimination and the many evenings they had spent socializing at each other's homes. In addition to fund-raiser cocktail parties, Brooklyn CORE members held potluck dinners and parties. Sometimes they used the meeting space at Siloam Presbyterian Church or the Bedford Avenue YMCA, which was also where they had some of their general meetings, but they gathered mostly in each other's homes. After Eva McGuire won her apartment, she became a regular host of Brooklyn CORE parties. People brought food, cheap wine, and records, and they ate, danced, and talked late into the night. Younger CORE members enjoyed the all-night dance parties at Arnold Goldwag's apartment. Sometimes the social events were fund-raisers for specific causes, but most of the time they were just for fun. Brooklyn CORE members also took turns babysitting for one another. Winnie Fredericks, who rarely had time to attend meetings or sit-ins, often did this important work for the chapter, and she also hosted parties at the Frederickses' home or cooked soul food delicacies for dinner parties. Friendships formed among the CORE children as well. By dining in each other's homes, hosting fund-raisers, and helping take care of each other's children, Brooklyn CORE members created a sense of camaraderie that made it possible for them to depend on one another during difficult, frustrating campaigns, such as the one against the Lefrak Organization.[52]

Developing bonds of friendship, especially across lines of class and race, was never easy for the people in Brooklyn CORE, especially for the white members who had never before interacted with or worked with African Americans. Rioghan Kirchner experienced some awkward social moments, both as a white woman and as a foreigner. The first time she attended a Brooklyn CORE potluck dinner, she asked Mary Ellen Phifer, a North Carolinian who had moved to Brooklyn in the 1950s and joined Brooklyn CORE during the Woolworth's boycotts, what would be a good dish to bring. Phifer told her most people brought chicken and various sides. Kirchner spent the afternoon before the social preparing a roasted rosemary chicken with basted potatoes, which was a typical dinner dish from her native region in England. Kirchner became the object of some good-spirited teasing when she arrived at the party. She remembered that Phifer, Fredericks, and others exclaimed, "That's not chicken! When we say chicken we mean *fried* chicken!" Years later, she still laughed at her own naïveté and recalled how everyone enjoyed sharing each other's food and afterward kept asking her to "make that British chicken" for future parties.[53]

Sometimes different ideas about race, gender, religion, and politics were not so easily laughed away. Many Brooklyn CORE members, especially African Americans, had to work patiently through white members' social blunders in order to remain friends and political comrades. Rioghan Kirchner remembered one instance when Robert Palmer visited her home and began talking about his Irish ancestry. She jokingly interjected that, "he must be the Black Irish," which Palmer did not find funny. She tried to explain that "Black Irish" was the British sobriquet for dark-haired people in Ireland, but he was still insulted by her remark. Another time, she was dancing with Maurice Fredericks at a party when he jokingly danced seductively with her. "I patted him on the head and said, 'Down, boy,' and then practically sank through the floor because he just went stiff. I didn't mean a thing by it. He was highly insulted." As soon as it was out of her mouth, Kirchner realized that what she had said sounded dehumanizing. These were the first African Americans with whom she had formed close personal relationships, and Kirchner admits that she "wasn't accustomed to the things you're not supposed to say."[54]

Similarly, many Brooklyn CORE members had to get accustomed to Kirk Flascher's kosher dietary restraints when they had dinner meetings at their homes, as well as his tendency to argue multiple sides of an issue late into the night. His harangues made meetings last for hours, but Brooklyn CORE's active membership, which was still fewer than a dozen, learned over time to accommodate members' different personalities. The chapter grew into a democratic, tolerant community. Like learning how to organize effective demonstrations and to mount productive campaigns against racial discrimination, overcoming personality difficulties within the organization was a necessary process in building a viable social movement organization.[55]

Over time Brooklyn CORE developed a supportive, almost familial atmosphere. Members called each other several times a week and encouraged one another to attend various meetings, rallies, and demonstrations throughout the city. "If about six or seven individuals are telling you to come back and participate, and getting on the telephone and calling you," remembered Mary Ellen Phifer Kirton, "it gives you a sense of belonging and that individuals really want you to be part of their organization." Elaine Bibuld, who joined CORE in early 1962, was also struck by how cohesive the group was. She recollected, "When you called an action everybody came. Everybody was there. One of the things that was so impressive was the loyalty of the group. No matter where it was going on, if you had to come later, you got there anyhow. You got there when you could. I remember bringing food because people would be coming from work to be on a picket line or to be at a sit-in."[56]

This tight-knit friendship and trust became a part of the chapter's culture, as did a tendency for brash, antagonistic behavior. Indeed, Brooklyn CORE's boldness became its trademark. Early on, its members enjoyed using audacious tactics that both articulated their disagreement with racial discrimination and annoyed or inconvenienced bigots and their supporters. During the Woolworth's boycotts, Arnold Goldwag lived in a ground-floor apartment of a private house in Flatbush, Brooklyn, and he proudly placed a CORE sticker that read "Boycott Woolworth's" on his front door. The landlord, who at the time was showing the house to potential buyers, removed Goldwag's sticker whenever real estate agents or couples came to view the house. Goldwag always replaced the sticker and eventually confronted the landlord, who told him he didn't support that "Communist crap," and "he didn't want it on *his* door," to which Goldwag replied that as long as he paid his rent on time he could put on the door whatever he pleased. The back-and-forth antics continued until Goldwag and other Brooklyn CORE members went to the landlord's office, which had a large front window that faced a busy thoroughfare, and plastered the entire facade with stickers that said, "Boycott Woolworth's."[57]

Later, on a Saturday morning during one of Brooklyn CORE's attempts to force an intransigent landlord to rent an apartment to a black person, Goldwag suggested that they move the picket line from outside the landlord's home to his synagogue. Most in the small group of picketers did not think it appropriate, so Goldwag decided to go to the synagogue by himself. The other picketers followed. Rioghan Kirchner remembered that not only did Goldwag picket outside the synagogue but, after the landlord arrived, Goldwag, "followed the guy in, and went all through the synagogue with his picket sign," which listed the landlord's name and announced that he discriminated against blacks. As irreverent and seemingly disrespectful as the tactic was, it worked. People in the synagogue began arguing with each other about whether they should forcefully remove Goldwag from the synagogue or let him stay, since they considered racial discrimination unjust and unholy. Eventually, the landlord changed his policy and rented the apartment to the black applicant.[58]

Actions such as these earned Goldwag a reputation as the "bad boy" of Brooklyn CORE and were the types of demonstrations that Palmer argued were counterproductive and unnecessary. Indeed, Palmer seemed reluctant in most cases to participate in even less provocative tactics. Despite members' criticisms of his leadership, Palmer was not totally averse to direct action. He participated in the sit-in at the Ira Management Company during Margaret Chapman's housing case in October 1961, but he disapproved of the Lefrak campaign after Brooklyn CORE members escalated their tactics. Palmer's absence from the sit-in at Lefrak headquarters and his refusal to participate in negotiations earned him a reputation as an ineffective chairman.[59]

Palmer, along with Brown, also poorly managed the chapter's various committees, and the two were terrible at organizing general meetings. During the fall of 1961 Brooklyn CORE's committee leaders experienced miscommunications and had arguments that brought the chapter to the brink of dissolution. Most problems revolved around the chapter's Constitution Committee, which was charged with the task of preparing a chapter constitution for approval by the membership and the national office. Palmer and Brown disappeared from committee meetings for weeks at a time without providing up-to-date contact information, and when they returned, they vetoed the Constitution Committee's work, chastised its volunteers, and revoked their power to call meetings on their own. Members of the committee reported Palmer to Gordon Carey, the National CORE field director, whose job it was to make sure local chapters ran smoothly. Carey tried to solve the problem by assigning representatives from the national office to monitor Brooklyn CORE's activities and mediate their conflicts. But Brooklyn CORE's members did not need outside advice; they desired a change in the character of the group's leadership.[60]

By the end of September there had not been a general chapter meeting in over a month. The active membership was still fewer than a dozen, but the affiliated members numbered more than forty. Since the chapter was growing and its active members sought leaders who were more supportive of direct-action campaigns, they moved to replace Palmer with someone who would be a better organizer and more militant. They found their new leader in Oliver Leeds.

Although not an active member at the time, Leeds had attended a few meetings since the Woolworth's boycott. Some Brooklyn CORE members knew him from his ongoing work with the Negro History Association, and others were familiar with his background as an experienced community organizer. Marjorie Leeds was the first member who asked him to get involved with the chapter, and others to whom he had become close over the preceding year, such as Maurice Fredericks and

Rioghan Kirchner, expressed similar feelings. "Come down, get involved, become the chairman. We'll get something done here, otherwise we're all quitting," Leeds remembered them saying. According to Leeds, he went to the next meeting, and, once again, Palmer did not attend. So the members elected him interim chairman.[61]

Oliver Leeds recalled that Brooklyn CORE's members "felt I would go for the direct action." National CORE did not challenge the coup, nor did its leaders reject Oliver Leeds because of his past membership in the Communist Party. Before accepting the position as chairman, Leeds sent word about his past to James Farmer, who had become national director of CORE on February 1, 1961. Farmer had no problem with a former Communist acting as chairman of Brooklyn CORE. Under Farmer's leadership, CORE was moving away from its staunch anti-Communist ideology, which had dominated the organization during the 1950s, and he worked to make CORE a recognizable national civil rights organization committed to nonviolence, direct-action protest, and interracial membership. In the heady times of the early 1960s, experienced local leaders like Oliver Leeds were essential to making those ideals a reality in local chapters.[62]

On January 26, 1962, Palmer sent an ambiguous letter of resignation to National CORE and the Brooklyn membership. The letter did not explain why he was stepping down as leader of Brooklyn CORE. He wrote only that "the most critical moment has arisen which is requesting an immediate decision about my future in this area of human relations. I have examined the problem carefully, and the prognosis is unfavorable." Although his time as chairman had come to an end, he said he would "be available for matters pertaining to Brooklyn CORE which have to be resolved because of my past position." Ben Brown remained a member of Brooklyn CORE, but he abdicated his position as vice chairman of the chapter and became less active in Brooklyn CORE's day-to-day leadership. As for Palmer, none of Brooklyn CORE's documents ever mention what happened to him, and former Brooklyn CORE members don't remember seeing him again at any of the chapter's activities.[63]

Brooklyn CORE transitioned to a new leadership cadre without any losses in its membership or bitter feelings toward Leeds from Palmer's supporters. In recognition of her leadership on housing issues, Rioghan Kirchner replaced Ben Brown as the chapter's vice chairman and remained the leader of the Housing Committee. Arnold Goldwag continued to serve as the public relations chairman and publicity coordinator, Maurice Fredericks became the chairman of the Employment

Committee, and Kurt Flascher and an African American working-class woman, Barbara Weeks, cochaired the Membership Committee. Indeed, the new leadership cadre reflected the type of interracial, democratic community Brooklyn CORE envisioned for the rest of society: it consisted of three blacks, three whites; Jews, Christians, radicals, and conservatives. Women, black and white, had influence over decisions and possessed real power within the organization. Brooklyn CORE's struggles, however, were far from over. Members often debated the appropriate uses of direct-action tactics during campaigns, National CORE continued to monitor the Brooklyn chapter's activities, active membership remained small, and alliances with other activist groups proved difficult to sustain. Brooklyn CORE members' vision of leading and participating in a mass movement against racial discrimination still seemed an unlikely possibility.

These struggles were largely a backdrop to Brooklyn CORE's strengthening culture of camaraderie and aggressive protest philosophy, which led it to spearhead a campaign against the Ebinger Baking Company. Ebinger's had a notorious reputation for discriminating against African Americans, Puerto Ricans, and Jews who sought jobs in their outlet stores and at their baking plants. Indeed, during the summer of 1962 the Ebinger's campaign established Brooklyn CORE as one of the more audacious local protest groups in New York City and one of the most noted CORE chapters throughout the country.

4

OPERATION UNEMPLOYMENT

Breaking through the Color Line in Local Industries

> Central to any understanding of the aggregate situation in Bedford-
> Stuyvesant or any large, black urban slum-ghetto must be the
> pervasiveness of income deprivation among the area's residents.
> Although it offers no guarantee against poor living conditions,
> illness, or poor nutrition, money does provide a certain access to
> more adequate levels of shelter, health care and parenthetically
> power. As long as blacks in Brooklyn or anywhere else continue in
> relative and/or absolute economic poverty, they will remain a
> deprived people, a people set apart.
> —Harold X. Connolly, *A Ghetto Grows in Brooklyn,* 1977

When Oliver Leeds became chairman of Brooklyn CORE in January
1962, he inherited a membership that was small, socially cohesive, and
very energetic, but also extremely disorganized. Aside from problems
with its leadership, Brooklyn CORE lacked a regular meeting space, and
the few general meetings that were held were unfocused and lasted for
over three hours. The chapter's Housing, Education, and Employment
Committees discussed initiating investigations and staging campaigns,
but they did little concrete planning. Brooklyn CORE's Membership
Committee also did a poor job of teaching CORE's organizing philosophy and principles. The chapter was eager to continue building a movement against local forms of racial discrimination, as it had done with
cases of housing discrimination, but if Oliver Leeds was going to keep
Brooklyn CORE from falling apart, he needed to bring order to its day-
to-day operations and steer it toward more manageable action projects.

The new leadership cadre resolved many of their organizational difficulties during a campaign to open employment at the Ebinger Baking

Company, which was the first major local action campaign under Leeds's stewardship. Members formed alliances with other local activist groups and slowly gained people's confidence. They debated protest tactics and honed their skills for creating nonviolent disturbances that captured newspaper headlines and forced Ebinger executives to sit down and negotiate. Indeed, experimenting with aggressive and inventive protest tactics during the Ebinger's campaign established Brooklyn CORE's activists' credentials throughout the city. The chapter's dramatization of employment discrimination at Ebinger's even garnered a bit of national press coverage. By the end of this campaign, Brooklyn CORE was not only a recognizable local civil rights organization, but also one of the most respected and radical CORE chapters in the country.[1]

Brooklyn CORE ran this successful campaign in spite of internal divisions and disagreements among some members. The Ebinger's campaign paints a revealing picture of how a social movement organization could become embroiled in petty arguments and internal factionalism. In fact, the chapter's democratic culture, which gave every member an equal voice, created an organizational structure in which a small number of people could hijack and derail the organization's operations. When this disruption occurred, as it did because of the behavior of one member, Kurt Flascher, some in Brooklyn CORE attempted to silence Flascher with strong-arm, undemocratic tactics. Kurt Flascher was an incredibly committed member of Brooklyn CORE, but some felt that his prickly personality and conservative politics were disruptive and destructive. The internal dissension that arose as a response to Kurt Flascher's membership threatened Brooklyn CORE's democratic ethos. In the midst of fighting to gain jobs for black workers, CORE members also had to manage their own personality differences and internal disagreements, which threatened to crush the group's camaraderie and cohesiveness. These were organizational politics that nearly every social movement group faces. Beneath the surface of a protest group's successful public campaign there sometimes exist potentially destructive fighting, tension, and personality politics.

In the midst of weathering those internal storms, Brooklyn CORE addressed an issue that was at the center of early 1960s black urban life: the need for good, stable jobs. As more and more black people came to Brooklyn and many other northern cities in the decades following the end of World War II, they entered a political economy in which manufacturing was on the decline and service industries were on the rise. Black people needed to escape from the perpetual instability of being "last hired, first fired." Brooklyn CORE and its local allies made protest demands that, in later years, would be called affirmative action. They wanted employers like Ebinger's to move "beyond tokenism" and to make an institutional, structural commitment to hire more black and, during this campaign, Puerto Rican workers. Brooklyn CORE's Ebinger's campaign represented one of the first early 1960s calls to combat urban employment discrimination with compensatory hiring practices that favored minority workers over whites. Such demands would echo in cities throughout the remainder of the decade and become major parts of black activist politics for the rest of the century. Just as affirmative action proved to be a contentious political issue later in the century, Brooklyn CORE's highlighting of employment discrimination in 1962 attracted a host of critics who blamed black people's social failings on their own cultural shortcomings. Brooklyn CORE, therefore, had to fight both a political battle against companies like Ebinger's for economic justice and an ideological battle against people who argued that black people's struggles for stable, secure jobs had more to do with black behavior than with racial discrimination.[2]

The Ebinger Baking Company, which had discriminated against minorities for decades, proved a formidable opponent. Founded in 1898 in the Flatbush section of Brooklyn, Ebinger's became famous for its German pastries, coffee rings, and cakes, especially its "blackout cake." By the early 1960s the company had expanded to more than fifty retail stores in Brooklyn, Queens, and Staten Island. Its retail clerks, all women, were popularly called "Ebinger girls," and they were known for their fast, friendly customer service, immaculately white uniforms, and spotlessly clean counters. Ebinger's boosters took pride in the company's history of serving the working- and middle-class residents of New York City's outer boroughs. Still, an unwritten policy was that only certain women could become Ebinger girls, and only certain men could work as bakers or store managers. During the early twentieth century and up through World War II, those were jobs for white Christians only: Jews and blacks need not apply. A handful of black men worked for the company as janitors, or as low level workers in the baking division; very few had attained coveted positions as delivery truck drivers. Such discriminatory practices continued into the postwar period, when working-class jobs in the city's manufacturing and service trades, such as those in the baking, apparel, retail, and jewelry industries, still provided economically stable wages that enabled individuals to afford the cost of living in New York City. Thus, into the 1960s, the Ebinger Baking Company represented white economic privilege closed to Brooklyn's black workers. The company's unofficial policies of racial discrimination barred African

Americans from attaining jobs—as bakers, retail clerks, managers—that provided stable lifestyles to many of Brooklyn's white working-class women and men. During the spring and summer of 1962, Brooklyn CORE investigated Ebinger's and demonstrated against its policies as a way to redress these economic and labor discrepancies. This jobs campaign attracted a great deal of media attention, and it even inspired teenagers in Brooklyn to form a CORE chapter. The results in terms of creating more jobs for black people, however, were not as significant as CORE members had hoped.[3]

Brooklyn CORE Joins with Operation Unemployment and Attracts a Following

The boycott against Ebinger's was not the first encounter between the company and Brooklyn CORE. When Robert Palmer was chairman of Brooklyn CORE, the chapter had investigated charges of discriminatory hiring practices at the company. After several meetings with its management, Palmer had negotiated a deal for them to hire "six Negro salesgirls." He thought the matter was settled. But members of another local organization, Operation Unemployment (OU), which operated through a black political club in Bedford-Stuyvesant, the Unity Democratic Coalition (UDC), had less faith in the company's willingness to keep its promise to Palmer. From OU's experience, Ebinger's was notorious for its refusal to hire people of color. When OU suspected Ebinger's had reneged on its commitment to hire black women, the group started its own investigation and found that the company had done nothing. A co-coordinator of OU, Andrew Cooper, suggested an immediate boycott, but Palmer refused to support it. In Palmer's view, the activists had not made every possible attempt to sway the hearts and minds of Ebinger's managers through negotiation, education, and reason. Until they reached that point, Palmer argued, direct-action protest was unnecessary and counterproductive because it would dissuade Ebinger's from further negotiations with the groups. Cooper and some members of Brooklyn CORE disagreed with Palmer's decision. OU tried to organize its own boycott of Ebinger's. On one occasion, a manager of Ebinger's referred to the coffee shop chain where Jackie Robinson worked as a company executive when he told black women picketers, "You'll never get a job here. Go to Chock Full o'Nuts, where you belong." The boycott, however, never gained momentum because OU was a small activist wing of a political club, and it could not mount an effective campaign on its own. It lacked the experience with direct-action protest campaigns needed to draw support and sustain a long protest. Still, OU was determined to integrate the baking company's workforce. "Ebinger's must know by now that we will not let them rest until they start hiring Negro, Puerto Rican and Jewish employees," Cooper wrote. "We will be out with our picket lines until they learn this simple lesson in Americanism and fair play."[4]

Brooklyn CORE wanted to expand its activities beyond individual housing cases, and OU hoped to focus local civil rights activists' attention on racial discrimination in employment, so the two groups formed a stronger alliance. Cooper helped Brooklyn CORE's new cadre find a permanent headquarters in a small storefront at 319 Nostrand Avenue, in the heart of Bedford-Stuyvesant. The lawyer who owned the space had few clients and deep sympathy for Brooklyn CORE's cause. He gladly shared his office with the chapter and charged them a minimal monthly rental fee (around fifty dollars), which they covered through membership dues and fund-raising parties. Before long the new headquarters became a virtual community center for local activists and residents. Leslie Campbell, a young teacher who lived and worked in Bedford-Stuyvesant, was attracted to Brooklyn CORE's militancy and dedication. "Their vision," he recalled, "was to wipe out racism of all types and create a society that was totally integrated." Campbell always admired Brooklyn CORE members for their relentless dedication to that goal and their willingness to engage in direct-action protests. At first, he just frequented the office and discussed politics and the civil rights movement with CORE members, but eventually Campbell began helping the Housing Committee with its testing projects. He remembered how young African Americans who were looking for work or trying to rent a decent apartment would come to the CORE office for assistance. The space became a nexus of information on housing laws, jobs, and reputable landlords. Indeed, Brooklyn CORE slowly became a trusted organization in the community. Many in Bedford-Stuyvesant welcomed the interracial activists and supported their dynamic efforts to create more opportunities for Brooklyn's black residents.[5]

With their base of operations established, Oliver Leeds and Maurice Fredericks, who was head of the chapter's Employment Committee, recommitted Brooklyn CORE to the Ebinger's campaign. OU had begun a weekly picket line in front of Ebinger's Brooklyn stores in mid-January. The demonstrations, held every Saturday, had sparse attendance and little effect on Ebinger's sales. The company's management ignored requests for further negotiations and refused to give any more concrete assurance it would hire more black workers. Brooklyn CORE's new leadership decided to make Ebinger's its main action project, and Fredericks helped OU plan its next organizational meeting for mid-March.[6]

Brooklyn CORE and OU's mobilization against Ebinger's caught the attention of high school students who wanted to start their own CORE chapter. They were initially attracted to Brooklyn CORE's reputation for militancy and grassroots activism, which it earned during its battles against prejudiced landlords and realtors who discriminated against blacks. John Akula, a senior at Erasmus Hall High School, contacted National CORE's Manhattan headquarters and expressed interest in forming a student CORE affiliate of the Brooklyn chapter. The national office sent Mary Hamilton to the students' first organizational meeting, which was held at Akula's home. Hamilton was a young black woman from the West Coast who had participated in CORE's 1961 Freedom Rides and had become an experienced field secretary in the South, where she organized CORE chapters in Louisiana before coming to New York to work with local chapters throughout the state. Over thirty students from five of Brooklyn's most academically competitive high schools attended, and Hamilton noted there was only one black student present. Unlike the adult chapter of Brooklyn CORE, which had an even number of black and white members, Student CORE (or SCORE) was overwhelmingly white. Part of the reason for SCORE's racial imbalance was that Brooklyn's elite public schools had very low numbers of black students. A trickle of blacks began to integrate these schools in the late 1950s and the 1960s, but of those black students, very few were a part of the social and political circles that organized SCORE. Most of the youngsters initially drawn to SCORE knew each other from other political clubs, especially high school chapters of the Committee for a Sane Nuclear Policy (SANE for short), and they shared common ethnic and religious backgrounds. Many were the children or grandchildren of Eastern European Jewish immigrants; some of their parents had been Old Leftists or Communist Party sympathizers during the 1930s and 1940s, and they also supported the 1960s civil rights movement. Since SCORE organizers recruited among their friends and their high schools' politically activist subcultures, its membership mirrored these predominantly white social networks.[7]

The overwhelming whiteness of the group was not a problem for the student organizers or Hamilton. John Akula assumed the role of chairman and presented Hamilton with an agenda. SCORE sought permission to become an affiliate of Brooklyn CORE and approval to do its own action project. Like many other young people who were eager to participate in the local civil rights movement, SCORE leaders were attracted to Brooklyn CORE's militant reputation. "Brooklyn CORE at that point was a group that was held in very high regard, and it was very heavily active in what was going on," remembers John Akula. Eleanor Stein, another early leader of SCORE, echoed Akula's thoughts. "The Brooklyn CORE group was fairly militant on the spectrum [of civil rights organizations]," she recalled, "and I think that we identified with that."[8]

But like a stern parent who cautions a child against socializing with troublemakers, Hamilton tried very hard to steer the youngsters away from Brooklyn CORE. She thought it better for them to work with Long Island University CORE, since members of LIU CORE were closer to them in age and experience. Although she did not say so to the students, Hamilton also felt Brooklyn CORE's organizational problems and radical culture would be a negative influence on them. In her notes she wrote, "The state of affairs in Brooklyn CORE is not one that is conducive to developing young people new to organization." SCORE members listened respectfully. When Hamilton finished speaking, Akula quickly informed her that the group had "already decided to work with Brooklyn CORE."[9]

Despite Hamilton's obvious distaste for Brooklyn CORE, Akula remained adamant about the students' choice. Brooklyn CORE inspired SCORE members, and they saw that chapter as their model for a local civil rights protest community. Many of their ideas for action projects mirrored the work of Brooklyn CORE. The group discussed spearheading an investigation into high schools' employment discrimination against blacks and Puerto Ricans. It also discussed leading its own tests of housing segregation in Brooklyn's predominantly white neighborhoods. SCORE leaders had already joined Operation Unemployment's protest against Ebinger's. They targeted an Ebinger's retail store not far from Erasmus Hall High School in a largely Jewish section of Flatbush and planned to organize a picket line there every Saturday. Akula also informed Hamilton that one of the girls had already formed a CORE study group at her high school. Hamilton gave them a strong endorsement, but she urged the national office to do whatever possible to keep them from joining Brooklyn CORE.[10]

In defiance of Mary Hamilton's efforts, the high school students met with Oliver Leeds, Rioghan Kirchner, and Fredricka Teer, an assistant to James Farmer, to discuss their affiliation with Brooklyn CORE. SCORE was eager for adult leadership, and, according to Teer, "they were practically begging us for direction." Leeds and Kirchner were interested in accepting the students but unsure how they should proceed. Mentoring

SCORE involved a serious time commitment, and they were not sure anyone in Brooklyn CORE could do it. National CORE could provide a temporary liaison to work with SCORE, but a permanent adviser had to come from Brooklyn CORE if the high school group was to be its official affiliate. Leeds and Kirchner found them the perfect mentor: Arnold Goldwag.[11]

Brash, energetic, and one of the more daring members of Brooklyn CORE, Goldwag was a part-time student at Brooklyn College, a part-time insurance fraud investigator, and a full-time activist. He had been raised in a strict Orthodox Jewish home, and his parents had planned for him to attend rabbinical school and become a Talmudic scholar. "I was scheduled to be a holy roller," he recalled. Indeed, his brother and sister followed their parents' wishes: the brother became a rabbi and the sister married a rabbi's son. Goldwag boasted with a chuckle that he was the "black sheep of the family." His parents did not approve of his involvement in the civil rights movement and thought he should let black people take care of their own problems. But Goldwag believed strongly that racial discrimination was America's greatest sin. It violated every principle he had grown up believing was fundamentally good: democracy, freedom, and equality. As an unmarried, idealistic, and adventurous twenty-four-year-old, he was close enough to their age that SCORE members could relate to him, and he had few obligations that would prevent him from serving as their adviser. With SCORE now part of Brooklyn CORE and the chapter settled in its new headquarters, the leadership turned its attention toward organizing a more aggressive campaign to open employment at the Ebinger Baking Company.[12]

"Don't Be Fooled by Tokenism"

Brooklyn CORE's April 1962 newsletter featured a blurb on the Employment Committee's activities. Its chairman, Maurice Fredericks, announced the chapter's alliance with Operation Unemployment and declared that Brooklyn CORE would picket the Ebinger Baking Company each Saturday until its managers agreed to hire more blacks and Puerto Ricans. Fredericks reported that on the previous Saturday Brooklyn CORE had sent members to a "joint street meeting" with Operation Unemployment. The two groups stood in front of the company's main retail store in Bedford-Stuyvesant, located on the corner of Fulton Street and Nostrand Avenue, and staged a public discussion on the company's discriminatory hiring practices. CORE and Operation Unemployment

members also handed out flyers that exclaimed, "DON'T CROSS THE FREE-
DOM LINE. DON'T BUY AT EBINGER. DON'T BE FOOLED BY TOKENISM."[13]

Months after the company agreed to hire a handful of black women
to work as salesclerks, nothing had changed. Its Ebinger girls were still
all white, even in the main store in Bedford-Stuyvesant. Brooklyn
CORE's previous investigations revealed that before the demonstrations
began, the company "had no Negro or Puerto Rican saleswomen in their
working force." There were no African Americans or Puerto Ricans in
the company's skilled trades, as bakers or chefs, and Ebinger's had very
few blacks and Puerto Ricans among the company's truck drivers. CORE
made its findings public in leaflets that advertised that the baking company had "never hired even a single Negro or Puerto Rican office
worker" and had "resorted to tokenism" when, after sixty-four years, it
hired two full-time and two part-time black salesgirls out of a total of
240 workers. "Must we wait another 64 years before Ebinger hires two
more?" the flyer asked. Brooklyn CORE implored citizens to join the
boycott and "PLEASE HELP US FINISH THE JOB."[14]

Brooklyn CORE also collaborated on the campaign with local ministers and the Brooklyn chapters of the NAACP and Urban League. The
NAACP recruited its members' children to picket the store at Nostrand
and Fulton and pass out leaflets throughout Bedford-Stuyvesant. The
Reverend Milton Galamison agreed to participate in negotiations with
the company's management and publicize the boycott among his parishioners. With Brooklyn CORE's approval, SCORE organized picket lines
in front of four different Ebinger's stores in Flatbush and Crown Heights.
Some police officers disapproved of the teenagers' activities. On one
occasion they threatened to give picketers from SCORE a summons for
disorderly conduct and to arrest Arnold Goldwag for endangering the
lives of minors. Anti-Communist sentiment colored some Brooklynites'
responses to predominantly white high school students picketing against
racial discrimination. Goldwag, who later recalled he was there every
Saturday with the youngsters, remembered someone approaching the
group and calling them "a bunch of little Commies," and him "a *big*
Commie!"[15]

But public criticism was low on the campaign's list of problems.
Despite the extra support Brooklyn CORE received from other civil
rights activists, the chapter poorly managed the campaign. It had too
many picket lines and not enough volunteers. Some lines, such as the
ones in Bedford-Stuyvesant and Flatbush, drew crowds of over twenty
people each week. Others, such as the one in Brooklyn's downtown
area, near Borough Hall and the County Courts, were fortunate to have

five people attend the Saturday picket line. Organizers also did a poor job of communicating with the police. Law enforcement officials disrupted picket lines and demanded to see participants' demonstration permits. The harassment stopped once CORE learned that it had to notify precincts before they formed a picket line.[16]

Minor problems on the picket lines aside, the spate of activity forced Ebinger's management to sit down and negotiate on May 25, 1962, this time with an alliance of local activists. Oliver Leeds, Milton Galamison, and W. J. Roy of the Brooklyn Urban League attended the conference with Cecil Trineer of the Ebinger Baking Company. Trineer maintained that Ebinger's hiring policies were democratic and not discriminatory, but he conceded that "a certain unbalance exists in the numbers and categories of Negroes employed." He admitted that it was in Ebinger's best interest "to change this unbalance and re-establish Ebinger's image as a corporation always willing to cooperate with community groups working in the interest of the community." Once again, he agreed that the company would immediately take steps to change its employment patterns.[17]

First, Ebinger's said it would immediately hire an African American woman as a full-time salesclerk no later than the first week of June 1962, which would bring the total number of black Ebinger girls to five. Trineer also declared that the company would immediately hire two black women to work part-time and would continue to hire black women to fill three of every five available positions for an indefinite period. Next, Ebinger's agreed to work with the Urban League to find qualified African American office workers. It also promised to request black salesclerks and truck drivers from the two unions that supplied new workers for those positions. And by the first week of June, Ebinger's would issue a public statement that repudiated racial discrimination and declared its intentions to increase its number of black employees.[18]

Despite Brooklyn CORE's advocacy for more Puerto Rican workers at Ebinger's, there was no mention of them during this round of negotiations. Trineer did not include Puerto Ricans in his promises to hire more women of color as Ebinger's girls, nor did the activists demand that Puerto Ricans be given as much representation as blacks in Ebinger's recruitment programs. Indeed, there were no Puerto Ricans even present at the negotiation. Though campaign organizers imagined them as part of "the community" that needed jobs at the baking company, they did not seem to make Puerto Rican people, or their interests, a priority during these talks.

But including Puerto Ricans at the bargaining table would not have made much of a difference in convincing Ebinger's to hire more people of color. Brooklyn CORE's Executive Committee was not optimistic that Ebinger's would honor its promises, and they planned to intensify the protest. At its meeting on May 30 chapter leaders agreed that if Trineer stalled past the first week of June, Brooklyn CORE would hold a sit-in at the company's Bedford-Stuyvesant store. On Friday, June 1, Arnold Goldwag attended a negotiation session with Ebinger's management. During the chapter's next general meeting he reported that the company was "hedging, especially in connection with the 3 out of 5 hiring question." Brooklyn CORE members postponed their sit-ins until after Oliver Leeds communicated with Ebinger's management. Leeds was also unsuccessful in convincing them to move ahead with the May 25 agreement, so the chapter was forced to make an important decision: either exercise patience and continue with the picket lines and negotiations, or initiate some form of direct action that would pressure the company into delivering on its promises.[19]

The chapter erred on the side of caution and waited to see what Ebinger's would do over the summer. As promised, the company had hired two new black women salesclerks, but it offered no tangible proof it would follow through with the rest of its agreement. This struck many Brooklyn CORE members as another example of Ebinger's tokenism. They were not satisfied with the campaign's results and tried to rally more support. Brooklyn CORE's June newsletter carried a blurb with the heading "CORE Makes Gains at Ebinger's but Continues Picketing," which noted that with the two new hires the total number of black women working in the company was only 6 of a total 240 salesgirls. Both CORE and SCORE declared they would continue organizing picket lines until Ebinger's met all their demands.[20]

A Call to Action

The picket lines and negotiations continued through June and July, and Ebinger's made no effort to hire more blacks or Puerto Ricans. Brooklyn CORE members realized the only way to make change was to force it on the company's management with more aggressive tactics. They planned a massive demonstration at all Ebinger's stores in Brooklyn on Saturday, August 4, 1962. CORE issued a call to action in the form of a letter in which it urged participation in a "mass demonstration against 39 of the Ebinger Baking Corporation's retail stores." The call invoked Ebinger's "long history of bigotry and unfair hiring practices in Brooklyn, where many of their stores are located in ghetto areas," and it derided Ebinger's for hiring only "2 'light-skinned' Negro sales clerks." The main sticking point was Ebinger's refusal to honor the agreement to allocate three of every five new employee positions to African Americans. "Since it has been impossible to come to any reasonable and working terms with the firm's representatives," the letter concluded, "we ask you to join us in this mass effort to once and for all end the discriminatory hiring practices of a firm earning the bulk of its profits from minority groups while refusing recognition of their rights to equal employment opportunities."[21]

Brooklyn CORE also sought cooperation with other CORE chapters. Maurice Fredericks wrote to Fredricka Teer at National CORE and implored her to publicize the August 4 demonstration to New York–area contacts. The logistical demands of the upcoming Saturday's event were more than Brooklyn CORE could handle, and it would need all the support it could muster. The chapter sought to organize picket lines and leaflet distribution tables in front of thirty-nine of the forty-two Ebinger's stores, and to assign at least five or six people to each store. They reached out to over sixty churches and recruited progressive ministers such as Milton Galamison to encourage other black pastors to form the ministers' movement to support the boycott and help make it an effective, meaningful protest. Fredericks named the meeting location and time when the picket lines would begin. He closed his letter to Teer by mentioning Brooklyn CORE's plans to intensify the campaign. "We, in Brooklyn CORE," he wrote, "have elected to stage a simultaneous sit-in in each of the stores picketed if we have enough people willing to do so, and unless legal counsel advises against it." Teer relayed the information to other CORE chapters and gave a summary of the Ebinger's campaign, but she omitted the plans for the sit-in. Given Brooklyn CORE's past organizational problems, she might have thought it would not be organized well enough to coordinate such a massive direct action tactic.[22]

Some citizens were more direct in their condemnation of the campaign. During the buildup to the August 4 demonstration, people wrote letters that criticized Brooklyn CORE's efforts and derided African Americans and Puerto Ricans. One unsigned letter stated: "To whom it may concern: All I can say is the NAACP and CORE is a trouble making organization. It should be wiped out. Down with Niggers and Spics: EBINGER'S IS OKAY BY ME."[23]

A letter from Linda Marks expressed ideas shared by many white residents of Brooklyn who were sympathetic to the boycott but did not see it as a solution for black people's problems. Marks differentiated between "good" and "bad" black people and argued that "respectable"

African Americans should work to "uplift" poorer blacks culturally. The main barriers to an integrated society, she contended, were not job discrimination, but black criminality and sentiments of black nationalism, which made whites fearful in their own neighborhoods. Her letter merits quoting in its entirety:

> I am in accordance with your rules about Ebinger's bakery and I would not purchase from them, but I thought this might be a good place to find help in what's going on in Brooklyn since the Negroes came to live here. Why should the nice refined people of your race suffer for the bad ones? We never were afraid to venture out after dark, we used to sit on Eastern Parkway until all hours on hot nights and go to Prospect Park after dark but now since the colored people came to Brooklyn, we have rape, muggings and robberies and it is up to *you* of your own *race* to get after this type of hoodlum and help us so we can have Brooklyn as in years gone by. This is not meant as an affront but pleading for help. You have to help your own, get after them, teach them not to be torrid *white haters*. Also as for discrimination, just look at the colored people. They never employ white help. I live in a house with Negroes, very nice families but my landlord wants only Negro families in his house and the colored people do not hide their feelings towards whites. They go only to their own shops if they can, hire colored taxi drivers mostly, in hospital and homes partiality is greatly shown. In Kings County the white people are badly treated by fanatic white haters. It is up to *you* to straighten these situations out before we can all be as one. The Jewish people work very hard to help the colored, but are mostly hated by them and it is very obvious. Please try to help us. We are afraid to go out. We live in fear at all times. It is up to the Negroes to get after their own. That's the only way.[24]

Marks made clear in her letter that she expressed concerns shared by others. She viewed social problems with race through a nostalgic lens of Brooklyn before African Americans moved into neighborhoods like Bedford-Stuyvesant, Brownsville, and East New York. She recognized that Ebinger's was culpable of racial discrimination through exclusionary hiring, which is why she supported the boycott. Still, Marks's argument that Brooklyn's problems (for both whites and "nice refined" black people) were caused by "fanatic white haters" and "hoodlums" was based on a notion of "respectability" that conflated social inequality with individuals' behavior. The black "underclass," in her mind, was inherently pathological and would remain the source of Brooklyn's worst social problems until "respectable" blacks vigorously policed their behavior. Until that happened, Marks argued, integration, whereby "we can all be as one," would remain a fantasy.[25]

The attitude that middle-class African Americans who were economically secure and socially "respectable" had a responsibility to "uplift" the black lower class, especially newcomers from the rural South, was a long-standing characteristic of African American communities in the urban North after the Great Migrations of the 1910s–1940s and beyond. "Established" blacks often looked down on newcomers from the South. They criticized their unkempt appearance and their "country" ways. Some, although by no means all, northern blacks took it on themselves to help acclimate new arrivals to the "proper" ways of urban living, such as the correct ways to dispose of their trash and monitor their personal hygiene and health. The latter issue was especially important since poor urban communities were rampant with communicable diseases. As can happen in any ethnic or racial group, class, religious, gender, and generational divisions pitted some blacks against each another as they vied for positions of power, status, and influence in their new urban environments.[26]

Unlike Linda Marks, who qualified her endorsement of the civil rights movement with commentary on black people's behavior, most supporters of the boycott shared E. J. Stelzer's sentiments. Stelzer wrote to Brooklyn CORE and thanked it for "calling to my attention by picketing Ebinger's bakeries the fact that this company denies equal employment opportunities to minority groups. As a result, I did not make any purchases in Ebinger's today. I join you in protest and shall not patronize the store until Ebinger's substantially alters its hiring practices." Some 3,800 others agreed with Stelzer and signed the pledge cards demonstrators handed out in front of Ebinger's stores during the August 4 demonstration. The cards, sent to the Ebinger Baking Company headquarters on Bedford Avenue in Brooklyn, stated, "I have pledged not to buy at any of the Ebinger's stores until you agree to hire without discrimination. My family enjoys your products and we would like to resume our patronage of your stores as soon as possible—so please let me know when you have come to an agreement with the Ministers' Movement and with CORE."[27]

Along with the cards, pedestrians received a flyer with the heading "Equal Employment Opportunity vs. Ebinger Baking Company," which framed the protest in a discourse on American democracy. "The Ebinger

Baking Company is denying equal employment opportunities to minority groups. This is contrary to the basic principles upon which this country was founded, and tends to undermine our democratic government." This flyer also reminded people of Ebinger's history of discrimination against Jews in addition to discrimination against African Americans and Puerto Ricans. It stated, "This company has a long history of defying any and all civil rights agencies. . . . We find it necessary today to picket Ebinger's Bakeries throughout Brooklyn to once and for all end the discriminatory hiring practices of a firm earning the bulk of its profits from groups—Negroes, Jews and Puerto Ricans—while refusing recognition of their rights to equal employment opportunities."[28]

But getting jobs for Jews at Ebinger's was not a priority of the boycott; getting jobs for African Americans was. Still, Brooklyn CORE's campaign discourse tapped into a latent historical memory of Ebinger's discrimination against Jewish Brooklynites during the early twentieth century and, consequently, won sympathy from some who might otherwise have ignored the protest. Arnold Goldwag remembered that some people in predominantly Jewish neighborhoods, at least those who were former leftists, supported Brooklyn CORE's boycott because of their memories of Ebinger's discriminatory policies against them thirty years earlier:

> The Brighton Beach Store was almost completely trashed by the old Jewish guys because Ebinger, during World War II, when Jewish women applied for work, he told them he would throw them in the oven—Mr. *head* Ebinger. So they remembered this stuff. You see, they had forgotten this, kind of, and they were buying at Ebinger's. But when we started with our signs that Ebinger's discriminates against Jews, and Negroes and Puerto Ricans and all that, *yeah,* they remembered. Their wife went to apply and she came home crying. So anyway, these old Jewish radicals from the '30s, they were ready to tear that store to pieces. They were like, enough already.[29]

Eleanor Stein, a member of SCORE, had a similar recollection of how Jews sometimes unknowingly supported the protests for blacks and Puerto Ricans because of their collective memory of discrimination and prejudice. One afternoon when the white SCORE group was picketing an Ebinger's store in a Jewish section of Flatbush, a woman approached Eleanor Stein's mother, Annie, and asked her in Yiddish, "What's going on here?" Annie Stein replied in Yiddish, "They don't hire," which clearly jarred the woman's senses. Eleanor remembered: "The woman looked absolutely shocked, assuming [my mother] meant they don't hire Jews. The woman said, 'No, they don't hire?' And my mother just very eloquently shrugged her shoulder and said, 'No, they don't hire.' The woman was outraged and said she was going to tell all her friends. So she walked off assuming it was a boycott because they didn't hire Jews, and my mother was happy to let her go ahead with that conclusion and tell her friends to stop buying their cake [from Ebinger's]."[30]

Indeed, Annie Stein insinuated it was a protest in support of Jews because she knew there was a strong chance this woman, like many other Jews of her generation, might oppose the idea of Jewish activists working to secure rights for people of color. The historian David Levering Lewis has maintained that Jews often fought to secure their own civil and social rights by advocating for other marginalized groups, especially African Americans. They would indirectly benefit from others' gains and incur less risk by working behind the scenes or in subtle, quiet ways. But while some Jews in Brooklyn supported Brooklyn CORE's protest, others believed that it was not in their interest to fight for jobs for African Americans and Puerto Ricans. Despite the commonly held assumption that Jews and African Americans were "natural allies" during the civil rights movement, there were palpable tensions, which caused conflicts between the two groups and within them as well.[31]

Some Jews, even those who supported the cause of black civil rights, often were deeply afraid that if they stepped outside the boundaries of their own group to help others, they would incur the wrath and discrimination of mainstream society. Mark Naison, who became a professor of history and black studies at Fordham University, was an Erasmus student who participated in the Ebinger's demonstrations. An anecdote from his memoir, *White Boy,* illustrates how his parents, who were both public school teachers, vehemently disapproved of his decision to join SCORE's picket lines. His mother asked, "Why are you trying to help the *schvartzes?* They certainly wouldn't do anything to help you. If you are going to help someone, why don't you help the Jews?" His father protested against his son's desire to participate in political activism: "You can throw away your whole future by signing a petition or marching on a picket line. Let the *schvartzes* fight their own battles. Don't be like the teachers we knew who joined the Communist Party and ended up losing their jobs. Jews always get in trouble when they try to help other people."[32]

To be sure, some local African Americans and Puerto Ricans were also reluctant to participate in Brooklyn CORE's demonstrations or picket lines. The potential for police to mistreat black and Puerto Rican protestors or for violent recriminations from angry whites dissuaded people of color from joining the line. Potential punishment from unsympathetic employers was also a factor that dissuaded others from participating in public protest. In addition, political differences explained why some blacks and Puerto Ricans did not support the goals of the Ebinger's campaign. Puerto Ricans and African Americans who rejected identity politics as viable ways to achieve economic advancement and social acceptance might have reasoned that this protest only exacerbated existing racial tensions and made people of color seem as if they were asking for special treatment. Hard work, not handouts, they argued, was the only way to advance in American society. In particular, Puerto Ricans, who saw themselves as the newest immigrant group in New York City's economic and social pecking order, probably adhered to this mentality more than blacks, but certainly some African Americans also looked scornfully at Brooklyn CORE's campaign and feared backlash from angry whites who resented such public challenges to the color line.[33]

Puerto Ricans also undoubtedly felt that they had little stake in the campaign's outcomes, since they were not represented in the protest's leadership. Brooklyn CORE's most glaring omission during the campaign was its failure to reach out to Puerto Rican citizens and organizations. All its flyers and placards were, up to this point, written in English, which excluded many Puerto Rican citizens who spoke only Spanish. Nowhere in its newsletters did it mention any attempts to form alliances with local Puerto Rican civic organizations or invite leaders from that community onto its negotiation team. At this stage of the campaign, Brooklyn CORE members did not make organizing with Puerto Ricans a priority. The tensions that may have resulted from an interracial, black-white organization acting as the spokespeople for Puerto Ricans were probably too intense for the young chapter to deal with that summer. But they would have to figure out ways to bridge those gaps if they hoped to become successful community organizers.

Although the August 4 demonstration was Brooklyn CORE's largest mobilization effort of the campaign, it still did not force Ebinger's management to accede to the protest's demands, nor did it attract large groups to join picket lines. Gaining employment at Ebinger's did not seem to be as important to local people as the chapter might have thought. Almost all its support came from the CORE chapters in the metropolitan area. Brooklyn CORE had recruited over one hundred members and friends from CORE chapters at City College of New York,

New York University, Long Island University, and Staten Island, and these volunteers covered more than twenty-five stores for at least six hours. Maurice Fredericks declared that Brooklyn CORE "would continue our demonstration indefinitely," until Ebinger's decided to honor its agreement "to correct the imbalance in minority employment." Oliver Leeds hinted at the possibility of stronger tactics in case the boycott did not produce results: "Applying the technique of non-violent direct action, we intend to bring every conceivable form of community pressure to bear upon the Ebinger Baking Company until it ends its discriminatory hiring policies." Since ten months of investigation, negotiation, and demonstration in the form of boycotts and picket lines had borne few tangible results, Brooklyn CORE was ready to intensify its tactics in order to expedite change.[34]

Debates about Tactics and Members' Behavior

Brooklyn CORE held a general membership meeting on August 6, 1962, the Monday after the August 4 mobilization effort. Two issues were at the top of the agenda: first was a petition to remove Kurt Flascher, who some members felt had acted inappropriately, as chairman of the Membership Committee and from the chapter's small central leadership group, the Executive Committee, which coordinated Brooklyn CORE's various committees; second was the next course of action in the Ebinger's campaign. Leeds called the meeting to order at 8:45 P.M., and immediately there followed a debate about when to discuss Flascher's demotion. Ben Brown motioned that the petition to remove Flascher as membership secretary be the first agenda item discussed and that only active members be allowed to remain during that time. He suggested that nonactive members go out and get coffee and return in a half hour. A discussion ensued. Brooklyn CORE members knew that there was serious business to discuss regarding the Ebinger's campaign and a debate over Flascher could derail the entire meeting. Blanche Byrd, an active member, suggested saving the Flascher debate until 11:00 P.M. No matter how far they had proceeded in the agenda by that time, they would stop, dismiss the nonactive members, and debate Kurt Flascher's removal. Byrd's motion was seconded and carried. The Flascher debate was important, but it would not disrupt important business regarding the Ebinger's campaign and other committee projects.[35]

Maurice Fredericks reported on the Ebinger's campaign's August 4 mobilization. There was a very good response from the New York City CORE chapters, but he was disappointed by the support given by the churches. From the thirty churches Brooklyn CORE contacted, only seven people turned out, five of whom were ministers. Fredericks argued that Brooklyn CORE needed to make winning the ministers' support its number one campaign priority. Without them and their congregations, Brooklyn CORE had a slim chance of getting large numbers of demonstrators each Saturday. Only 110 persons participated in the demonstrations, and twenty-seven stores were picketed from eleven in the morning until five in the evening; about three stores were picketed until six at night. Ebinger's stores in Brighton Beach and Flatbush attracted large groups because those neighborhoods had high numbers of whites sympathetic to the movement. Large white turnouts also might have discouraged African Americans, who were wary of white-dominated organizations, from participating in the protest.

Despite Brooklyn CORE's improving reputation with African Americans in Bedford-Stuyvesant, without black ministers, neighbors, and coworkers strongly endorsing the campaign, it was unlikely everyday people would show their support in large numbers. Jews who may have had leftist backgrounds or experiences with trade union organizing responded more favorably to the campaign's message than blacks or Puerto Ricans, a development that Fredericks argued might have reflected a problem in their publicity. He thought Brooklyn CORE needed to be more specific when it referred to Ebinger's discrimination against Jews and cautioned that the chapter should "investigate and ascertain the number of Jews employed by Ebinger's before we print up new leaflets and make new posters." No one argued that Jewish support was detrimental to their campaign, but the skewed information seemed to have an adverse effect on black participation. Fredericks also made no mention of Puerto Ricans and their response to the mobilization. In his conclusion, he declared with confidence that Brooklyn CORE would continue to picket each Saturday until more blacks and Puerto Ricans were hired.[36]

Oliver Leeds questioned the possibility of maintaining such high numbers on the picket lines each week. He suggested that on the following Saturday, Brooklyn CORE concentrate on four stores and try to close them. He also wondered how effective it was to picket stores that already had African American salesclerks. A few people felt it would hurt the campaign's image, and possibly decrease the African American employees' salaries, if they urged people to boycott stores that had black workers. After some discussion, the majority agreed that they should not avoid picketing those stores because the demonstration had to "educate the Negro communities of the fact that those sales girls are there only as tokenism."[37]

The chapter then discussed options for intensification of their protest, which would be essential if it failed to amass hundreds of participants each Saturday. They raised the possibility of having some volunteers demonstrate during the week and of conducting an education campaign in black neighborhoods that emphasized that the protest was against token hiring. When the group arrived at the question of whether to stage a sit-in, a lively debate ensued about its necessity and possible effectiveness. The sit-in had been Brooklyn CORE's most powerful tactic during its housing discrimination cases. When landlords or realtors refused to rent to black tenants, Brooklyn CORE threatened to hold around-the-clock sit-ins in the space. The threat of a sit-in in a vacant apartment, or the appearance of half a dozen people with placards, pillows, and blankets was usually enough to make a landlord more accepting of African Americans. When Brooklyn CORE staged sit-ins at real estate companies such as Lefrak, management was usually not concerned about their sleeping in an office waiting room; to avoid more negative press, they refrained from calling the police to arrest the protestors. But with Ebinger's, the chapter had to consider what it meant to occupy a store filled with food and cash. Bakery managers would most certainly have them arrested, and Brooklyn CORE members had to ask themselves if they were willing to go to jail for this cause.[38]

Arnold Goldwag continued to be a zealous advocate for more dramatic tactics. He reminded people that the membership had voted in May that if negotiations failed, the Employment Committee could call a sit-in. He also noted that at a recent meeting of the Metropolitan Action Council, which was composed of representatives from local CORE chapters, the subject of a sit-in was "discussed and rehashed for three hours." The final vote was in favor of using the tactic if Brooklyn CORE's leaders sanctioned it. Goldwag saw the boycott as ineffective and felt that further attempts to solicit the support of local ministers was useless. He suggested a sit-down at the company's main truck depot instead of a sit-in at a store. "If we sit down where the trucks leave to make deliveries," he argued, "they might negotiate, and it will be widely publicized—especially a sit-in in New York City." Through this tactic the campaign would "become known to more people than we could hope to reach otherwise."[39]

The general membership had mixed feelings about Goldwag's idea. Those who favored nonviolent tactics in principle desired to continue the boycott and to make it more effective before Brooklyn CORE resorted to more dramatic forms of direct action. They questioned the tactic's timing. Escalating the campaign before it had time to gain mass appeal, they argued, could be a disastrous blow to Brooklyn CORE's image with moderates. Surprisingly, Ben Brown agreed with Goldwag, and he pushed the idea of a sit-in one step further, suggesting that "a sit-in with jail and no bail would be very effective." Another black member, Mineral Bramletta, also supported the call for a sit-in. He argued that "CORE is an organization to end discrimination of the Negro people and the sit-in is not only an excellent method of direct action, but it would enhance Brooklyn CORE, weaken Ebinger's, and call attention to the public." Some supported the idea of a sit-in but did not agree with a steadfast rule against participants accepting bail. They argued that to accept jail without bail was a personal decision and not something that should be demanded of all volunteers. There was also talk about how Brooklyn CORE would raise money if it needed to bail out demonstrators. Leeds suggested going to labor unions, whereas Ben Brown mentioned possible assistance from local politicians and reform clubs. Goldwag was the most vociferous supporter of the sit-in. He ended the discussion by declaring that "a sit-in would shame the ministers to join us."[40]

The membership was evenly divided on the question of escalating tactics, and competing camps did not form along racial lines. At this moment in Brooklyn CORE's and the local movement's history, black and white activists did not use racial ideologies to explain tactical or strategic decisions in a campaign. Some blacks in Brooklyn CORE supported a patient approach and others were allied with Goldwag and Brown; whites both criticized and applauded Goldwag's heady ideas, which was a testament to Brooklyn CORE's relative success at fostering a movement culture that welcomed diverse opinions from its interracial membership. Still, most members agreed that more intense forms of direct action would generate media coverage and inspire more volunteers and might be the only way to force Ebinger's to negotiate. Unable to reach a consensus, Leeds and Fredericks postponed the vote on a sit-in and turned to the question of Flascher's status.[41]

At 11:00 P.M. the active membership discussed the petition to remove Kurt Flascher as chairman of the Membership Committee and from the chapter's Executive Committee. The debate over the petition to remove Flascher reflected the chapter's internal conflicts and democratic culture as much as differences over the Ebinger's campaign did. The fight over Flascher also revealed how Brooklyn CORE members preserved their respect for one another and the chapter's culture even in the midst of a stressful, frustrating protest when the members were tired and irritable. Some former members remembered Brooklyn CORE in the early 1960s as a second family in which spats, such as the one with Flascher, were common. Rioghan Kirchner recalled that Brooklyn CORE was "very tight," but that its members still argued a great deal. She remembered most clearly the arguments with Flascher. Kirchner smiled as she recollected that Brooklyn CORE meetings "would go on until two o'clock in the morning because Kurt wouldn't shut up." In the end he always agreed with the majority, but he had to argue a position for all possible sides to get there. "I guess it was good to have somebody who said the hell with what anyone thinks," she recalled.[42]

At the August 6 meeting nine active members of Brooklyn CORE presented a petition for Flascher's removal as chairman of the Membership Committee. It listed grievances with his behavior that extended over a year. Most of the instances involved Flascher's "violent outbursts" toward people at CORE conventions, picket lines, and demonstrations. At the 1961 CORE national convention in Cincinnati, Flascher had a verbal altercation with Gladys Harrington, the chairperson of New York CORE. He kept the fight going on the bus to New York City, "with hysterical screaming and yelling," and then created another scene in a restaurant at a bus stop where he "had a violent argument and threatened a fistfight with nineteen-year-old Wesley Sutton from New York CORE." People also claimed that Flascher "caused violent scenes at Executive Committee meetings." He was banned from the home of Dorothy Thorne, a Brooklyn CORE member, because of his behavior. On two occasions Kurt Flascher prolonged meetings held at Oliver Leeds's home "into the wee hours of the morning" because his harangues "made it impossible to complete Executive Committee business." During Brooklyn CORE's participation in a project in Englewood, New Jersey, the woman at whose home Flascher stayed said he raised his voice and had violent arguments with other CORE visitors. He also burned her teapot, used her phone excessively, and left the room strewn with papers.[43]

Kurt Flascher became involved in the civil rights movement after CORE's Freedom Rides. When he learned that whites in Anniston, Alabama, had bombed the bus carrying interracial demonstrators and nearly beat some to death, Flascher had said to himself, "I can't take this anymore." Born in Austria on November 7, 1928, Flascher, with his family, who were Orthodox Jews, escaped the Nazis and arrived in New York in late 1939. "I had never seen a black person before in my life," he recalled. Spending his teenage years and young adulthood in New York, Flascher never forgot the inhumanity of the Holocaust that had shaped his childhood. In the early 1960s, when he worked as a social worker and was a rabbi at a synagogue in the West Village, Flascher followed the southern civil rights movement in the papers. Seeing a photo of James Peck's bloodied face and head after the violence in Anniston incensed Flascher. He considered such violence "unfathomable in the United States of America, where all men are created equal," especially since Flascher had lived in Nazi-occupied Europe, where the civic culture was the exact opposite. He joined CORE and became active in the Brooklyn chapter, Flascher insisted, for his own freedom, not because he wanted to do something good for black people. "I fought for my right to have a friend who was black and go out for coffee and not take our lives in our hands."[44]

Flascher sometimes sensed that Brooklyn CORE members ostracized him. He felt he struggled to fit in with the chapter because he was an Orthodox Jew. Although many members of Brooklyn CORE respected Flascher's fierce dedication to the civil rights movement, Flascher recalled feeling isolated from the chapter's emerging cadre, especially if it held organizational meetings on the Jewish Sabbath. "I was an outsider in CORE," he later summarized. He had fierce debates with Oliver Leeds and was deeply critical of Communism. As the only Orthodox Jew in the chapter, although not the only Jewish member, Flascher also suspected, years later, that anti-Semitic sentiments of some members of Brooklyn CORE had caused them to attack him during the Ebinger's campaign.[45]

Flascher's behavior at an Ebinger's picket line was the final act that caused members in Brooklyn CORE to call for his removal. Dorothy Thorne and Rioghan Kirchner were monitoring a table with Ebinger's campaign literature in front of the Masonic Temple on Bedford Avenue. The table also had some leaflets that announced a civil rights benefit at the famed Apollo Theater in Harlem on August 11, which was sponsored by the Southern Student Freedom Fund of the U.S. National Student Association. According to the petition, Flascher questioned why those flyers were on Brooklyn CORE's table and demanded to know if Thorne had "checked to see if this was a Communist-front organization." Unsatisfied with Thorne's answer, Flascher "snatched up the leaflets and carried them to a box being used for trash, shouting at the top of his voice, 'I refuse to allow these leaflets to remain here!'" Flascher's behavior, the petition argued, was completely unprofessional and detrimental to Brooklyn CORE's image.[46]

Some Brooklyn CORE members believed that Flascher was "not qualified to orient new members in the CORE philosophy of nonviolence when he persists in conducting himself so violently on so many occasions." Those who signed the petition, including Ben Brown, Maurice Fredericks, Arnold Goldwag, Barbara Weeks, and other key members of Brooklyn CORE, said that if Kurt Flascher was not removed from his position on the Executive Committee, they would "have no alternative but to resign forthwith from Brooklyn CORE." After over two hours of discussion, active members voted to remove Kurt Flascher as membership chairman but not as an active member.[47]

Despite such acrimonious feelings toward Flascher, Rioghan Kirchner and others disapproved of the methods used to unseat him from the Executive Committee. At the following week's membership meeting, Kirchner read a petition that stated the impeachment of Kurt Flascher as membership chairman was unconstitutional and illegal, according to the chapter's constitution, and therefore the decision was null and void. Oliver Leeds added that the procedure was not handled according to the chapter's standards. A committee would be formed to investigate the charges; it would present its findings to the membership at large; and the membership would vote either to accept or to reject its recommendations. Leeds's solution was favored by a vote of nine to two, with two abstentions.[48]

With the debate over Flascher tabled, Arnold Goldwag again raised the question of using more militant direct action on the Ebinger's picket lines. He suggested that Brooklyn CORE hold a "stand-in," in which members would stand in line at bakeries and purposefully disrupt the store's service by placing obnoxious, long-winded orders. The tactic, Goldwag argued, would catch Ebinger's off guard and maintain the campaign's momentum. Members defeated that suggestion and agreed to continue the picket lines as they had the past several months.[49]

Brooklyn CORE's Innovative Tactics Force Ebinger's to Make a Deal

Brooklyn CORE had a meeting with Ebinger's management on Friday, August 17, and lawyers on each side drew up a declaration of intentions. The agreement reiterated Brooklyn CORE's earlier claims to "encourage and promote equality of treatment for, and prevent discrimination against, any such persons by reason of racial, religious or ethnic backgrounds." Ebinger's would cooperate with unions to recruit qualified African American and Puerto Rican workers and meet with Brooklyn CORE periodically to discuss progress and any problems. One difference from the past promises was that this declaration established a time line. Ebinger's agreed to hire a part-time saleswoman immediately in its Bedford Avenue store and, after September 1, to hire two part-time saleswomen to work Fridays and Saturdays each week. They also agreed to a trial period during which Brooklyn CORE would cease all demonstration activities in front of the company's stores and plants. Arnold Goldwag and Benjamin Brown signed the declaration. Brown stood in for Leeds, who had to work at the time of the negotiations. James Farmer issued an immediate press release that announced a meeting on Tuesday, August 21, among himself, leaders of Brooklyn CORE, and Arthur C. Ebinger, president of Ebinger Baking Company. At that time both sides would publicly state the details of their agreement.[50]

Some Brooklyn CORE members saw this as a tactic to diffuse any momentum that the demonstration had gained over the preceding several months, and they did not want to give the Ebinger's management another opportunity to delay changing its hiring policies. Despite the dissenting voices within the chapter that rejected the proposal for an escalation in direct-action tactics, eight members of Brooklyn CORE, including Brown, Goldwag, Kirchner, and Fredericks, went ahead and held a special sit-in. Instead of taking over one of Ebinger's most popular retail stores, this faction of members from Brooklyn CORE decided to take the protest to the heart of the baking company's operations: its delivery truck depot. On the morning of Saturday, August 18, 1962, just as Ebinger's was preparing to make its morning deliveries, seven Brooklyn CORE members sat down in front of the bakery's trucks and refused to move. They held signs that read, "The Cause Is Freedom Now" and "Don't Buy Where You Can't Work." Realizing they had missed opportunities to communicate the campaign's message to Puerto Ricans, they also had a placard with the same message written in Spanish: "Aquí no se puede trabajar! Entonces no comprar!" For several hours Ebinger's main Brooklyn distribution hub was effectively closed and business as usual ceased until the police hauled the protestors off to jail.[51]

The tactic brought Brooklyn CORE local and national media attention. Oliver Leeds remembered how they "sat two pickets in front of each truck and defied them to run over us." Police arrested seven Brooklyn CORE members for blocking the trucks. This one dramatic event generated more publicity than the entire previous year of organizing picket lines and boycotts. Newspapers, radio programs, and television news shows all covered Brooklyn CORE's demonstration. Brooklyn CORE also employed a tactic that was not common in nonviolent demonstrations in 1962: they made their bodies go limp and forced arresting officers to carry them off the premises. Going limp, according to a manual on direct-action tactics, was "the relaxation of all of the body in a kind of physical non-cooperation" so that the demonstrator employing the tactic "has to be dragged or carried to wherever authorities want him moved." The idea was for nonviolent activists to present no physical signs of struggle; if others struck them, especially police officers, it would be apparent to any witnesses where the source of any injury lay. Instructors informed participants in nonviolent workshops to cover their heads and vital organs if they were attacked while going limp. This was a tactical breakthrough for CORE chapters in their demonstrations against employment discrimination. Meier and Rudwick wrote that, to other CORE chapters, these tactics "seemed radical at the time. . . . This was the first time a CORE affiliate had used this technique since Wally Nelson had demonstrated at Coney Island Amusement Park in Cincinnati a decade before." "That was the straw that broke Ebinger's back," Leeds recalled. "Once they realized that we were going to harass them not only at the stores but also at the plant, they agreed to negotiate." Brown brokered the deal to end the boycott with Arthur C. Ebinger himself. On September 19, 1962, Ebinger's agreed to hire at least twelve African American and Puerto Rican saleswomen by the end of the year and have at least 40 on the staff of 240 within one year. Leeds remembered it as "a solid victory and . . . probably one of the best things we ever did."[52]

But hiring more people of color would not be as simple as Brooklyn CORE expected, nor was the campaign as clear a victory as Leeds remembered. Ebinger's found more subtle ways to reject black and Puerto Rican job applicants. In a letter from the baking company's lawyer, Joseph Eckhaus, to Carl Rachlin, the lawyer who handled Brooklyn CORE's affairs during the campaign, the company revealed its new tactics for discriminating against black candidates. The Brooklyn chapter of the National Urban League recommended two women who had applied for jobs as salesclerks. One was Chiogu V. Aghaji, a twenty-year-old from Nigeria who had been in the United States for three months. The other, Mary Anne Wyatt, was an eighteen-year-old who lived in Brooklyn. Eckhaus reported that Aghaji was unsuitable because of her Nigerian accent. "Probably due to the fact that she has been in this country for such a short time," he wrote, "it is difficult at times to understand her." Still, he noted that her appearance was "fair." Wyatt, on the other hand, was rejected because her "experience is very limited. She has resided in New York only for approximately three months, having come here from Virginia where she was born and raised." He also remarked that her "appearance and language" were "poor to fair." Another applicant referred by CORE was Joan E. Myers. Eckhaus commented that her "appearance and speech" were "good" and that she "would have been hired except for the fact that she resides in Manhattan." Myers was also younger than most Ebinger girls. Eckhaus said he would have been willing to overlook her youth in the interest of hiring a black woman, but Ebinger's managers had a hiring policy "established over many, many years whereby it attempts to hire its sales people who live as close to the stores' location for which they are hired as possible." He wrote that one of the company's basic policies was "to hire the residents of Brooklyn in our stores as well as in the plant. We believe that there is ample good material available to us through the Urban League and other similar organizations who reside in Brooklyn so that we do not have to go outside the Borough in any new hirings."[53]

Eckhaus's explanations were a smokescreen. Ebinger's planned to stall for as long as possible before it radically changed the racial composition of its workforce. Subjective factors, such as a candidate's looks and speech, worked against immigrants, southern migrants, and those who did not fit into a manager's notion of what constituted "good appearance" for an African American woman, which may have included the "right" complexion, hair texture, or any number of other racially based physical attributes.

An even greater impediment to Ebinger's ability to hire black workers was its residential policy. Mandating that workers reside in areas near the stores and plants placed a restriction on blacks who might not have been able to acquire housing or apartments in certain areas of Brooklyn. The Ebinger's campaign demonstrated how patterns of discrimination used by realtors, landlords, and banks denied black people more than just housing in white neighborhoods. They also established where black children went to school and where black adults might be able to work. Overall, whites in Brooklyn had access to the best residential areas, which had choice housing and excellent public schools, and they had more access to secure employment and higher wages. Blacks, on the other hand, were limited in their housing choices, their schools, and their employment. The result in many cities was that there were often two lived experiences, one for black residents and one for whites. With respect to Ebinger's, the different reasons its managers used for rejecting black candidates may have been nonracial, but the result was the same as if they posted signs that read "Negroes Need Not Apply": Ebinger's workforce remained practically all white throughout the 1960s and even up until the company folded in 1972.

Over the years some African Americans secured jobs at Ebinger's, but their numbers never reached the goal Brooklyn CORE had set. By the early 1970s, 100 of the company's 625 employees had been with Ebinger's for over thirty years, and most of the rest had been there for more than twenty. When Ebinger's closed in 1972, it blamed low sales owing to competition from larger corporations such as Entenmann's and the company's failure to follow its customer base to the suburbs. Indeed, many of these problems might have been avoided if, instead of shunning black and Puerto Rican newcomers to the outer boroughs, Ebinger's had welcomed them as customers just as it had other working-class immigrants who had settled in outer-borough neighborhoods since 1898. Failing to hire blacks and Puerto Ricans and to create relationships with these new residents sealed the company's fate. When people of color became the majority in neighborhoods where Ebinger's bakeries once thrived, they chose to spend their money elsewhere.[54]

The Ebinger's campaign made Brooklyn CORE one of the most recognizable CORE chapters in the country. Thirteen jobs fell far short of expectations, but the attention from this action produced more faith in the value of dramatic tactics. Indeed, Meier and Rudwick wrote that throughout the early 1960s "it was Brooklyn CORE that was most consistent in its application of new tactics." National CORE leaders were conflicted about when it was appropriate to use tactics that disrupted and disturbed public spaces. At that time Farmer openly disapproved of such tactics, but other national leaders contemplated their usefulness in the urban North. Members of CORE's field staff thought that "more controversial techniques will have to be adopted as the problems become more subtle. . . . People might have to resort to more shocking methods of protesting."[55]

These were the very types of tactics that Brooklyn CORE members mastered over the next two and a half years. The chapter continued with its individual housing cases, and it launched campaigns in 1963 to win jobs for black and Puerto Rican workers at other industries in Brooklyn, such as Sealtest Dairy Company and the Schafer Brewing Company. But Brooklyn CORE also took on more community-based issues as a way to try to spark a mass movement against racial discrimination in Brooklyn. By the fall of 1962 its new challenge was how to make something that had become such a normal, everyday part of life for black people in Brooklyn, such as dirty streets and irregular garbage collection, into a major local civil rights campaign.[56]

5

OPERATION CLEAN SWEEP

The Movement to Create a
"First-Class Bedford-Stuyvesant"

Twelve years of neglect! That's the story of Bedford-Stuyvesant.
Years of allowing a good community to go to pot.
—Robert Law and Oliver Leeds
to Mayor Robert F. Wagner Jr., 1962

Brooklyn CORE members chose to address the issue of inadequate garbage collection because the excessive trash was such an odious part of
people's everyday life in Bedford-Stuyvesant, and, by late 1962, after
their work on housing and employment discrimination, they understood
that, to build a powerful local protest movement, they would have to
develop campaigns that connected with the grass roots and with local
organizations. The housing cases and Ebinger's campaign created a sense
of camaraderie and trust among Brooklyn CORE's members. The
group's unique ethos, represented in its democratic culture and penchant
for audacious protest tactics, gave its members strength to tackle
entrenched structural inequality within an agency of city government
such as the Department of Sanitation (DOS), which controlled garbage
collection policies for neighborhoods throughout the city. The chapter
also pressed borough-level politicians to advocate for better services in
Bedford-Stuyvesant, which gained publicity for the cause. But because of
the structure of city government, neither Borough President Abe Stark
nor local representatives on the New York City Council had direct power
to redress the situation. Brooklyn CORE also hoped that everyday people in Bedford-Stuyvesant might become emboldened by a community-
wide effort that fought city hall for improvements in their quality of life
and that demanded recognition and respect from the highest seats of city

government. Chapter leaders imagined that mobilization spurred by the sanitation issue would spark a wider movement against local forms of racial discrimination. Dubbed Operation Clean Sweep, the campaign was a test of Brooklyn CORE's ambition and creativity.

The chapter's efforts attracted black college students, working-class African Americans, middle-class black and white professionals, and interracial married couples, some of whom brought their own political ideologies to the organization. Sometimes these new members advocated ideas that did not always reflect CORE's basic principles of interracialism and nonviolence. After Operation Clean Sweep ended, members of Brooklyn CORE, mostly younger black men, argued for a more black nationalist influence in the local, and even national, movement. Black nationalist sentiments were popular among black urban youth, even the college-educated ones attracted to Brooklyn CORE, early in the 1960s. Indeed, the critiques of interracialism that flourished in the national movement during the mid- to late 1960s were not new, nor did such criticisms begin to affect activists' thinking until after 1966, when Stokely Carmichael popularized the black power slogan and ideology. In the urban North black activists involved in interracial, nonviolent, direct-action protest and community organizing articulated critiques of race and class inequality with black nationalist ideas and language much earlier than historians usually recognize. Young people in Brooklyn CORE wanted to put the needs of poor people at the center of the northern civil rights agenda, and they also wanted to transform civil rights leadership. In the early 1960s Brooklyn CORE's democratic culture allowed these ideas to coexist with the national organization's and some chapter members' values of interracialism. The chapter did not dissolve over ideological battles that pitted black nationalism against interracialism. Instead, more people in Brooklyn used CORE to further their own protest agendas through the chapter's innovative demonstrations and widespread interests. And Brooklyn CORE's action-oriented cadre was eager to accommodate such new energies.[1]

During Operation Clean Sweep the chapter developed dramatic street theater tactics and skillfully employed the media, which forced the DOS to defend itself against charges of racial discrimination. Evidence also indicates that the city subsequently increased sanitation services in north-central Brooklyn. A small group of African Americans in their twenties was largely responsible for this small, much-delayed, but nonetheless important victory. Through editorials in Brooklyn CORE's newsletter, the *North Star,* named after Frederick Douglass's nineteenth-century abolitionist organ, Brooklyn CORE's young black college students issued bold criticisms of the racial and class characteristics of national and local civil rights movement leaders and articulated their belief that the black poor, especially in cities, should be at the vanguard of the movement. Their militancy, which was often supported by whites such as Arnold Goldwag and Jerome Bibuld and older African Americans like Maurice Fredericks, reflected Brooklyn CORE's growing aggressiveness and desire to develop campaigns that worked directly with black people living in Brooklyn's ghettos.

Existing leaders such as Oliver and Marjorie Leeds, Rioghan Kirchner, Arnold Goldwag, and Maurice Fredericks mentored new members and tried to shape Brooklyn CORE as an interracial group that promoted nonviolent, direct-action protests. External political obstacles and internal organizing difficulties, however, put a strain on Brooklyn CORE's ability to transform its philosophy and tactics into a mass movement. The city government's bureaucracy and liberal politicians' tacit indifference stymied the chapter's progress. Over time members became frustrated with the lengthy process required just to force power brokers in government, business, and real estate to meet with Brooklyn CORE at a negotiation table. Exasperated and tired, some in Brooklyn CORE began to move away from focused, single-issue protests and toward more aggressive and unfocused demands for immediate ends to all forms of racial discrimination in Brooklyn and New York City. On top of that, Brooklyn CORE struggled to hold on to enthusiastic members, such as the Brooklyn high school students who had formed a student CORE chapter during the campaign to open jobs for black workers at the Ebinger Baking Company. After that boycott campaign and the loss of key student leaders when they graduated and went to college, the student CORE group dissolved. As Brooklyn CORE became less effective in achieving practical results and retaining activists who developed their politics through CORE's culture and philosophy, it began to concentrate more effort on dramatizing the deteriorating living conditions of working-class and poor African Americans in Brooklyn and throughout the city.

Still, in late 1962 and early 1963 demonstrations like Operation Clean Sweep were transformative events for many of the chapter's members, especially the younger African Americans who had grown up in New York City feeling it was free from the types of racial discrimination that affected their parents and grandparents in the South. Participating in Operation Clean Sweep introduced them to creative applications of direct-action protest and showed them how inventive, bold tactics could be used to bring about social change. It also put them in direct contact with their neighbors and the quotidian nature of structural forms of racial discrimination in Bedford-Stuyvesant. More important, this campaign gave young black members a feeling of personal empowerment and achievement and further radicalized their ideas about community activism and politics.

Overpopulated and Underserved

Environmental Problems Pile Up in Bedford-Stuyvesant

As Bedford-Stuyvesant's population quadrupled from the 1940s to the 1960s, the number of daily sanitation pickups remained the same. More than ten years before Brooklyn CORE began Operation Clean Sweep, in November 1950, the Bedford-Stuyvesant Neighborhood Council's Sanitation Committee met with Commissioner Andrew Mulrain of the New York City DOS and made two requests: daily garbage collections in Bedford-Stuyvesant and a change in the DOS's classification of the neighborhood. The DOS classified Bedford-Stuyvesant as a neighborhood of one- and two-family houses. Representatives from the Bedford-Stuyvesant Neighborhood Council (BSNC) informed Commissioner Mulrain that three or more families occupied most of the homes in the area. The committee reported on the accumulation of "rubbish of all sorts" in the neighborhood's streets and argued that Bedford-Stuyvesant's garbage problem "requires attention not inherent in the physical size of the area." Commissioner Mulrain conceded that the group raised a valid issue with implications for other parts of Brooklyn, too, but he could not promise to increase garbage collection in Bedford-Stuyvesant. Both Commissioner Mulrain and the BSNC agreed that the neighborhood could expect "a steady improvement which should result in a cleaner neighborhood," but they recognized that there were factors at work beyond the department's control, namely, "the human element that is inherent and must be considered in matters such as these." Mulrain and the BSNC members recognized they could never completely stop people from littering. Both parties agreed that the "human element" would always affect the environmental conditions of urban neighborhoods, no matter what the DOS did.[2]

Still, if people's behavior produced the trash, city government's policies did nothing to stop it from piling up in Bedford-Stuyvesant's streets. By the 1960s the situation had not improved. About half of Brooklyn CORE's members lived in other parts of the borough, and they received different types of sanitation services. Some blacks and whites within the chapter used this anecdotal evidence as the basis for an argument that

Bedford-Stuyvesant's problems with garbage were brought on by discriminatory treatment from the city. Arnold Goldwag had a basement apartment in the Marine Park section of Brooklyn. He recalled the stark contrast between the two neighborhoods' trash collection. Marine Park was 99 percent white and composed of one- and two-family detached homes, each with small front lawns or backyards. Bedford-Stuyvesant was 95 percent black, and over half of its housing contained multiple apartments. Many parts of Bedford-Stuyvesant received three-days-a-week garbage collection service (one of those days was supposed to be reserved for bulk trash, which included large items such as refrigerators, scrap metal, and furniture) and three-days-a-week street-cleaning services. And though Marine Park's population density was half of Bedford-Stuyvesant's, the whiter, less populous community received comparable, if not better, sanitation collection service. Since Goldwag's work with Brooklyn CORE allowed him to travel around the borough, he knew that the neighborhood's garbage problem had less to do with residents' behavior and more to do with city policies. Garbage-production levels and the concentration of trash in residential areas were related to concentrations of people. Population densities in Bedford-Stuyvesant census tracts in 1960 were double, and some were even triple, the densities in census tracts in which Marine Park sat. The different racial demography, population densities, and percentages of single-family and multiple-family housing units in these areas revealed that, for the number of people and their concentration, Bedford-Stuyvesant was grossly underserved. The city's infrequent service caused sights and smells that characterized Bedford-Stuyvesant, in many people's minds, as a ghetto and a slum. "For the population in Bedford-Stuyvesant," Goldwag recalled, "they should pick it up maybe [every] three hours, 'round-the-clock, compared to Marine Park." Three-days-a-week service was not sufficient for the area, so as Goldwag later remembered, "the streets were always dirty, of course, because the garbage always overflowed." Brooklyn CORE determined that, compared to Marine Park, Bedford-Stuyvesant was underserved precisely because its residents were black, the community was a ghetto, and elected officials stereotyped the social problems in such areas as products of residents' behavior, not municipal discriminatory policies.[3]

Following CORE's guidelines, Brooklyn CORE investigated the problem and scheduled negotiations with the city. Goldwag, Robert Law, and Marjorie Leeds compiled statistics on demographics and housing conditions in neighborhoods that received three-days-a-week collection services. Bedford-Stuyvesant had more black people and poorer-quality housing than other areas in their survey. Using data from

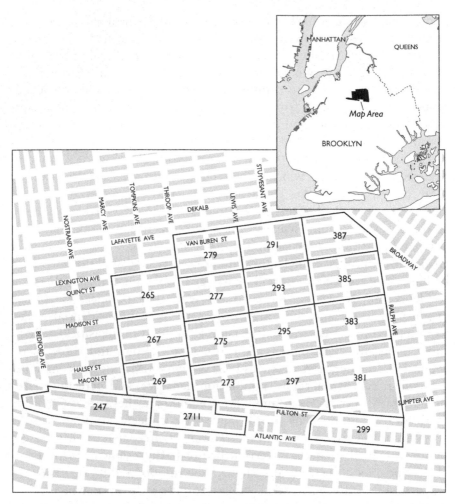

Sampling of majority-black census tracts in Bedford-Stuyvesant, 1960 (based on Social Explorer Tables [SE], 1960 Census, Tracts-Only Set, Social Explorer and U.S. Census Bureau—DUALabs).

the 1960 U.S. Census, Brooklyn CORE determined that the housing conditions in Bedford-Stuyvesant contrasted sharply with those in other neighborhoods that received three-days-a-week service. Only 75 percent of Bedford-Stuyvesant's housing was classified as "sound," whereas 90 percent of housing was "sound" in all other neighborhoods with three-days-a-week service. In Bedford-Stuyvesant, 18.6 percent of housing was "deteriorating," and 5.6 percent was "dilapidated," versus 8.6 percent and 1.4 percent, respectively, in all other areas with three-days-a-week service. The data confirmed Brooklyn CORE's suspicion that there

Table 3. Population Density, Race, and Housing in Bedford-Stuyvesant, 1960

Census tract #	Total population	Total area (sq. miles)	Population density (per square mile)	Race White	Race Black	Housing 1-family	Housing 2-family	Housing 3–4-family	Housing 5–9-family	Housing 10+-family
247	3,009	0.08	39,770.41	12.4%	87.4%	0.9%	19.0%	24.3%	19.5%	36.3%
265	5,603	0.06	90,062.22	3.0%	96.7%	21.0%	20.3%	21.6%	24.8%	12.2%
267	5,312	0.06	85,226.50	1.5%	98.3%	8.2%	8.8%	29.0%	37.5%	16.5%
269	3,449	0.05	67,765.54	1.2%	98.8%	26.6%	10.6%	17.4%	33.1%	12.4%
2711	1,711	0.05	32,441.81	6.1%	93.7%	20.9%	48.5%	29.6%	0.9%	0.0%
273	3,513	0.06	61,258.95	0.9%	98.8%	3.7%	10.5%	51.7%	20.7%	13.4%
275	4,928	0.06	77,523.35	1.3%	98.1%	3.8%	12.9%	29.5%	27.4%	26.5%
277	4,462	0.06	69,625.13	2.6%	97.4%	1.6%	14.9%	63.4%	13.3%	6.8%
279	6,157	0.06	96,002.77	6.3%	93.3%	4.1%	9.4%	55.3%	20.4%	10.8%
291	4,923	0.06	76,683.79	2.4%	97.1%	0.8%	5.8%	55.6%	32.0%	5.8%
293	4,874	0.06	75,657.93	5.3%	94.5%	2.3%	14.1%	49.6%	24.9%	9.2%
295	4,933	0.06	78,206.89	2.8%	96.6%	4.7%	21.2%	48.0%	17.8%	8.4%
297	4,054	0.08	51,176.83	3.4%	95.7%	5.9%	17.9%	39.7%	33.8%	2.8%
299	2,956	0.06	48,539.40	12.5%	87.4%	6.7%	54.5%	28.8%	10.1%	0.0%
381	7,855	0.09	83,933.82	7.4%	91.9%	3.4%	14.7%	19.5%	20.2%	42.2%
383	5,398	0.07	79,865.25	6.2%	93.1%	3.2%	51.6%	11.8%	27.2%	6.3%
385	5,000	0.07	73,862.15	19.3%	80.2%	6.8%	32.9%	26.8%	30.0%	3.4%
387	5,324	0.08	70,773.57	28.8%	70.7%	7.3%	18.7%	24.1%	33.2%	16.6%
Median	4,926	0.06	74,760.04	4.4%	95.1%	4.4%	16.4%	29.3%	24.9%	10.0%

Source: Social Explorer Tables (SE), 1960 Census, Tracts-Only Set, Social Explorer and U.S. Census Bureau—DUALabs.

was a connection between Bedford-Stuyvesant's environmental conditions and the overcrowded, stressed housing infrastructure in which its overwhelmingly black population lived.[4]

Arnold Goldwag, who spent much time in Bedford-Stuyvesant investigating housing discrimination and illegal evictions, recalled that drug users and negligent landlords contributed to the problems caused by excessive garbage in the streets. Goldwag remembered how residents avoided junkies and rats that lurked in alleys by way of the "airmail express": "The landlord would not provide covers for the garbage cans. Now there were hot and cold running junkies, there were all kinds of things happening in the streets, and there were rats and cats in with the garbage. Well, why would you send your kids down five flights to put garbage next to an open can, and risk whatever? You open the window and it's the airmail express. It comes right down and splatters by where the garbage is. So one thing leads to the other."[5]

Through their investigating into irregular garbage collection, Brooklyn CORE leaders recognized the limitations of fighting against racial discrimination one issue at time. Civil rights activists in Brooklyn would never bring about noticeable, lasting changes if they only concentrated on a single problem—employment discrimination at one company, for example, or infrequent garbage collection in one neighborhood. Instead, activists began to learn that systemwide policies and practices, such as the ones that limited garbage collection in Bedford-Stuyvesant, made Brooklyn and, by extension, all of New York City a racially segregated society. Bedford-Stuyvesant's garbage problem, Brooklyn CORE realized, was bigger than the trash that lined the streets and the rats that filled the alleys. Infrequent trash collection in Bedford-Stuyvesant was connected directly to governmental policies and racial ideologies. The single issue of infrequent collection, which helped turn parts of north-central Brooklyn into a trash-filled "slum," was part of larger systems of discrimination that put residents of Bedford-Stuyvesant at a social and economic disadvantage because of their race, class, and residential location. Brooklyn CORE would never eradicate racial discrimination in Brooklyn, or transform completely Bedford-Stuyvesant's environmental conditions, if it tackled only one issue, one civil rights campaign at a time. The chapter realized that to attack racial discrimination in Brooklyn, it had to develop campaigns that targeted the systematic, political nature of racially discriminatory policies. It also had to fight against racialist ideologies that blamed black individuals' culture and behavior for problems that were, in effect, deeply woven into social and political practices. On the surface, the neighborhood's garbage problem seemed like a simple matter—attain more trash collection, or punish more people who threw garbage on the street. But infrequent garbage collection in Bedford-Stuyvesant, Brooklyn CORE learned, was not a simple, single issue: it was deeply connected to government agencies' budgets, to networks of political power within communities, and to the ways power brokers in government thought about the people who lived in particular communities. In short, infrequent garbage collection in Bedford-Stuyvesant reflected the ways race, class, and location shaped who held, and who lacked, political and social power in New York City. To eradicate Bedford-Stuyvesant's problems with infrequent trash collection, Brooklyn CORE members found that they had to address the policies, practices, and ideologies that gave life to racial segregation in *all* facets of the city's life, from where people were forced to live, to the types of education to which they had access, to the limited employment opportunities that structured their economic lives and their larger social communities.

Of course, its assault against infrequent garbage collection in Bedford-Stuyvesant also taught Brooklyn CORE that orchestrating a dramatic, coherent, focused direct-action campaign that attacked the socially systematic, political, and ideological nature of racism was easier said than done. To appeal to people who were not hard-core activists and to force negotiations with political power brokers, Brooklyn CORE had to limit the scope of its campaign. The enemy—a municipal agency that treated poor black communities differently from the way it treated middle-class white ones—had to be clear, as did Brooklyn CORE's campaign goal: garbage collection and services that reflected the needs of Bedford-Stuyvesant's massive population and overcrowded housing. Brooklyn CORE members found that, to win some of their specific campaign demands, they could not wage an amorphous political and ideological battle against racism in the city. Winning small victories on specific campaign issues, Brooklyn CORE learned, was the best its movement could hope to achieve.

Brooklyn CORE slowly learned these political lessons throughout the course of Operation Clean Sweep. Oliver Leeds remembered when National CORE Director James Farmer attended a Brooklyn CORE meeting as a guest speaker, and Marjorie Leeds questioned him on the usefulness of individual protest campaigns. "Look, where are we going with all these discrimination cases?" Oliver Leeds recalled her asking Farmer. "The problems in Bedford-Stuyvesant are community-wide problems," Marjorie Leeds had argued. "They're not just the case of some landlord, or even an Ebinger's store. The city is discriminating

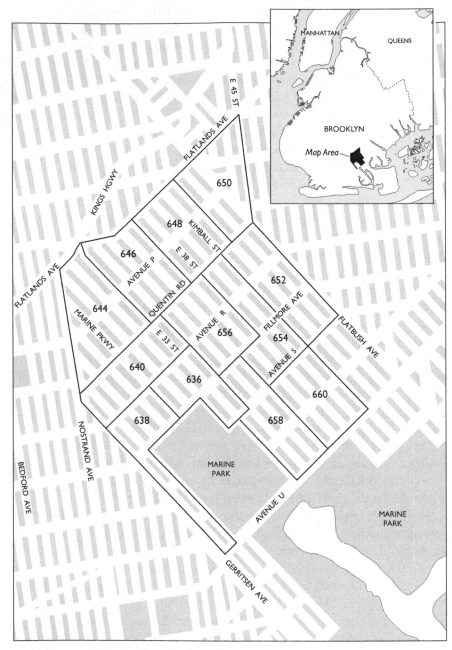

Sampling of majority-white census tracts in Marine Park, 1960 (based on Social Explorer Tables [SE], 1960 Census, Tracts-Only Set, Social Explorer and U.S. Census Bureau—DUALabs).

Table 4. Population Density, Race, and Housing in Marine Park, 1960

Census tract #	Total population	Total area (sq. miles)	Population density (per sq. mile)	Race White	Race Black	Housing 1-family	Housing 2-family	Housing 3–4-family	Housing 5–9-family	Housing 10+-family
636	1,482	0.04	34,359.16	99.9%	0.1%	88.6%	10.3%	1.1%	0.0%	0.0%
638	2,002	0.05	36,520.17	99.6%	0.3%	48.6%	50.6%	0.8%	0.0%	0.0%
640	1,834	0.06	30,246.33	99.1%	0.2%	78.6%	19.5%	1.9%	0.0%	0.0%
644	2,778	0.08	35,687.79	99.9%	0.0%	54.7%	31.5%	0.6%	9.6%	3.7%
646	2,425	0.06	38,703.60	99.5%	0.1%	100.0%	0.0%	0.0%	0.0%	0.0%
648	2,283	0.06	40,390.77	99.8%	0.1%	65.4%	23.3%	3.3%	8.1%	0.0%
650	2,015	0.07	29,364.79	99.1%	0.2%	40.8%	30.8%	2.8%	3.3%	22.3%
652	1,372	0.07	18,741.35	99.6%	0.1%	81.6%	17.2%	1.2%	0.0%	0.0%
654	2,007	0.05	39,951.15	99.9%	0.0%	79.0%	20.1%	0.9%	0.0%	0.0%
656	2,154	0.06	35,839.50	99.7%	0.0%	97.6%	2.4%	0.0%	0.0%	0.0%
658	2,248	0.06	37,551.65	99.7%	0.1%	60.6%	39.4%	0.0%	0.0%	0.0%
660	2,101	0.05	39,384.61	99.8%	0.1%	84.9%	15.1%	0.0%	0.0%	0.0%
Median	2,058	0.06	36,179.84	99.7%	0.1%	78.8%	19.8%	0.9%	0.0%	0.0%

Source: Social Explorer Tables (SE), 1960 Census, Tracts-Only Set, Social Explorer and U.S. Census Bureau—DUALabs.

against this community." Until then, National CORE and other CORE chapters throughout the country had organized demonstrations with usually one clearly defined objective: desegregate a restaurant or a pool; end race-based job discrimination at a local business; or, with the Freedom Rides, force state compliance with federal laws. Brooklyn CORE argued that Bedford-Stuyvesant's problems with trash collection were endemic social ills that both the city and local residents were responsible for correcting. Brooklyn CORE would mobilize the community to demand equal treatment from the city and, in the process, organize residents to take charge of their neighborhood's improvement. Although such an approach was uncommon for CORE, Farmer did not protest. "James Farmer said he was tickled pink that we would take on the city," remembered Oliver Leeds.[6]

Taking on the city began with a letter-writing campaign throughout the spring and summer of 1962. Marjorie and Oliver Leeds contacted the mayor's Rent and Rehabilitation Administration in April 1962 and petitioned for a variety of improvements on Gates Avenue between Broadway and Bedford Avenue, which covered an entire residential section running across Bedford-Stuyvesant. "This area," they wrote, was "completely and physically run down." Electrical fires that occurred frequently in the winter were due to old, faulty wiring in overcrowded buildings. They characterized garbage collection, and street and sidewalk cleaning, as "BAD." Houses on the block were in a "complete state of disrepair," and there was almost a "complete lack of recreational facilities in schools and neighborhoods." Street lighting was poor on Gates Avenue, which also had old, rusted traffic signs, an insufficient number of traffic lights, and inadequate police protection around P.S. 129. Marjorie Leeds was president of P.S. 129's Parent-Teacher Association and knew the school's needs. Enrollment, they wrote, was "100% de facto segregated," which affected the caliber of its teachers. "Poor conditions of the neighborhood," she argued in the petition, "leads to difficulties in staffing the schools."[7]

At the end of the letter, Marjorie and Oliver Leeds offered a two-part solution. First, the city should declare the area a "'Special Service Area' for emergency rehabilitation" and have "all city agencies concerned move in for an 'Operation Cleanup.'" Then the city was to provide people on Gates Avenue with "new housing in [the] neighborhood." Residents should not be evicted during Operation Cleanup. Instead, the Leedses suggested inhabitants have access to new housing regardless of income or marital or welfare status. "We regard this as essential," they underscored, "if the City is not to merely transfer these people to another ghetto slum area." The petition concluded with requests for "consideration and action," and an "early response." City hall gave neither, and the summer passed without the city's taking any action to correct these problems. By late August Brooklyn CORE had formed a delegation on sanitation conditions in the Bedford-Stuyvesant area and scheduled appointments with Mayor Wagner's Citizen Complaint Office. This committee's volunteers represented some of the chapter's new members, who became its most imaginative strategists and determined activists during Operation Clean Sweep.[8]

Young and Old Flock to Brooklyn CORE

Members of this new delegation reflected the multigenerational, action-oriented, middle- and working-class cohort of black community activists attracted to Brooklyn CORE during this period. The chapter's active membership, which numbered around twenty by late summer 1962, was still evenly divided between blacks and whites. By that time SCORE, the high school student CORE group that had participated in the campaign against Ebinger's, had ceased to exist because its main organizers, John Akula and Eleanor Stein, had graduated from high school, and no other students replaced them. During and after Operation Clean Sweep, African Americans in Brooklyn CORE began to outnumber white members, but not by many. Brooklyn CORE's willingness to challenge the city's sanitation policies in Bedford-Stuyvesant attracted some local black residents to the chapter. They became active in the chapter and were empowered by its bold, creative use of nonviolent activism.

At thirty-nine years of age in 1962, Vincent Young was part of the older cohort of African Americans in Brooklyn CORE and a member of the Operation Clean Sweep Action Committee. A tall, slim, handsome man, Young worked as a city bus driver. He found CORE after searching for an organization that fulfilled his desires for a sense of fraternity and political action. Orphaned at a young age, he had had an unstable childhood. He bounced from one foster home to another. His wife, Jacqueline Young, recalled that as a youngster, Vincent was "sort of like a juvenile delinquent." In his late teens, he came to live with a Trinidadian family named Lewis, who, like many black families seeking to escape the overcrowded tenements and congested sidewalks of Manhattan, moved from Harlem to Brooklyn. Young stayed with the Lewis family until he was a young adult, but he still engaged in petty criminal activities. At the age of eighteen he was arrested twice on charges of forgery. By age twenty he had graduated to petty larceny, but he was never imprisoned for his crimes. Although not proud of his actions, Young never hid his history. When he applied for employment with the New York City Transit Authority, Young revealed his criminal past on his application. It did not prevent him from attaining a job driving a bus on the Ocean Avenue line, a boulevard that cut north to south in Brooklyn and took Young through some of Brooklyn's segregated white neighborhoods. Some of his passengers were not accustomed to seeing a black man driving a city bus. "He got in trouble," Jacqueline Young recalled, "because this white man got in and said, 'What is this nigger doing driving this bus?'" Unable to control his anger, Vincent "socked him and the guy fell off the bus."[9]

Luckily, a supervisor vouched for Young's integrity, and he received only a stern warning. The incident was a turning point in his life. It compelled the young man to seek more productive ways to channel his anger at racial injustice. He joined Siloam Presbyterian Church and was deeply influenced by the Reverend Milton Galamison, who encouraged church members to be politically active in community improvement efforts. Dissatisfied with the general church membership's low commitment to activism, Young joined the Prince Hall Masons because, as his wife recalled, "he said, 'I need to be a leader of something.'" Young tried to encourage the Prince Hall Masons to participate in local civil rights demonstrations, but no one seemed interested. He was often the only Mason at local rallies, demonstrations, or community meetings. Frustrated with the Masons' inactivity, Young gravitated to Brooklyn CORE during the Ebinger's campaign. Throughout the 1960s (and for the rest of his life), Vincent Young participated in social and political activities with Oliver Leeds, Maurice Fredericks, Jerome Bibuld, and others he met in Brooklyn CORE. At the time of Young's death in 1988, Paul Robeson Jr. eulogized him in the *Amsterdam News* as more than a participant in the civil rights movement, but as "a leader, an organizer, a gentle warrior."[10]

Vincent Young fit in immediately with Brooklyn CORE's activist culture and the nurturing, mentoring relationships that older participants, such as Young, Fredericks, and Leeds, formed with some of the younger African Americans who joined after the Ebinger's campaign in late summer of 1962. James Steward and Robert Law were two black men in their twenties who saw Brooklyn CORE as the perfect organization to develop their ideas about black politics and activism. James Steward, who joined the New York City Police Department as a way to pay for his college education, and Robert Law, a senior at Pratt Institute, immediately became leaders of Operation Clean Sweep.

The student sit-in movement in the South spurred the political awakening of Robert Law, James Steward, and other young African Americans in Brooklyn. Law was attending Pratt Institute when the sit-ins began. He and a few other young men, including Steward, wanted to start a political club that would address civil rights issues, but they organized it halfheartedly. "We were still very much coming out of the partying era, being stylish, listening to jazz records," Law remembers. The first thing he, Steward, and others did when they formed a political group was host a party. But sitting around having political bull sessions while listening to records by John Coltrane, Miles Davis, Freddie Hubbard, and Art Blakey and the Jazz Messengers, or drinking cheap wine and dancing to rhythm and blues music, was not what Law initially had in mind. Steward rallied the group to become more serious, and he suggested they join Brooklyn CORE. Of the small group, only Steward and Law attended the next Brooklyn CORE meeting. They met Oliver Leeds, Maurice Fredericks, and Vincent Young, who became their mentors. Law remembered how this older cadre of black activists "understood that we were not really aware that all these things were going on . . . inequalities in the school system, in jobs, in housing. We lived in New York City, where everybody was thinking of themselves as upwardly mobile and free." Brooklyn CORE's conclusive research into cases of racial discrimination shattered their naïveté. The chapter's dramatic demonstrations inspired young activists like Law and Steward to believe that change for Bedford-Stuyvesant was both possible and imminent.[11]

"The Collection of Garbage . . . Is Disgracefully Inadequate"

On August 24, 1962, Marjorie Leeds, Vincent Young, and James Steward arrived at the mayor's office. After months of letter writing, investigation, and petitioning the city for improvements, Brooklyn CORE's delegation was prepared to argue its case for increased garbage collection and improved sanitation services in Bedford-Stuyvesant. The city, however, seemed unwilling to make major changes in policies that shaped Bedford-Stuyvesant's environmental conditions. When administrators in the mayor's Citizen Complaint Office tried to bury the issue by referring CORE's prepared statement to other departments, Steward demanded that the delegation be allowed to discuss the situation with someone in authority. The secretary for the Citizen Complaint Office called the DOS's main office and gave them an immediate appointment. Before leaving, the CORE representatives left a statement with the Mayor's Office demanding action by September 8, 1962; otherwise, they threatened, they would move ahead with plans for direct-action protest.[12]

The delegation's statement differed from Oliver and Marjorie Leeds's earlier letter because it concentrated only on the problems of excessive garbage and dilapidated sidewalks. Brooklyn CORE members realized they had to concentrate on one issue if they hoped to have any success petitioning city officials. Gates Avenue between Broadway and Bedford Avenue, they declared, had become "the most depressed street in the Bedford-Stuyvesant community . . . a completely rundown and filthy thoroughfare." Sidewalks were in disrepair and streets were constantly littered. Moreover, Brooklyn CORE charged, "The collection of garbage by the Sanitation Department is disgracefully inadequate." They claimed that inspectors did not regularly investigate landlords or enforce minimal sanitation standards, which allowed building owners and managers to neglect the upkeep of their buildings. Garbage collectors also left lots, alleys, and stairwells filled with "discarded furniture and other refuse." PTAs and block associations had previously brought this issue to the attention of city authorities, but nothing happened. Brooklyn CORE explained that "this disgraceful situation" was "something that can only happen in a ghetto" and was caused by discriminatory treatment. The petition concluded with a request for "emergency measures," such as daily collection of garbage, enforcement of sanitary regulations, and immediate repair of sidewalks "no later than September 8, 1962."[13]

At the Commissioner of Sanitation's Office, the delegation met with Henry Liebman and Marty O'Connell of the Community Relations Department, who assured them that Sanitation had requested funds for increased pickup service in Bedford-Stuyvesant. O'Connell also confirmed what Brooklyn CORE already knew from its investigation: because of difficulties maintaining trucks during World War II, the city had instituted an austerity program and cut back from six-days-a-week pickup services to five days in some parts of the city and three days in others, depending on the area's population. Liebman suggested that Brooklyn CORE "form a committee to make the area 'cooperative' with the Sanitation Department." The collection districts had orders to pick up any trash they saw on the street, so the garbage epidemic Brooklyn CORE described must have been the result of area residents' behavior. He asked the delegates to "survey the district and report any filled lots." The city would clean them right away and issue summonses to owners of private lots who neglected the upkeep of their property. Liebman rejected the idea that trash baskets on each corner would lessen the amount of garbage in streets and on sidewalks because "people misuse them." Exactly how they would misuse the trash baskets Liebman did not say. He probably feared a spike in reported cases of people using the bins to start fires for warmth in the winter, or juveniles kicking them over for fun. Still, those issues did not *cause* Bedford-Stuyvesant's massive garbage problem, and Brooklyn CORE's sanitation delegation resented Liebman's attempt to blame the people in the community for the department's inadequate attention to such a large community.[14]

Marjorie Leeds could not contain her anger. She exploded in the middle of Liebman's explanations with complaints about the horrendous sanitation service on her block. Oliver and Marjorie Leeds lived at 272 Van Buren Street. They rented a small apartment in a brownstone that belonged to Oliver Leeds's mother. The Leedses lived at the corner of Lewis Avenue, four blocks north of Gates Avenue and directly in the middle of the Bedford and Broadway swath Brooklyn CORE's research targeted. Conditions on their street reflected the problems in the rest of the neighborhood. The DOS officials, hoping they could distract the delegation from demanding widespread service changes, tried to redirect the rest of the conversation to Marjorie Leeds's specific situation, but she remained steadfast. Her individual issue was not the point of the delegation's visit, she reminded the officials. "We came about the dirty conditions throughout Bedford-Stuyvesant." James Steward then showed photographs of conditions in the neighborhood—empty refrigerators, broken-down cars, heaps of rusty metal and splintered debris, children playing near caved-in sidewalks—and demanded action before September 8. The delegation left and went to Borough Hall in Brooklyn to try to see the borough's president, Abe Stark. They were denied a meeting. They left a copy of their petition and requested an appointment before the deadline passed.[15]

September 8, 1962, was the scheduled date for Operation Clean Sweep. If there were no improvements in services by ten in the morning that day, Brooklyn CORE would mobilize citizens in Bedford-Stuyvesant to take matters into their own hands. Brooklyn CORE prepared for Operation Clean Sweep the week of September 1 by distributing leaflets in the neighborhood that summarized CORE's talks with the city and announced the chapter's plans to stage a community demonstration the following week. The exact details of Operation Clean Sweep were purposefully vague. Publicizing Brooklyn CORE's plan to collect trash along Gates Avenue and dump it on the steps of Borough Hall would have attracted unwanted attention from the police, who might have tried to thwart the action by arresting key members of Brooklyn CORE's leadership. According to Robert Law, some members of Brooklyn CORE suspected there were police informants in their ranks. To ensure there were no problems, organizers of Operation Clean Sweep kept secret the specific details of the action. They did not discuss at general meetings where they planned to dump the trash, so even some chapter veterans remained in the dark.[16]

Abe Stark called for a meeting with chapter representatives on September 7, 1962, the day before CORE planned to implement Operation Clean Sweep. Members of Brooklyn CORE's Public Relations Committee met to speak with him about the unsanitary conditions of the Bedford-Stuyvesant community, which they argued reflected "the woeful neglect of this area" by city and borough leaders. The committee reiterated the main arguments about infrequent garbage collection and emphasized that "this situation is a menace to the health and welfare of the residents . . . as well as degrading to them." At the same time, they again argued that infrequent garbage collection was part of larger community-wide problems, brought on by "years of neglect." Using Gates Avenue as an example, they complained to Stark that the area suffered from slum housing, inadequate transportation, segregated and overcrowded schools, a lack of nurseries, playgrounds, and libraries, unemployment, inadequate traffic lights, and of course, poor sanitation. The representatives assured Stark that Brooklyn CORE would remain interested and involved in the area's rehabilitation "until the Bedford-Stuyvesant community becomes a neighborhood to be very proud of instead of the eyesore that it is now."[17]

Stark promised to intercede with the DOS on Brooklyn CORE's behalf and bring about a speedy resolution to this situation, but his timing for meeting with Brooklyn CORE and making these promises was suspicious. Stark probably wanted to delay or prevent Operation Clean Sweep, which had been planned for the very next day, more than he wanted to improve conditions in Bedford-Stuyvesant. Residents in Bedford-Stuyvesant had practically no political clout. Aside from the Unity Democratic Coalition (UDC), the neighborhood had very little political organization and practically no influence with the city's Democratic political machine. Though the neighborhood's population was approaching half a million residents, gerrymandered voting districts prevented Bedford-Stuyvesant and north-central Brooklyn from having a congressional representative. Its citizens were not wealthy or even solidly middle class. Instead, this was one of the poorest areas with some of the highest crime rates in the city. In the eyes of politicians up for reelection or reappointment, money that could have been put toward rehabilitating Bedford-Stuyvesant was better spent in districts that had more political and economic power.[18]

Still, the delay in action did not last long. Brooklyn CORE moved quickly after it received the DOS's response to the chapter's leafleting drive. Henry Liebman wrote a letter to the Brooklyn chapter, which told it that Bedford-Stuyvesant was in the "alternate parking program," which meant that streets received machine cleaning service three days a week and garbage collection the other three days a week, so technically the area received six-days-a-week service from the DOS. Liebman noted that he would pass Brooklyn CORE's complaints along to area supervisors, who would ensure that "corrective measures be taken wherever necessary to maintain street cleanliness." Nothing significant would change in the near future, however, because Bedford-Stuyvesant's housing stock did not require additional garbage collection. "Refuse collection pick-ups," he explained, "are generally made in accordance with neighborhood requirements." Neighborhoods with tenements received five-days-a-week service, which, according to Liebman, was "the maximum that can be provided by our Department." All other areas received service three days a week. Unless the DOS received "budgetary authorization for additional equipment and personnel," Bedford-Stuyvesant would not receive additional service. "Please be assured," Liebman stated, "that the matter will be given careful consideration and study."[19]

In the minds of Brooklyn CORE members, more was at stake than garbage in the street. Dirty streets in an all-black neighborhood and politicians' reluctance to correct the situation revealed patterns of racial discrimination in city services. Gilbert Banks, a black World War II veteran and skilled construction laborer, joined Brooklyn CORE during the Ebinger's campaign after he experienced tremendous difficulties getting work on unionized construction jobs. Banks remembered that Brooklyn CORE justifiably took action with Operation Clean Sweep because the DOS's negligence and politicians' noncommittal attitude were reflections of how the city discriminated against poor people of color. "We were dissatisfied with the way the Sanitation Department was viewing the community," Banks recalled. "The Sanitation Department comes to pick the garbage up, but they have more garbage out in the street than they have in the damn truck. So we complained to city hall, but they weren't hearing us."[20]

In fact, Banks, Goldwag and other Brooklyn CORE members felt the city made the garbage problem in Bedford-Stuyvesant worse. According to Maurice Fredericks, "The garbage men would come by, supposedly to collect the garbage, but when they left, the place would be very filthy." Mary Ellen Phifer, an African American migrant to Bedford-Stuyvesant from Kannapolis, North Carolina, who became an active member of Brooklyn CORE during the fall of 1962, felt this practice was a clear case of racial discrimination. If garbage collectors spilled trash on the streets, "they didn't clean it up. They left it there. And that's what was so disturbing about them taking up garbage in black neighborhoods. . . . In other neighborhoods, if they spilled some garbage on the sidewalk or in the street, because they have brooms and shovels on the side of the truck, I'm sure they put that garbage in the truck. They didn't leave it lying in the street." Among Brooklyn CORE members, and perhaps throughout north-central Brooklyn, everyday perceptions of municipal neglect, mixed with the evidence that white areas received qualitatively different treatment, proved that racial discrimination was real and damaging the community.[21]

If Brooklyn CORE strictly followed CORE's "Rules for Action," it would have continued its letter-writing campaign and leafleting. Stark and Liebman conceded that the city would act on some of Brooklyn CORE's demands, but in the eyes of Brooklyn CORE members the city's promises were meant only to appease their protests and would take too long to implement. Winning the hearts and minds of racially prejudiced people through education and mobilization, although it was "the CORE way" and in this case seemed to be succeeding, did not bring about tangible results fast enough to match Brooklyn CORE members' anger, frustration, and impatience. A desire for action and visible changes replaced their adherence to CORE's beliefs in the strict practice of compassion, discipline, and patience. In the garbage issue Brooklyn CORE saw an opportunity to rally the Bedford-Stuyvesant community and instill residents with a sense of political empowerment, and it did not want to waste that organizing opportunity.

Stark's meeting with Brooklyn CORE on September 7 delayed Operation Clean Sweep for one week. Brooklyn CORE members discussed Stark's comments at an emergency meeting of the Executive Committee, which decided to wait and see if the city brought any noticeable changes to Bedford-Stuyvesant's trash collection that week. When nothing happened, Brooklyn CORE went forward with the protest on Saturday, September 15, 1962. The day before it planned to implement Operation Clean Sweep, Brooklyn CORE leaked some details about the demonstration to the press. On the morning of September 15 readers from all over the city learned that "a city official is in for a surprise today" because "a load of garbage from Bedford-Stuyvesant is to be dumped on his doorstep." Arnold Goldwag, the chapter's public relations chairman, did not reveal to the press where demonstrators would dump the garbage "for fear the police and sanitation people would show up first and send their truck away." He did, however, reveal that after Brooklyn CORE collected garbage that Sanitation workers passed by in Bedford-Stuyvesant, the demonstrators would take it by truck and "dump it at the office of one of the city officials who they say promised better garbage collection but did not keep his word." Demonstrators would then leave before police arrived. In his anonymous press release, Goldwag stressed that this action was necessary because city officials refused to provide Bedford-Stuyvesant with proper services. "The area is being discriminated against because it is a neighborhood in which mostly Negroes and Puerto Ricans live," and after a year of negotiations, CORE got only promises from Mayor Wagner, Borough President Stark, and officials at the DOS.[22]

Brooklyn CORE launched Operation Clean Sweep on that Saturday morning, which was when the DOS collected bulk trash in Bedford-Stuyvesant. The demonstration created quite a scene. An interracial group of about twenty CORE members waited until the garbage trucks finished collecting on Gates Avenue. Then, with their own U-Haul trailers attached to several cars, Brooklyn CORE collected trash that Sanitation workers had left in the street. Maurice Fredericks remembered, "We went *after* the truck, and the garbage *we* picked up was the garbage that *they* should have picked up but for whatever reason they didn't. We collected what they *failed* to collect." Women and men swept Gates Avenue with brooms and used shovels to load dirt and debris into the trailers. Men carted off large boxes, old mattresses, broken refrigerators, and hunks of metal. Marjorie Leeds and Barbara Weeks, an African American member of Brooklyn CORE, even wore aprons that featured Brooklyn CORE logos. Bob Law captured the festive atmosphere of the demonstration. After the participants collected the garbage that the DOS had left behind, Law recalled, the demonstrators "marched down the street with the garbage in a parade."[23]

Residents came out and some stared with interest, others with amusement. Between twenty-five and thirty joined the group from CORE. One newspaper reported that close to fifty people, including children, participated in the demonstration. For the most part, Law believed, the community supported Brooklyn CORE for its action because "when we did things like that it said to the community for the first time, you don't have to accept this. You can actually do something about your condition." In his mind Brooklyn CORE's Operation Clean Sweep was a turning point for many black Brooklynites who had grown up accepting second-class status and double standards. They had never before believed that "if you go down to the Department of Sanitation and say pick up the garbage and they won't do it, that we would have dramatized this with a demonstration." Indeed, Operation Clean Sweep may have represented a brief moment in which residents of Bedford-Stuyvesant witnessed a new way of using direct-action protest to make their political voices heard and force negligent politicians to listen to their demands.[24]

The city expected that CORE would dump the garbage at the Mayor's Office in City Hall. According to Oliver Leeds, police closed off the Brooklyn Bridge, which denied easy access to that area. Instead, after Brooklyn CORE members filled the trailers, they made their way to Borough Hall, the political and judicial center of Brooklyn and location of the borough president's office. With no police or sanitation officials to stop them, demonstrators unloaded the broken mattresses, refrigerators, old rugs, splintered wooden crates, and other garbage and placed it on the steps of Borough Hall nearest the corner of Court and Remsen Streets. Shortly before noon, they formed a picket line and marched with placards that stated, "Taxation without Sanitation Is Tyranny," "Operation Clean Sweep," "Give Us a First-Class Bedford-Stuyvesant Community," and "Show Us Integration with Better Sanitation." Crowds formed to watch the demonstration and a few police officers arrived just as Oliver Leeds and others were unloading the last of the garbage. One police officer ordered the demonstrators to stop, but Leeds and others ignored him and continued the dumping. No one was arrested, but the police issued a summons to appear in criminal court for "violation of littering sidewalk." Marjorie Leeds accepted the ticket because, among CORE's leadership, she was available to go to court that Monday, September 17. The crowds dissipated and demonstrators made their way home. Aside from the court summons, the only other penalty was a ticket police gave to Oliver Leeds for illegally parking his station wagon and U-Haul trailer.[25]

Operation Clean Sweep had a strong effect on demonstration participants and local politicians. Brooklyn CORE's October 1962 newsletter had Operation Clean Sweep as its lead article. "Borough President, Abe Stark, has felt the wrath of Brooklyn CORE and the entire Negro community," the piece began. "The action prompted Mr. Stark and City officials to tour Bedford-Stuyvesant where he found what he termed 'shocking conditions of poverty.'" Some participants, like Robert Law, were empowered by the demonstration. "Throwing that garbage was emotionally gratifying. It was like, here, take this garbage back! You got the sense of fighting back." When Marjorie Leeds went to court that Monday, the judge found her guilty of littering and issued her a fine of ten dollars. When Leeds refused to pay and said she preferred jail, the judge summarily dismissed the case. Successfully evading fines and prison motivated Brooklyn CORE members and affirmed that Operation Clean Sweep was a just action. Dave Snitkin, a white garment worker and member of Brooklyn CORE, wrote to the editor of his union's paper and argued that Operation Clean Sweep should be mimicked by other neglected neighborhoods in the city. After summarizing the campaign and the demonstration, Snitkin declared, "Now the powers that be know what poor people have had to live with for many years." City officials probably wanted to avoid more demonstrations, but Brooklyn CORE members were prepared to continue Operation Clean Sweep if politicians ignored their requests. "We will come back again next week until you pick up this garbage," Law exclaimed. "Until you pick up this garbage, we will bring it back out here again and again." After Operation Clean Sweep, Brooklyn CORE leaders said the chapter would wait two weeks and see if the city took any action. If nothing was done, they promised to carry out another "dramatic action."[26]

Officially, Borough President Stark expressed more concern over the health and housing conditions in Bedford-Stuyvesant than the threat of more Brooklyn CORE–led demonstrations like Operation Clean Sweep. Repudiating the dramatic demonstration, a defensive Stark told reporters, "There was no need of any action of this kind. Although I have no jurisdiction over garbage and refuse collection, I assured [Brooklyn CORE] that I would make every effort to obtain for this neighborhood the services it needs—and I am living up to my word." Operation Clean Sweep led the borough president to make some strong statements that he was politically unable to match with strong action. Stark agreed there was "an urgent need for daily collection of garbage" on Gates Avenue between Bedford and Broadway. "The condition is a bad one and I feel that action should be taken . . . at an early date." He also pressed Harold Birns, the city building commissioner, to tour parts of Bedford-Stuyvesant and Brownsville and witness the "appalling" living conditions of those predominantly black neighborhoods. Stark said he had been "concerned for some time with the terrible conditions under which some of our residents have to live," and he described some of the houses in those neighborhoods as "unfit for human habitation." For all his supportive words, however, Stark was largely powerless in matters of public policy. At that time the borough president's only formal political authority at the municipal level consisted of his vote on the Board of Estimate, which determined the city's annual budget. Stark declared that he would support any appeal for funds to increase garbage collection in congested Brooklyn neighborhoods, and he urged the DOS to expedite those requests. Making suggestions and showing support with his one vote on the Board of Estimate, however, represented the extent of Stark's power and could hardly bring about the type of changes Brooklyn CORE demanded.[27]

Sanitation Commissioner Frank J. Lucia stated outright that Bedford-Stuyvesant would not receive five-days-a-week pickup service without changes in the department's budget. Lucia claimed he needed funds to hire thirty-nine extra workers, and until the city approved his new budget, Bedford-Stuyvesant had to make do with three-days-a-week service. He did, however, have a two-part plan that he argued would decrease the amount of garbage in the neighborhood. First, Lucia planned to send more officers into Bedford-Stuyvesant to enforce the city's health code and issue summonses and fines to negligent landlords. Second, he planned to work with Bedford-Stuyvesant civic groups to implement an education program that discouraged people from littering on the street and instead encouraged them to deposit trash in garbage cans. The Sanitation commissioner also refuted Brooklyn CORE's allegation that the city racially discriminated against Bedford-Stuyvesant. Harlem and Brownsville, Lucia pointed out, were also predominantly black and Puerto Rican neighborhoods, and those areas received five-days-a-week garbage collection service. Population density determined the frequency of a neighborhood's garbage collection, according to Lucia, not the residents' class or race. Bedford-Stuyvesant's garbage problem, he argued, resulted from its inhabitants' behavior, not racism or the city's negligence.[28]

Lucia's two-part plan and color-blind arguments disregarded Brooklyn CORE's empirical evidence of Bedford-Stuyvesant's large population density and poor housing conditions that warranted emergency attention. The DOS commissioner seemed content, however, to characterize people in Bedford-Stuyvesant as adherents to a "culture of poverty." He implicitly blamed residents' behavior for problems that reflected more than a decade of political neglect. Mayor Wagner was silent on the issue, which made the city appear unwilling to admit any responsibility for Bedford-Stuyvesant's complex problems. Lucia's solutions, while proactive, were insufficient and somewhat condescending. Summonses and fines were rarely an effective means of influencing slumlords' actions; and Lucia's proposed education program ignored the garbage already amassed around buildings, in empty lots and alleys, and on sidewalks.

No matter how many behavior-modification programs Lucia would implement, Bedford-Stuyvesant's population required extra sanitation services, which the city seemed unable or unwilling to provide.

Somehow, Brooklyn CORE misinterpreted Lucia's intentions and ran the headline, "Five Day Pick-up Achieved," on the cover of the October 1962 edition of the *North Star*. Later in the month, Oliver Leeds and others met with the Sanitation commissioner, and Lucia reiterated the department's position: there was not enough money or manpower to switch from three-days-a-week to five-days-a-week collection. Lucia stressed that he had already made a request for more funds and expressed regret that the budget director had not taken action. He was hopeful, however, that despite "budgetary stringencies," it would be possible to obtain the necessary money for expanding services in Bedford-Stuyvesant. Indeed, Lucia recognized that the area had a serious problem, but he refused to admit publicly that the city was responsible both for exacerbating the situation with inadequate services and correcting it with emergency increases in garbage collection.[29]

Brooklyn CORE ignored Lucia's explanations and continued to complain that there was no change in services on Gates Avenue. Apparently, the chapter misunderstood his promises and thought at least Gates Avenue would immediately begin receiving five-days-a-week service. Befuddled and annoyed, Lucia responded in early December that he was "at a loss to understand [Brooklyn CORE's] complaint. . . . The schedule of services on this street was not changed nor was five-day service instituted." In the six weeks since the October meeting, however, the DOS had initiated some measures to alleviate the garbage situation in Bedford-Stuyvesant. Sanitation workers placed 237 additional litter bins on corners throughout the neighborhood and posted seventy-five "No Dumping" signs at vacant lots "to help curtail the illegal disposal of refuse." Lucia sent "additional supervision" into the neighborhood, which he claimed would "make possible increased control over the general situation." In November Sanitation patrolmen issued 1,124 summonses "for various infractions of the Health Code." These steps—inadequate as they were—gave the impression that the city was not ignoring the predominantly black community. Lucia assured Brooklyn CORE that he would continue to advocate for increased collection in Bedford-Stuyvesant and that the department would service the community "to the fullest extent of our capabilities."[30]

The DOS did make one change in Bedford-Stuyvesant's pickup services: it increased collection of bulk trash from one to two days per week. Lucia explained that the department added the extra day as a way to discourage residents from littering. The neighborhood's people, Lucia implied, were solely responsible for such high levels of trash, not the DOS or the city. Brooklyn CORE grew dissatisfied with superficial solutions that placed all the blame for the problem on the residents. The chapter remained committed to five-days-a-week collection as the only solution to Bedford-Stuyvesant's problem and took their complaints above Lucia to Mayor Wagner. "It is our view," Oliver Leeds and Robert Law wrote to the mayor, "that a community as overcrowded as ours should get *preferential* treatment from the agencies of the City and not *prejudicial* treatment." They insisted that the DOS deliberately discriminated against Bedford-Stuyvesant by providing inadequate remedies to the neighborhood's garbage situation. Leeds and Law also admonished the mayor for his silence on the issue, which they found "quite shocking," since Wagner ran as "an independent fighting mayor" in the last election. Enclosed with the letter was a copy of a 1950 article in the *Stuyford Leader,* which highlighted Bedford-Stuyvesant's fight for five-days-a-week collection service. "Nothing had been done to help the neighborhood for over a decade," Leeds and Law argued. "Houses, schools, sanitation, bus service—even the local park—Tompkins park is in shambles. If something isn't done about the sanitation—and quick— Brooklyn CORE and a few prominent ministers will circulate the [1950 *Stuyford Leader* article] to every organization in this area."[31]

Similar correspondence continued throughout 1963. Brooklyn CORE members tried to recruit local participants to stage more direct-action protests, but they had difficulties gaining support. The chapter lacked the personnel to initiate a door-to-door community organizing campaign, and a onetime dramatic action like Operation Clean Sweep did not necessarily inspire ordinary people to dedicate their time, energy, or resources to a social movement. The one group directly in touch with the black masses was the black church leaders, but most black ministers in Brooklyn (except for Milton Galamison) were much more politically cautious and tended to avoid direct-action protest. The Brooklyn chapters of the NAACP and Urban League did not have memberships large enough to mobilize for future Clean Sweeps. Support from elected officials was also not forthcoming. State Assemblyman Thomas Russell Jones, president and founder of the UDC and a staunch supporter of civil rights activism in New York City, was the only elected official who wrote a letter to Mayor Wagner encouraging him to meet with community leaders in Bedford-Stuyvesant and stating that he supported Brooklyn CORE in any conference, community-wide demonstration, or picket line that it might organize to bring about the desired changes. This statement notwithstanding, Lucia made no attempt to provide the community with emergency services and remained steadfast in his claim that the department needed to wait for increased funds.[32]

Since it could not organize more direct-action protests alone, Brooklyn CORE joined other community groups in the Central Brooklyn Coordinating Council. The council presented various complaints, including Bedford-Stuyvesant's problem of infrequent garbage collection, to the New York City Commission on Human Rights. Bernice Fisher, one of the original founders of CORE, was in charge of the Brooklyn office for the commission. All she could do to help Brooklyn CORE was to set up another meeting, on March 26, 1963, between Frank Lucia and Bedford-Stuyvesant community leaders. Fisher and the commission were powerless to force the DOS into an immediate commitment for five-days-a-week collection. As late as May 1963 the Central Brooklyn Coordinating Council issued another statement that protested against discriminatory practices in Bedford-Stuyvesant. The declaration demanded five-days-a-week garbage collection and resolved to set up the "necessary machinery for community-wide action" if the city did not change its policies.[33]

Winning Concessions from City Hall

Demonstrations similar to Operation Clean Sweep did not occur in Bedford-Stuyvesant throughout the fall or winter of 1962. In 1963 community activists began two other efforts to redress Bedford-Stuyvesant's garbage problem, but they were even less effective than Brooklyn CORE had been the previous autumn. On February 5, 1963, at the behest of Oliver Leeds, the Community Relations staff of the City Commission on Human Rights agreed to investigate Bedford-Stuyvesant's garbage problems, and it promised it would do whatever was possible to make tangible improvements in the neighborhood's quality of life. One month of the commission's investigations culminated with a meeting between Sanitation Commissioner Lucia and several specially invited community leaders from Bedford-Stuyvesant. Marjorie Leeds was one of the activists who received an invitation from the Human Rights Commission's Intergroup Relations officer, Bernice Fisher. In the letter Fisher exhorted Leeds and others to attend this special gathering because the people from the community were the ones who had "repeatedly told us the urgency" of the garbage problem in Bedford-Stuyvesant, and "now is the time to act."[34]

Later that spring, community activists in north-central Brooklyn still petitioned the city to do something about the area's trash problems. In May the Central Brooklyn Coordinating Council (CBCC) issued a statement demanding five-days-a-week garbage collection in two of Bedford-Stuyvesant's most crowded sanitation districts. The CBCC rehashed arguments that the neighborhood's population density warranted increased service and noted that less dense, predominantly white areas received more frequent trash collection. It echoed Brooklyn CORE's criticism that "by giving 5-day collection service to others less deserving [by which it meant white neighborhoods] and denying such service to us," the DOS racially discriminated against Bedford-Stuyvesant, "whose people are predominately Negroes and Puerto Ricans." The CBCC did not want to "deprive" other neighborhoods of "needed service," but at the same time it "could no longer accept the logic which requires that we, though more deserving, must continue to be deprived." Its prescribed action, however, was vague and unimaginative. The CBCC called for community groups to issue statements to the mayor and the commissioner of the DOS that demanded five-days-a-week service. It also declared that it would "set up necessary machinery for community-wide action," but it was unclear what form the "machinery" would take or what type of "community-wide action" the CBCC could possibly design that would force Lucia and Wagner to bring about tangible changes.[35]

A different campaign in Bedford-Stuyvesant, this one for more traffic lights on streets that surrounded three elementary schools and one junior high school, had more immediate and tangible results than the community's campaigns for improved garbage collection services. A broad coalition composed of community-based organizations with ties to the CBCC—the P.S. 129 PTA, the Lexington-Lewis-Sumner Avenue Block Association, the P.S. 129 Community Association, the UDC, Brooklyn CORE, and an all-black community action group called the Fellowship of the Concerned Negro, which was headed by the Reverend George Lawrence of Antioch Baptist Church—staged a one-day direct-action protest on January 17, 1963, in which more than four hundred women and children assembled at three o'clock in the afternoon on the corner of Lexington and Lewis Avenues, created a human barricade, and blocked traffic. They carried signs that read, "We Want to Live"; "Save Our Children"; "We Love Our Children"; and "Will I Be Next?" For at least two years, according to Dorothy Titus, president of the PTA, community activists had petitioned Traffic Commissioner Henry Barns for more traffic lights. In the preceding three years, ten children, including one of Titus's, had been struck and injured by speeding vehicles; twenty-nine accidents had occurred in the area the activists identified as in need of traffic lights; and there had been two pedestrian fatalities. "We have stopped asking and begging," Titus told reporters, "and now we are taking things into our own hands." Titus declared that the group of protestors would remain in the intersection "until we get our lights." Titus declared that if police officers "come and haul away 100 of us, 100 more will come; and 100 more after that." Ironically, as a group of protestors drove away from the demonstration, their car was hit by a speeding motorist, and all five passengers were injured.[36]

The following week, representatives from the City Traffic Commission, the Police Department, and the Brooklyn Borough President's Office promised the community groups that they would investigate their demands and report back in early February. Officials of the Traffic Commission admitted that the locale under discussion was ranked as one of the worst accident areas in the entire city. Community activists gave the city until February 6 to install lights at four intersections: Quincy Street at Lewis Avenue; Quincy Street at Stuyvesant Avenue; Lexington Avenue at Summer Avenue; and Lexington Avenue at Lewis Avenue. Otherwise, they would resume their demonstrations. By mid-February the activists began to mobilize for more community support. "Every year more of our children are being struck down in the streets," a new flyer read, "yet we still *do not have a minimum number of traffic lights.*"[37]

By late August the mobilization, demonstration, and negotiation efforts paid off. Leaders from the various block associations wrote Brooklyn CORE a letter thanking the chapter for its members' "strength and determined aid in helping us to obtain the traffic lights that are now installed on the corners in our area." The campaign was hard-fought but ended in a solid victory, one that ostensibly saved young people's lives. It also proved to residents and activists that they could use direct-action protest and community organizing successfully. Indeed, they could mount a movement that fought city hall and win.[38]

The garbage collection campaign also produced a victory for Brooklyn activists, but tangible signs of change took longer to arrive than the new traffic lights. Operation Clean Sweep certainly established inadequate garbage collection and poor municipal services in Bedford-Stuyvesant as a major civil rights issue. The direct-action protest and various community organizing efforts forced people to consider the disproportionate amount of trash in north-central Brooklyn as a reflection of insufficient service, not residents' improper behavior. Brooklyn CORE's research and statistics also revealed the unfair treatment that predominantly black and poor areas received from the city, especially in light of the attention the DOS gave white, middle-class neighborhoods. As early as July 1963, City Building Commissioner Birns promised to flood the area with more inspectors, who would crack down on landlords and building owners whose properties violated city environmental codes. He increased the number of inspectors working in the area from sixty-one to eighty-five and assured the community that more inspectors would investigate slumlords, issue citations, and identify target areas to receive special attention from the DOS. Over the next few years, DOS services in north-central Brooklyn, especially in bulk trash collection, increased.[39]

"The Take-Charge Negro": Black Nationalism and Gendered Ideas on Leadership in Brooklyn CORE

In the aftermath of Operation Clean Sweep, young people in Brooklyn CORE became more involved in writing for the chapter's newsletter. They began to frame civil rights activism in Brooklyn as a reflection of a new, younger spirit of militancy. Such rhetoric and ideology, especially in the form of revolutionary critiques of class inequality, black nationalist emphasis on cultural activism, and criticisms of black middle-class complacency, would become commonplace throughout the country later in the decade. As early as 1962 and 1963, in the wake of Operation Clean Sweep and the traffic light demonstrations, Brooklyn CORE members began to debate how these sentiments should influence the culture of their organization and local activist efforts.

"Concern comes late, Bedford-Stuyvesant, but it comes . . . on the wings of a new generation, an uncompromising, take-charge genera-tion," Robert Law wrote in a front-page article for the *North Star.* Par-ticipating in Clean Sweep galvanized the small group of young black men in Brooklyn CORE to advocate for all-black leadership in the civil rights movement. Robert Law also wrote an article in that same newslet-ter called "The Take-Charge Negro," which called for an end to compla-cency among middle-class blacks and a black freedom movement that was not so reliant on white supporters. Law's article challenged CORE's belief that interracial activist communities were the best way to organize against racial discrimination. He wrote, "The Negro must take charge! For too long the Negro has been removed from the forefront of the bat-tle for his freedom. For too long the fight has been in the hands of liber-als and sympathizers. How can a man that doesn't feel your pain know the extent of your injury? In short, how can the white man tell me what I must do to acquire freedom?" Law then railed against "the tokenism that has swayed the bourgeoisie into their life of counterfeit freedom." The black middle class, "because of eagerness to be accepted or fear of rubbing their white benefactors the wrong way," had feigned participating in the fight for black freedom, "forsaken [their] forefathers," and "denied their heritage." He concluded with a call to "all factions of the Negro Community"—middle-class, working-class, southern, northern, Baptist, Methodist, Catholic, Episcopalian, Muslim, light-skinned, and dark-skinned—to "forge together in a great and grand alliance" to fight against "the common enemy of man: tyranny and bigotry." The leaders in this movement would be "a new generation, an uncompromising, unyielding generation," strengthened by its commitment to the struggle for black freedom and disciplined by its connection to a proud heritage of black resistance.[40]

James Steward echoed Law's ideas, but he also claimed black people's humanity and historic contributions to the nation's economic development earned for them full civil rights and equality. The black freedom struggle, he wrote, had to become "a way of life" for black people. He used masculinist rhetoric that would also become popular among young men drawn to black nationalism during the mid- to late 1960s. "Though bigotry is the nation's problem," he wrote, "it is the black man's fight." Steward's emphasis on black participation and leadership was not meant to discredit or disparage the contributions of white activists; he felt, however, that "the man who is struck" should be "the one to cry out. The protest must come from [him] who is violated. . . . My people must be the leaders in this struggle, for no one has the right to tell me or my brethren how to fight for our freedom; and as long as I live, no one will." Steward then condemned black leaders who advocated assimilation and acceptance from whites over basic respect and black autonomy in the United States. "I do not wish to be accepted by white America," he wrote. "I demand respect from white America as a human being. . . . I demand to be referred to as a human being whose forefathers bled, died for this nation's wealth, but never received the fruits of its wealth."[41]

Probably the most trenchant arguments Steward and Law put forward were for poor African Americans to lead the civil rights movement. Both derided and rejected the black middle class as natural leaders of the race. Black men from America's inner cities, Steward argued, were the vanguard of the new black freedom movement. In a diatribe against the black middle class that Steward wrote in the *North Star,* he argued, "The black man today is not Ralph Bunche or any other 'Bourgeois Leader.' He is the man in the ghetto of Harlem and Bedford-Stuyvesant . . . the man without a job, the man who fights the rats away from his baby's crib. . . . These are my people and wherever they may be or whatever they are, I am proud of them. For to claim the fight for freedom,

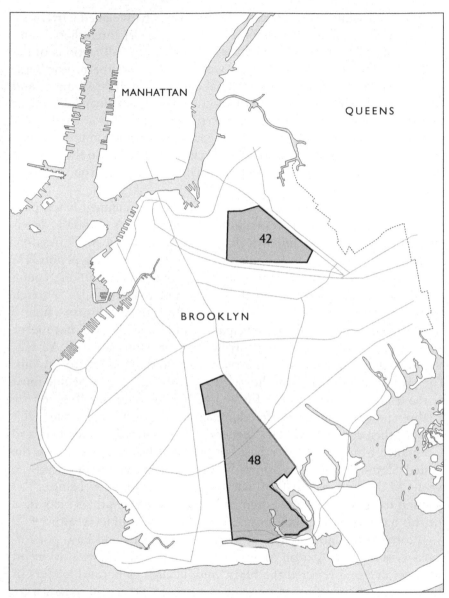

New York City Department of Sanitation Locations 42 (includes Bedford-Stuyvesant) and 48 (includes Marine Park), 1960 (based on Department of Sanitation, City of New York, *Annual Report, 1961–1962,* p. 11, Municipal Archives, City Hall Library).

Table 5. Department of Sanitation Services in Locations 42 (Bedford-Stuyvesant) and 48 (Marine Park), July 1960–June 1964

		Man days worked		Routine compactor collections Mixed household, institutions, baskets*		Bulk trash collections		
		Refuse collection	Street cleaning	Loads	Tons	Loads	Tons	Man days
1960–61	42	19,700	4,911	16,545	51,895	1,065	2,346	1,087
	48	20,173	4,828	18,334	53,257	1,090	2,033	853
1961–62	42	20,723	4,752	15,357	49,443	1,212	2,837	1,286
	48	22,415	3,836	18,235	52,854	1,337	2,199	1,080
1962–63	42	20,193	5,281	15,296	48,657	1,108	2,321	1,058
	48	22,052	3,446	17,249	48,475	1,277	2,245	1,220
1963–64	42	25,185	6,027	17,059	51,986	2,009	4,110	1,671
	48	21,952	3,410	17,467	50,021	1,193	2,748	1,290
1960–64 % change	42	+27.84	+22.72	+3.11	+0.18	+88.64	+75.19	+53.73
	48	+8.82	−29.37	−4.73	−6.08	+9.45	+35.17	+51.23

* *Baskets* refers to public trash receptacles located on sidewalk corners.

Source: The City of New York, Department of Sanitation, Bureau of Administrative Services, *Statistical Review and Progress Report,* New York City Department of Records and Information Services, City Hall Library. Data collected from the following separate reports: July 1, 1960–June 30, 1961; July 1, 1961–June 30, 1962; July 1, 1962–June 30, 1963; July 1, 1963–June 30, 1964.

and yet scorn and turn in shame upon one's own people is a folly of self-destruction."[42]

Law's and Steward's expressions of affinity for the black poor reflected Brooklyn CORE's growing commitment to organize people in "ghetto areas." As time passed and dramatic demonstrations like Operation Clean Sweep became common for Brooklyn CORE, the chapter developed a strong identification with people living in Bedford-Stuyvesant. Other CORE chapters in New York City, particularly those in Harlem, the Bronx, and Queens, also identified themselves as the "ghetto chapters," a term leaders used to separate themselves from the predominantly white, less militant college chapters and National CORE leaders and field secretaries. Such shifts in identity and allegiance, however, were not yet fully developed in late 1962 and early 1963. Instead, Law's and Steward's ideas indicated the beginnings of ideological differences that would eventually change National CORE's organizing philosophy as well as the ideology and political direction of the national movement.[43]

Young whites, like Arnold Goldwag, agreed with aspects of Law's and Steward's analyses. "The great American dream," Goldwag wrote, "was on paper. It was an empty reality. It was real only if you were white, all your friends were white and you were able to ignore . . . the ugly realities that occurred and reoccurred." Law, Steward, and Goldwag were adamant that racial discrimination was the driving force of American life and politics, and it was this belief that attracted them to remain with CORE's program, at least for the time being. For these three young men, and many others like them, CORE appeared to be the best organization for actively fighting racial discrimination in Brooklyn and the rest of the country. Steward wrote a short article in November 1962, entitled "Why You Should Join CORE," which stressed that CORE's values were in keeping with the country's highest ideals. "The principles of CORE," Steward wrote, "are also the principles of this Nation's heritage: that justice, equality and freedom shall be for all men." CORE was the only civil rights organization, Steward argued, that challenged one to view threats against another person's freedom as a danger to one's own coveted rights. CORE called on everyone to "live up to and struggle for that which he believes in" by "directly participating against instances of discrimination." CORE, Steward concluded, was an organization based on "action for freedom" and a group "America has learned to be proud of."[44]

Articles written by Law, Steward, and Goldwag dramatized the evolution of new strategies for organizing that occurred in Brooklyn CORE after Operation Clean Sweep. According to Maurice Fredericks, the articles caused "torrid discussions" among Brooklyn CORE members. Fredericks wrote a letter in the November 1962 issue of the *North Star,* which commended Law, Steward, and Goldwag for writing "forthright, interesting, and enlightening pieces." He was amazed at the opposition some expressed toward ideas he felt were "undeniable truths," namely that black people should be the top leaders in the struggle for African Americans' civil rights. His letter combined criticism of people who bashed Law's and Steward's articles with suggestions about how CORE could still be "the cure" for racial discrimination in America. Whites, according to Fredericks, did have a role to play in the "momentous drive toward full freedom through complete integration." Still, "the responsibility of top leadership, with but a few worthy exceptions, should of necessity be borne by Negroes." African Americans were suspicious of civil rights organizations, Fredericks argued, because whites tended to dominate their leadership and contributed most of their financial backing: "Many Negroes simply will not allow their civil rights struggle to be led by whites, reds, yellows, or any hue other than black." According to Fredericks, this idea was not "nationalistic," because for every righteous white participant in the movement, there might be "a thousand Ross Barnetts, Eastlands, Bull Conners, [and] plain John Citizen 'sitting this one out' and advising the Negro to 'slow down,' 'don't push so hard and so fast.'" Commenting on Brooklyn CORE's own difficulties in building a large black membership, Fredericks suggested that black apathy toward the movement stemmed from white control of civil rights organizations. He nevertheless concluded with a strong endorsement of CORE as the best organization for African Americans in their struggle for civil rights. Fredericks asserted, "CORE could indeed be the cure for ending discrimination, particularly if we keep before the public the image of a dramatic, direct action, non-violent group led by Negroes and whites. Our emphasis should be on an integrated leadership and active members with the top leadership mainly Negro. We are climbing Jacob's ladder and the bottom must, if we are to reach the top, be resting on solid rock."[45]

The "solid rock," in the minds of Fredericks, Law, and Steward, was black leadership and an organizational base in black urban communities. Without both, they believed Brooklyn CORE would continue to have problems, as it had during the Ebinger's campaign's early picket lines. Operation Clean Sweep, with its dramatic street theater and vocal condemnation of the mayor and the DOS, created an opening in the chapter for a debate on the role of African Americans as leaders in an interracial organization. Similar debates on the role of whites were occurring in other CORE chapters throughout the country during the early 1960s. In 1961 Newark CORE discussed restricting the chairmanship to blacks. Advocates of the position argued that having a black chairman was the only way the chapter could relate to the local black community. In New York CORE in early 1962 Gladys Harrington, the chairwoman, publicly stated that civil rights organizations "should basically be run by Negroes"; and in May 1962 several influential black members of Baltimore CORE expressed criticism of white participation. In some instances changing attitudes toward whites produced rifts. In 1961 in Detroit, CORE broke apart over the issue. Those who felt all-black leadership and white acquiescence to a "Negro point of view" were "racist violations of CORE's color-blind traditions" formed a new CORE chapter called Metropolitan Detroit CORE. New Orleans CORE split over a debate on interracial dating, which ended with most whites leaving the chapter because they insisted that interracial socializing was central to CORE's goals, whereas most black members felt that it was an expendable goal if it damaged the group's reputation in the black community.[46]

During Operation Clean Sweep, black members of Brooklyn CORE expressed ideologies that in later years would dominate the chapter and the national movement's organizing philosophies. For the time being, black nationalist tendencies did not replace Brooklyn CORE's commitment to maintain an interracial membership. From the end of 1962 on, Brooklyn CORE debated the question of interracialism versus all-black leadership, but unlike the CORE chapters in New Orleans and Detroit, Brooklyn CORE did not split apart over this issue. African Americans in Brooklyn CORE felt secure in their relationships with the whites in the chapter, and white members supported the unwritten rule of having a black person as chairperson. Throughout these debates, people in Brooklyn CORE adhered to CORE's principles of nonviolence and interracial membership, although black nationalist sentiments would intensify in coming years and eventually dominate the chapter's organizational culture.

Although rhetoric about the need for black men to become leaders of the local and national movement shaped discussions in Brooklyn CORE and the wider civil rights movement, women were ever-present and important leaders at the national and local levels. This was especially true in Brooklyn CORE. Their most important leadership roles were as committee chairs, in which roles women, black and white, made vital contributions to the chapter's everyday operations and supplied visionary leadership. The chapter never seemed to limit women's involvement to specific jobs or committees. Frances Crayton, whose family migrated to Brooklyn from Georgia, joined Brooklyn CORE shortly after graduating from high school. In 1964 she was Brooklyn CORE's vice chair, but when she became an active member shortly after Operation Clean Sweep, her role models for leadership were both women and men. Crayton remembered that there were women "like Mary Phifer, who was very active and played a major leadership role," and she emphasized that women were central to Brooklyn CORE's leadership cadre:

> We held offices. Our opinions were taken seriously. . . . A lot of us devoted so much time, [and] we were openly accepted. I had keys to the office and Mary had keys. I don't ever remember doing any female kind of work. I'm not a cook, so I never was asked to do any cooking or cleaning. It wasn't that we were put in that role. I think we were recognized as equal partners in this organization, and the organization, as I remember, was a real democracy, that people actually voted on issues and concerns, on actions that we were to take. And sometimes we were voted down and sometimes we weren't.[47]

To be sure, some women whose husbands were very active in Brooklyn CORE took on a great deal of their family's "home work," but even these labors were essential to the chapter's political organizing. Winnie Fredericks, Maurice Fredericks's wife, went to demonstrations but did not regularly attend meetings. She left that part of political activism to her husband. "We had youngsters at home, so I always said, well, somebody's got to be home to mind the kids." For all Marjorie Leeds's activity, she also took on more "private sphere" responsibilities in terms of managing their home and children. At the same time, taking care of families was not always women's work. Rioghan Kirchner remembered that other wives "had to stay home and mind the children" but "my husband had to stay home and mind ours." Minding children was work for the movement just as leafleting and picketing were, and in some families like Rioghan Kirchner's and Elaine Bibuld's, women took on much more public roles than did their husbands. There was also a communal aspect to the "home work" of the local movement, and Brooklyn CORE families often took turns babysitting people's children when there were all-day sit-ins or when members were occasionally arrested at demonstrations.[48]

Still, women took leadership roles in areas where they had interest and expertise. In essence, black women in Brooklyn CORE were exemplary "take-charge Negroes," and white women like Kirchner were significant leaders, too. Mary Phifer argued that women could easily have become chairs of the Employment or the Rent-Strike Committees. She eventually became the chair of the Education Committee, not because it was "woman's work," but because she was involved in everything that pertained to public schools and local education issues. These were not merely political concerns for Phifer. She recalled that she "attended most of the meetings dealing with education . . . because I had eight children that I was raising and they were in the public school system."[49] The same was true for Rioghan Kirchner, who chaired the Housing Committee and was the chapter's first vice chair. Women were just too incredibly important to the local movement in Brooklyn, which became readily apparent in late 1962 and early 1963 during CORE's campaign against inequality in Brooklyn's public schools.

In fact, Brooklyn CORE's involvement in this fight came at the behest and leadership of Elaine Bibuld, a black woman who joined Brooklyn CORE during Operation Clean Sweep.[49]

6

"A War for the Minds and Futures of Our Negro and Puerto Rican Children"

The Bibuld Family's Fight to Desegregate Brooklyn's Public Schools

Since the Supreme Court Decision of 1954 in *Brown vs. Board* of Education, school systems throughout the North have made excuses for the all-Negro school by attributing its presence to de facto segregation. . . . The word de facto segregation was never heard of until the historic Supreme Court decision of 1954. Before that year the North could get away with segregation in their schools by pointing to the more blatant and vicious form found in the South. Now the law was clear, segregation by legislative act was illegal and in violation of the Constitution of the United States. Now the North needed a rationalization to continue its brand of racial segregation.
—Paul Zuber, "The De-facto Segregation Hoax," *Liberator* 3.8 (August 1963)

There are those in our society who are coming more and more to understand that not only are our children being destroyed, but that the destruction is connived and deliberate and inevitable unless Negroes call a halt to this inhuman process.
—The Reverend Dr. Milton Galamison, "What Child Is This?" sermon delivered December 29, 1963

A Story about Quality and Access

In New York City during the 1960s, the race and class of a neighborhood's inhabitants powerfully shaped the quality of education in its public schools. In economically stable communities, where residents' incomes were at or above the city median, the schools seemed to work well. But in residential areas where the majority of people lived below the poverty line, public schools were plagued by numerous problems. In the twenty years after World War II, the poorest areas of Brooklyn became almost completely African American and Puerto Rican, and many children in those communities attended schools that were over-crowded, poorly staffed, and underresourced. Inadequate books and inexperienced, overworked teachers contributed to their low scores on reading and math tests. Many of the children performed poorly in their academics, which was startling; perhaps more startling, given the condi-tions and resources of schools in predominantly black neighborhoods, is that some children managed to succeed.[1]

When Douglass Bibuld lived in a mixed-income area of Crown Heights during the early 1960s, his school had a Gifted and Talented Program, took children on field trips to the city's museums and historic landmarks, provided music and art programs, and offered advanced classes in reading and math. After his family's home caught fire in the fall of 1962, the Bibulds moved to a run-down section of Park Slope, where his new school, which was more than 70 percent African Ameri-can and Puerto Rican, offered substandard academics and few extracur-ricular activities. Bibuld went from a fifth-grade class in which he studied algebra and international current events to a class in which teachers assigned rudimentary arithmetic and basic spelling. He began murmur-ing to himself in class to stifle his boredom. Teachers wondered if he had emotional problems and suggested he might be better served in special education classes.[2]

Douglass's parents, Elaine and Jerome Bibuld, were members of Brooklyn CORE, and they asked the chapter for help. So began a four-month campaign to improve education for the entire city's poor African American and Puerto Rican children. CORE allied with other grassroots activists from the Parents' Workshop for Equality and made the Bibuld case a cause célèbre. They staged one of the first public school sit-ins in New York City history, occupied the Board of Education headquarters, and picketed in front of some of Brooklyn's poorest public schools. Crit-ics harassed the Bibuld family with offensive phone calls and letters, and some even threatened to kill the children. This was one of the first times Brooklyn CORE members received such threats, which revealed the ugly backlash against racial integration that simmered beneath the surface of everyday life in New York City. If that were not enough, Elaine and Jerome Bibuld faced imprisonment for parental neglect when they refused to send their children to a segregated, substandard public school.

In New York black parents and children who demanded equal education faced a reactionary, potentially violent public and an intransigent government bureaucracy that preferred to maintain the status quo rather than institute policies that created racially and economically integrated public schools.

The Bibuld family and Brooklyn CORE members, however, were not easily intimidated or cowed. Elaine Bibuld became the first chair of Brooklyn CORE's Education Committee, and, with the assistance of other chapter members such as Mary Ellen Phifer, Marjorie Leeds, and Gilbert Banks, she transformed her personal cause into a political campaign that contributed to the city's education reform movement. Unlike many narratives of early 1960s black activism regarding public schools, Brooklyn CORE's campaign did not use integrationist rhetoric to argue for black students' inclusion in an education that favored white students. The rhetoric of racial integration campaigns emphasized the belief that black students' educational and civic advancement came only when they attended schools with their white peers. But, as Jack Dougherty argues, viewing black activism solely through the lens of racial integration "distorts our understanding of the past" and causes us to overlook how there were "struggles for numerous reforms." Racial integration of predominantly white schools was only one vehicle, one tool in a long struggle for black access to high-quality education. It was a strategy that Brooklyn's own Reverend Milton Galamison, and the citywide Parents' Workshop he led, promoted for much of the first half of the 1960s. Galamison's strategy said, in short, that if the white-dominated educational system was leaving black children to rot academically in inferior Jim Crow schools, then the only solution was for black children to integrate white schools. Brooklyn CORE adopted a different strategy. Brooklyn CORE's rhetoric in the Bibuld campaign underscored the consistent structural inequality—in resources and curriculum—that defined New York City's Jim Crow public school system, and therefore the chapter demanded systemic structural changes, not merely racial integration. Rather than fight for a policy that racially integrated some schools, Brooklyn CORE hoped to make the entire school system more equitable and just, so that it would not matter if a black student attended an all-black school or a predominantly white school: the education would be the same for all students throughout the city. Brooklyn CORE also called attention to the faulty logic behind "culture of poverty" arguments that rationalized the inferiority of black schools as a reflection of black students' cultural deficiencies. Brooklyn CORE argued instead that black students' culture, or level of academic motivation, had not created New

York City's racially segregated public school system. Instead, the city's racially segregated public schools had been created, and maintained, by a history and politics of white privilege. Brooklyn CORE hoped to help the Bibuld family smash through this system of white privilege and to take the entire city with them.[3]

"I Want Some Help! I Want You to Hear Me!"

In the fall of 1960 the Bibulds lived on the second floor of a brownstone at 1633 Union Street in the Crown Heights section of Brooklyn. The family had moved to Brooklyn after living in several different public housing complexes in Queens, and Elaine and Jerome saw it as a chance to live in a safer environment and to send their children to better public schools. The three children, Douglass, Carrington, and Melanie, attended school around the corner from their home, at P.S. 167. The school was racially mixed. Most of the 37,000 African Americans in Crown Heights (one-quarter of the neighborhood's population) lived in areas just south of Bedford-Stuyvesant, which by 1960 were fast becoming predominantly black. Only a little more than 6 percent of all blacks in Crown Heights lived where the Bibulds did, but the area did not remain that way long. Douglass Bibuld remembers that when the family first arrived at the house on Union Avenue, the Irish, Italian, and Jewish families began to leave. Three years later, he recalled, the racial demographics had dramatically changed: "I don't think there were any white people left on the block." This was one of Douglass's earliest memories of experiencing racial discrimination.[4]

Still, the Bibulds raised their children to be proud of their nationality and to better themselves through education. They emphasized that African Americans were a strong nation with a rich history, not a "race," which they viewed as an oppressive concept designed to mark some humans as superior and others inferior. The Bibulds wanted their three children to identify as part of an African American nationality, a point of view they had both developed from their personal histories and participation in radical politics.

Jerome Bibuld's parents were eastern European Jews. When he turned three in 1931, his mother abandoned him and his younger brother, Seymour, at a Jewish orphanage in the Bronx. After six years, their father found them and took the boys to live in the Bronx with him, his new wife, and his parents. Jerome Bibuld grew up during the Great Depression. He was poor and bitter. He recalled that he often went to bed hungry and used newspapers to fill holes in his shoes during the winter. His stepmother and grandmother quarreled often, which made the home an upsetting place to live. Although he felt loved and cared for, Jerome remembered his youth as a time of suffering and misery. Growing up in poverty sparked his interest in radical politics. As a teenager, Bibuld was involved in American Youth for Democracy, a spin-off organization of the Young Communist League. Later he attended meetings sponsored by the Communist Party, the American Labor Party, and other radical organizations, which was where he met his future wife, Elaine Jones, and best friend, Oliver Leeds.[5]

Elaine Carrington Jones's mother died while giving birth to the baby girl in 1930, and a distant cousin of her mother adopted Elaine as an infant. The Carringtons, according to stories Elaine heard as a child, were leaders in a self-sufficient black community outside Gilbert's Corner, Virginia. In the family's oral tradition, the Carringtons never bowed down to whites, even in the face of intimidation and terror, and safeguarded their independence. The only time they interacted with whites was when they traveled to town to buy and sell goods. According to lore, Elaine's great-uncle once went to town and had an argument with a white man over the price offered him for goods. Carrington defied the racial mores of his day and stood up for himself. After the exchange, some whites rode to the black settlement and tried to terrorize the residents, but Elaine's great-uncle frightened them into a hasty retreat by firing his rifle just over their heads. Though the story was framed to teach youngsters about courage and honor in resistance, it also had a gloomy caveat: sometimes black folks' resistance could go too far and have a grave price. The next time Elaine's great-uncle went to town, whites beat him unconscious, and he lived the rest of his life as an invalid.[6]

Still, Elaine Jones recognized from her family's oral tradition the importance of activism and resistance. When she turned seventeen, she left her childhood home in the Williamsbridge section of the Bronx and moved to Harlem. Her first activist experience was as a volunteer for Benjamin Davis's reelection campaign in the late 1940s. Davis was the first African American member of the Communist Party elected to the City Council, and he became an icon to both black and white leftists and progressives. Elaine Jones worked with other young black and white boosters handing out flyers, registering voters, and knocking on doors in black neighborhoods to collect signatures on petitions. Canvassing exposed her to some of the most serious conditions of urban poverty: cold-water flats, vermin, overcrowding, faulty plumbing, and hazardous electrical wiring. Her background, coupled with these experiences, made her more empathetic to poor people's struggles and receptive to leftist critiques of class inequality in America.

Jerome and Elaine raised their children to see themselves as African American, and to believe that as black people they had a duty to contribute to their people's liberation with a firm knowledge of history and a disciplined work ethic. Elaine Bibuld often read the children biographies of famous black Americans such as Frederick Douglass, Paul Robeson, and Harriet Tubman; and both parents were very rigorous when it came to their children's schoolwork. Academic success would be their children's main weapon against racism. At night the children left their homework on the kitchen table for their father to review when he came home. Jerome Bibuld worked late nights as a manager at Group Health Incorporated (GHI). If he found errors in his children's work, he roused them from sleep and helped them correct their mistakes. "As tired as he was," Douglass Bibuld recalled, "he would get us up to do the homework and then try to see that it was done right. We'd be falling asleep over the homework."[7]

The Bibulds' emphasis on education and African American pride helped their children excel in school. At P.S. 167 Douglass Bibuld enrolled in the third-grade class for Intellectually Gifted Children (IGC), in which he developed a love for science fiction and an appreciation for poetry. In the late 1950s schools in Crown Heights were evenly mixed: whites constituted 51 percent of the public school population, and blacks and Puerto Ricans combined made up the remaining 49 percent. During their first few years in school, the Bibulds were in a multiracial, academically competitive learning environment. They felt comfortable being with other black students in a place where their academic achievements were encouraged, not scorned.[8]

Douglass especially thrived at P.S. 167. Each classroom had a library, and he remembered that, after he read all the books in his classroom, he went on to the fourth grade's library and finished those as well. Third-graders in the IGC program at P.S. 167 had weekly current events assignments from the *New York Times*. "I would get a huge article on the arms race between Eastern Europe and the United States and then I would go through at least the first column or two and break down all the words into words I could understand," Douglass Bibuld recalled. He developed a rigorous work ethic with his studies, and the friendly competition from his classmates encouraged him to excel. Children at P.S. 167 also took field trips to cultural and historical sites around the city and connected those experiences with their classroom lessons. Elaine Bibuld accompanied her son's class to the Statue of Liberty, where they read Emma Lazarus's epigraph and the teacher led students in lessons on history and poetic imagery.[9]

For two years the Bibuld children's education progressed at P.S. 167, and their family lived a comfortable life. Elaine and Jerome attended CORE meetings and parties, and they sometimes sponsored social gatherings at their apartment. Their peace, however, came to an abrupt end in the fall of 1962.

On September 27, 1962, an electrical fire destroyed the Bibulds' apartment. They found a new place to live in a two-family house at 342 Fourth Street in the Park Slope section of Brooklyn. Named for its proximity to Prospect Park and a westward slope going toward the river, Park Slope was once a suburb where Brooklyn's gentry lived. In the 1930s middle- and working-class people began renting apartments in the area, and its class and composition changed. "In this neighborhood," one community study noted, "on the avenues as well as on the side streets, the income level and the quality of the housing have moved downward with the slope of the ground to the East River." Moving west from the park, the area's housing changed from mansions and large, single-family homes to brownstones, multifamily houses, and apartments above storefronts. The large brownstone homes that once housed a single family were now carved up into three and four apartments. In the late 1950s the neighborhood still had specialty food shops, furniture stores, and businesses that sold handmade crafts, all of which catered to the wealthy, but these were being abandoned or replaced by chain stores.[10]

The Bibulds lived in one of Park Slope's poorer sections, where the median family income was below the borough average. Douglass Bibuld recalled the area's housing as run-down and dangerous compared to that where they had lived in Crown Heights. In the late 1950s over three-quarters of the residents of Park Slope were whites born in the United States, and a fifth were immigrants from Italy, Ireland, Russia, Poland, Germany, England, Canada, Scandinavia, and Greece. African Americans combined with the small Puerto Rican population to make up less than 3 percent of Park Slope's population.[11]

There were several elementary schools from which Elaine and Jerome Bibuld could choose to send their children, and they sought one comparable to P.S. 167. The Bibulds asked the Assistant Superintendent's Office about the area schools' conditions, racial populations, and programs. Specifically, they did not want to send their children to a Special Service (SS) school, which had lower standards, more remedial programs, and fewer resources than other schools. A representative of the

Board of Education (BOE) strongly recommended P.S. 282, a newly built public school just a few blocks from where the Bibulds lived. P.S. 282 did not have an IGC program, but the BOE promised that its small classes and new facilities would give their children an appropriate learning environment. All three children enrolled in early October 1962. Douglass entered the fifth grade, Carrington the fourth, and Melanie the first. Despite the small population of African Americans and Puerto Ricans in Park Slope, they were the overwhelming majority (over two-thirds) of students at P.S. 282. Elaine and Jerome Bibuld were assured their children would be enrolled in the most challenging classes.[12]

The Bibulds' lives quickly settled into a familiar routine until Douglass returned home sulking during his second week of school. His mother assumed he missed his old school and playmates and assured him he would adjust to his new environment. The young boy slid a piece of paper toward his mother across the kitchen table. All Elaine Bibuld saw was the "100%" written in red ink above the heading for a spelling test. "Oh, that's great!" she exclaimed, to which her son cried back, "No! Look at it Mommy! Look at it!" She glanced down and saw that the words were of a first- or second-grade level: "bag," "bank," "bit," "bill," "bet," "band," "bath," and "basket." Douglass complained he was unhappy and bored because his work was too easy. He then showed his mother his math homework, a drill on single-digit multiplication. Compared to the basic algebra he had started to learn at P.S. 167, these exercises were rudimentary. "The work that they were doing was just nothing," Douglass Bibuld remembered. "It wasn't work to me at all. It was like I was going to do my sister's work [and she] was four grades below me." The school also provided him with inadequate supplies. After almost two weeks in school, he had received only two books, and one was a dictionary that was missing its cover.[13]

Douglass had complained to his teacher that the material was too easy, but the teacher assigned him busy work writing random reports from an encyclopedia while the rest of the class participated in the day's lessons. Douglass cried to his mother that he felt awkward and embarrassed when others labeled him the "smartest" student in the class. "I had never been considered the brain in a class before. It was just so foreign to me." The social stigma of being the class brain and lack of stimulation caused Douglass Bibuld to murmur aloud unconsciously. Teachers chastised him for disturbing the class, and students began to mock Douglass as a "crazy" person who talked to himself. Douglass was not even cognizant of his behavior. He denied the accusations and became reluctant to socialize with his new classmates. Years later Douglass Bibuld realized he probably did talk to himself unknowingly: "That was a mark of how out of it, how bored and disconnected I was in that classroom."[14]

Elaine Bibuld recognized the seriousness of her son's dilemma. The following day she and her husband met with the school's principal, Jennie Montag. They asked Montag if there was anything more the school could do for their son since he was not learning. Elaine Bibuld suggested his skipping a grade, but Montag assured her that would not be possible. Instead, the principal took the Bibulds to each of their three children's classrooms, introduced them to the teacher, and said, "This is Mr. and Mrs. Bibuld. I want you to make sure that their children get homework." "I saw what the system was," Jerome Bibuld recalled. "I said this is ridiculous. Our children still won't learn . . . or if they do learn, they will learn in opposition to their peers!"[15]

The Bibuld children's predicament revealed the paradoxical effects race and class had on many of the city's public institutions, especially its school system. New York City officials touted their public programs as some of the most democratic in the country. Architects of the city's public school system designed it to provide equal educational opportunities for all New Yorkers, regardless of their language skills or academic proficiency. Immigrant students had special service programs for remedial language instruction and citizenship training. Academically proficient and artistic students like Douglass Bibuld had the IGC programs and highly selective high schools that specialized in the liberal arts, music and dance, and math and sciences. Young men and women who sought training in a specific trade, such as secretarial work or automotive repair, also had vocational schools. The school system tracked students through proficiency examinations and gave children opportunities to advance into more rigorous programs through special examinations. For much of the century, New York City's public school system prepared students either to go to college or to enter the workforce with marketable skills. Over time, however, public schools reflected, and reproduced, the class and racial inequalities that shaped the city during the postwar era. Many of the city's poor people, African Americans, Puerto Ricans, and other immigrants, were forced to live in neighborhoods that were quickly deteriorating because of political neglect and economic disinvestment. Public schools in those neighborhoods often became overcrowded, underresourced, and poorly staffed.[16]

Elaine and Jerome Bibuld's options seemed limited and bleak. If the Bibuld children remained enrolled at P.S. 282, which Board of Education officials argued was the best of all the schools in their zoned area, they would be stifled by its low standards and ostracized by teachers and students. Teachers and administrators who wanted to do the least amount of work saw the Bibulds as an annoyance. To them Elaine and Jerome Bibuld were needy, pushy, and demanding; and their ambitious children were anomalies among youngsters who, over the years, had come to expect nothing but mediocrity from their public schools. Among the other children at P.S. 282, Douglass became an oddity as the smartest child in his class. His new peers looked at him as different, even strange. This scenario had already had an effect on his emotional state, and Elaine and Jerome Bibuld feared the same for their two younger children. The Bibulds took their complaints to various levels of the Board of Education's chain of command, but they received no satisfaction. Education officials told them they were not permitted to send their children outside their prescribed area and offered alternative schools in their district. None of the choices matched the achievement levels of P.S. 167. The Bibulds demanded a school that performed at or above the national median level for reading and math, but none of the schools in their area, which all seemed to be predominantly black and Puerto Rican, matched those criteria.[17]

The Bibulds attempted to home-school their children, which lasted for about seven weeks. Home-schooling the three children demanded a great deal of time. Jerome Bibuld sometimes worked eighty hours a week, and both parents wanted to remain active in Brooklyn CORE. The BOE began sending truancy summonses to their home because the children were still enrolled at P.S. 282. After the Bibulds informed BOE officials of their protest, the BOE informed Elaine and Jerome Bibuld that they had violated the mandatory attendance law, which stated that children had to attend an accredited school or show proof that they were privately taught by a certified teacher. Legally, the state could remove the children from the Bibuld's custody if they did not immediately return them to P.S. 282. Faced with the traumatic, destructive possibility of losing their three children, the Bibulds panicked and sent the youngsters to live with relatives in New Jersey. They planned to visit them on weekends while the children were home-schooled in New Jersey. The separation, however, was too painful. After the trauma of the fire and the abrupt move, being separated from their children was too emotionally difficult for Jerome and Elaine. Eventually, they brought them back to New York City.[18]

Desperate and seemingly out of options, the usually shy, reserved Elaine Bibuld spoke up at the next CORE meeting. The couple had heard about Brooklyn CORE from Oliver Leeds and joined during

Operation Clean Sweep. She became anxious as members went through the usual routine of making reports from different committees and endlessly debating minor points of a protest's strategy or tactics. After almost two hours, Elaine felt the group would never get to her and the meeting would end with her problem unresolved. She stood behind the podium, slammed her hands down and said, "I want some help! I want you to hear me!" Brooklyn CORE's small cadre sat rapt as she explained her family's situation. Many concluded that this case demonstrated how the BOE maintained two separate school systems: one for middle-class, largely white neighborhoods, and another for the city's poor, who were increasingly black and Puerto Rican. After she spoke, Oliver Leeds suggested the formation of an education committee that would investigate the Bibulds' case and devise an appropriate action plan. He asked for volunteers to work with Elaine Bibuld. Arnold Goldwag, Gilbert Banks, Marjorie Leeds, and Mary Ellen Phifer raised their hands. Brooklyn CORE's Education Committee formed and Elaine Bibuld became its first chairwoman.[19]

Marjorie Leeds, Goldwag, and Banks were veteran organizers, but Phifer and Bibuld had little leadership experience in organizing a long-term investigation and a possible large-scale demonstration movement. Still, the Education Committee formed a unique matrix in which women with little formal leadership experience were able to perform very public roles as spokespersons for Brooklyn CORE. Mary Ellen Phifer, a southern migrant who had spent half her life living under Jim Crow, was very familiar with racially segregated public schools, which was why she expressed interest in the Bibuld campaign. Like Elaine Bibuld, Rioghan Kirchner, Marjorie Leeds, and other women in Brooklyn CORE, Phifer became an influential leader of the chapter and an important public figure. Although her role in the Bibuld campaign is not prominently recorded in extant sources, she was involved in a significant way: she attended local PTA meetings, investigated patterns of racial discrimination in the BOE's zoning policies, and helped host meetings and fundraisers, all while raising a family of eight children. As in other campaigns for public school reform in New York City, women were vital leaders in Brooklyn CORE's campaign to help the Bibulds.[20]

"Fighting . . . for All Children
Who Attend Segregated Schools"

Members of Brooklyn CORE's newly formed Education Committee developed a three-part plan that would help the Bibulds, but members also agreed they wanted to use this protest to press for larger changes in the public education system. First, Brooklyn CORE planned to form strong alliances with other grassroots civil rights organizations. CORE members who were also a part of other local organizations and churches would influence those groups to support the Bibulds' campaign. Second, Brooklyn CORE would collect and review data on the level of segregation in Brooklyn's public schools. The last component, a large-scale direct-action campaign, would publicize the city's racially segregated school system.

Marjorie Leeds and Mary Ellen Phifer, who were both involved in the Parents' Workshop for Equality in New York City Schools, petitioned its members and leaders for support. Brooklyn CORE members had learned from past campaigns the importance of building and maintaining strong alliances with other activist groups. By the end of 1962 public education had emerged as the single most important political issue among African American New Yorkers, and Brooklyn CORE's success in this area would depend on outside help.

Brooklyn CORE's campaign received an endorsement from the Parents' Workshop on November 8, 1962. A group of fifty parents met at Siloam Presbyterian Church. After sharing in a potluck dinner, Leeds and Phifer presented the facts of the Bibulds' case, and the Parents' Workshop voted to support them and any other families that withheld their children from attending public school because of substandard conditions. The Parents' Workshop declared it would help the Bibulds' campaign with "legal and social action," and it would also "recruit parents with children in substandard schools who will be prepared to withdraw them." Galamison, president of the Parents' Workshop, said the organization would press for a meeting with the BOE and request a specific program for integration. He also affirmed that the grassroots organization would prepare to strike at specific problems such as overcrowding, low standards in black and Puerto Rican schools, and part-time education programs, which split a full school day in half to accommodate overcrowded schools. Brooklyn CORE's small membership welcomed this added participation.[21]

The very next day members from the Parents' Workshop and Brooklyn CORE accompanied Elaine and Jerome Bibuld to a meeting with Dr. Bernard Donovan, the superintendent of schools. Donovan "expressed shock" at P.S. 282's low standards and "promised to investigate," but in the meantime he firmly stated that the children must return to school. The Bibulds refused to send their children back to P.S. 282. They gave the superintendent a copy of a telegram they had sent to the mayor and the governor that listed their reasons for protesting the school and their demands. The Bibulds withdrew their children "because the standards are so low that Douglass [who was] in . . . the most advanced class in the 5th grade was getting third grade work!" They refused to send their children to any school designated by the BOE until they received written assurance that the school had median reading and arithmetic levels of 6.5 or higher in the sixth grade and a proportion of permanently licensed teachers not lower than the city norm. Donovan offered them three alternative schools, but each one was racially segregated, a special service school, overcrowded, or inconvenient for the Bibulds to travel to by public transportation. Donovan's office also refused information regarding the reading and math levels in the schools' six grades or the proportion of permanently licensed teachers. He assured them only that the schools had ICG programs. Elaine and Jerome Bibuld summarily rejected Donovan's offer.[22]

While Marjorie Leeds and Mary Phifer worked as liaisons with the Parents' Workshop, Arnold Goldwag and Elaine Bibuld gathered evidence that proved Brooklyn's public schools were racially segregated. Goldwag visited the BOE posing as a parent who wanted to move to Brooklyn. He inquired about schools in different neighborhoods, their racial populations, and their achievement levels in math and reading. A BOE office worker supplied him with a set of maps and lists of the information he requested. The data confirmed what activists had claimed for years: the BOE's neighborhood zoning patterns created racially segregated schools. Schools that were predominantly black and Puerto Rican were two grade levels behind "white" schools in reading and math.[23]

Brooklyn CORE created flyers that listed racially segregated schools, their neighborhoods, the percentages of African American and Puerto Rican students, and sixth-grade reading levels. The Education Committee planned to distribute these flyers to the public and submit them to the press at an opportune time. With more press coverage of the campaign, newspapers and evening news shows would be forced to take its research seriously. Without that, the media would ignore the committee's findings. CORE also wanted to help the Bibulds, who were under a great deal of pressure from the BOE to return their children to P.S. 282. In the middle of November Elaine and Jerome Bibuld received a summons to appear in Family Court on December 15, 1962. The city charged the Bibulds with neglect for keeping their children out of school. If the judge found them guilty, they faced up to a year in prison and would lose custody of their children.

Brooklyn CORE devised a tactic that would exonerate the Bibulds and challenge racial segregation in the city's public school system. The Education Committee planned an unorthodox sit-in that involved the Bibulds' children. Elaine Bibuld had a friend who lived in the Bath Beach section of Brooklyn. Her children attended their local elementary school, P.S. 200, which fulfilled all of the Bibulds' requirements. P.S. 200 was an underutilized school, which meant there was ample space for new students. The school also had high performance levels in reading and math, and was accessible by subway from the Bibuld's apartment. One last factor made P.S. 200 a suitable school for this demonstration: it was overwhelmingly white. A sit-in at P.S. 200 would dramatize the inferior education in predominantly black and Puerto Rican neighborhood schools compared to that in white school zones. Of 1,700 total students, 25 to 35 were African American, a paltry 1.5 to 2.1 percent of the student body.[24]

CORE knew the BOE would refuse the Bibuld children official admission to P.S. 200 because it was outside their zoned district. Still, the tactic would counter charges that Elaine and Jerome Bibuld were guilty of child neglect, since they were attempting to send their children to a school that had standard achievement levels. Brooklyn CORE welcomed the sit-in because it forced BOE officials to defend its racially segregated system, compromise with the Bibulds, or devise a concrete plan to desegregate the borough's public schools. CORE saw the Bibuld sit-in as a catalyst for changes in the entire public school system. Many politicians, policy makers, intellectuals, and citizens argued that schools failed in African American and Puerto Rican neighborhoods because of the people's cultural deficiencies and behavioral practices, rather than because of discriminatory treatment by the BOE and the city. Public schools historically had helped uplift poor minorities and immigrants, they maintained, and could do the same for African Americans and Puerto Ricans if only they adjusted their speech, styles of dress, attitudes, family compositions, work ethics, and consumption patterns.[25]

Brooklyn CORE, the Parents' Workshop, and other activists challenged these claims. Behavior modification would do little to help black and Puerto Rican children if they were forced to attend underresourced, poorly staffed public schools. African Americans' and Puerto Ricans' problems in the schools were material, not cultural or behavioral. If given the same type of facilities, numbers of experienced teachers, student-teacher ratios, and resources such as libraries and science labs, poor students of color would perform just as well as middle-class white students. The lead article of the November 1962 issue of the *North Star* articulated Brooklyn CORE's arguments and its vision of the Bibuld campaign's purposes and intentions. Jerome Bibuld wrote: "We are fighting not only for our children, but for all children who attend segregated schools in the City of New York. . . . We charge that the Board of Education runs a dual system of education. It provides a substandard program for Negro and Puerto Rican children and a somewhat better system for white children, particularly those of the upper economic classes. Under the insulting label of 'culturally deprived,' the Board of Education deliberately and purposely miseducates minority children."[26]

Rhetoric, however, would not be sufficient to improve the quality of education for the Bibuld children, let alone "for all children who attend[ed] segregated schools." City officials, citizens, and editorialists used arguments about the "culture of poverty" to ignore activists' petitions. Predominantly black and Puerto Rican schools were substandard, most argued, because the students and the parents made them that way. Brooklyn CORE and the Parents' Workshop prepared to counter these popular beliefs with empirical evidence and public demonstrations.

The Education Committee assembled at the Bibulds' apartment one evening in late November and finalized plans for the sit-in. Elaine Bibuld's friend told her the location of the classrooms where their children would perform their sit-in. Elaine planned to accompany Douglass, Carrington, and Melanie to school, walk them into their classrooms, instruct them not to move, no matter what the teacher told them, and then speak to the school's principal and request their official admission to P.S. 200. Some members of Brooklyn CORE planned to form a picket line in front of P.S. 200, and Arnold Goldwag assured them that newspaper reporters and photographers would cover the event.[27]

Before the meeting adjourned, Elaine Bibuld brought Douglass in front of the Education Committee. Although Carrington and Melanie Bibuld would participate, CORE members predicted that much of the media attention would concentrate on Douglass and his frustrations at P.S. 282. Douglass Bibuld's situation proved that the BOE's segregated system failed bright students forced to attend schools that could not nurture their talents. Elaine Bibuld explained the plans for the sit-in to Douglass and asked how he would feel if he received a lot of negative attention. She feared the possible backlash might be too traumatic for the young boy and maybe even physically dangerous.[28]

He assuaged his mother's fears by recounting his past experiences at political protests. Before his parents joined CORE, Douglass had often accompanied his father to union rallies and picket lines that supported striking workers. He participated in Operation Clean Sweep with his parents and remembered feeling a sense of accomplishment in cleaning up abandoned lots and streets. For ten-year-old Douglass Bibuld, the sit-in at P.S. 200 seemed adventurous, but he also recognized its political importance. "I was excited at the prospect, maybe a little bit nervous," he recalled, "but also I had admired [CORE]." Carrington and Melanie were also eager to protest. Douglass remembered that his brother and sister "identified with protesting . . . more than I did." About a year before the fire forced the family to move, there had been a teachers' strike. Picket lines were set up in front of P.S. 167, and Douglass and his siblings had refused to cross it. When they turned around to walk home, a police officer stopped them and said they had to go to school. "I was just going to say something like, Yes we forgot our books at home, just something to get out of the situation and go home," Douglass recollected, "but Melanie, and Carr too, said, 'Oh no, we don't cross picket lines. They're striking and we're not going to cross. We stand for solidarity.'"[29]

Despite Douglass's positive attitude, the sit-in at P.S. 200 would not be as adventurous or exciting for the Bibuld family as he hoped. The family underwent a traumatic few weeks in which people threatened them. Elaine and Jerome Bibuld defended themselves in Family Court, and they still faced possible imprisonment. With the future of the children's education still unknown and the chance that their family might be broken up by the state, Brooklyn CORE members attempted to muster supporters for standing in picket lines, canvassing neighborhoods, and recruiting more African American and Puerto Rican families with children in the schools to demand improvements in schools where they were majorities. The chapter hoped the sit-in would be dramatic enough to spark enthusiasm for school reform among local people and force change in the entire public education system. It got much less than it wanted in both areas.

"Another 'Meredith' Case": The Bibuld Children Sit-in at P.S. 200

The morning of November 26 was brisk. Douglass, Carrington, and Melanie bundled up in winter parkas and rode the subway with their mother to the Bath Beach section of Brooklyn. A dozen members of Brooklyn CORE and the Parents' Workshop for Equality waited for the Bibulds near the front of the school, their placards and flyers concealed so as not to draw attention. Students and teachers at P.S. 200 had no idea that in the coming weeks their school would become the focal point of a major protest that attracted swarms of newspaper photographers and reporters. Elaine and the three children made their way into the school and inconspicuously slipped into the first-, fourth-, and fifth-grade classrooms.

Elaine Bibuld went to the office of P.S. 200's principal, Frederick Nislow. She stated her case and requested that he allow her children to enroll in the school. She also showed him the picket line that had formed in front of the school. Demonstrators marched silently and handed out flyers to parents and passersby. Some of their placards pointed out the racial and economic disparities between schools in white school zones and schools in African American and Puerto Rican districts. One sign stated, "Our children want schools as good as P.S. 200," and another read, "Equal Taxes—Equal Schools." Flyers bore the headline "Sit-in for Equality in P.S. 200," and listed the spelling words and math homework from Douglass's fifth-grade class at P.S. 282. Brooklyn CORE's flyer explained the reasons for the Bibulds' sit-in:

> It is because the Board of Education refuses to place [them] in a decent school that we have placed [them in] P.S. 200. They [Bibulds] have withdrawn their children from P.S. 282 because they refuse to allow the destruction of the minds of their children. The Board of Education is denying the Bibuld family children the education for which their parents pay. . . . The Board of Education now threatens the Bibulds with arrest for the "crime" of insisting on the proper public education of their children. The Bibulds have chosen P.S. 200 because the Board of Education refuses to designate any school available by one means of transportation and that meets reasonable standards.

Nislow checked with officials at the BOE, who instructed him not to enroll the Bibuld children, but not to remove them from the classrooms. Nislow told Elaine Bibuld that her children would be allowed to attend P.S. 200 as "guests" for an unspecified period, which meant they could attend classes as unofficial students. Her children were not permitted to enroll, Nislow told Bibuld, because they did not live in P.S. 200's district. He then accompanied Elaine Bibuld to each classroom where her children had "sat-in," and explained the situation to the teachers.[30]

All the major New York City newspapers covered the Bibuld family story the following day, but the extent and tone of coverage varied widely. The *New York Post,* which tended to be more attentive in its coverage of civil rights stories, focused on Douglass. Its story featured a medium-sized picture of him conversing with his new classmates, and the story focused on his difficulties at P.S. 282. Pictures of Douglass and Elaine Bibuld, as well as Marjorie Leeds holding a placard and flyers, appeared on the front page of the *Brooklyn Eagle*, which tried to attract Brooklyn readers by highlighting local newsworthy events. The *Daily News* buried the event on page 72 and derisively headlined the story, "Negro Tries to Crash White School." Still, this was the only story to feature a quote by one of the Bibuld children: Douglass told a *Daily News* reporter, "I don't like P.S. 282 because the work is too easy. They made me do work I had already done in the second and third grade." The Brooklyn section of the *World Telegram and Sun* concentrated its story on Elaine Bibuld and her defiant stance toward the courts. "I will go to jail," she reportedly stated, "before letting my children attend a school with an inferior curriculum." The *Daily News* also reported that Elaine Bibuld charged the BOE with "crippling" her children by insisting that she put them in a substandard school.[31]

On the first morning of the sit-in at P.S. 200, CORE members also distributed another flyer in front of P.S. 282. This flyer, written in both Spanish and English, was entitled "Parents Face Jail," and it used forceful rhetoric to emphasize the severity of racial discrimination in public schools. Near the top it told readers, "Your children are being mentally crippled for life at P.S. 282, by the Board of Education which deliberately maintains low academic standards in schools of predominantly Negro and Puerto Rican areas." After listing the facts of Douglass Bibuld's experience at P.S. 282, Brooklyn CORE charged the BOE with "using dual standards for curriculum, teaching staff, and classroom facilities in Negro and white areas." Readers were encouraged to confront their children's teachers and ask the reading and arithmetic level of their classes. According to Brooklyn CORE's research, "By law, they *must* tell you!" At the bottom of the flyer, Brooklyn CORE announced that the Education Committee's next information and strategy session would be held in the Bibulds' apartment that Thursday.[32]

Few new people joined the campaign. Brooklyn CORE's outreach to Spanish-speaking families did not generate an outpouring of support from Puerto Ricans in Park Slope or the surrounding neighborhoods that had higher concentrations of Puerto Rican residents. During the early 1960s alliances between black and Puerto Rican activists were tenuous and in many cases, such as the Bibuld campaign, nonexistent. The reasons are varied and speculative. Some Puerto Ricans did not identify with African Americans and sought to distance themselves and their needs from those of blacks. They struggled to adapt and assimilate into mainstream society, not challenge and change it. Others participated in various types of "diasporic" cultural and political projects, which ranged from forging mainland groups that supported the independence movement in Puerto Rico to constructing new identities through poetry, music, dance, and literature. Like earlier activism to improve public schools in New York, Brooklyn CORE's support for the Bibuld campaign failed to usher in a new moment in black-Latino political solidarity.[33]

Even though it failed to attract new members, the small cadre of organizers from CORE and the Parents' Workshop continued to picket in front of P.S. 200 and distribute flyers near P.S. 282. During that last week of November the Bibuld children attended school as "guests," with few problems. The fifth-grade teacher and students welcomed Douglass as a member of the class. After his picture appeared in the newspapers, some students treated him as a minor celebrity and playfully asked for his autograph. Douglass also came to class determined to participate. Elaine Bibuld spoke with the fifth-grade teacher at P.S. 200, who remarked on how determined Douglass was to get an education. He "would not permit the class to go on if he did not understand something. He would *stop* them," Elaine Bibuld remembered. Douglass had learned to play the recorder while at P.S. 167, and when the fifth grade at P.S. 200 practiced for a winter recital, he happily joined them. Carrington, on the other hand, was not warmly received, and, of the three children, the sit-in was most difficult for him. Douglass recalled that Carrington's teacher "would not recognize him in the classroom. . . . She would not call on him if he raised his hand, would overlook him and really made him feel isolated. He was very hurt by that experience. In my class, they made me a part of the class, I was accepted into it and I had a good time." Melanie Bibuld, although only in the first grade, had an experience similar to her older brother Carrington's.[34]

To make matters worse, the Bibulds began receiving hate mail and threatening phone calls. One letter, signed by A. Shapiro from New York City, expressed disdain for interracial schools because "Niggers belong among niggers not among humans." He addressed Elaine Bibuld as a "monkey faced animal," and demanded that she "keep your papoose among his own kind instead of trying to force him among whites who resent his freakish looks." An unsigned letter was just as derogatory: "We had a lot of respect for your race until this past year. Now we consider you and your color only niggers—and real ones too." Both writers' ideas were emblematic of the racial animosity and fear that shaped many white New Yorkers' thoughts, private conversations, and jokes, as well as their opinions of demands for racial equality in the city. Though these types of raw sentiments rarely surfaced in public political or intellectual conversations, they emerged as powerful ideological underpinnings of many white New Yorkers' politics during the mid- and late 1960s. Racial antagonism fueled resistance to residential and school integration. Coupled with economic changes in housing and job markets, racist ideas provided the rationale for why so many whites moved farther and farther away from African Americans and Puerto Ricans. The unsigned letter also indicated how black people's political activism and community organizing for racially integrated public schools offended white people. Many New Yorkers resented activists' pointing out racial discrimination and inequality in New York City's public sphere. As Brooklyn CORE became more militant with its protest tactics, most people—whites and even some blacks—began to dismiss them as troublemakers.[35]

Brooklyn CORE received a letter responding to its leaflets that contrasted academic performance levels of predominantly black and Puerto Rican schools with those of white schools. Compared to the letters the Bibulds received, this writer, who chose not to sign his name for "obvious reasons," refrained from using racial epithets or berating remarks. Still, the letter's content was no less derogatory. In the main text the writer listed twelve comparisons between schools that were predominantly black and those that were predominantly white, which the writer argued were just as important to examine as the differences in reading and math scores. The list is worth quoting in its entirety:

1. Number of prostitutes
2. Number of illegitimate children
3. Number of fathers in homes
4. Number of known drunkedness [sic]
5. Number of people on relief
6. Rate of crime wave
7. Degree of immorality
8. Number of children belonging to library
9. Number of children mercilessly beaten
10. Number of drug addicts
11. Number of people who do not want to work
12. Number of filthy homes

According to the author, if Brooklyn CORE really wanted to get at the root problems of African American and Puerto Rican children, it should "start a crusade in the homes instead of lambasting the school."[36]

The BOE's racially segregated school system, in which students of

color had fewer resources and fewer qualified teachers, was not perpetuated by the conditions of black and Puerto Rican homes. These types of
cultural and behavioral arguments allowed critics to dismiss the economic arguments school reformers made about racially segregated
schools. Urban crime, single-parent homes, abusive parenting, and anti-
intellectual behavior were some of the many stock images people had of
the poor. Critics used these images to attack, belittle, and ignore urban
protest movements, and to justify the deteriorating neighborhoods and
social instability of American cities. The "culture of poverty," as
explained by this anonymous writer, did not articulate why predominantly black and Puerto Rican public schools were so poorly resourced
or why a student like Douglass Bibuld could not receive a suitable education in the New York City public school system. Black and Puerto
Rican culture and behavior did not justify P.S. 282's fifth-grade class
doing third-grade work, nor was it responsible for Douglass Bibuld's
receiving a book there that had no cover. Carrington Bibuld's fourth-
grade class had no books at P.S. 282, and his sister's first-grade class at
P.S. 200 had four. What, one might ask the anonymous writer, was the
relationship between those disparities and the number of people on public assistance?[37]

In addition to these questions about resources, the Bibuld campaign
revealed a tragic flaw in the BOE's racially segregated system: the "neighborhood schools" policy funneled academically talented students of
color into schools without rigorous scholastic programs. Beginning in
the early 1960s, public schools that challenged students to excel in math,
the sciences, and the arts were disappearing in neighborhoods that had
become all black and Puerto Rican, and this unfortunate development
left parents to choose the least worst school from a pool filled with
below-average choices. Brooklyn CORE experimented with different
ways of framing this complex issue. In one press release the chapter
emphasized that "the issue involved is the lack of special classes for
intellectually gifted Negro children." But over time the Education Committee members realized that so much more was at stake in this battle
over equal education for blacks and Puerto Ricans, and they adjusted
the rhetoric of the campaign to go far beyond their initial critique that
predominantly black and Puerto Rican schools did not have enough academic enrichment programs for very smart children such as Douglass
Bibuld. CORE flyers began to highlight the economic consequences of
racial inequality in public schools. "Unequal Education = Unequally
Qualified," headed one flyer. Another, prepared in both Spanish and
English, proclaimed, "Inferior Schools—NO JOBS!!" "Do you know why

almost 30% of Bedford-Stuyvesant is UNEMPLOYED?" asked the flyer. Underneath the rhetorical question, parenthetically, it compared Bedford-Stuyvesant's unemployment rate with that of the rest of the city, which stood at only 5 percent. "Each and every one of us are products of a *segregated, inferior* school system. By the time our children get out of schools, they are YEARS behind white children and thus CAN'T compete equally for the available jobs. . . . The Board of Education is *crippling* your children." Brooklyn CORE's Education Committee planned to force these ideas into mainstream political discourse with hopes they would bring about concrete changes in the educational system.[38]

The Bibulds consistently stated these arguments to the press. After they received the hate mail, Elaine and Jerome Bibuld held a press conference and reiterated their charges: "There are two separate education systems in this city—one for Negroes and Puerto Ricans and one for whites." The principal of P.S. 282, Jennie Montag, defended her school. She argued that P.S. 282 was a "special service school," because children in the neighborhood required special services, such as remedial English classes and instruction in Spanish for students from Puerto Rican families who did not speak English. She claimed children who could carry on regular studies were not held back. To further discredit the Bibulds' claims, she told the *Brooklyn Eagle* that Elaine Bibuld allegedly admitted to the school's secretary that she really wanted the children to be in an all-white school. Jerome Bibuld emphatically denied the allegation and argued that Elaine and he were not criticizing the teachers or principal at P.S. 282, but only acting on the belief that their children would not receive the same educational opportunities as other pupils received elsewhere. "We are not asking for anything special," he told reporters. "We just want a school that is on par, where our children can get an education that is not substandard. They can't do that in a segregated school."[39]

The Bibulds' fight occurred at the same time as another, more prominent protest against racially segregated public education in other parts of the country. In the fall of 1962 James Meredith enrolled as the University of Mississippi's first black student. State officials and students were vehemently opposed to racially integrating the school, and many threatened Meredith's life. Attorney General Robert Kennedy sent federal troops to protect him from a possible lynching, which set off a bloody counterdemonstration. Two bystanders, including a French reporter, were killed; 160 troops were injured, 28 by gunfire. Some 200 people were arrested, and less than a quarter of them were University of Mississippi students. Meredith continued to attend the university, but this incident had a national significance. The riot's carnage startled people who watched news footage of overturned, burning cars and enraged young whites in pitched battle against club-wielding Guardsmen and soldiers armed with rifles fixed with bayonets. The message was clear to people in the North: racial integration would come to the South in the wake of death and destruction.[40]

Many in New York saw that type of racial discrimination and violent backlash as a strictly southern phenomenon. Racial segregation, most citizens believed, did not exist in New York, at least not like it existed in the South. The sit-in at P.S. 200 exposed New York City's dual education system to an otherwise ignorant or ambivalent public. Brooklyn CORE used the incident at Ole Miss and the discrimination against the Bibulds to argue that life in New York was not as different from life in Mississippi as most wanted to believe. Brooklyn CORE rejected the idea that New York was a bastion of liberalism and cosmopolitanism. Numerous flyers exclaimed, "Just as Mississippi is trying to kick James Meredith out of a 'white' school, the City of New York is trying to keep the Bibuld children out of a 'white school!'" The *Liberator,* a monthly journal of commentary on African American and African diaspora activism, politics, culture, and economics, ran an article on the Bibulds. Next to a picture of Elaine reading to her three children it ran the headline "Another 'Meredith' Case." The story implied that New Yorkers and Mississippians were partners in the same program of racial discrimination and injustice toward African Americans and their families. A quote from Jerome Bibuld read, "The difference between our struggle and that of James Meredith is one of degree—and very little degree at that. This difference itself will be erased if the City of New York is allowed to kidnap our children and send us to prison."[41]

Indeed, similarities between the Bibulds' case and what happened to James Meredith became more apparent in early December. With the Bibuld case, southern forms of racism spilled over into a northern civil rights movement campaign. The Bibulds had received crank calls when the story of the sit-in at P.S. 200 first broke. In addition to the letters they received by mail, people who claimed to be from different racist organizations dropped off notes at their home. Harassment became so bad that Jerome Bibuld eventually bought a large attack dog to guard the house, and he slept with a shotgun under the bed. One evening Elaine Bibuld received a threatening call from a man claiming to be Robert Shelton, leader of the United Klans of America (UKA), which was an Alabama-based spin-off of the Ku Klux Klan. She hung up quickly, but he called back and warned her about the evils of integration and "race mixing."

He said he had heard the Bibulds were "kicking up a little noise," and suggested that he could "break Jerry in" to the ways of white supremacy, but that probably "wouldn't do any good." According to Elaine Bibuld's notes on the conversation, Shelton said, "It might change your ideas if I threw acid in your face [and] it would also change your ideas if we took care of the children." The caller said the attack would happen soon, probably over the weekend. Curious if this caller was really from the South, Elaine checked with the operator, who traced it to a Virginia area code.[42]

Elaine Bibuld became worried. She immediately contacted Arnold Goldwag at the Brooklyn CORE office and told him about the threat. Goldwag was shocked. While participating in protests to desegregate parts of Cambridge, Maryland, he had become familiar with Robert Shelton's reputation for terrorism against civil rights workers. Goldwag called the Bibulds' police precinct, reported the threat, and demanded protection for the Bibulds. He got the impression that the police did not think the situation serious enough to warrant special treatment. Goldwag then called his newspaper contacts, informed them of the caller's threat to "take care of the children," and encouraged them to ask the police about their course of action. The Bibulds told reporters they had received "many malicious calls," but this was the first time someone threatened to use violence. Goldwag's pressure worked, and the local precinct captain eventually posted a squad car in front of the Bibulds' home for the weekend. Arnold Goldwag also arranged to have three officers accompany Elaine Bibuld and her children to and from P.S. 200 each day. On Monday, December 3, 1962, when the Bibulds made their morning commute to school, a New York Police Department (NYPD) officer walked them from their home to the subway station, a Transit Authority police officer rode the subway with them, and another NYPD officer accompanied them as they walked from the subway station to the school. The escort would continue, Police Department officials said, until it was no longer necessary.[43]

Tension and fear wore on the family's nerves. Elaine Bibuld felt besieged by the constant media attention, phone calls, and hate mail. "Every single time I looked the press was there," she remembered. "It was scary because first of all you're making a point and you're trying to keep focus on that. Of course, I was nervous. I had diarrhea every morning. I had the worst time getting out of the house, I was so tense." The hearing in Family Court also weighed on the family's minds. Douglass Bibuld remembered fearing that any day he would wake up and find his parents in jail and himself and his siblings split up into different foster homes. At school the children were still treated as "guests," which meant that "no official cognizance is taken of their presence," and they were still considered truants by the BOE. George Lent, a spokesman for the BOE, also dismissed the Bibulds' demands for a school with above-average reading and math levels. Lent commented that this was "an ideal situation in any school," and that the BOE's "neighborhood schools" registration policy was designed to give "justice to the whole community," even if it did not please individual families. The Bibulds, like every other black and Puerto Rican family who lived in racially segregated neighborhoods, would have to make do with the substandard schools near their homes.[44]

Elaine and Jerome Bibuld repeatedly stated that they were willing to go to jail for their children's education and became even more vocal in their criticisms of the school system. According to a handwritten note by Oliver Leeds, either Elaine or Jerome Bibuld attended a local Parent-Teacher Association meeting and "created an unpleasant scene." Leeds was not present at the meeting and he heard the information second-hand, so, unfortunately, the note leaves pertinent questions unanswered. What was the location of this PTA meeting, P.S. 282 or P.S. 200? What words or actions transpired during this "unpleasant scene?" But Leeds's note remains valuable because it reveals his strategy during a precarious moment in the campaign.

After the flurry of articles appeared on the threatening phone calls and the family's police escort, newspaper reporters quickly lost interest in the Bibulds' campaign. Editors and beat reporters moved on to whatever was the next buzz-worthy story, and without media attention on the campaign, the Bibuld family's case was in danger of disappearing from the public's eye. On top of that, Elaine Bibuld also recalled that some people criticized the police escort as an unnecessary use of taxpayers' money; and after a little over a week police officers stopped accompanying the Bibulds to school. Leeds recognized that the campaign was in danger of losing its moral high ground. Indeed, the Bibulds were powerful symbols of thousands of other hapless black and Puerto Rican families whose children were forced to attend racially segregated public schools that were academically behind predominantly white schools. For the campaign to continue building momentum, the public had to see them as unfortunate victims of an unjust system. If a story about one of the Bibuld parents causing an uproarious scene at a PTA meeting leaked to the press, the Bibulds would appear as aggressors and agitators, and the tide of public opinion might quickly turn against the family and Brooklyn CORE's cause. Thus, in his note, Leeds apologized for the Bib-

uld's unruly behavior and stated that Brooklyn CORE "does not condone discourteous behavior." As the campaign entered the final cold
weeks of December 1962, members of Brooklyn CORE brainstormed
about more militant tactics to put the Bibulds back into the press as the
champions of a just cause, and thus save the campaign and prevent them
from going to jail.[45]

"'Jim Crow' Must Go!!"

Several postponements delayed the Bibulds' hearing in Family Court.
Court officials waited for a lull in media coverage, and by early January
there was less grist for the sensationalizing mill as articles on the sit-in
and the resultant hate mail and threatening phone calls vanished from
newspaper pages. Family Court Judge Leonard E. Ruisi ruled on the Bibulds' case on Wednesday, January 2, 1963. He declared Elaine and
Jerome guilty of violating New York City's compulsory education laws
because they had willfully kept their children out of school since mid-
October. The sit-in at P.S. 200 was a clever tactic, but since the BOE had
not allowed the Bibuld children to enroll, the parents still violated the
neighborhood schools' policy. Ruisi probably wanted to avoid rekin-
dling protest and to pressure the Bibulds into compliance with the law,
so he postponed their sentencing until January 28. The maximum punishment was three years' imprisonment and state seizure of the children.
Ruisi added that the state would drop all charges if the Bibulds put their
children back into P.S. 282, or any of the other elementary schools in
their zone. An article in a newsletter, the *Worker,* declared the sentencing
was "the first conviction in the struggles by Negro parents against discriminatory zoning."[46]

Brooklyn CORE intensified the campaign. It issued a press release,
written by Oliver Leeds, with a statement by the Bibulds that reiterated
their charge that the BOE "operates two separate school systems: an
inferior group of schools" for African American and Puerto Rican children and an "education on par with the best in the nation" for privileged
white children. The statement argued that the Bibulds' demands were
not extraordinary. They merely sought a school where the median sixth-
grade reading and arithmetic levels were 6.5 or higher, which was "not
extraordinary among 'white' schools" in New York City and "not high
by national educational standards." Still, the BOE refused the Bibulds'
request and now even punished them for demanding a good education
for their children. The BOE argued that P.S. 282 was the best school in
the district, with which the Bibulds agreed. But they charged it was a

"gerrymandered Jim Crow school district." Oliver Leeds noted the broader implications that this fight had for African American and Puerto Rican families throughout the city. He explained in the press release that this campaign "represents an attempt to desegregate New York City's schools," and Leeds encouraged people to write protest letters to Bernard Donovan, the superintendent of schools. He also offered to have Brooklyn CORE representatives speak at organization meetings about the specifics of the Bibuld case and "the Jim Crow school system operated by the City of New York." Brooklyn CORE was taking one family's fight and turning it into a citywide effort to transform the educational opportunities for black and Puerto Rican children.[47]

CORE also increased its activities in the streets. The Education Committee and members of the Parents' Workshop picketed six schools throughout Bedford-Stuyvesant on January 9, 10, and 11. They distributed the bilingual flyers that linked the area's unemployment rate with inferior and segregated schools and carried placards that read, "Inferior Schools, No Jobs!" and "Johnny Can't Read, He Is Not Taught!" Arnold Goldwag spoke with reporters and compared P.S. 44, a school that was

Table 6. Sixth-Grade Reading Levels in a Sampling of Brooklyn's Predominantly Black and Puerto Rican Public Schools, 1962

School	% Black/Puerto Rican	Level
P.S. 3	99	4.0
P.S. 25	97	4.9
P.S. 26	96	4.6
P.S. 44	100	4.4
P.S. 93	99	4.5
P.S. 129	100	4.7
P.S. 147	95	3.9
P.S. 270	98	4.1

Source: "Inferior School—No Jobs!!" flyer in Elaine Bibuld personal papers.

Table 7. Sixth-Grade Reading Levels in a Sampling of Brooklyn's Predominantly White Public Schools, 1962

School	Location	Level
P.S. 102	Bay Ridge	7.4
P.S. 103	Borough Park	7.6
P.S. 179	Flatbush	7.7
P.S. 185	Bay Ridge	7.2
P.S. 193	Flatbush	7.6
P.S. 197	Marine Park	7.8
P.S. 222	Flatbush	7.9
P.S. 254	Sheepshead Bay	7.8

Source: "Inferior School—No Jobs!!" flyer in Elaine Bibuld personal papers.

100 percent black and Puerto Rican and had a 4.4 median reading level in the sixth grade, with P.S. 222, which was predominantly white and had a 7.9 median reading level in the sixth grade. Lower education standards, he argued, had a direct relationship to higher unemployment rates for African Americans and Puerto Ricans.[48]

As the sentencing date drew near, Elaine Bibuld was invited to address a large black congregation in Brooklyn, and she used the opportunity to drum up support for the campaign. On Sunday, January 13, 1963, she spoke to over five hundred mostly black worshipers at the morning service of Washington Temple, an affiliate of the Church of God in Christ (COGIC). The church's founder, Associate Bishop Frederick D. Washington, had built his church into the best-known COGIC center in Brooklyn. Through members' support he had purchased a Loews theater at Bedford Avenue and Bergen Street in Crown Heights in 1952 and transformed it into a church. Washington Temple became known among Brooklyn's black churches for sponsoring a well-organized youth group, holding testimonial social banquets, and hosting radio station WWRL's Fifth Annual Gospel Singing Contest, which attracted more than five thousand people.[49]

Education in Brooklyn, Elaine Bibuld told the audience, was "inferior, segregated, and humiliating to minority groups." She emphasized that her family's struggle was no different from what all people of color faced in New York City: it was "a war for the minds and futures of our Negro and Puerto Rican children." These children, she argued, "spend precious hours of their youth in classrooms with no permanent teachers and with the same lessons day after day." They are "frustrated by the lack of books and materials" and with the teachers who consider them "culturally deprived, inferior, and unteachable." Members of the congregation burst into applause after she charged that the schools were low-grade and when she vowed to accept incarceration rather than abide by the court's ruling. Frederick Washington agreed with Bibuld's arguments and urged drastic measures to combat "conditions of segregated schools." Deacon William Thompson, a member of the congregation who lived in Bedford-Stuyvesant, hoped the Bibulds and CORE would "continue fighting until victory is won." The Bibulds' protest received active support from one audience member, a prominent teacher named Gene Lovitt. In 1956 Lovitt became the first male kindergarten teacher appointed in New York City. On Monday, January 14, he announced his resignation from the BOE in support of the Bibulds' protest. That Friday would be his final day teaching. He said Elaine Bibuld's speech inspired him to take this stand.[50]

Brooklyn CORE tried to generate more active support among African Americans, Puerto Ricans, and elected officials in Brooklyn. The chapter wanted large turnouts at two major upcoming demonstrations. The first one was on Friday, January 25, at BOE headquarters, which was located at 110 Livingston Street in downtown Brooklyn, and the second on Monday, January 28, at the Family Court's sentencing hearing. National CORE's Department of Organization sent notice of the demonstrations to all New York area CORE chairmen and encouraged their chapters to support Brooklyn's effort. Members from Brooklyn CORE and the Bibuld family held a small "protest walk" throughout Bedford-Stuyvesant and promoted the upcoming demonstrations with leaflets that proclaimed, "A NEGRO FAMILY WILL GO TO JAIL UNLESS YOU HELP!! Join our Picket Line, Pack the Court!" Another flyer declared that the New York City Board of Education violated the U.S. Supreme Court's ruling in *Brown v. Board of Education* by forcing parents to send their children to racially segregated schools. During the walk, Elaine and Jerome Bibuld held placards that read, "Don't Let the Board of Education Kidnap Our Children," and "We Ask for Education. We Face Jail." Brooklyn CORE also solicited support from Brooklyn's borough president, Abe Stark. Gilbert Banks, a member of Brooklyn CORE's Education Committee who volunteered to organize the upcoming demonstrations, wrote to Stark and asked him to support the picket line in front of BOE headquarters. After recapitulating the facts of the case and the sit-in at P.S. 200, Banks emphasized that the Bibuld children were being discriminated against racially because they could not register at "a white school where they are being properly educated." He closed with an appeal to the borough president's hometown pride: "Don't let this injustice happen in Brooklyn." Apparently, Stark seemed content to leave schools in Brooklyn as racially segregated as others throughout the city. He did not respond to CORE's letter, nor did he support the picket line.[51]

While Brooklyn CORE promoted the upcoming demonstrations, the Bibulds expanded their attack against the school system and filed a complaint against the BOE with the New York State Commission on Human Rights (SCHR) on January 24, 1963. They charged that Frederick Nislow, principal of P.S. 200, and the BOE had discriminated against their three children on the basis of their "race and color." The Bibulds argued that the reason for P.S. 282's neglectful approach to homework, lack of resources, and substandard curriculum was that it was "a segregated school containing approximately 73% Negro and Puerto Rican students." In the complaint, the Bibulds stated that P.S. 282's principal, Jennie Montag, even admitted that "the most advanced class in the fifth grade was working on a third-grade level." P.S. 200's Principal Nislow told them they could not register at his school because they did not live within the school district. The Bibulds argued that this reason was a "subterfuge, used to keep P.S. 200 a segregated, predominantly white school and in effect to deny enrollment to our children . . . because of their race and color." Both Nislow and the BOE violated New York State's law against discrimination when they denied the Bibulds full access to public school facilities at P.S. 200. Filing the complaint bought more time for the Bibulds. A representative of the commission responded that the Bibulds had a "prima facie case of discrimination" and encouraged them to ask for a postponement of sentencing pending the outcome of the investigation. If the commission decided in favor of the Bibulds, P.S. 200 would be ordered to register the children.[52]

Elaine and Jerome still had to appear in court that Monday to hear the judge's ruling. During the week leading up to the January 25 demonstration at BOE headquarters, CORE members continued promoting it in front of schools in Bedford-Stuyvesant, but their efforts did not generate much of a showing. Friday morning, in near-zero temperatures and biting winds, about two dozen supporters marched in front of 110 Livingston Street, waving placards that continued to compare New York City's racially segregated schools with the situation in Mississippi. Protestors' signs read, "This Is New York Not Mississippi (So They Say)," "Segregated Education Is No Education," and "'Jim Crow' Must Go!!" The events in Little Rock, Arkansas, five years earlier may have been a more appropriate comparison, but Arkansas did not carry the same symbolic power as the Magnolia State. Despite the cold, demonstrators stirred up a lively chant to remind passersby that Jim Crow schools were in the North, too. They chanted, "Hey, Hey! Ho Ho! Jim Crow Schools Have Got to Go!" The small group also created a dramatic scene as Jerome Bibuld and another participant marched with an empty coffin, which had a sign that read, "Bury Jim Crow." Another call-and-response chant bellowed, "What'll we do? Bury Jim Crow! When'll we do it? Now!"[53]

That Sunday the Bibulds received a major endorsement from the Reverend George Lawrence, pastor of Antioch Baptist Church and leader of the Fellowship of the Concerned Negro. Lawrence presented Elaine Bibuld with the FCN Woman of the Year Award at Antioch's Sunday service and commended her courage and activism. Lawrence urged his congregation to back the Bibulds' fight. "What we need today," he exhorted, "is people who will stand up and fight for freedom." Elaine Bibuld took the podium and reminded the audience that she was no different from them. She and her husband "did not look for this fight, it was thrust down our throats. . . . The choice was permitting the Board of Education to retard our children or doing what we did, protesting actively."[54]

The congregation's thunderous applause gave her confidence to face the following day's court hearing. Monday, January 28, was also when Brooklyn CORE planned to begin an around-the-clock sit-in at BOE headquarters. Members of the Education Committee expected that the judge would grant a continuance while the SCHR reviewed the Bibulds' complaint. If the Bibulds received a postponement of their sentencing hearing, CORE had to use the time to put more pressure on the BOE. In the worst case, a prison sentence for the Bibulds, CORE's response would also be a dramatic, militant demonstration. In the absence of press coverage, a disruptive sit-in would draw attention from the media and get the Bibulds' campaign back in the pages of the city's major newspapers.

On the morning of January 28 Elaine and Jerome Bibuld arrived at the Family Court building on Adams Street in the bustling center of downtown Brooklyn. Fifty supporters attended the routine procedure. Judge Leonard Ruisi summarily granted a continuance pending the SCHR's investigation and set February 13 as the tentative date for sentencing. When the hearing ended, Elaine and Jerome Bibuld led the group in an orderly procession to BOE headquarters and began the sit-in at the main offices. Demonstrators spread out on waiting room chairs, the floor, and in the halls. A dozen people agreed to be the first group to spend the night. Gilbert Banks told reporters they planned to stay until the BOE did something about "realistic desegregation in the schools." They propped up their placards, set up a chessboard, and began playing and reading to pass the night. Newspapers in Newark and Jersey City, New Jersey, ran stories on the sit-in and printed photos of the scene that featured a prominent poster with the statement "The Bibulds want their children EDUCATED . . . IS THIS A CRIME?"[55]

CORE posed that question to two of New York's most powerful elected officials: Congressman Adam Clayton Powell Jr. and Senator Jacob Javits. Jerome Bibuld handwrote letters to each on January 30, 1963, telling them about the campaign. Bibuld showed that P.S. 282 was "inferior" to P.S. 200 with a list that compared the different resources available to his children and the drastically different levels of class work and homework teachers assigned at each school. Bibuld mentioned that they demanded a desegregated, high-performance school, but the Board of Education "insists that our children return to a school like P.S. 282, where, by the principal's unsolicited statement, *the most advanced class in the fifth grade is working at the third grade level.* These are not schools, but concentration camps of the mind and soul." He closed the letter asking them to urge the BOE to negotiate with Brooklyn CORE and "help us assure the future of our children." Attached to each letter was a copy of a centerfold from the *Metropolitan Daily,* which featured three pictures under the headline "Racial Question—Figures in the News." The first picture showed an armed soldier guarding James Meredith as he walked across campus. The second contrasted Ole Miss with Clemson University, where Harvey Gantt was able to enroll as the school's first African American student without violence and bloodshed. At the bottom, there was a picture of Brooklyn CORE members camped out at the Board of Education offices and a blurb on the undecided campaign. The implication was clear: Which scenario for desegregating public schools would New York City follow—Mississippi and violence or South Carolina and peace?[56]

CORE's message spurred Powell's office to action. At that time Adam Clayton Powell Jr. was chairman of the House Committee on Education and Labor. Almost immediately after Powell received Jerome Bibuld's letter, Odell Clark, chief investigator for the committee's Investigative Task Force, sent a short, forceful letter to the BOE, asking for its leadership, "in the interest of justice, democracy, and equal opportunity for all citizens, to sit down with CORE for the purpose of arriving at a satisfactory transfer for the Bibuld children." Clark also invoked New York City's position as "the greatest city in the world." Such a place, Clark argued, "cannot afford to have any children of any nationality receiving inferior education."[57] The editorial board of the *Brooklyn Eagle* also recognized that the Bibuld case had become "a very ugly situation" and "an explosive issue" that had to be addressed immediately by the BOE and the SCHR. *Eagle* editors tried to diminish the Bibulds' arguments about racial discrimination and segregation in public schools. They proposed that the Bibulds might have been "mistaken, or unduly sensitive to imagined discrimination," but the BOE's "retaliatory action" was "deplorable" and made it seem "utterly blind to what it is getting into." "New York is not Mississippi," the *Eagle* declared, "and it should not be made to appear so either because of emotionalism in a family or bureaucratic rigidity in the Board of Education." The only solution seemed to be for the BOE to allow the Bibulds to transfer their children to the school of their choice.[58]

Despite the *Eagle*'s harsh criticism, the New York City Board of Education did not "blindly" pursue its course of action against the Bibulds. If the BOE did not stick to its color-blind "neighborhood schools" policy, public education could quickly turn into the city's most contentious, racially polarized political issue. Neighborhoods were increasingly becoming segregated along racial and class lines. Black and Puerto Rican areas often also had the worst housing, dirtiest streets, lowest-performing schools, and highest rates of unemployment and crime. These social and economic conditions were not initially caused by people's behavior. Public policies, private-public economic development plans, real estate companies, banks, and credit agencies were major influences on neighborhoods' social and economic development. In many people's minds, however, conditions in schools and neighborhoods reflected the "quality" of their people. The BOE and the Wagner administration preferred to ignore advocates of school integration and put off making radical changes to the educational system. Their biggest fear was a well-organized, powerful reform movement that called for racial equality in public schools. When Brooklyn CORE and the Bibulds made it clear they were going to fight as hard on this issue as they had on sanitation, employment, and housing, the BOE used the mandatory attendance law and Family Court system to force the Bibulds to back down on their demands or compromise on its terms. The tactic, which to some seemed foolish and overly harsh, was politically calculated and strategic.

The Bibulds' campaign had offered an alternative to the BOE's strategy: a "busing" program whereby students from districts in which all the schools were substandard could attend a better-performing school outside their prescribed zone. A few reform groups such as the Parents' Workshop pushed for an open enrollment program that would allow students in low-performance schools to transfer to underutilized schools with average or above-average academic performance levels. The BOE had begun slowly to allow these types of transfer programs in overcrowded elementary schools, but it was up to active civic groups and parents' associations to help guide people through the lengthy bureaucratic process, and even then there was no guarantee a child would be able to attend a "receiving school" near his or her home. And even if students did successfully transfer to predominantly white schools, they then had to deal with painful ostracism that often accompanied the stigma of being one of the few black or Puerto Rican children in a class. No wonder few people of color participated in such an arduous and emotionally taxing process.[59]

Busing might have worked in theory, but such programs would be hotly contested throughout New York City. Rioghan Kirchner's husband, Paul Kirchner, who supported the Bibulds, explained these social and political realities in an article he wrote for the *North Star*. He argued that schools were substandard in black and Puerto Rican areas not because people of color are biologically inferior to whites, but because their schools are located in slum areas that landlords and politicians let deteriorate into social and economic wastelands. Since African Americans and Puerto Ricans were poor and gave the city less money through taxes, Kirchner believed they had little political power and, therefore, "the richer neighborhoods are more vocal, pay more taxes, and get better service." He contended that the only solution for the unequal, unjust public school system was "two way 'bussing' of children": "If children from the 'better' neighborhoods, the ones that are listened to because they 'pay more taxes,' had to go to these substandard schools, then the community as a whole would rise up and in equal voice demand better schooling for everyone." Paul Kirchner knew, however, that racial prejudice toward African Americans and Puerto Ricans was the main deterrent to any busing program. Backlash against busing and open enrollment "would be much louder than the cry for general improvement." Signs of these reactions had already begun to appear. When Brooklyn CORE began the sit-in at the Board of Education, white parents in Bensonhurst staged a small protest over the admission of a black student to a local public school. After this brief spurt of anger, the white parents' outrage simmered. They would peacefully allow one black student to enroll, but they remained vigilant against the threat they imagined more African Americans could bring to their neighborhoods and schools.[60]

Still, Kirchner's letter articulated a bona fide "liberal" stance on race relations and public schools. He wrote that the social problems that created substandard schools concerned all citizens because "the concentration of poverty and prejudice" would "produce both apathy and crime," and the only solution was for the city to provide "more, not less education in the schools of the poorer, Negro community." If city government took such an active role in reforming public education, Kirchner argued that citizens "may hope too that our children, better educated, more qualified, will be able to break the restraints of poverty, encounter society on an equal level, and eventually break prejudice."[61]

But no elected officials or members of the BOE publicly voiced support for this type of investment in public education and poor neighborhoods. Since politicians seemed unwilling to listen, let alone dole out money to improve conditions in failing schools, Brooklyn CORE and its supporters from the Parents' Workshop used the power of protest to demand an overhaul of the public education system. By Friday, February 1, the sit-in at BOE headquarters had gone on for four straight days. Gilbert Banks reported that about seventy people had taken part, and Brooklyn CORE continued to organize fresh replacements for the people who had spent long hours on hard floors and in cramped chairs. Banks made CORE's intentions clear: "We'll stay here until the court resolves the case in favor of the Bibulds or until we're arrested."[62]

Victory?—"This Is Only One Family"

After a six day sit-in, the BOE offered the Bibulds a compromise: they could enroll their children at P.S. 130, which was outside their district but met their academic requirements. If the Bibulds rejected the offer, Brooklyn CORE was prepared to continue the sit-in and launch a massive picket line at the BOE offices. It even reached out to the famed actor-activist Ossie Davis, who was a member of New York CORE, for support, and he agreed to lead the demonstration that day if the Bibulds did not accept the BOE's deal. CORE activists had also solicited support from wealthy citizens at a Carnegie Hall jazz benefit concert the previous Friday evening, at which they passed out flyers that continued to compare New York's brand of racial discrimination to practices in Mississippi. The BOE was now besieged with criticism from all angles. CORE embarrassed the city every time it distributed flyers that compared the Bibulds to Meredith and New York to Mississippi. Coverage of the sit-in had spread to newspapers beyond the tristate area. Additionally, Brooklyn CORE had a motivated, well-organized cadre of activists who had disrupted BOE headquarters for a week and were prepared to continue until it settled. All these factors forced the BOE to accede, in part, to the Bibulds' demands. P.S. 130 was a short subway ride away from the Bibulds' home; it was 20 percent black and Puerto Rican, had 7.1 median sixth-grade reading and arithmetic scores, and had classes for academically talented students. Even though the Bibulds had wanted to send their children to a school within their district that had high academic performance, they also compromised and accepted the BOE's offer. Ossie Davis never led the march, and the Bibuld children enrolled as students at P.S. 130 on Monday, February 4, 1963.[63]

Shortly after his first week attending P.S. 130, Douglass Bibuld spoke to reporters from the *Amsterdam News* and summarized the protest's success with his comments on his new school: "It's fine. There is a challenge in this school, a big one. It is better than P.S. 200 or P.S. 282. This is an integrated school." Elaine and Jerome Bibuld expressed heartfelt thanks to Brooklyn CORE for its role in fighting to improve their children's education. By the end of the seven-day sit-in, over three hundred people had participated, which made this the largest Brooklyn CORE project to date. In a letter to Marjorie and Oliver Leeds, Elaine Bibuld wrote: "I know that the school sit-in case was a CORE project—it was that and more to me. . . . Thanks for the long exhausting hours you both put in it. From where I sit, well content, and think back on the last unbelievable week, your help, encouragement, and fidelity deserve our deepest gratitude." After three months, the campaign officially ended on February 13 when Judge Joseph Doran dismissed all charges against the Bibulds.[64]

The Bibulds, Brooklyn CORE, and allies from the Parents' Workshop may have won this battle, but the larger struggle for public education reform continued. The Bibulds' statement in Brooklyn CORE's newsletter hinted at the limitations of their victory: "We feel that our position has been vindicated. What we need is organization to completely desegregate the schools. This is only one family." Years later Jerome Bibuld argued that the campaign was a failure: "We didn't win," he lamented. "We lost. But it appeared that we won."[65]

Despite Jerome Bibuld's grim assessment, the campaign was a significant victory for Brooklyn CORE. The chapter brought a tremendous amount of local and national attention to the complex problem of racially segregated public schools in New York City, the supposed center of American liberalism. The campaign also proved that change was politically possible with aggressive agitation, inventive demonstrations, and disciplined organization. Probably most important was the way that the Bibuld campaign sent the signal that other people could also fight this problem. And in the long run, the campaign laid the groundwork for future massive direct-action protests against racial segregation in New York City's public schools. Milton Galamison and the Parents' Workshop continued the movement the following year when it staged a one-day boycott of the public schools that drew support from over 400,000 students. Over the next five years, public education became the most prominent and contentious issue within New York City's racial politics. Later mobilization on "community control" that centered on the Brooklyn section of Ocean Hill–Brownsville, and battles between the teachers' union, city hall, the BOE, and black and Puerto Rican parents over decentralization, involved many complex issues, but one root motivation was identical to what had driven the Bibulds' fight: a desire to provide students of color with a sound education, which they were not receiving in their local public schools.[66]

Low academic performance in New York City's predominantly black and Puerto Rican schools stemmed from the BOE's policies and bureaucracy, which produced schools that were overcrowded, underresourced, and inadequately staffed in the city's most high-need areas. At the same time, these failing schools were microcosms of their communities, which suffered from a host of social and economic crises related to residential segregation, joblessness, police brutality, and a slow drain of human capital that resulted from pressures on families and individuals caused by poverty, substance abuse, crime, the lure of a lucrative illicit economy, and, over the course of the 1960s, the rising death toll and psychological sicknesses caused by the war in Vietnam.[67]

Over time black and Puerto Rican families in Brooklyn and the rest of urban America found it harder and harder to crack though the impenetrable wall of political bureaucracy in government agencies such as the Board of Education. They also found it increasingly difficult to avoid being sucked into the dizzying downward spiral of their own communities' deterioration. Brooklyn CORE's campaign was one of a string of moments when community activists and parents successfully mobilized and organized to take power over their children's educational futures, which they saw as their effort to regain control over the future of their communities. But, given the deep roots of the structural inequality and attendant social ills that devastated cities in the thirty years after World War II, these campaigns (and the ones that followed in New York City in 1964 and 1967–68) were but brief moments in the sun before people turned around and marched slowly back toward the darkness of a dual school system that did little in the way of preparing children of color to participate as skilled workers in a knowledge-based economy.[68]

While Brooklyn CORE remained active in local education issues, it also turned its attention to another major civil rights issue: racial discrimination in construction and building trades unions. During the Bibuld campaign, Brooklyn CORE had skillfully used direct-action tactics and media resources to force the BOE to accede to the Bibulds' demands. The chapter had expanded its connections to different local activist groups and leaders, and it had benefitted from prominent, powerful individuals' support. Brooklyn CORE would attempt the same approach during the summer of 1963, with very different results.

7

"WE HAD STRUGGLED IN VAIN"

Protest for Construction Jobs and Specters of Violence

> It comes to my mind that at least a quarter of a century ago we sat in on the City Commission for Human Rights, a bunch of black working folk, because it was not doing its job. And as a matter of fact, in twenty-five years it still hasn't done its job as it pertains to the building trades and now we are having another hearing.
> —James Houghton, president, Harlem Fight Back, speaking at a public hearing on the construction industry in New York City sponsored by the New York City Commission on Human Rights and the New York City Office of Labor Services, 1990

Brooklyn CORE's campaign to integrate the construction workforce building the Downstate Medical Center inspired tremendous community support and attracted over one hundred new affiliate members to the chapter's ranks. The movement also set in motion conflicts between militants and reformers that would ultimately cause the chapter to move away from the types of demonstrations that made Brooklyn CORE able to gain audience with power brokers, as it did during the Ebinger's campaign, the demonstrations against Lefrak, and its protests against infrequent garbage collection. For many reasons, the issue of discrimination in employment, especially discrimination in the construction industry, would be a particular source of rage and frustration, not only for CORE members and leaders, but also for the city's black population. The construction trades were palpable symbols of entrenched white economic privilege; their powerful unions refused to give African Americans jobs in one of the highest pay niches of the city's blue-collar labor market.

Even when the national civil rights movement was at the height of its power and prestige, northern urban construction unions stubbornly refused to desegregate their ranks, especially in skilled trades. Indeed, racial discrimination in construction industries was one of the most important civil rights issue in cities throughout the Northeast and Midwest during the summer of 1963. Most African American and Puerto Rican construction workers were relegated to menial, low-skilled jobs. The Downstate Medical Center construction project revealed how the state and city government and the powerful building trades unions perpetuated these discriminatory labor patterns.[1]

The attack by northern, urban civil rights activists against employment discrimination in the building trades industry marked a significant moment when activists applied pressure tactics for blacks' immediate entrance into one of the most racially segregated and well-paying sectors of the U.S. workforce. In the short run these protests achieved little in terms of breaking down the racial barriers in construction unions. But as some of the largest protests to sweep northern cities during the early 1960s, these campaigns served as the catalysts to transform first-time demonstrators into lifelong political activists. Campaigns like Downstate also helped create new, more militant organizations, such as Harlem Fight Back, which spent decades struggling to secure jobs for black workers in the building trades. And these campaigns against discrimination in the construction trades focused the attention of the larger black freedom movement on employment discrimination, job-creation initiatives, and calls for economic justice through affirmative action. In fact, calls for economic justice in northern cities occurred at the same time as southern movements for voting rights and access to public accommodations. Demands for increased black employment opportunities did not first emerge in the mid- to late 1960s. When historians pay closer attention to black social movements outside the South, they see the ways desegregating jobs and racially segregated unions were always part of the postwar struggle for black rights. In the early 1960s this ongoing struggle gained much-needed energy, direction, and attention through northern efforts to desegregate the construction trades unions.[2]

The Downstate Medical Center expansion project was typical of the types of state-funded construction work that black workers were systematically shut out from during the early 1960s. It consisted of two new additions to the sprawling Kings County Hospital complex: a new, 350-bed teaching hospital and renovations of the State University of New York (SUNY) medical school in New York City. The construction was part of the $353 million that the state had earmarked in 1960 to expand the entire SUNY system by 1965. Upgrading the state's two medical schools was a main priority of this overhaul. Albany had allocated $20 million for construction costs of new facilities at SUNY Downstate Medical Center in Brooklyn, and $22 million for its counterpart, SUNY Upstate Medical Center in Syracuse. With these improvements, SUNY Downstate would be able to increase its student capacity from 587 to 800, and SUNY Upstate's capacity would go from 308 to 400.[3]

The state funds allocated to the Downstate construction project seemed to be a boon for almost everyone—the SUNY system administrators, the Kings County Hospital complex, city residents who wanted affordable medical school training, and the citizens of Brooklyn, who received a new state-of-the-art medical facility. But one group that criticized the construction project was composed of unemployed black laborers who found it difficult to break into all-white building trades unions. They were especially outraged because Downstate was situated in the Flatbush section of Brooklyn, a historically white community of private homes. By the 1960s parts of Flatbush were slowly becoming racially mixed; East Flatbush was also becoming surrounded by predominantly black sections of Brownsville and Crown Heights. The border between white and black neighborhoods had moved steadily south from Atlantic Avenue, to Eastern Parkway, and during that decade it began to reach Linden Boulevard. Black people who lived in these communities were denied jobs at the building site, whereas some white laborers commuted to the site from as far away as Connecticut and New Jersey. Brooklyn CORE members were outraged at these discriminatory practices and wanted more skilled jobs set aside for people of color. They demanded that construction trade unions "open the books" to allow more blacks and Puerto Ricans to become members, enter apprenticeships, and learn skilled trades. Oliver Leeds and others on the Employment Committee devised a plan to picket the site and disrupt the work, but Downstate was too big for CORE to handle alone.[4]

To shut down the site effectively, Brooklyn CORE needed hundreds of volunteers to march in picket lines and commit acts of civil disobedience. It could not muster those numbers on its own. Leeds decided the best way to attract masses of people would be to enlist Brooklyn's leading black ministers, who, after reluctantly agreeing to participate, took over as the campaign's titular leaders in mid-July and assumed control of all negotiations with union leaders and politicians. Though the ministers were the public leaders of the protest, Brooklyn CORE had more experience in dramatizing demonstrations and generating excitement through the press. Thus, Brooklyn CORE members, who shaped the atmosphere on the picket lines with their willingness to engage in direct action and inventive tactics for disrupting the work site, were everyday leaders of the campaign. They initiated audacious actions that kept newspapers focused on the protest and black workers' nearly total exclusion from construction trades. They also pushed the usually moderate ministers to be more confrontational and militant. But when specters of violence appeared on the picket lines, the Downstate campaign grew into something neither Brooklyn CORE nor the ministers could control. The culture of symbolic aggressiveness that emerged at the Downstate demonstration foreshadowed the interracial, dynamic Brooklyn CORE chapter's not-too-distant future. The inability to win concrete victories from the state or union power brokers also highlighted reasons for the Brooklyn chapter's eventual decline as a powerful force in direct-action protest politics.[5]

"No Way of Fighting It"

Historically, African Americans worked in the construction industry's "trowel trades" as low-skilled, menial laborers. Although black workers earned good wages hauling materials, excavating rock, or performing other low-end construction work, jobs in the "trowel trades," and even construction jobs that required specialized skill, were rarely permanent, always physically taxing, and often dangerous. When common laborers were no longer needed at a work site, they were cut loose. African American construction workers in the postwar era found it almost impossible to advance to positions that required more skills. Black workers who wanted to break into the construction trades also found it difficult and, in some industries, impossible to attain apprenticeships with construction unions that helped novices become experienced journeymen. With no union protection or job placement assistance, they wandered from site to site, or even city to city, in search of work. Unlike many white construction workers who had political or familial connections, black workers could not use the building trades to climb the economic and social ladder into the American middle class.

This discrimination made a record $345 million in construction work unavailable to African Americans and Puerto Ricans. Whites dominated the industry; in 1960 they made up 92 percent of the 189,122 workers enrolled in the 121 New York City building trades unions. As African Americans and Puerto Ricans grew to almost one-quarter of the city population, they still held only just under 8 percent of city construction jobs, mostly in the lowest, meanest positions available. Some unions had no black members, or only a token number: Local 1 Plumbers had 3,000 members and only 9 blacks; Local 2 Plumbers and Steamfitters had 4,100 members and only 16 blacks; Local 28 Sheet Metal Workers had no blacks among its 3,300 members. Only the forty-two Carpenters and Joiners locals had a sizable number of black members: of 34,000 members, 5,000 were African American. At a time when the construction industry was booming, thanks to government-funded building projects, unions excluded African Americans from lucrative jobs, denied them access to apprenticeship programs, and barred them from advancement in one of the most promising labor markets for unskilled men with little or no specialized education.[6]

From the union locals that ran apprenticeship programs and trained new workers to the small contracting firms or large companies that employed them, networks built through friendship, familial ties, organized crime, and political cronyism determined who received jobs and the type of work they performed. The highly skilled, best-paying jobs, such as those for electricians, steamfitters, and sheet metal workers, passed down from fathers to sons, uncles to nephews, and among cousins and neighborhood buddies as ethnic groups created specified niches within the construction industry and its unions. Over time, Italian, Irish, and Polish Americans amassed political power and became economically mobile through their monopolization of construction jobs.[7]

In New York City this industry was almost entirely white. Black workers made some gains during the two world wars, but those advances quickly receded during the Great Depression and the postwar period. Some union locals made no attempts to cover up their exclusion of blacks. Local 3 Electrical Workers outright refused to admit African Americans. Local 2 Plumbers enforced racial exclusiveness by not issuing licenses to black workers who gained experience or completed apprenticeship programs in other states. Local 28 Sheet Metal Workers was strictly a father-son local with no black members at all. Carpenters were a less highly skilled group and had more black workers, but their unions also segregated members. After World War I all black carpenters were assigned to Local 1888, a racially integrated union local based in Harlem. As whites transferred out and the local became exclusively black, union councils relegated black workers to jobs that were only in Harlem. When work sites outside Harlem needed carpenters, Local 1888 never received the assignments. The union's insidious practices and racist policies segregated these skilled black workers from jobs in predominantly white residential areas and in bustling downtown business districts; and in a business where job opportunities were seasonal or often temporary, these were the work sites that paid well and lasted long enough to provide workers with a semblance of job stability and income security. With only one neighborhood from which they could draw work, skilled black carpenters were in limited demand, and membership in Local 1888 fell from 440 members in 1926 to a meager 65 in 1935.[8]

For Gilbert Banks, the subtle, informal methods of racial discrimination that denied construction jobs and advanced training to African Americans became all too clear when he left the army in 1953. An expert diesel mechanic during World War II, Banks could not find work in his field after nine years of service and becoming a high-ranking noncommissioned officer. He searched for any type of work on construction sites, but foremen usually hired blacks only when they were behind schedule. Men like Banks found sporadic work in the worst jobs at the least pay. Sometimes he landed temporary jobs as a "chipper." Chippers operated a pneumatic hammer that broke concrete; their work was one of the most low-level, dangerous, and unhealthy jobs in the industry. Banks noticed that men who had been chippers for years did not live long. Many contracted silicosis from breathing airborne particles and spending hours in deep holes with little or no ventilation. Whenever Banks asked for work that was permanent or more related to his expertise, he experienced the catch-22 that many skilled black laborers faced from foremen and union administrators: no job meant no union card and no union card meant no job. Whenever he attempted to attain skilled work on a construction site, Banks remembered that the foreman at a job would ask him, "'Have you got a [Union membership] book?' I'd say, 'No.' 'Well,' they said, 'Go get a book and we'll give you a job.' And I'd go to the union and ask them for a book. They'd say, 'Listen, if you get the job, we'll give you a book.'"[9] Banks struggled with this cycle for over twenty years. Day-in and day-out he experienced the ways unions masked their racist sentiments and discriminatory policies behind such subtle tactics. According to him, there was just "no way of fighting it."

Banks's resigned attitude seems justified given events that transpired at the start of the summer of 1963. After multiple reports and statements from the Urban League, NAACP, and Negro American Labor Council, which criticized the inaction and apathy of elected officials and labor leaders, New York's politicians and union power brokers responded with tough talk and empty promises. "Whatever we have been doing in the field of human rights until today is still not enough for tomorrow," Mayor Wagner declared in a statement to aides charged with monitoring racial discrimination in private organizations that had contracts with the city. "By law and by mayoral direction," he proclaimed, "every agency and department is under mandate to advance the cause of equal rights and equal opportunity." New York's labor commissioner, James J. McFadden, echoed the mayor's sentiments. "Statistic after statistic," he wrote to twenty-four construction union leaders, "clearly indicate that right here in New York City many of our Negro and Puerto Rican workers are making little true progress in the vital fields of wages and employment." Blacks and Puerto Ricans were underrepresented in construction unions, McFadden argued, because of the "historical hiring patterns that have been allowed to develop." "The time to correct this inheritance is now," he declared. "Change is long overdue." And in a separate meeting with two of the city's most powerful labor leaders, Peter J. Brennan, president of the Building and Construction Trades Council, and Harry Van Arsdale, president of the Central Labor Council, Mayor Wagner demanded "more jobs and more job opportunities for members of the minorities who have a much greater unemployment ratio than the rest of the city's population." "The goal," Wagner explained, "is not headlines." Nonetheless, no jobs or investigations into patterns of bias resulted from these meetings, and the statements by the city's mayor and its most powerful labor leaders did not produce any tangible changes for skilled black workers.[10]

"The Time Is Now"

The year 1963 promised to be one of intense action in the national civil rights movement. During the spring of 1963 the violent suppression of demonstrators in Birmingham sent shocking images across the nation as people watched televised scenes of children being blasted with high-powered water hoses by firefighters and attacked by vicious police dogs. This dramatic campaign, and Martin Luther King's stirring "Letter from a Birmingham Jail," in which he reminded moderates that "freedom is never voluntarily given by the oppressor; it must be demanded by the oppressed," reinforced northern activists' commitment to improve conditions in their hometowns, especially with respect to employment opportunities for blacks.[11]

Some national civil rights leaders became frustrated and angered by the empty rhetoric from mayors and labor leaders around the country. Unlike Banks, though, they actually believed that blacks could crack through the racial barriers that barred them from jobs in the construction industry. What was needed was a much more aggressive approach. In early June 1963 Herbert Hill and James Farmer of CORE made

harsher critiques of politicians' inaction and called for direct-action protests that demanded jobs and an end to discrimination by construction
unions. "For years," Hill declared, "we have attempted through conferences, memoranda and interminable negotiations to make progress for
Negro workers in the building trades' craft unions. This has been an
exercise in futility." On June 12, 1963, James Farmer appeared on *The
Open Mind*, a nationally televised interview program hosted by Richard
D. Heffner, which featured live debates on current events among political leaders, prominent intellectuals, and social activists. That evening
Heffner moderated a conversation among Farmer, Wyatt Tee Walker of
the Southern Christian Leadership Conference, Allan Morrison, an editor of *Ebony*, and Malcolm X. The theme for the discussion was "Race
Relations in Crisis." James Farmer spoke at length about the boycotts
and demonstrations that had won jobs in cities throughout the country.
Furthermore, he made some of the first public arguments in favor of
affirmative action programs. Employers and government leaders, he
argued, should begin "compensatory, preferential hiring" in industries
that for years had excluded African Americans from the labor force: "It
is necessary for there to be a new push. We say to the employer now that
he has a responsibility not only to the best qualified person who applies,
but to seek qualified Negroes, and if they are not qualified for the specific job to help train them, and to admit them to apprenticeship training
classes. We say the same thing to the trade union, because we've got to
break out of this box where the Negro is at the bottom of the economic
totem pole." When Heffner stated that his arguments sounded like
Negroes now wanted something "more than equality," Farmer concluded that black people in the United States had received "special treatment of a negative nature for three hundred to four hundred years. Now
we're asking for the kind of special treatment that is positive and
affirmative."[12]

Just as Farmer was arguing for protests that demanded affirmative
action in employment sectors, New York City CORE chapters took to
the streets in Harlem and demanded that contractors immediately hire
qualified African American and Puerto Ricans as construction workers.
New York CORE started a direct-action campaign at the construction
site of the Harlem Hospital annex at 135th Street and Lenox Avenue.
On June 12, 1963, after several days of picketing, demonstrators used
more intense tactics to disrupt the site. Protestors formed groups of three
and five, sat down in front of entrances to the work site, and blocked
trucks and workers from entering and leaving the area. After police
arrested one group, another took its place. Police action proved ineffec-

tive, and one officer called for assistance. When an additional three hundred police officers arrived on the scene, minor scuffles broke out between law enforcement and picketers. Morris De Lisser, a member of the Harlem NAACP chapter, sustained head and neck injuries while allegedly resisting arrest. Passersby noticed the action and joined the demonstration, swelling its ranks to over 150 people. Eight black laborers from the construction crew left work and joined the demonstration. Feeling solidarity with the cause, they added their voices to the chants: "If we don't work, nobody works." Fearing an uncontrollable riot, the general contractor, Julius Nasso, suspended work and sent his crew home.[13]

The following day protestors returned and blocked the entrances. More fights erupted between police officers and demonstrators. While tensions mounted in Harlem, Mayor Wagner was in Hawaii attending a conference. In his absence, Paul Screvane, the acting mayor, officially shut down the Harlem Hospital project. Concern for "public safety," he said, was the reason for his decision. Work on the annex would be suspended until the mayor conferred with labor leaders and investigated the demonstrators' charges. Protestors in Harlem cheered when they heard Screvane's decision. Their jubilation echoed in the black press. The *Amsterdam News* hoped the Harlem Hospital demonstration would serve as a template for other protests that summer. In an editorial titled "The Time Is Now," James L. Hicks, the activist editor of the paper from 1955 to 1965, called on political leaders to make the work crew at the Harlem Hospital annex a model of racial integration. Substantial numbers of black construction workers in Harlem would be a model for the rest of the city's building projects. With success secured in Harlem, Hicks encouraged the same protest groups to "immediately turn their attention to some other city project and force home the same conditions." Nonstop protest would be the only way to ensure equal job opportunities for African Americans in New York City: "The course is now clear," he concluded. "We have waited too long and the only thing that will help us is direct action."[14]

Other New Yorkers, however, were not as overjoyed about the results of the Harlem Hospital protest, nor were they as optimistic about the use of disruptive tactics to further the cause of equal employment in construction unions. In a letter to the *New York Times*, Marilyn Rubin wondered why the Mayor's Office could not fix problems with racial discrimination while construction of the annex continued. This ordinary citizen probably spoke for many when she acknowledged that "racial discrimination does exist in the Union" but wondered, "Cannot corrective measures be taken without hampering progress on a vitally needed community structure?" Though directed at the mayor, Rubin's question became a point of contention for activists: How high a price should citizens be expected to pay for increasing the number of blacks and Puerto Ricans in the construction unions? Was achieving that goal worth preventing the construction of a much-needed community facility, such as a hospital or a school? Which was more important?[15]

In many ways, answers to those questions depended on how one chose to spin the issue. Racial discrimination in the building trades was a widespread, systematic condition that prevented black and Puerto Rican workers from attaining lucrative jobs and marketable skills. To change those patterns, civil rights activists simultaneously had to expose the problem to the public and force politicians and labor leaders to negotiate changes in union hiring practices. Disruptive tactics were the only effective weapons they had at their disposal. According to demonstration supporters, the temporary inconvenience of shutting down a work site, even a construction project that benefited the entire community, was worth the long-term gains in employment that potentially could result from the protest. At the same time, opponents of these disruptive tactics often painted a powerful picture of demonstrators as reckless agitators whose actions denied citizens a much-needed facility and therefore wreaked havoc on the entire community. Northern urban civil rights activists who led these campaigns had to deal with the ways their opponents in government and the press manipulated definitions of what was best for "the community," which was often a major obstacle in their campaigns.

Despite these extra battles, Brooklyn CORE activists wanted to build from the momentum generated by the Harlem Hospital demonstration, and the massive, million-dollar, state-funded Downstate Medical Center project, with its predominantly white workforce in a residential area that was experiencing changes in its racial demography, seemed an ideal target. But before Brooklyn CORE could implement disruptive tactics at Downstate, it needed to find hundreds of participants. The construction project was a seven-story medical school facility and a new hospital building that was four blocks wide and one large block long. To make matters even more difficult, the work site had several entrances. Oliver Leeds, Gilbert Banks, Maurice Fredericks, and Vincent Young investigated the scene. Leeds saw hundreds of workers, large cement trucks, bulldozers, and cranes constantly entering and leaving the site. Except for a handful of carpenters' assistants, there were few black workers. They immediately realized that it was too large for

Brooklyn CORE to picket alone. At most, the chapter had thirty to forty members, only ten or twelve of whom could be counted on to attend every meeting and demonstration. If Brooklyn CORE wanted to stage an effective protest, it would need help.[16]

Leeds contacted Warren Bunn, president of the Brooklyn chapter of the NAACP, and John Parham, leader of the local Urban League chapter. In early July the three went to the Downstate construction site to gather more data. While walking around the work area, they witnessed how the few black workers there performed only menial labor. Bunn, Leeds, and Parham took their complaints to leaders of local construction unions and tried to convince them to recruit more black members. The union leaders' responses were not pleasant. "They wouldn't even listen to us," Leeds recalled. "One of them almost threw us down the stairs."[17]

The three men went back to Downstate and planned a demonstration strategy. The main construction area had one large entrance on its far west side. A large picket line in front of that area could effectively slow down the work, and if enough people sat down in front of trucks, they could repeat the success of the Harlem protest. But Leeds knew Bunn and Parham could not rally enough members to pull off that type of disruption. According to him, "Johnny Parham's Urban League had no troops," and "the NAACP had a big paper membership, but it undoubtedly couldn't get ten people out there on a Monday morning at 7 o'clock." Brooklyn CORE could guarantee twenty people, but that number would not be enough. Demonstrators had to maintain the picket line from 7:00 A.M. to 4:00 P.M., five days a week. Hundreds, if not thousands, would be needed to make Downstate as successful as the protest at Harlem Hospital. Some of the larger black churches in Brooklyn had over one thousand members. With support from their ministers, Leeds felt confident they would have enough troops to lead an effective protest at Downstate. But getting the ministers' support for a Brooklyn CORE project proved difficult.[18]

For the most part, Brooklyn's black church leaders held cautious (some might argue conservative) views on civil disobedience. With the exception of the Reverend Milton Galamison, Brooklyn's black clergy rarely participated in Brooklyn CORE's early-1960s civil rights activities. Politically prominent ministers probably did not want to risk their reputations by being associated with militants in Brooklyn CORE. The two Brooklyn ministers with the most political power in Brooklyn were the Reverends Sandy F. Ray and Gardner Taylor. Ray, the sixty-five-year-old pastor of Cornerstone Baptist Church, was an avid supporter of Governor Nelson Rockefeller. The governor made an annual visit to

Cornerstone and spoke there several times during campaign season. Taylor, pastor of Concord Baptist Church, was a leading Democrat in Brooklyn and had a close relationship with Mayor Wagner. In 1958 the mayor appointed Taylor to the Board of Education, and in 1962 Wagner also made Taylor Brooklyn's Democratic leader. Like Ray and Taylor, most of Brooklyn's black ministers thought of themselves as moderate power brokers. They believed they could use their influence over thousands of black voters as leverage with elected officials. Brooklyn CORE had a reputation for rabble-rousing and militancy. If the ministers participated in anything led by CORE, they might lose all clout with their friends in City Hall and Albany.[19]

The Harlem Hospital demonstration, however, made fighting against racial discrimination in the building trades the most important civil rights issue in the city. Other demonstrations developed, but only in Manhattan. East River CORE, a chapter from the Lower East Side of Manhattan, began a similar protest at the construction site of the Rutgers housing projects, and a coalition of activists from different organizations began a round-the-clock sit-in at the mayor and governor's downtown offices. Calling themselves the Joint Committee for Equality, they demanded that New York's elected officials enforce the state's anti-discrimination laws, especially in the building trades. By early July, Leeds remembered, "You couldn't pick up a newspaper anywhere in New York City without seeing demonstrations at construction sites all over the city, all over, except Brooklyn." If the ministers did not support Brooklyn CORE's demonstration at Downstate, they knew that they would seem out of step with a majority of everyday black citizens during a high point of civil rights activism.[20]

Not wanting to lose face, fourteen of Brooklyn's African American ministers agreed to encourage their congregations to support the Downstate campaign. Most, like Gardner Taylor, hesitated when Leeds approached them with CORE's idea for the protest. "Well, Ollie," Leeds recalled him saying, "I think that's a good idea. I'll do the best I can. I got a busy schedule. I don't know if I can make it, but I'll give it a try." Eventually, Taylor and other ministers not only gave the campaign their full support, but also became its most ardent spokesmen and leaders.[21]

Many factors influenced their change of heart. According to the historian Clarence Taylor, the ministers were inspired by the example of Martin Luther King Jr., whose leadership in the South motivated clergymen around the country to see nonviolent direct action as a powerful weapon for social and political change. Brooklyn's ministers were also motivated by the opportunity to demonstrate their local influence. They were confident they could get hundreds, if not thousands, of their members to participate nonviolently in the demonstration and take the media spotlight off of Brooklyn CORE. They formed the Ministers' Committee for Job Opportunities and planned to make their first appearance on the picket lines on Monday, July 15. Using the power of the pulpit, they would drum up support from their congregations by delivering rousing sermons that Sunday, connecting the righteousness of the protest to the message of the Gospel.[22]

The Ministers' Committee members positioned themselves to become the de facto leaders of the campaign. If they were going to expend their political capital with elected officials and use their influence with their congregations to send participants to picket lines, then the ministers probably reasoned that they wanted to be the public faces associated with the nonviolent campaign. Not wanting to feel controlled by outsiders, members of Brooklyn CORE organized their own picket line in front of Downstate on Wednesday, July 10, a few days before the ministers planned their debut appearance. By seven o'clock that morning, only thirty people had come. Some blocked the work site's entrance, but they failed to disrupt the site for long. Police arrested Gilbert Banks for disorderly conduct when he blocked a truck from entering the construction site. The Bibulds, who were also there with their children, were arrested for assaulting police officers. Their confrontation with the police on the picket line and Elaine Bibuld's subsequent outburst at the judge during her arraignment foreshadowed the types of unruly behavior that soon would become common on the Downstate picket lines. The *New York Times* reported, "Mrs. Bibuld had kicked one policeman and her husband had punched two others when the policemen tried to move them out of the path of cement-mixing trucks." The details are sketchy, but, according to the *Times,* the Bibulds were clearly the aggressors and their arrest was justified.[23]

Elaine Bibuld, on the other hand, told a story in which she and her husband were singled out by police officers and attacked, and they were merely defending themselves. She said one officer pointed at her and her husband and said to his partner, "Get those two." She cautioned Jerome to keep close to their children. When Jerome and Douglass passed the police officer, Elaine saw him push her son. Jerome came to Douglass's defense and wrestled the cop to the ground. The officer rolled on top of Jerome Bibuld, pressed a knee into his groin, and used Jerome's jacket zipper to choke him. When Elaine saw this, she said she sprang into action. "I was going to kick this cop's testicles as far up through his head as I could get them. I meant to hurt him," she recalled, "but he was getting up just as my foot was connecting so my foot hit him in the middle of his back."[24]

Police arrested both Elaine and Jerome and charged them with disorderly conduct and third-degree assault. Jerome Bibuld was immediately released on bail. Elaine's hearing, on the other hand, was a fiasco. She lashed out at her judge after he lectured her on the impertinence of civil disobedience. "You know who you are?" she screamed at the African American judge. "You're Uncle Tom with Jim Crow sitting on his shoulder!" The judge held Elaine in contempt and sentenced her to ten days in the Women's House of Detention. She was pregnant at the time, and the trauma of the fight and prison sentence proved too much. Shortly after her release, Elaine had a miscarriage.[25]

In part, Elaine Bibuld's memories of her arrest at Downstate were shaped by the dramatic months her family had spent fighting the Board of Education. She had been besieged by threats for almost two weeks, and her suspicion of the officers at Downstate might have stemmed from her feelings of distrust that remained after the previous winter's ordeal. And her descriptions of her courageous, retaliatory response portrayed her as a fearless protector of her family, provoked to fight. "I personally had not, up until that point, been ready to attack anybody," she recalled, "but that was my husband and my child!"[26]

Regardless of whether the arrest happened as described by the *Times* or according to Elaine Bibuld's memory, her actions on the picket line—and in court—indicated how frustrated, impatient, and daring some Brooklyn CORE members had become. The ministers believed they could bring more order and discipline to the protest and reduce the potential for outbreaks of disorder, which could lead to violence. The ministers attempted to borrow from Martin Luther King Jr.'s leadership style. King skillfully conflated demonstrators' use of nonviolent direct-action protest with American traditions of Christian morality and political ideologies of democracy and freedom, and many members of the Ministers' Committee presented themselves as the strategic *and* moral leaders of this campaign. They crafted their unified public persona to be a composed vanguard at the head of a phalanx of hundreds of peaceful demonstrators. This image, they believed, would embody the protest's legitimacy and position it on a moral high ground in the eyes of the public. If disorder occurred, as it had in Birmingham that April, it would not stem from actions of the ministers or their troops; it would be at the hands of racist construction workers who fought to maintain the whiteness of their unions and indifferent police officers who disdained agitation for social change. Thus, the ministers saw it as their role to keep the public focused on systematic practices of racial discrimination in the construction unions, and this attention would easily be lost if the demonstrators, not the white workers or the cops, were the ones who initiated violence or disorder.

Brooklyn CORE, which had a reputation for militancy, could not be this protest's public face because its members did not carry the same moral or political clout as the ministers. Leeds, Fredericks, Kirchner, Young, and Goldwag went along with this plan and for the most part followed the ministers' leadership. Thus, from July 15 onward, the black ministers of Brooklyn effectively took over as leaders of the Downstate campaign. Still, the ministers' strategy, though appropriate, was incapable of attaining the type of moral legitimacy that King's efforts won in Birmingham. For many reasons, Birmingham was not Brooklyn. Brooklyn CORE members had to use their expertise as direct-action tacticians to keep the protest alive. Still, Downstate attracted certain protestors who were interested neither in following the ministers nor in adhering to CORE's principles of nonviolence. The actions of these newcomers had the potential to greatly undercut the movement's success.

Direct Action at Downstate

From the start, newspaper reporters and politicians treated members of the Ministers' Committee as the titular leaders and practically ignored Brooklyn CORE's role in organizing the protest. Black churches became the "local movement centers" of the Downstate campaign, and almost all the demonstration's participants came from the various congregations. The churches themselves served as bases of operation. Ministers held rallies in their church halls, petitioned their members during Sunday services for donations that went into bail funds, and inspired them with weekly sermons on the righteousness and justice of their cause.[27]

Still, Brooklyn CORE's members were a significant force at the picket line. Their experiences during campaigns against Lefrak, Ebinger's, the Department of Sanitation, and the Board of Education made them much more experienced than the ministers in working with the press and devising tactics to disrupt the work site. At Downstate, Brooklyn CORE members led picketers in committing disruptive acts that put a media spotlight on their cause for three solid weeks. The ministers, on the other hand, were overly cautious when it came to disrupting work at the site. Protective of their reputations, they tried to choreograph their every move on the picket line, including the exact day they would get arrested. They even sought to control the demonstrators' behavior, a task that became more difficult as time wore on.[28]

Monday, July 15, was the Ministers' Committee's first day at Downstate, and fourteen of Brooklyn's most prominent black clergymen arrived at the site at 7:00 A.M. Their Sunday sermons had drummed up noticeable support as well. Over seventy-five of their parishioners attended the early-morning picket line. The ministers planned to make their presence known by giving interviews to reporters and posing for pictures, but they decided against arrest until Wednesday, July 17, at which time the ministers thought they would have generated sufficient buzz in the media and the tactic could be seen as their leading the campaign to greater militancy.

As it had been in the past, media attention would be an essential tool for the campaign's success. CORE leaders and the ministers wanted photographers and television cameras to capture images of demonstrators lying in front of trucks, blocking entrances, singing freedom songs, and being carried away by police officers. Images of the most prominent black ministers in Brooklyn engaged in civil disobedience would be one of the campaign's most important weapons. The public had seen similar images from the South, especially from Birmingham during April 1963. Pictures and news footage of peaceful demonstrators attacked by fire hoses and police dogs swayed northerners' opinions to support the southern civil rights movement's calls for basic human rights to extend equally to black and white Americans. Brooklyn CORE and the ministers hoped Downstate would elicit the same amount of public empathy for their cause as the events in Birmingham had generated for the movement to desegregate lunch counters in that city's downtown district. But the building trades industries were, in the words of the historian Nancy Banks, "the last bastion of discrimination." Systems of white privilege that excluded black workers from building trades unions proved to be just as intractable as the southern Jim Crow system that barred black workers from certain "white" jobs and banned black people from "whites-only" public spaces and accommodations.[29]

Organizing the press even to appear at the construction site, however, was the first hurdle protest organizers had to overcome. A mixture of the cult of personalities and black nationalist rhetoric almost sabotaged the campaign's effective use of newspaper coverage. Though Arnold Goldwag, Brooklyn CORE's public relations chairman, had experience working with the press, some ministers were uneasy with a white person's having an important leadership role. The Reverend George Lawrence, who had been a news reporter before he became a minister, guaranteed Leeds that the media would be at Downstate on Monday morning. Oliver Leeds wanted to give that job to Goldwag, but Lawrence protested. Whites, he argued, should not be allowed to have authority in a black-led movement. "*We* have to take care of business *ourselves!*" he told Leeds. Goldwag's involvement, he argued, showed that blacks were too dependent on whites for assistance, especially in public matters like press conferences and communication with political leaders. Lawrence chastised Leeds, saying, "*You can't let other people take care of our business!*" Leeds did not argue with him. It was more important for him to maintain unity with the ministers than quibble over Lawrence's black nationalist politics. For all his rhetoric, Lawrence failed to deliver. On Monday morning, when the ministers arrived at Downstate with their parishioners, George Lawrence was conspicuously absent, and so were the many reporters and TV cameras he had promised.[30]

The ministers and demonstrators formed a picket line and marched peacefully for an hour. Some newspaper reporters and one television camera arrived, which Leeds believed was due to Goldwag's last-minute work. Gardner Taylor and the other ministers approached Leeds and made plans to return on Wednesday and be arrested. Years later, Leeds derided this staged arrest by calling it the "big show" because of the way the ministers demanded that when they were arrested, the event receive maximum coverage in the press. A handful of newspaper reporters would not meet their tactical needs and was not worth the trip to jail. Mimicking Gardner Taylor's Louisiana accent, Leeds told the historian Clarence Taylor that the Reverend Taylor turned to him while they were huddled on the sideline of the demonstration and declared, "We've got to stop this discrimination in these construction places, and I don't mind going to jail for it, but if I go to jail I'd like to get my picture took." No longer wanting to put his faith in George Lawrence, Taylor also told Leeds to "get that Arnold Goldwag to take care of the TV people" for Wednesday. The ministers were ready to leave the demonstration when Leeds saw a truck about to enter the site. "I'll go for the 'big show' Wednesday," he told the departing ministers, "but I'm taking this one *today.*" Leeds went by himself, sat down, and blocked the large truck. All fourteen ministers followed him and sat down, too.[31]

They blocked the truck for over an hour, and during that time more cameras arrived. The arrest of fourteen of Brooklyn's most prominent ministers on the first major day of picketing was a dramatic event. It inspired twenty-seven others also to lie down in front of the trucks. They, too, were arrested. Even though Leeds was the leader of the spontaneous sit-down, neither he nor Brooklyn CORE was mentioned in the news. A story appeared on the front page of the *New York Times*, which lauded the Reverend Taylor as "one of the most prominent Negro religious leaders in the city" and highlighted the minister's leadership of the protest. The *Times* also featured a picture of the ministers who went limp and forced police officers to carry them into the wagon, a tactic they probably copied from Leeds when he was arrested.[32]

Later in the day more than four hundred people, mostly from the ministers' churches, attended their arraignment at the Brooklyn Criminal Court. The Reverend George Lawrence arrived at the courthouse just in time to greet reporters as the demonstrators' spokesman. He mentioned that "the Bedford-Stuyvesant section is on the brink of a very violent outburst," but he and the other ministers would do their best to maintain peace. "The reason why our clergymen took part [in the demonstration] is that we feel anything concerning our people is our concern since they look to us for leadership and guidance. The militant action was forced upon us by the inaction of the Governor and the Mayor." Reporters also interviewed the Reverend Taylor, who emphasized the ministers' role in bringing about justice: "Most of the prophets spent time in jail. This is a long tradition. When a government is corrupt, as this one is about discrimination, it must be challenged, particularly by those who love it and certainly by religious people." Neither mentioned Leeds's or Brooklyn CORE's influence, and no one bothered to interview any members of CORE.[33]

That evening, at a postdemonstration rally at Bethany Baptist Church, the Ministers' Committee for Job Opportunities decided it would control the negotiations with the mayor, governor, and labor leaders without the input of Brooklyn CORE. In some ways the decision made sense. Combined, the fourteen ministers on the committee had over 75,000 parishioners. Their congregations would be ideal sources of participants and funds, and the ministers' personal connections with the mayor and governor gave them some leverage. The Ministers' Committee kept Leeds informed and invited him to speak at rallies, but Brooklyn CORE had no voice in the negotiations.

The July 15 rally at Bethany attracted over 1,500 people. The Ministers' Committee made their demands public that night. Governor Rockefeller, Mayor Wagner, and Building Trades Council President Brennan had to make the workforce on all publicly funded construction jobs at least 25 percent African American and Puerto Rican. If New York's political and labor leaders refused, the ministers would continue the protest, which they promised would lead to a record number of arrests. "We need more jailbirds for freedom," George Lawrence told the crowd. He encouraged the twenty-six ministers in attendance to support this campaign by leading their congregations in sit-ins at Downstate. Other ministers hinted that uncontrollable violence might also result. Taylor exclaimed, "Blood may flow in the streets of Brooklyn, and if it does the streets will be cleansed. If necessary we will die like heroes."[34]

The ministers allowed Oliver Leeds to speak, and he made one of the most memorable speeches of the evening. He told the audience about his experiences with racial discrimination in the construction trades, which energized the crowd and swayed many who attended to support the goals of the Downstate campaign:

> I went in the army and I tried to join the Tank Corps. When I got down to Louisiana I found I was in the Corps of Engineers. And you know what we did? We *worked* to win the war. We built anything that could be built: bridges, tunnels, houses, officers' quarters, mess quarters, roads, and airstrips. We loaded and unloaded ships. We did anything in the way that involved *work, construction work.* You know, when I got back to the United States, after the war, I couldn't get a job in construction, that there was no union that would let me in. And there was damn little that I couldn't do in the way of construction work. They'll take you and turn you into construction workers in the army, in a *segregated* army, and then when you get back into civilian life, you can't get a construction job.[35]

Leeds may have been an effective spokesman and leader, but he later remembered how the ministers distanced themselves from him and Brooklyn CORE. "They wanted to control it," he declared years later. They wanted to "be able to say that this was a civilized, well-organized demonstration, no radicals, nothing wild about it, even though it was wild. They were well-intentioned but they wanted to control it, and within days they took it over."[36]

One deficiency in the ministers' monopolizing the campaign's leadership was their apparent lack of outreach to Spanish-speaking communities. Although they advocated for more jobs for Puerto Ricans, they included no Puerto Rican organizations or leaders in their inner circle. No doubt some of the fault rested with Puerto Ricans who did not want to participate in a predominantly black protest. A letter to the *Daily News* from A. H. Rivera captured the sentiment of many Puerto Ricans in New York who felt the local civil rights demonstrations did not address their concerns and did not see Puerto Ricans' political struggles as tied to black people's. "I don't understand why these groups fighting for racial equality insist on dragging us Puerto Ricans into it," she wrote. "We have our own problems here without being dragged into this." Rivera also noted that Puerto Ricans should not be grouped with African Americans because of their mixed-race ancestry. "We have Negroes, whites and mixed among us," she argued. "I believe that our main problem is not racial but economic and educational and personally I don't think we are doing so badly. Given enough time and understanding I'm sure we can take care of our problems ourselves." Some African Americans agreed with her. Howard Bell of Brooklyn wrote to the *Amsterdam News,* "We are fighting for the Negro and all the time we bring in the Puerto Ricans alongside of us. They can get what they want: jobs, housing without the Negro going to bat for them. They even have a better chance for passing for white than we can."[37]

No matter how many times civil rights leaders spoke of African Americans and Puerto Ricans having common interests and facing similar forms of racial discrimination during the early 1960s, the two groups did not form political alliances easily or naturally. Different ideologies of racial identity sometimes drove a wedge between blacks and Puerto Ricans, especially when Puerto Ricans distanced themselves from African heritage and African American culture. Some Puerto Ricans, like A. H. Rivera, also often situated themselves in a discourse of upward social and economic mobility common to European nationalities and ethnic groups that immigrated to the United States. For Puerto Ricans such as Rivera, involvement in African American struggles was a step backward in her climb up the social and economic ladder. Of course, Puerto Rican activists involved in labor union organizing or community organizing that put them in direct and everyday contact with African Americans were more likely to see Puerto Rican socioeconomic advancement tied to black people's progress. The African American–Puerto Rican political, social, and economic relationship in New York City was historically complicated. Even though Downstate leaders claimed to represent Puerto Rican interests, and to put black and Puerto Rican workers in the same struggle, it is unclear if that was actually the case. The ministers who led the Downstate campaign do not seem to have invested much time in using the movement to strengthen black–Puerto Rican coalitions. Given Brooklyn CORE's efforts to reach out to Puerto Ricans during the Ebinger's campaign and the Bibuld family campaign, it may have had more success in this area.[38]

Brash Tactics Revive the Downstate Campaign and Attract New Participants

The ministers felt confident members of their churches would supply most of the troops for the protest and keep numbers high at the demonstration. Some of the more prestigious members of the committee also tried to make alliances with other major religious leaders in the city, in hopes that they would encourage their followers to join the movement. Gardner Taylor called on the leader of New York's Catholics, Francis Cardinal Spellman, the Reverend Dan M. Potter of the Protestant Council, and Rabbi Israel Mowshowitz, president of the New York Board of Rabbis, "to let us know how many clergymen they have under them who are willing to offer their bodies for our demonstration." But the Catholic, Protestant, and Jewish leaders did not offer significant public support, either in words or in deeds. They were not swayed by the black ministers' example to volunteer to walk in picket lines or sit in jail cells, nor did they issue any significant statements endorsing the Downstate campaign and its calls to create more jobs for blacks and Puerto Ricans.[39]

Aside from trying to widen their support among other religious leaders, the ministers also argued for the protest's broader historical significance. A rally on Sunday, July 21, at Tompkins Park in Bedford-Stuyvesant drew more than six thousand people. Ministers gave speeches meant to broaden people's understanding of the protest. Sandy Ray declared that the Downstate campaign was a part of the national struggle for both civil rights and human dignity. "We are here in response to the call of history," he exclaimed. "There will be no turning back until people in high places correct the wrongs of the nation." Gardner Taylor, a magnificent orator, also placed Downstate in the context of the national civil rights movement: "We're ready!" he shouted. "We're not going another step and America is not going anywhere without us!" "Revolution has come to Brooklyn!" he cried. "Whatever the cost, we will set the nation straight." He implicitly compared the Brooklyn protest's strategy with that of the King-led movement in Birmingham when he said, "The protest will be peaceful, but if the ruling white power structure brings it about, our blood will fill the streets." The crowd responded with loud cries of "Yes, sir!" and "Amen!" The ministers were also superb fundraisers. At the Tompkins Park rally they announced that over $2,000 had been collected and another $3,140 was pledged to assist with legal fees. Those donations did not go to waste. Downstate made history with the number of people arrested for disruptive acts of civil disobedience. On July 22 more than 1,200 people attended the demonstration and over 200 were arrested. This was the largest mass arrest since 500 people had been jailed during the Harlem riot on August 1, 1943.[40]

Still, as eloquent and powerful as the ministers were, they could not carry the demonstration by themselves. Participation waned over time as arrests took their toll on the ministers' funds and ability to supply fresh troops to the site. Days with hundreds of people on the picket line and many arrests—143 were arrested on July 23 and 84 on July 25—were followed by days with low turnouts and few arrests. Fewer than fifty people were arrested on July 30. By July 25 there were only 150 protestors on the picket line and more than half of them were arrested that day, leaving a bare-bones crew on the picket line at the site. For the protest to be effective, hundreds of demonstrators had to occupy the site all day. This proved too difficult for the ministers to organize. Most of the participants were working people who could not afford to lose more than a day's wages. Newspapers responded to these lulls in attendance with scant coverage. The demonstration was in danger of fading from the headlines and politicians' attention. Protestors had to think of new ways to disrupt the work site and maintain the campaign's momentum.[41]

In these kinds of situations, Brooklyn CORE delivered. CORE members and other protestors who were not beholden to the ministers kept the media focused on the demonstration by using innovative tactics the ministers thought were too outrageous, inappropriate, or antagonistic. At a strategy meeting some members of the Ministers' Committee suggested using children in the sit-downs, in the same way children in Birmingham took to the streets and filled the jails during desegregation protests that spring. Eventually, the committee rejected this idea because a majority felt it was too dangerous and they might lose public support if people saw pictures of children sitting down in front of steamrollers and bulldozers. Brooklyn CORE did not go along with their decision. On a day when sixty people attended the picket line and there were only twenty-seven arrests for blocking entrances to the site, two members of Brooklyn CORE organized seventeen children to block the main entrance. They too were arrested. Barbara Weeks, a member of Brooklyn CORE since the Ebinger's campaign, and Isaiah Brunson, a twenty-one-year-old from Sumter, South Carolina, who joined Brooklyn CORE during the Downstate campaign, orchestrated the children's sit-down. They were charged with endangering the lives of minors. When the patrolman asked them to escort the youngsters away from the entry roadway, Weeks and Brunson refused. The tactic made the front page of the *Times* on what otherwise would have been a lackluster demonstration day.[42]

On another day with a low turnout, fourteen picketers chained their wrists together and refused to move from the work site's main entrance. They chanted, "Jim Crow Must Go," and sang "The Battle Hymn of the Republic." Two women at the site also grasped each other's arms and locked their legs together as they sat in front of a truck. They struggled and kicked as police attempted to separate and arrest them. On another occasion Arnold Goldwag and six others climbed to the top of a crane shovel, which prevented it from bringing bricks into the work area. Twenty police officers climbed after them. After a long struggle, police arrested the seven demonstrators. All the major city newspapers featured a picture of the dramatic scene. Shelly Spector, a young white woman who joined Brooklyn CORE during the Downstate campaign, was one of those who climbed the crane with Goldwag that day. Climbing that crane, she remembered, made her feel "the exhilaration of doing something meaningful and being part of a dedicated community." Brooklyn CORE lacked impressive political contacts and hundreds of members, but the few dedicated members it had helped inspire others to do audacious acts for the movement.[43]

Veteran members of CORE expressed a similar sense of pride participating in the Downstate campaign. Maurice Fredericks worked as a postal carrier from six in the morning until two in the afternoon. Every day after work he went home, changed his clothes, and attended the picket line. Sometimes he had to use vacation days or sick time when his arrests prevented him from going to work. Indeed, getting arrested at the Downstate site became a badge of honor in Brooklyn CORE. Some of the younger members, such as Goldwag and Brunson, were arrested multiple times. Oliver Leeds claimed that Brunson and Goldwag "were arrested every day, literally every day, and sometimes twice a day at Downstate." Leeds probably exaggerated their arrest record, but other CORE members also remembered that going to jail during the Downstate demonstrations became a source of pride and a way they built camaraderie. "You'd be ashamed if you didn't get arrested," Rioghan Kirchner remarked. She was arrested twice at Downstate, once after she called in sick to the library where she worked. She almost lost her job that day when her supervisor recognized Kirchner's picture in the next day's newspaper. "Everyone at work kept saying, 'Gee, that looks like you,'" she recalled. "I said, 'No. No, I was so sick.'"[44]

Losing employment was one fear many had, and being killed was another. "They would rev the engines, make you think they were going to run over you," Kirchner recalled. Maurice Fredericks was confident no one would be killed. "Honestly, I didn't expect to get killed," he remembered, "because there were a lot of people there and a whole lot of cops. You just assumed that the man wasn't going to run you over." His confidence also stemmed from his belief that white people in the North, unlike whites in the South, would not kill demonstrators. "There was always a more humane white person in the North than in the South," he argued. "That was our feeling, anyway." Cameras and reporters certainly offered some protection to the demonstrators. "Whatever we were doing, there was plenty of press there," Elaine Bibuld recalled. Indeed, the overwhelming media presence prevented police or workers from attacking demonstrators out in the open the way southerners did; and the stigma of being likened to southerners also probably mitigated their harsh treatment of the protestors. With so much public attention on the Downstate protests, the police and union leaders were careful to prevent any fatal accidents.[45]

Daily news coverage of dramatic, heroic acts of civil disobedience and record numbers of arrests made the Downstate site a magnet for activists from all over the city. Malcolm X attended the protest daily, but he never participated in the demonstration's direct-action tactics. Some Brooklyn CORE members approached him and invited him to join the picket line, but he declined because the lines were interracial. According to Maurice Fredericks, Malcolm X told him, "I'd be only too happy to walk with you just as soon as you get them devils off your line." Fredericks and other black members of Brooklyn CORE who were committed to interracial solidarity assured him that was impossible. "We were fighting against discrimination," Fredericks explained, "and we couldn't possibly do that."[46]

Still, Malcolm X remained on the sidelines at the protest and preached about the futility of integration and nonviolent demonstration. He caught the eye of a young Sonny Carson, who was drawn to the Downstate protest because of Brooklyn CORE's militancy and dramatic tactics. Carson, a onetime street hustler and member of a gang called the Bishops, had, when the Downstate protests began, recently been released from prison for robbing a UPS worker. Meeting Malcolm X that day turned him into a political activist. According to Carson, Malcolm X approached him, shook his hand, looked him in the eye, and then anointed him a political activist, saying, "You look like you can get something done." Malcolm X spoke with many young people on the picket lines at Downstate, and after his fateful meeting with the famed black nationalist leader, Carson began to direct his energies and leadership abilities toward black nationalist politics and community activism.[47]

To Carson the only civil rights organization that was worth joining at the time was Brooklyn CORE because, as he recalled, the chapter "was in the papers more so than anybody else." Carson also appreciated Brooklyn CORE's boldness and willingness to be confrontational, which appealed to the young militant's aggressive personality. Brooklyn CORE's sit-ins, as Carson remembered, "weren't altogether nonviolent"; and since Carson rejected completely the idea that "when he hits you, don't hit him back," he was drawn to the way the Brooklyn CORE members sometimes "became confrontational, and some of them fought back" during demonstrations. Brooklyn CORE members almost never physically attacked others (except for Elaine Bibuld's encounter early on in the Downstate campaign), even in self-defense. But their militant persona struck some, such as Carson, as coming as close to an endorsement of those types of tactics as any other civil rights organization he had seen. Though Brooklyn CORE never advocated the use of violence or physical intimidation as a campaign tactic, most of its members were not philosophical adherents to nonviolent pacifism. Brooklyn CORE was aggressive, dynamic, and confrontational, which was why Carson chose it as his first official activist organization.[48]

For Carson and others, Brooklyn CORE's leadership at the Downstate site signaled a newer, more confrontational approach to civil rights activism. The campaign attracted many young people and first-time activists, some with black nationalistic tendencies like Carson, and others who just wanted to get involved in something exciting and meaningful. Pastors appealed to their church's choir members and deacons to devote at least one day on the picket line, and these people continued to constitute the bulk of the demonstrators and arrests. For Yuri Kochiyama and Frances Crayton, who were not members of the local churches, participation in the Downstate protest was a chance to do something they felt would make a contribution to the larger freedom struggle. Their motivation also stemmed from personal experiences with racial discrimination and the inspiring examples of others at Downstate.[49]

In 1963 Kochiyama was a forty-two-year-old Japanese American living in Harlem with her husband and six children. She had been politically active since her internment in one of the prison camps established for Japanese American citizens during the Second World War. Her activism in the camp, however, was mostly as a journalist and social events coordinator. Afterward, she and her husband, Bill, organized letter-writing campaigns to free Japanese American political prisoners. During the late 1950s and early 1960s, Kochiyama had read a great deal about the southern civil rights movement, but not until she and her husband moved to an apartment in a Harlem housing project did she become involved in that struggle. She attended local political meetings and met people who were leaders in the national movement. The Kochiyamas hosted gatherings on Saturday nights at their apartment, which attracted many prominent activists, including Ossie Davis, Ruby Dee, Malcolm X, and Bayard Rustin. Arnold Goldwag was also a regular. He remembered that "anyone who was anyone in the movement knew Saturday night at the Kochiyamas' was the place to hang out. This was the place where you brought a bottle of wine, you sat there, and you bullshitted." James Peck, the famed CORE leader who was hospitalized in Birmingham, Alabama, during the Freedom Rides, began visiting the Kochiyamas' Saturday night socials in 1961. They became good friends, and she developed a deep respect for CORE and its action-oriented activities.[50]

When the Downstate campaign began, she volunteered to stand in the picket line. Yuri Kochiyama was inspired by the demonstration's charged atmosphere. She brought her children to the picket line every day. The Downstate demonstration's nonviolent methods and interracial protestors motivated Yuri to get arrested for the first time. She and her oldest son, Billy, were carried off by police for blocking a truck. Kochiyama said she felt proud and excited to "be a part of the actions, to be doing something to fight discrimination."[51]

Another person who was introduced to protest politics and Brooklyn CORE at the Downstate campaign was Frances Crayton. Born in 1943 in Columbus, Georgia, Crayton moved to Bedford-Stuyvesant with her mother and sister in 1956. While living in the South, Crayton's family shielded her and her sister from the nastiness of Jim Crow racism. She spent most of her childhood in environments that were all-black. When she shopped in the city, Crayton recognized the segregated buses and second-class treatment blacks received in stores, but she also remembered that her mother and grandmother "made sure that we were never in a position of being insulted or accosted in any way." Older women in her family had mastered southern mores well enough that Frances never had serious trouble with whites—until, that is, she moved to Brooklyn.[52]

Crayton attended George Wingate High School, which was a new school in Crown Heights. To attend, she traveled by bus and walked through white residential areas. Crayton felt tortured in those neighborhoods. Young people would yell slurs at the black Wingate students who passed through their streets. In the afternoons, Crayton recalled, some white teenagers would drive around and "throw rocks at us and say, 'get out of our neighborhood,' 'niggers go home.'" The experience stuck with her: "It always bore heavy on my mind that we weren't wanted in the neighborhood, that we were treated differently, that we were told that we better not be there after sundown. And it reminded me of the kind of thing that I had been hearing about in the South." When the demonstrations began at Downstate, she empathized with the African Americans who could not get work, who she assumed were also ostracized and terrorized when they were the minority in an all-white environment. "I know how those workmen must feel," she recalled. "I mean, the fact that we can't get jobs there and when we do get jobs we're chased and told that we shouldn't be there." She joined Brooklyn CORE during the Downstate campaign and over the next few years became one of its most militant young members.[53]

Procept Attempts to Infiltrate and the Ministers' Committee Hurries to Negotiate

Brooklyn CORE members' outlandish tactics, bold spirit, and strong camaraderie kept the Downstate campaign alive during its uneventful moments, and inspired new members and demonstrators like Carson, Kochiyama, and Crayton, but they also appealed to a rowdier element that neither CORE nor the ministers were prepared to deal with. During the last few days of July, as the campaign threatened to fizzle without any gains, some activists wanted to employ more destructive and violent measures to gain politicians' and labor leaders' attention.

After three weeks of demonstration, some on the Ministers' Committee felt they might no longer be able to control people in the crowds who were increasingly not from their churches. They wanted to end the protest, but not just because of feared violence. Most felt the demonstration was taking up too much of their time and causing them to neglect their parish duties. Others, like Gardner Taylor, argued that the campaign lacked a proper exit strategy. They did not know what to do if Rockefeller, Wagner, and Brennan chose to ignore their demand that 25 percent of construction workers on publicly funded projects be African American and Puerto Rican. Taylor publicly remarked that some of the ministers were "not particularly wedded to the quota idea." After 691 arrests, politicians and labor leaders had ignored their demands. Rockefeller and Wagner repeated their commitment to enforce the existing legislation and support investigation committees, but both refused to consider the ministers' demands. Brennan denounced it as "blackmail." His only concession was to establish a six-man panel that would screen job applicants, which replaced the old system whereby newcomers needed two current members to sponsor them for union membership. The Ministers' Committee wanted to negotiate while they still had at least a modicum of influence with elected officials. They were looking for an exit from the campaign that allowed them to save face with their political contacts and parishioners, and an opportunity came at the end of July.[54]

Brash antics like climbing cranes and chaining wrists almost escalated into violence when members of a fringe protest group called Procept approached the picket line around four o'clock on the afternoon of Tuesday, July 30. The Police Department's Bureau of Special Services (BSS), which investigated radical or subversive political groups, monitored their activities at the Downstate site. BSS officers noticed three men, two black and one white, conversing with younger picketers. According to the BSS report, Procept members were at Downstate to "get the picketers to engage in more violent acts and to resist the police to a greater degree." Some of the youngsters left the line and spoke with the Procept representatives. One of the ministers, the Reverend J. Morgan Hodges, suspected the three men might be troublemakers and broke up the meeting. The Procept members left the scene. According to the BSS, they agreed to "meet some of the pickets at an undisclosed location that night to plan strategy for the following day at the demonstration site."[55]

BSS officers later identified the Procept members at Downstate as Anthony Maynard, Frank Mabry Jr., and Jeff Neff. The three men were between twenty-two and twenty-nine years old. The police sent an undercover BSS detective to gather more information from Procept's Manhattan office. Mabry told the undercover detective that Procept was an "inter-racial, inter-faith, non-violent peace group" that worked "to help bring peace, harmony and understanding between all mankind regardless of race, creed or color." Procept sensed that the rift between Brooklyn CORE and the Ministers' Committee had grown. Its members wanted to help reconcile the ill will and bring both sides together. Mabry told the undercover detective he had approached Arnold Goldwag of CORE and the Reverend Jones of the Ministers' Committee "and offered to act as mediator to help bring the two groups together." But overall, Mabry said, Procept was critical of the campaign's tactics. "The pickets show no self-respect by chaining themselves together and trying to stop the trucks," he explained. The best solution, Procept felt, was to bring together the ministers, Brooklyn CORE, and the governor, and have public debates on the issue of discrimination in the construction unions. Mabry also made sure to emphasize that "Procept does not believe in violence."[56]

Mabry's statement was most probably a subterfuge meant to divert the police's attention from what were probably Procept's real motives. The day after Procept members first arrived at the Downstate site, the picket line erupted in a "near riot." Newspapers did not mention Procept or its members as the ones responsible for the confrontation, but most of the antagonists were young people who heckled and fought with police. Teenagers also started a new tactic that day. Ten would lock arms and block a truck until police asked them to disperse. Just as soon as they left, another ten were in their place. Officers became so frustrated that they formed a double column and used their batons to ram protestors away from the trucks' path. The crowd of about one hundred demonstrators spilled into the streets, scuffled with police, and taunted them with repeated chants of "storm trooper!" One protestor kicked a cop in the groin, which sent the officer to the hospital. The Reverend Jones tried to calm the crowd and halt the demonstration. He climbed atop a stack of lumber and proclaimed, "This proves there's no difference between New York and Alabama, no difference between the United States and South Africa. This nation is going straight to hell!" Gardner Taylor blamed the police for the disturbance. Later he sent a telegram to the governor and the mayor that said, "Violence has occurred at Downstate Medical Center. People can no longer be restrained. Police apparently cannot be controlled. Public safety is threatened." This incident was the breaking point for the ministers.[57]

Oliver Leeds attended the Ministers' Council meeting that night at Berean Missionary Baptist Church. "The tenor of the meeting was that everyone was looking for an excuse to get out," he remembered. Sandy Ray voiced concern over the ministers' loss of control and the potential for more violence. "This is the first time in my life that I ever got into anything like this and I'm not ready to get into any more violence," Leeds recalled him saying. Leeds also represented Ray's strong desire not to associate himself with even a hint of violence by paraphrasing his exclamation, "Anything violent takes place, I am out!" Rumors flew around the room that some unknown militants were threatening to destroy construction property at the Downstate site. After more than twenty minutes of this type of talk, Milton Galamison refocused the ministers on the next day's plans. Leeds recalled that Galamison stood up and shouted to the room, "As far as I'm concerned, we are only responsible for our congregations. When I bring my people down there, they do what I tell them. When you bring your congregation down, they do what you tell them. We're not responsible for anything else. If somebody wants to burn up some trucks or blow up Downstate, LET 'EM!"

The Ministers' Committee stayed involved for the next few days, but it took precautions to avoid any more serious violence. Many members eagerly awaited their meeting with Governor Rockefeller on August 6, when they planned to work out a solution and end the campaign.[58]

Before they officially withdrew from the demonstration, the ministers collaborated with the police to diffuse Procept's involvement in the Downstate campaign. On the morning of August 1 the Reverend Jones informed the police officer in charge that they expected troublemakers to disrupt the lawful protest. He promised the police the ministers would help remove Procept members if they interfered. Maynard, Neff, Mabry, and another Procept member, Joseph Mills, returned that morning. At 10:15 A.M. they arrived with four or five dozen eggs in a paper bag. The ministers asked the police to arrest them. When a patrolman tried to question the four men, they pelted him with the eggs and attempted to run away. All four were arrested.[59]

One member of Procept, twenty-five-year-old Donald Washington, wanted to do more than just throw eggs at cops. On August 5 he went to the picket line, and on five different occasions he sat down in front of trucks, but he left each time officers threatened to arrest him. As he walked away, he taunted the cops. One time he asked a patrolman to "come around the corner for five minutes with me and I'll show you some black supremacy." That evening he attended a Brooklyn CORE meeting and proposed sabotaging equipment at the work site. According to Leeds, he wanted to "put some bombs underneath some trucks and put a match to it." CORE members refused to actively participate in his plan, but as Oliver Leeds remembered the conversation, they rejected him the same way Frederick Douglass rejected John Brown's invitation to join his raid to incite slave insurrection throughout the South. "On the day you want to blow up a truck," Leeds said he told Washington, "stop by and pick up a dollar from me and let me know so I won't be there. You can blow the truck up. I have no problem with that, just don't do it in the name of CORE or the civil rights movement." Leeds may have been willing to support such violence financially, but he was not willing to ruin the chapter's reputation or risk his own life by endorsing such a foolhardy proposal.[60]

Leeds and most other Brooklyn CORE members, like many civil rights activists, saw nonviolence as a useful tactic, not a way of life. Many in Brooklyn CORE were not philosophically opposed to using violence, especially in self-defense, but they knew there was no way activists could use violent tactics and expect to keep public support and convince politicians to negotiate. Brooklyn CORE's leadership felt Procept's tactic would be counterproductive to their cause, even though destroying construction property seemed like a logical thing to do to some of Brooklyn CORE's more radical-thinking members. Still, they valued their affiliation with the national organization and did not want to participate in something that would alienate the chapter from its allies in the movement or besmirch their reputation as an effective protest group. Washington and Procept never followed through with the plan for more violence at the Downstate site. After those few episodes, they disappeared from the campaign.

Procept's proposal to destroy property and the spate of violence at the demonstration on July 31 were more antagonistic and confrontational than anything Brooklyn CORE had done previously. The increasingly militant character of people at the picket line and at Brooklyn CORE meetings signaled imminent changes in the chapter. Toward the end of the Downstate protests, Brooklyn CORE was moving in a younger, more radical, and—with new members like Sonny Carson—increasingly black nationalist direction. For the first time in its history, membership, which had usually been half white and half black, was more than half African American, and the more militant members, led by Brunson and Goldwag, wanted to take over the leadership. They seized their opportunity in the aftermath of the Downstate campaign. Leeds, Fredericks, Young, Kirchner, and the other veterans did not stand in their way.

The Campaign Ends; the Struggle Continues

When the Ministers' Committee met with Governor Rockefeller on August 6, it dropped demands for the quota. After three hours, the ministers and Rockefeller had worked out a compromise. In exchange for an immediate end to the demonstration, the governor would appoint a representative to monitor the construction industry and report cases of discrimination to the State Commission on Human Rights. Rockefeller also promised a special investigation into charges of racial discrimination in the Sheet Metal Workers Local 28, a union notorious for its discrimination against blacks. Last, a recruitment program would be created to place qualified African American and Puerto Ricans in unions and apprenticeship programs. Except for the promised apprenticeship program, nothing new resulted from their talks. Moreover, there was no guarantee that the Building Trades Council or the unions would support the governor and ministers' apprenticeship program; nor did it make promises regarding immediate jobs at the Downstate construction site for black and Puerto Rican workers.[61]

The ministers held a rally that evening and announced their victory. They invited Oliver Leeds to speak and publicly endorse the settlement, which he did. In a letter he sent to Galamison, Leeds remarked, "While the accord was less than satisfactory, it was, nevertheless, a good beginning." Twenty-five years later, however, he remarked that his decision was "the biggest mistake I've ever made in my life." Logistically, Leeds realized, the demonstration was over without the ministers. "Basically, I felt what the hell, I can't carry it by myself," he said. "CORE can't carry it. The NAACP isn't anywhere. Urban League's got no troops and the ministers are pulling out. What's left? There's nothing. So I agreed to go along." Members of Brooklyn CORE who were standing in the back of the church burst into protest. They accused the ministers of selling out just when it seemed possible to win on the hiring quotas.[62]

Brooklyn CORE's outrage carried over to their next meeting, which attracted over one hundred people. People spilled out the door of Brooklyn CORE's tiny storefront office. Many were attending a CORE meeting for the first time. Brooklyn CORE did not follow strict rules on voting or decision making, and so the raucous assembly rejected a resolution to support the ministers' settlement. Everyone there wanted to continue the demonstration. Leeds put the question to a vote and the decision was unanimous. Some of the older members of CORE were doubtful the demonstration would have any meaningful effect without the ministers' involvement. "I just didn't believe that those hundred people would be out there the next morning," Leeds remarked.[63]

His prediction was correct. Only forty-four demonstrators arrived at the site on August 8, and by the end of the week the attempted resurgence fizzled. Unlike other demonstrations that Brooklyn CORE led, the Downstate protest required a steady supply of more than a hundred people willing and able to demonstrate all day and go to jail for disrupting work at the site. Brooklyn CORE could not generate the necessary numbers after the ministers abandoned the campaign; and CORE members were pariahs in the eyes of many churchgoing African Americans after the ministers publicly denounced the chapter's call for renewed demonstrations.[64]

In many ways the Downstate campaign seemed like a failure. The promised apprenticeship programs did not produce many jobs, at least not immediately, and not at the Downstate construction site. After the settlement, Gilbert Banks worked hard to get unemployed black construction workers into the unions' programs. He remembered the unions and politicians "got a construction team to review the two thousand people who applied for these jobs. There were six hundred who could do anything they wanted: electricians, plumbers, carpenters, steamfitters; all that stuff. The deputy mayor got this committee together, and two years later, nobody was hired. So we had struggled in vain." Almost thirty years later the city still had to deal with the problem of racial discrimination in the building trades unions and the low numbers of black and Puerto Rican workers in the construction trades. In the 1990s James Houghton, a leader of the group Harlem Fightback, which was one of the city's leading organizations fighting for blacks to enter the building trades industry, reflected on the demonstrations of the 1960s and remarked that the state's antidiscrimination laws and the city's Human Rights Commission were basically impotent when matched against the political power of the construction trades unions. "I think in large measure that relates to the political nature of the struggle that we are talking about," Houghton summarized, which meant that the political power of unions and the weakness of antidiscrimination legislation served to maintain racial imbalances and white workers' privileged access to jobs in the building trades industry. Decades after the Downstate campaign, Houghton lamented that black workers still struggled to break into skilled construction jobs for the simple reason that "the building trades have been able to flout the law and get away with it."[65]

The Downstate campaign proved to be a mixed blessing for Brooklyn CORE. Oliver Leeds was a masterful strategist, first by convincing the ministers to sacrifice their time (and possibly their reputations) to join the campaign, and then by deftly handling their egos and personalities to ensure unity between them and members of CORE. For Leeds, staging a successful demonstration and achieving its goals were more important than having a spotlight on Brooklyn CORE as the protest's leaders. And at the Downstate site, Brooklyn CORE's members did what they had learned to do best: they created imaginative, dramatic scenes that disrupted the work site and grabbed the media's attention. Record numbers of arrests for civil disobedience took place at Downstate, and the tactics inspired a diverse coterie of new members to join Brooklyn CORE.

Many of these new members were young and willing to continue the antagonistic style of protest they experienced on the picket lines at Downstate, and Brooklyn CORE became a very different chapter after that campaign. It lacked the cohesiveness that had held CORE members together in previous campaigns. New members had not been together long enough to develop the strong sense of camaraderie that came from months of socializing and working together. The personal relationships among the scores of people who called to continue the demonstration were weak, and their enthusiasm lacked commitment. Leeds foresaw the lack of follow-through after the vote to continue the demonstration at Downstate as an omen of the chapter's future, but there was nothing he could do about it. When Brunson, Crayton, and Goldwag challenged him for the leadership of the chapter, he merely handed it over to them and remained a regular, active member.

Within Brooklyn CORE, the more youthful and militant cadre, whom Leeds, Fredericks, and other older members referred to as the Young Turks, wanted to continue in a more radical direction. Brooklyn CORE's Young Turks were in their twenties, but age was not necessarily what bound them together and set them apart from the older cadre headed by Leeds, Fredericks, Kirchner, and Bibuld. They shared an outlook that, to remain a significant local activist force, the chapter had to escalate its tactics. Goldwag, who had been a member of Brooklyn CORE from the chapter's inception and was several years older than Brunson and Crayton, had always attempted to push the chapter to use tactics that were antagonistic and brash. In the aftermath of the Downstate campaign, as Leeds and his cohort found themselves exhausted from that struggle, Goldwag's approach took center stage within the new leadership cadre. In 1964 the Young Turks took the chapter in radical directions that made Brooklyn CORE the most notorious CORE chapter in the country.

Aside from the chapter's members pushing for a more antagonistic approach to protest tactics, many who had been in Brooklyn CORE since the Woolworth's demonstrations also felt it was time for new leadership, not so much because Leeds had done a poor job during the Downstate campaign, but because they recognized the national movement was becoming younger in age and bolder in approach. Rather than destroy the organization through power grabs and factionalization, Leeds and his contemporaries just moved aside. Elaine Bibuld, with both resignation and relief, admitted, "It was time the youngsters took over. We were too old to climb the fences and do the things that we had been doing." Bibuld, Leeds, and others were also tired and frustrated after three straight years of meetings, demonstrations, and negotiations with few clear-cut victories to show for their efforts. The time was right for them to move to the chapter's background and take a more supportive role.[66]

Isaiah Brunson and Frances Crayton became the chapter's chairman and vice chairwoman, and Goldwag remained as public relations chairman. The chapter's new leadership faced some difficult questions after the Downstate campaign: How extreme would Brooklyn CORE need to be to challenge racial discrimination effectively? And could it produce results without sacrificing its credibility? Confronting those issues became Brooklyn CORE's focus after Downstate. And these Young Turks, headstrong and a bit impulsive, were responsible for what became Brooklyn CORE's most outrageous and dramatic campaign against racial discrimination: the World's Fair stall-in.

And the fears of potential outbreaks of violence that emerged during the Downstate campaign paled in comparison with the public's hysterical reactions against the stall-in.

8

"A Gun at the Heart of the City"

The World's Fair Stall-in and the Decline of Brooklyn CORE

> I am ashamed of my fellow Negroes who have threatened to sabotage the opening of the Fair and suggest that . . . No Negroes be admitted on the opening day despite the fact that some may be planning to attend with no bad intent.
> —Mary Caraballo to Robert Moses, April 14, 1964

After the Downstate campaign, the Young Turks waited for an opportune moment to launch their first full-scale attack against racial discrimination. The upcoming 1964–65 World's Fair, which would take place in New York City, seemed like the ideal event. Nearly all the construction companies building the pavilions for the World's Fair hired only white workers from racially exclusive unions. Brooklyn CORE's new leadership saw this as an opportunity to continue the movement they had started during the Downstate campaign. But the Young Turks also had other plans for the World's Fair, which would focus the attention of the entire nation on New York City. With the right type of action, they could raise the awareness of the entire country about the practices of racial discrimination that ruined the quality of life for African Americans and Puerto Ricans living in New York City. Brooklyn CORE would turn this celebration of the future and of American progress, hosted by America's great "melting pot," into one of the country's largest demonstrations against urban forms of racial discrimination.[1]

For the civil rights movement in New York City, 1964 was a period of transition. More people participated in protest campaigns, and a vocal opposition movement emerged. Probably the most significant action in the city and arguably one of the largest civil rights demonstrations in the nation's history occurred in February when the Reverend Milton Galamison and a citywide consortium of parents, teachers, and activists called the Parents' Workshop staged a one-day boycott of the New York City public school system. The boycott occurred roughly one year after Brooklyn CORE and the Bibuld family concluded their protest against racial inequality in the city's public school system. Rather than merely attacking inferior resources and academic work in predominantly black and Puerto Rican schools, as the Bibulds and Brooklyn CORE had, Galamison and the Parents' Workshop based the 1964 boycott on specific demands for racial integration. Racially balanced public schools, Galamison argued, would bring about an equitable redistribution of resources such as books, teachers, and classroom space. The city's black and Puerto Rican children would not have an inferior education, the boycott organizers reasoned, if they sat next to white children in public schools: white parents, and the system, simply would not allow white children's education to suffer and, by extension, black and Puerto Rican children's educational opportunities would improve. Nearly half a million students skipped school on the day of the boycott; thousands attended the Parents' Workshop's "freedom schools," which Galamison and his allies organized throughout the city. The boycott movement was an impressive demonstration of solidarity among black, Puerto Rican, and white New Yorkers, but it failed to persuade the Wagner administration to initiate immediate action.

As he had in past demonstrations against racial segregation in the city's public schools, the mayor promised to investigate the issue. Opponents of racial integration were also busy organizing during this period. After Galamison's boycott, the mostly white Parents and Tax Payers (PAT) emerged as a political force. PAT members opposed "forced integration" programs, and they did not want the city to preempt their ability to send their children to neighborhood schools, which were almost completely racially homogeneous. Galamison attempted to organize a second boycott in March, but very few people participated. After that disappointing demonstration, and the city's continued failures to deal directly with school segregation, even Brooklyn's radical reverend, who had spent a decade advocating, petitioning, organizing, and demonstrating for racial integration of New York City's public schools, believed that the moment for racial integration of public schools had indeed passed.[2]

Perhaps inspired by the success of the February boycott, some in

Brooklyn CORE wanted to use the World's Fair, and all the national attention and press it would receive, to protest dramatically *all* the ways urban liberalism failed its black citizens. After several years of attacking racial discrimination in different sectors of public life, Brooklyn CORE wanted to stage one major nonviolent direct-action campaign that targeted all the ways black New Yorkers experienced second-class citizenship: in racially segregated schools; in segregated housing markets; in jobs that were off-limits to black workers; and in police brutality that targeted black citizens. Chapter members, however, were not of one mind about whether Brooklyn CORE should invest its energies in a large-scale mobilization campaign centered on the World's Fair. Some members believed the chapter should discontinue those types of onetime dramatic events and find other ways of becoming involved in the everyday, community-based struggles that promoted self-empowerment and political organization. This philosophical split did not destroy the Brooklyn chapter, but it did signal the ways it would evolve during the mid-1960s: toward community organizing and deeper immersion in Brooklyn's black communities, and away from the types of interracial, dynamic, direct-action protest campaigns that had defined Brooklyn CORE's culture during the early 1960s.

The World's Fair, then, represented the last major campaign of the chapter's interracial, nonviolent, direct-action phase. The Brooklyn chapter and the local movement that emerged after the World's Fair, and after New York City's "long, hot summer" of 1964, were very different from the civil rights movement that Brooklyn CORE activists had led. Brooklyn CORE's earlier uses of dramatic protest to try to force urban liberalism to become more inclusive of black and Puerto Rican citizens, and more responsive, in tangible ways, to issues of racial discrimination and white privilege, fell out of favor in the aftermath of the tremendous backlash that arose against Brooklyn CORE's World's Fair protest. Such tactics also probably seemed ineffective and passé after residents of Harlem and Bedford-Stuyvesant expressed their frustration with systematic poverty and racism, especially police brutality, through a violent summertime uprising in 1964.

After that tumultuous year, Brooklyn CORE's interracial membership, action-oriented culture, and protest campaign strategies effectively ended; its focus on community organizing within Brooklyn's black communities began. Over time, community-organizing efforts coincided with the chapter's embrace of black nationalism under the leadership of Sonny Carson. In this respect, the chapter's development mirrored National CORE's change in organizational culture, as well as the national black freedom movement's shift toward black power. But as Brooklyn CORE contemplated its future in 1964, those transitions toward all-black organizations and community organizing within all-black communities had not become dominant ideologies or strategies. When they did emerge in the mid- to late 1960s, they represented only one part of the borough's dynamic black power movement. In addition to Sonny Carson's leadership of Brooklyn CORE, the black power movement in Brooklyn involved the push for more black elected officials, federal investment in economic development, community control of public schools, and independent black institution and culture building. None of these developments, this history of Brooklyn CORE demonstrates, caused the dynamic Brooklyn chapter's interracial, direct-action period to end. The black power movement of the mid- to late 1960s probably had less to do with the breakup of interracial civil rights activist groups than historians have previously thought.

The failures of urban liberalism to permanently and tangibly affect local forms of racism did more to cause the breakup of Brooklyn's civil rights movement than the black power movement or black nationalism. Indeed, there were only so many political and social changes that action-oriented activists like the ones in Brooklyn CORE could win from a liberal city power structure that consistently delayed dealing with the systematic racial discrimination that infected its public schools, housing options, and employment opportunities. The city's political inattention brought activists and citizens to a boiling point in 1964. The antiracist movements and political responses that followed that turning point in the city's history were qualitatively different from the civil rights movement that Brooklyn CORE led during the early 1960s. Whereas many histories of northern activism start with episodes like Brooklyn CORE's World's Fair campaign and the summertime violence that rocked Harlem and Bedford-Stuyvesant in 1964, this history of Brooklyn CORE ends at those moments to show what happened to a dynamic, inventive, interracial activist organization, and to a politically and socially neglected black neighborhood, when New York City's liberal power brokers ignored the screaming demands of its very own civil rights movement.

One glaring effect of both increased civil rights militancy, which Brooklyn CORE's World's Fair protest embodied, and liberal power brokers' negligence was growing public resentment toward civil rights activism. When Brooklyn CORE made demands that struck at the heart of inequality throughout the borough, elected officials simply refused to negotiate with the chapter. National CORE censured its rogue chapter, and other national civil rights organizations decried the Brooklyn chapter as misguided and foolish. Rather than deal directly with Brooklyn CORE's charges of systematic racism, critics dismissed Brooklyn CORE's audacious nonviolent protest as an inappropriate form of political dissent. Citizens throughout the country, such as Mary Caraballo, categorically ignored Brooklyn CORE's arguments regarding racial discrimination in the city and instead blamed black people for the joblessness and failing schools that plagued black neighborhoods. "My family has lived in this city for over 70 years," Caraballo wrote to the World's Fair Corporation's president, Robert Moses, "and I never heard a member utter one word of criticism against it. There are plenty of jobs available, and only the lazy, irresponsible, dependent negroes who want handouts complain. The so-called leaders are publicity seekers who inflame the negroes with false stories of injustice. Those who do not like our city should return to wherever they came from and where they never had it so good."[3]

Over time, such blame-the-victim arguments would dominate the ways citizens and conservative politicians discussed racial and economic inequality in American cities. This backlash discourse, which framed civil rights activists as liars and agitators, had always been present in the northern movement. When Brooklyn CORE moved away from focused campaigns and staged a more symbolic protest, backlash discourses and wholesale dismissal of social problems that stemmed from racial discrimination became an obsession of news media, elected officials, and the general public. Rather than dealing honestly and directly with the very real social effects of decades of discrimination, urban liberals embraced these discourses. Black people in north-central Brooklyn, whose everyday lives were defined by the effects of widespread racial discrimination, eventually responded with a backlash of their own.

Brooklyn CORE's Community-Organizing Efforts

During early August 1963, just as the Downstate campaign was winding down, several Brooklyn CORE members formed a Rent Strike Committee and began working with a citywide community-organizing movement that sought to improve living conditions in some of the city's worst apartment buildings. The Harlem activist Jesse Gray, a tenant organizer since 1953, was the public leader of this grassroots effort and a media darling.

Starting in the fall of 1963, Gray began organizing residents who lived in the city's most deplorable housing conditions to withhold their rents until landlords brought their buildings up to the standards of the city's housing and health codes. These buildings suffered from a wide range of problems, such as rodent infestation, faulty electrical wiring, mildewed, rotting floors, and inadequate heating systems. During that period, which followed New York City's long, hot summer of direct-action protest, Gray captured headlines in city newspapers with his flamboyant personality and audacious press conferences, where he publicly displayed evidence that Harlem's citizens lived in inhuman conditions. Gray often posed for newspaper photographers with dead rats he had taken from apartments in buildings where residents were engaged in a rent strike. The rent strike movement quickly spread to other neighborhoods, and a small group of CORE activists, led by a man named Major Owens, took these actions across the river to Brooklyn.[4]

Born in Memphis, Tennessee, in 1936, Owens was a graduate of Morehouse College and Atlanta University, where he received a master's degree in library science. In 1958 he moved to Brooklyn to pursue what he hoped would be a long career as a famous novelist. He worked as a librarian at the Brooklyn Public Library and began writing a novel, which he finished but never published. The solitary life of a writer took a backseat to the exciting world he found after attending his first Brooklyn CORE meeting in late 1962. He remained an affiliate member throughout most of the Bibuld campaign and was not very much involved with the chapter's day-to-day leadership. His responsibilities to his wife and two young sons prevented him from becoming a full-time activist, although the chapter's charismatic members and bold protest style drew him further into its ranks over time. He did not become a zealous member of Brooklyn CORE until the rent strike movement began during the spring of 1963 and gained its momentum that fall.[5]

Major Owens felt that the rent strike movement was the best way to mobilize and empower the black community in Brooklyn, and for a while Brooklyn CORE's new leadership cadre gave him their full attention and support. By early October Brooklyn CORE's Rent Strike Committee, under Owens's leadership, had organized the borough's first significant rent strike in Bedford-Stuyvesant. Tenants in five buildings (four in Bedford-Stuyvesant and one in Brownsville) agreed to withhold their rent until their landlords improved their living conditions and upgraded their buildings so that they adhered to various standards and codes. Brooklyn CORE's press release listed the following "abominable conditions" in these buildings: leaking walls, maggots in bathtubs, faulty electrical wiring, no locks on front doors, inadequate garbage disposal, and absentee superintendents, as well as chronic infestation with rats, mice, and other assorted vermin. The chapter kicked off the rent strike with picket lines at each of the landlords' homes. It also demanded not only that these slumlords "alleviate the intolerable conditions" but also that they turn each and every building into "a first-class dwelling." Oliver Leeds, who still served as a spokesman for Brooklyn CORE, summarized the situation, saying, "No one expects people to buy stale bread or rotten meat; housing should be provided on the same basis: it should be decent, or it shouldn't exist at all." Two weeks later Brooklyn CORE was organizing rent strikes on another block in Bedford-Stuyvesant.[6]

Owens and a handful of others believed that the chapter should continue organizing rent strikes throughout the borough because they empowered black people to become leaders of their own action movements. Rent strikes required long, painstaking hours of knocking on people's doors, endless informational meetings and organizing sessions, and the time-consuming work of setting up and monitoring escrow accounts into which striking tenants deposited their withheld rents until landlords improved the buildings. During these campaigns, members of Brooklyn CORE's Rent Strike Committee adopted what the sociologist Charles Payne referred to in his study of grassroots movements in Mississippi as a "community-organizing" approach, the goal of which was to have the tenants themselves become the leaders and organizers of their own strike. Community organizing also laid a solid foundation of local leadership for future political movements. What started as a rent strike and resulted in improvements in living conditions could eventually empower everyday people to take control of the politics in their own communities. According to Payne's study of Mississippi, the main goal of a community-organizing campaign, whether it took the form of a rent strike in Brooklyn or a voter registration drive in Mississippi, was to wrest power from indifferent or corrupt power brokers and place it in the hands of ordinary citizens. For a while it seemed as if the rent strikes in Brooklyn could become the basis for this type of painstaking, slow-moving effort to organize everyday African Americans into a much more formidable political force.[7]

Brooklyn CORE's Rent Strike Committee achieved great success over the next several months. From the fall of 1963 through the beginning of the spring of 1964, the entire chapter was engaged in this work. Goldwag mobilized the local press to cover rent strike rallies. Leeds and Fredericks petitioned city agencies to investigate buildings and force slumlords to repair and maintain their property. Kirchner, Marjorie Leeds, Kirton, Brunson, Banks, the Bibulds, and Crayton, along with other new active members, such as two white college students named Paul Heinegg and Stanley Brezenoff, participated in the investigation teams and led initial educational classes with tenants on how to stage a successful rent strike. After Brooklyn CORE's campaigns to test housing segregation in the borough, the rent strikes were the chapter's most successful attempts at establishing a noticeable activist presence in Brooklyn's black neighborhoods. Major Owens summed up the philosophy of the Rent Strike Committee and its leadership in a new phase of civil rights activism in a conclusion to the committee's first progress report. "The major aim of the rent strike committee," he wrote, "is to teach people to fight for themselves. On the specific problem of living conditions and, in the future, on civil rights problems concerning the human condition, we expect each building organized by CORE to serve as a fighting unit. The people will never again become victims if they themselves lead the fight."[8]

Despite these lofty goals and the success of the rent strikes as a community-organizing tactic, in the early spring of 1964 the Young Turks decided that the time was right to begin organizing a massive mobilization campaign coinciding with the opening day of the World's Fair. Owens and a few others disagreed with the idea of diverting the chapter's energies from the rent strikes. They argued that a large, dramatic onetime mobilization tactic was not as effective as the slow work of community organizing in bringing about lasting social change. Edwin Lewinson, a professor of history at Seton Hall University, was a member of Brooklyn CORE and also held a seat on National CORE's central governing body, the National Action Council. He was one of the chapter's active members who voiced strong objection to the Young Turks' plan for a dramatic action at the World's Fair.

Lewinson had joined Brooklyn CORE in 1961 as the chapter began to make headway with its housing campaign. Blind since birth, Lewinson made headlines when the Society for the Prevention of Cruelty to Animals brought him up on charges of endangering the health of his seeing-eye dog by taking it to picket lines during the Ebinger's campaign. At the time of the World's Fair Lewinson thought the chapter should have spent more time negotiating its grievances with the mayor and the governor. He sensed that the new leadership cadre would rush into a direct-action protest without clearly defining its agenda, goals, and demands. Instead, Lewinson felt Brooklyn CORE should have exercised patience, continued to build a base of support in black communities with the rent strikes, and pressed city and state leaders for specific changes. The plan to target the World's Fair with a dramatic, nonviolent protest caused intense debate within the chapter ranks, and it eventually resulted in a rancorous split between Brooklyn CORE and the national office.[9]

But despite these internal conflicts, Brooklyn CORE itself did not split into factions as the Young Turks prepared for their audacious protest at the World's Fair. Owens and the cadre that made up the Rent Strike Committee continued with their various campaigns throughout the borough and supported the action against the World's Fair, but they had little to do with organizing it. Brunson, Goldwag, and Crayton, along with the rest of the active membership, geared up for their most audacious demonstration to date: the stall-in.

The 1964–65 World's Fair: "All New York Says—'Welcome!'"

The 1964–65 World's Fair, which was being held in Flushing Meadows Park, Queens, was one of New York City's largest public works projects in the twentieth century. The city's master builder, parks commissioner, and fair president, Robert Moses, received over $1 billion to finance the redevelopment of Flushing Meadows into a new "Central Park" for the people who were fleeing the city to live in Queens and Nassau Counties. Flushing Meadows was the site of the 1939 World's Fair, and before that it had been a dumping ground for Brooklyn's garbage. Planners for the 1964–65 event projected that it would attract between 70 and 100 million visitors over the course of one year. A caption in the *New York World-Telegram and Sun* summarizes what the fair meant in the imaginations of most New Yorkers: "It's an epic event for the city and for guests from all over the world. Sixteen million residents of the metropolitan area, with an unofficial but deep-seated interest in the exposition, invite fellow countrymen and people of other lands to this fair of fairs. To a large degree it was New Yorkers who planned and designed when there was nothing but an open field and untouched blueprint paper. Then other New Yorkers built the shining towers, the architecturally exciting buildings and the exhibits. Now it is done and all New York says—'Welcome!'"[10]

Clearly, "all New York" was not welcome. Planners of the fair knew that extending subway lines to Flushing Meadows would be necessary to make it easier for the city's poorer families, who did not own cars, to attend the fair. The existing subway line skirted the edge of the park, and the proposed extension would terminate in the heart of the fairgrounds. As Robert Moses's biographer Robert Caro writes, however, the park that Moses envisioned would remain after the fair closed was not designed for low-income people, "particularly the Negro and Puerto Rican people who made up so large a percentage of the city's lower-income families. So, Moses vetoed the Transit Authority's proposed new subway extension to the Fair."[11]

The most powerful of New York's politicians—ranging from Republican Governor Nelson Rockefeller and Democratic Mayor Robert Wagner to Republican U.S. senator Jacob Javits from New York and Robert Moses, who controlled several seats of power in state authorities and city agencies—were working together to make the 1964–65 World's Fair a national showcase that celebrated American democracy and trumpeted future technologies that would modernize and improve urban life. Given such political consensus on this event, Brooklyn CORE planned to devise a tactic that expanded its attack on racial discrimination and forced the highest politicians in the state to address its charges that racial discrimination limited social, economic, and political opportunities for the vast majority of black and Puerto Rican citizens in the city. Brooklyn CORE's tactic was called a stall-in, and its premise was quite simple. Brooklyn CORE would send hundreds of cars with near-empty gas tanks onto highways that led to the fairgrounds in Queens. With over a quarter-million people projected to attend the fair's opening, the resultant traffic jam would be a political statement unlike any the city had seen in recent memory.

The stall-in represented a departure from other Brooklyn CORE mobilization campaigns, such as Operation Clean Sweep and the sit-down during the Ebinger's campaign. Whereas in the past its members had focused entirely on local problems of housing, employment, and schools, with the stall-in they wanted to articulate a protest that would target the effects of racism throughout the entire city and, on a symbolic level, the entire country. The stall-in would bring together all the issues of New York City's civil rights movement agenda, namely, unemployment, racial discrimination in unions, overcrowded and underfunded schools, housing discrimination, and inner-city decay. In a telegram addressed to Mayor Wagner and Governor Rockefeller, the planners of the stall-in explained their reasons for such a demonstration:

> For many years you have given lip service to the just demands of Black people of this city for equal jobs, decent housing, first class education and the right to live in peace and dignity—and for just as long, you and your agency heads, have done everything in your power to thwart these demands. . . . You have disregarded the rampant discrimination in the building trades, the brewery industry and even in your own office. You have acqui-

esced in the jailing of civil rights demonstrators, but have never seen fit to imprison or indict those who discriminate.

The people of this community are fed up with empty promises and pious pronouncements. Unless you formulate and begin to implement a comprehensive program, by April 20th, which will end police brutality, abolish slum housing and provide integrated quality education for all—we will fully support and help organize a community backed plan to immobilize all traffic leading to the World's Fair on opening day, Wednesday, April 22.[12]

Brooklyn CORE's leaders reasoned that the previous campaigns, as bold as they were, never went far enough in their use of disruptive tactics. Indeed, with each previous campaign—against housing discrimination in the Lefrak Organization, against employment discrimination at the Ebinger Baking Company, against the Department of Sanitation's discriminatory treatment of Bedford-Stuyvesant, and against racism in the building trades unions—as soon as Brooklyn CORE had dramatized its point by using creative, newsworthy tactics, chapter leaders agreed to negotiate a settlement, which cooled the public's anger and signaled to the press that the problems addressed by the demonstration had been solved. Yet the problems seemed only to worsen, an outcome that demanded that activists become more aggressive and confrontational.

Goldwag, Brunson, and Crayton also designed Brooklyn CORE's traffic-snarling stall-in with the city's increasing suburbanization in mind. Some demonstrators would lie down in front of subway cars and buses, effectively shutting down all means of travel to the fair, but the major disruption would occur on the roads. One motivation for this was to create a large enough traffic jam so that women and men trapped on highways that ran through some of New York City's most impoverished areas would be forced to observe up close the effects racial discrimination had on the everyday lives of New York City's black and Puerto Rican citizens. Stall-in organizers believed such an experience would prevent people from continuing to ignore the plight of the urban poor. As Oliver Leeds told reporters at a press conference, "Our objective is to have our own civil rights exhibit at the World's Fair. We do not see why people should enjoy themselves when Negroes are suffering all over the country."[13]

"There Will Be No Peace or Rest"

In the midst of the maelstrom of controversy that developed around the stall-in, one newspaper described Isaiah Brunson, the new chairman of

Brooklyn CORE, as a young, unpretentious, soft-spoken man "who smiles easily and who appears wholly unruffled by the nation-wide storm of protest surrounding him."[14] Indeed, some members of Brooklyn CORE pegged Brunson as a bumpkin because he lacked formal education and spoke with a slow southern drawl, and they questioned his appointment as chairman. Black nationalists in the chapter saw him as a puppet of Arnold Goldwag, who had formed a friendship with Brunson during the Downstate campaign. But in truth, Brunson and Goldwag became close because they were about the same age and advocated the use of tactics that were disruptive and antagonistic, even if they violated National CORE's rules for direct action. Since the chapter was forced to compromise on its demands with each campaign, and members had become more and more frustrated, Brunson and Goldwag reasoned that its only recourse was to put the entire city in a position that forced power brokers to take seriously their demands for an end to racial discrimination.[15]

Brunson, Goldwag, Crayton, and others thus prepared to use the stall-in to expose the widespread racial discrimination that shaped everyday life for black and Puerto Rican citizens in New York City. One of the first mentions of the stall-in in local newspapers was an article in the *New York Journal-American* that covered a speech made by Louis E. Lomax, the renowned African American journalist and author. In July 1963 Lomax insinuated during a lecture at Queens College that a stall-in might disrupt the forthcoming World's Fair. He told an audience of one thousand, "Imagine the confusion which might result if 500 people get in their cars, drive towards the Fair grounds, and run out of gas, or somebody loses a distributor."[16] The next day, a *New York Journal-American* editorial denounced the proposed stall-in as "going too far." The paper's editors believed that "stalling hundreds of autos on crowded highways is not peaceful assembly. It is a clear threat to law and order that must be prevented. . . . What [these activists] are proposing would only harm their cause by alienating the innocent citizens who would suffer untold hardship."[17]

Later editorials that appeared closer to the date of the stall-in echoed this belief that the demonstration was inherently violent and the work of a mischievous group. The *New York Journal-American* asked, "How irresponsible can some civil rights leaders get? The answer is: very. As reflected in the threat of the Brooklyn chapter of CORE to paralyze every highway to the World's Fair . . . a spokesman for national CORE repudiates the plan as 'extremely childish and silly.'"[18] The *New York Post* ruminated on essential characteristics of a proper and productive demonstration:

It is axiomatic that any effective civil rights demonstration must have both tangible and symbolic meaning plainly intelligible to the unaware bystander. Otherwise it merely serves to crystallize hostility without mobilizing any body of sympathy. It becomes an exercise in futility, or worse. . . . The projected traffic tie-up can win few converts to the civil rights banner. It will provide new ammunition for the racists—here and in Washington and in many other cities. It will create dangers as well as harassment for many innocent citizens who are not adversaries of the Freedom movement. It will leave a residue of rancor and confusion. It will in short be a form of sound and fury, carrying no clear message to most of the populace.[19]

Radio station WMCA acknowledged that "not enough progress has been made" in the civil rights movement, and it claimed it "would favor any plan that would help to wipe out bias in any part of our city and nation. But we have to oppose the plan . . . to create a mammoth traffic jam on highways leading to the World's Fair. . . . The proposed 'stall-in' would only cause an irksome, and possibly dangerous, disorder on the highways without making any civil rights advances."[20] WLIB, "Harlem Radio Center," commented that "most demonstrations for civil rights have been carried out with dignity and singleness of purpose. The March on Washington last August 28 was, of course, the greatest. It was distinguished by thoughtful planning that focused clearly on the struggle for human rights." Knowing that in some ways the March on Washington was more reflective of the movement's national leadership and not its rank and file, WLIB went on to say that "there have been other demonstrations for equality, well planned and executed. Noteworthy was the recent March on Albany, which gave citizens at the grass-roots level an opportunity to be seen and heard by their legislators." The station then went on to lambaste Brooklyn CORE:

We believe that the traffic stall-in proposed to block arteries to the World's Fair on opening day Wednesday could have disastrous, even tragic, consequences.

We doubt seriously that the Brooklyn chapter of the Congress of Racial Equality, in announcing this move, considered all the ramifications. For example, did Brooklyn CORE consider that the ordinary citizen, white or Negro, has the right to travel to the fair free of any harassment?

Did Brooklyn CORE consider that on March 3rd just one

car stalled on the East River drive and caused a 34-car collision?

In other words, what is Brooklyn CORE's purpose? Is tying up traffic on expressways with possible loss of life and limbs to innocent persons calculated to improve race relations in this city? We think not.[21]

Of course, analyses that marked the March on Washington as the pinnacle of nonviolent civil rights activism ignored the range of ideas and voices regarding the movement's tactics, leadership, and strategies present in the capital that day. SNCC leader John Lewis prepared what many march organizers considered an inflammatory speech. The original content was peppered with the word *revolution;* included incendiary criticism of the Kennedy administration's civil rights bill, calling it "too little, too late"; and closed with a rhetorical flourish that exclaimed civil rights activists would "pursue our own 'scorched earth' policy and burn Jim Crow to the ground—nonviolently" and "fragment the South into a thousand pieces and put them back together in the image of democracy."[22] Malcolm X was among the crowd on the Washington Mall, listening to the speeches and making a few informal ones of his own. So was the militant activist Gloria Richardson, who was known for carrying a gun during the sit-ins she led in Cambridge, Maryland, which attracted violent white mobs and civil rights activists who advocated armed self-defense over nonviolence. Indeed, the meaning of the March on Washington changed depending on where you looked: on the dais where the speakers professed unwavering faith in nonviolence, or in the crowd where the masses of movement foot soldiers represented a wide array of opinions on the movement's goals and the best tactics and methods of organizing for achieving them.[23]

Editorialists may have dismissed Brooklyn CORE's new tactic, but the stall-in foreshadowed what would become a radical shift in Brooklyn CORE's use of nonviolent tactics. Frustrated by the ineffectiveness of gradualist protest techniques to bring about meaningful change, stall-in organizers planned to disregard National CORE's rules for direct-action protest. They abandoned the prolonged investigations and negotiations that National CORE believed must precede nonviolent direct action. With the stall-in, Brooklyn CORE members attempted to circumvent municipal reform mechanisms and effect change on their own terms. Stall-in organizers stated in their demands that they wanted "the Mayor and City Council [to] take immediate action to right the wrongs that have been perpetrated upon Negro and Puerto Rican people for so long as a result of the apathy and callousness of the city of New York." While the national civil rights movement, particularly in the South, concentrated on securing black voting rights and eradicating racial segregation through participatory democracy, local activists in New York determined that staging an act of civil disobedience that affected the entire city was the only way to alter practices of racial discrimination as they occurred in the urban North. New forms of activism were needed to end the cycles of conciliatory tokenism. Such a shift in tactics created openings for critics to label this confrontational but still nonviolent demonstration as violent.[24]

At the same time, the stall-in appealed to other frustrated individuals and activist communities. A press release addressed to the officials of New York City and the general public from the Bronx and Brooklyn chapters of CORE summarized local frustration and ushered in a more antagonistic approach to fighting racist power structures. "More severe direct-action methods" were needed to bring attention to the city's inferior, segregated schools and inadequate housing in black and Puerto Rican neighborhoods. The press release continued its demands:

> The officials of this city must also realize that they can no longer let citizens be subjugated to beatings by "criminals" who hide behind a badge—not if there is to be any peace in this city. There will be no peace or rest until every child is afforded an opportunity to obtain high-quality education, and until significant changes are made in all areas mentioned. The World's Fair cannot be permitted to operate without protests from those who are angered by conditions which have been permitted to exist for so long—conditions which deny millions of Americans rights guaranteed them by the Constitution of the United States. We want all our freedom!!! We want it here!!! We want it Now!!![25]

"The Means Will Only Bring the Negro Further from His Goal": The Stall-in Violates Accepted Rules of Nonviolent Protest

In the weeks leading up to the fair's opening on April 22, Brooklyn CORE members distributed leaflets that encouraged people to "drive awhile for freedom" and "take only enough gas to get your car on EXHIBIT." The World's Fair showcased the country's technological and social progress, but the stall-in would exhibit the power of the grass roots to draw attention to the government's negligence regarding urban poverty and racism. The protest's demands were listed on flyers that organizers handed out on street corners throughout New York City: "We want jobs now, integrated quality education, [and an] end [to] slum housing."[26] Ed Miller was one of CORE's volunteers who distributed flyers around Bedford-Stuyvesant. A white high school student involved in Brooklyn CORE rent strikes, Miller had been born in Bedford-Stuyvesant and his family later moved around the New York City Housing Authority low-income projects in the Brownsville section of Brooklyn. Miller had joined CORE after seeing its picket lines at the local Woolworth's stores in Bedford-Stuyvesant. During the buildup to the stall-in, Miller remembered, the media attention excited many people in the community and brought "lots of unsolicited phone calls and drop-ins from people who simply liked the idea and wanted to be part of the stall-in. I did a lot of the mimeographing and sign painting, lots of putting up posters and distributing leaflets along Nostrand Avenue and at the subway stations and distributed a lot of leaflets at the projects where I lived."[27]

In addition to the stall-in, Brooklyn CORE concocted a scheme to drain the city's water supplies. "Operation Turn on the Water" called for all people living in black and Puerto Rican ghettos to open their household water faucets on the opening day of the World's Fair and simply let the water run. Frank Elder, the city's chief engineer of the Bureau of Water Supply, responded that such a tactic would have a terrible effect on the entire city's water system. Brooklyn CORE claimed that this protest was a way for people who did not own cars to express their frustration with the city's failures to address widespread forms of racial discrimination. A member of Brooklyn CORE told reporters that Operation Turn on the Water was "a sort of sit-at-home and fight-for-freedom drive."[28]

The ploy to waste water was probably a publicity stunt. Some of Brooklyn CORE's Young Turks relished their ability to devise audacious antics that sent the city's political leadership into hysterics. But, along with the stall-in, the threat to waste water drew attention to Brooklyn CORE's broader social demands. The stall-in and Operation Turn on the Water were forms of guerrilla activism: theatrical campaigns designed to disseminate a particular message, which in this case was that frustrated residents of the ghettos and activists were capable of disrupting everyday life in New York City, thereby forcing otherwise apathetic citizens and power brokers to take seriously complaints about racial discrimination and inequality. Such tactics generated an enormous response on both the local and national level, much of it shaped by the dominant discourse of the national movement. As Congress debated civil rights legislation, and national organizations such as CORE and SNCC prepared for intensifying the voter registration movement in the Deep South with a campaign called Freedom Summer, Brooklyn CORE's stall-in appeared to some people as a radical anomaly that threatened to hurt the civil rights movement. New York City's liberal Democrats saw the stall-in not only as a threat to the city's economic and social stability, but as a setback for the local and national civil rights movement. Mayor Wagner declared that he would not deal with any group that held "a gun at the heart of the city." Furthermore, he declared, "Such undertakings as the stall-in do more harm to the civil rights cause, both in Congress and here in New York City, than anything that Dixiecrat Senators can do in Washington, or that the forces of bigotry can do in the city." Brooklyn CORE had apparently become more dangerous to the civil rights movement than southern defenders of racial segregation and northern bigots.[29]

Ordinary citizens echoed these criticisms and concerns. A letter from Mary R. MacArthur, a white resident of Glen Ridge, New Jersey, and a self-defined "active participant in the Civil Rights movement," warned Brooklyn CORE of the repercussions the stall-in would have on the national movement: "I feel very strongly that the recent actions of the Brooklyn chapter of CORE may set the civil rights movement back from 2 to 4 years. . . . There are certainly hundreds of thousands of people who believe as I do . . . and among them may be MANY workers in this struggle whose support you may lose if you continue along this path."[30] John Keating from Yonkers, New York, echoed these sentiments. He wrote to Isaiah Brunson, the chairman of Brooklyn CORE, "I am a white man. I was all for the Civil Rights bill to help the colored people. I don't like the violence that's being used now such as the Stall-In. If I had to vote now, I would vote against it. It shows by the actions of your people they are not ready for us to accept them as equal. P.S. I shall write to Washington hoping to stall the Civil Rights Bill now."[31] Black citizens also encouraged Brooklyn CORE to rethink its plans for the stall-in. Myra Zuckerman, whose daughter had died en route to a hospital because of traffic tie-ups, wrote: "After hearing your threats to stall cars on roads . . . I can only feel shock and fear. I am a Negro myself, and I know and understand what you're fighting for. . . . These demonstrations you proposed can only cause other Americans to call and think us unpatriotic and unfit for the rights of citizens. . . . Many times the end justifies the means but in this case the means will only bring the Negro further from his goal." The same held for Brooklyn CORE's threat to waste water. Mary Caraballo, a black resident on 213th street in the

Bronx, hoped the city's response would be to turn off all water lines that fed into black neighborhoods, even if that decision harmed black citizens who were not involved with Brooklyn CORE. In the face of such a seemingly dangerous protest, Caraballo concluded, "The good will have to suffer along with the bad."[32]

Robert Moses, president of the fair, concentrated on ways to punish participants in the stall-in. Moses, like many New Yorkers who opposed the stall-in, was quick to enlist the power of the state to thwart the protest. Some in the press believed the stall-in participants should be fined, but Moses did not think a financial penalty was harsh enough. Existing laws allowed police to revoke registrations of all vehicles that were driven recklessly or endangered public safety, which included running out of gas. They also empowered the state commissioner of Motor Vehicles to revoke drivers' licenses for the same reasons; and Moses believed that participation in the stall-in was also legal grounds for cancellation of a person's automobile liability insurance. "A fine is not the answer," Moses told the president and publisher of the *Daily News*. Moses thought that people who participated in the stall-in essentially created a menace on public roads and highways and therefore forfeited their right to drive.[33]

The public weighed in with more inventive solutions to the potential traffic nightmare. Meier Steinbrink, a New York Supreme Court judge from Brooklyn, suggested that if people who blocked roads did not move their automobiles, the Department of Sanitation should use bulldozers and road scrapers to push cars off the highways. "If the cars in the process should be damaged," Steinbrink reasoned, "that will be the fault of the drivers." Louis Cook of Long Island City, New York, agreed with that idea and thought motorists on their way to the fair should be allowed to use their own vehicles to push the stall-in participants off the road. Robert Nehring of Scarsdale, New York, agreed with scores more who suggested that Robert Moses "post numerous volunteers with quantities of five-gallon containers of gas to be distributed free along affected highways every 100 feet." He thought Moses should seek volunteers first from civil rights groups that opposed the stall-in, and call the effort "Gallons for Galamison," in honor of the activist reverend. Other citizens thought the mayor and Moses should mobilize helicopter and motorcycle squadrons. The motorcycle patrols could quickly identify stalled cars, dispatch officers to fill gas tanks of those vehicles, and then drive the protestors' cars off the road. If a car was completely disabled, one citizen thought a large helicopter could lift it over to a side street. Probably the most outrageous suggestion Moses received came from William Sunners, a teacher at Junior High School 227 in Brooklyn. The solution was not trucks, motorcycles, or helicopters, Sunners argued. "All you need are about 200 strong wooden bridge ramps," he wrote to Moses, along with a sketch of his proposed contraption. "When a car stalls, just place one of these ramps over the stalled car and let traffic proceed. . . . You can place these bridge ramps at strategic spots along the main traffic arteries a day in advance and foil the efforts of the plotters." The stall-in inspired wildly inventive plans in which the full power of the state stymied protestors, but such power seemed unavailable to stop the discriminatory practices the stall-in sought to redress.[34]

Other letters reflected more violent and racist opposition to the stall-in. An unsigned letter to the Brooklyn CORE office told Arnold Goldwag, the chapter's public relations chairman, that "it is Communist kikes such as you that cause the hatred by so many for law abiding Jewish people. Watch out!"[35] Margaret V. Martyn, the chairwoman of the White Teachers of America, wrote: "Why you miserable black sonofabitch! How dare you threaten the Worlds Fair and the Christian White Power structure of this City? You nigger bastards belong in Africa not here among genteel white Christian folk! We hope the police break your black ape heads on Wednesday! So drop dead!" Brooklyn CORE's plan to waste water stoked the anger of one citizen who succinctly evoked a host of stereotypes about the black "underclass" in a postcard to Brooklyn CORE that read, "Waste water? How heroic! Maybe you misfits don't use the stuff (judging by the leeward odor) but we bigots, racists, mugger-victims and relief payers – we do." The writer chose not to sign the card and instead voiced support for "Apartheid Now!"[36]

Letters to local papers were equally reactionary. Jerry H. Gumpert wrote to the *Post* that "close to half a million people from all corners of the globe are expected to witness the opening of the New York World's Fair and a group of fanatics plan to shame us all with their stall-in."[37] "A. White" wrote to the *Daily News:* "To the Negro voicer who wrote 'We shall overcome,' all I can say is that you might have a very long wait, like maybe another 100 years. These current animalistic tactics will only set you big bunch of idiots back about that much."[38] Mrs. L. W. from Queens pleaded with the *New York World Telegram and Sun* that "it is time for your newspaper to cease giving so much space to the little dictators of the Brooklyn CORE. Having magnified their position by the continuous limelight you give them, it is difficult for them to back down without losing 'face.'"[39] On the other hand, Charles T. Jackson, from Woodmere, New York, wrote to the *New York Herald Tribune* and voiced a need for cooperation from both protestors and government officials. He also predicted the repercussions that would result if politicians failed to make good on their promises to ameliorate conditions afflicting a majority of the city's poor African American and Puerto Rican citizens. "For Brooklyn CORE the moral would seem that the wisest course is negotiation spurred by non-violent demonstrations relevant to specific grievances. The authorities must see that the need for sympathetic negotiations followed by effective action is urgent—before frustration does lead to such attacks as are now just beginning to be advocated."[40]

From editorials and letters we can discern a public discourse on protest violence that demonized stall-in supporters and marginalized their critiques of policies of racial discrimination and demands for political change. During the postwar civil rights movement, a national public discourse that supported nonviolent civil disobedience developed after televised images showed police and white citizens violently suppressing peaceful demonstrations in the South. White southerners, however, criticized nonviolent civil rights activists who demanded social and political equality as "troublemakers" who instigated violence among generally peaceful people. Black ministers even criticized Martin Luther King Jr. for leading demonstrations in Birmingham that invited intense levels of violence and disturbance. In the context of the Cold War, however, the White House feared how images of violent attacks on peaceful demonstrators would be seen around the world, especially as Communist propagandists used them to expose lies behind American claims of spreading freedom and democracy among former European colonies in Africa, Asia, and Latin America. Thus, at the national level the Kennedy and later the Johnson administrations reluctantly supported the calls for protection of voter registration workers and nonviolent protesters working to desegregate public facilities in the South. Newspapers and television stations also shaped this public discourse with their dramatic portrayals of police dogs mauling peaceful demonstrators and fire hoses blasting nonviolent protestors to the ground. The dominant public discourse placed the stall-in as completely outside any hierarchy of acceptable protest tactics. People perceived the stall-in as violent and its participants as irresponsible and reckless. For many editorialists, citizens, politicians, and national civil rights leaders, these perceptions shaped the ways they dealt with Brooklyn CORE.[41]

Indeed, there was nothing "violent" about the idea of a stall-in. In a letter to the New York Post, Frederick Lydecker explained that the actual motive and purpose of the stall-in was "to demonstrate power," not to gain supporters for black and Puerto Rican people's civil rights. He predicted that "extensions of the stall-in technique can be expected until the Negro's aspirations are fully met." "Is it really so difficult to meet these aspirations?" Lydecker wondered. "They consist merely of immediate, effective and complete school integration, preferential hiring and promotion to correct economic injustice, and weightage of the Negro vote to attain political equality." Given the simplicity and necessity of these goals, Lydecker marveled "not at the Negro's importunity" with the dreaded stall-in, but instead at the demonstration's "restraint." Mrs. Freeman, a resident of Bedford-Stuyvesant, expressed her support of the stall-in in a letter to Brooklyn CORE. "More power to you and your chapter for the stall-in at the World Fair," she wrote, and stated that "many people are behind you and money will be sent to keep your unit alive." She compared the stall-in with "white race strikes against the government when their grievance is not met." "They never give up till they get what they want," Mrs. Freeman concluded, "and we have to have guts too."[42]

Large traffic jams are practically part of everyday life in modern cities, so it was not the stall-in's disruptive property that was "violent." Rather, when compared with other protests and demonstrators of the era, the rhetoric and tactics of the stall-in were an aberration. Pictures of events in the South defined the "reality" of civil rights protest for most people in 1964. The movement was black schoolchildren being turned away from schools, or black citizens being terrorized for attempting to eat at a department store lunch counter or to vote. The meaning of the movement was most commonly associated with the August 1963 March on Washington and Martin Luther King Jr.'s mantra, "I Have a Dream!" According to the dominant televised discourse in 1964, it was also about whites committing *real* violence against protestors. With the stall-in, Brooklyn CORE planned to affect as many people as possible because of its belief that all members of society were responsible for maintaining racist structures *and* for eventually eradicating them. Up to this point, social protest advocated this idea in theory but did not incorporate it into its public demonstrations, which were mostly limited to economic boycotts and civil disobedience that targeted specific institutions: department stores, five-and-dime lunch counters, schools, voter registration drives. Thus, most stall-in critics felt that they were being victimized. To those people the World's Fair and American racism had nothing to do with each other. The idea of sitting in miles and miles of traffic "violently" intruded on most people's belief that racism was someone else's problem—namely, the government's—to remedy.

The most vocal criticisms of the stall-in came from politicians and from the ranks of moderate leaders of national civil rights organizations, who viewed the stall-in as a threat to the movement. Roy Wilkins of the NAACP dismissed the stall-in and marginalized its organizers as "strictly Brooklynese," which, given Brooklyn's reputation for scrappy, uneducated, working-class immigrants, was a tongue-in-cheek way to characterize Brooklyn CORE members as uncivilized and backward compared to the mainstream civil rights organizations and leaders.[43] James Farmer, national director of CORE, suspended the Brooklyn chapter for its plans to go through with the stall-in. In a telegram sent to Isaiah Brunson, Farmer stated, "Your chapter and all members thereof are immediately ordered to refrain from making any public statements and any news releases or taking any actions in the name of CORE."[44] In a newspaper article Farmer commented that the stall-in would "merely create confusion and thus damage the fight for freedom." The city traffic commissioner said that the stall-in would "paralyze the whole city. It would take a week to untangle the mess." And the police commissioner commented that the stall-in "ignored the civil rights of others to work and play without interference."[45] Senators Hubert H. Humphrey (D-Minnesota) and Thomas Kuchel (R-California), the floor managers for the civil rights legislation in Congress, expressed concern about the white resentment and violence the stall-in would generate. "Violence," they said, "is the very antithesis of law and order. Illegal disturbances, demonstrations which lead to violence or to injury, strike grievous blows at the cause of decent civil rights legislation." Their short-term memories had forgotten that King's movements were based on provoking whites into violent retaliation against peaceful demonstrators or imprisoning them for demanding basic civil and human rights. Humphrey and Kuchel wanted to ignore the reality that violence against protestors had actually spurred them to expedite civil rights legislation. Instead, in their criticisms of the stall-in, they stated that the fight for black equality would be furthered if rights advocates conducted "their peaceful crusade with the same good manners, forbearance and devotion so abundantly displayed in last August 28th's civil rights march on Washington."[46]

Brooklyn CORE did not waver in its radical plans. Its members were certainly devoted to equality, but they had learned that politicians ignored civil rights activists the most when demonstrators exhibited good manners and patience. In fact, members reveled in their status as a radical chapter in the seemingly conservative National CORE organization. Gilbert Banks, who had been radicalized by his inability to gain employment in construction unions despite his expertise as a mechanic and heavy equipment operator, explained his attachment to Brooklyn

CORE: it "was a very radical CORE. National CORE didn't want us to do the World's Fair in '64 and they wanted to kick us out of National CORE and we took the blows. We don't care what you do."[47] The rogue chapter did receive support from other CORE chapters in Manhattan and the Bronx, who claimed they would help stall cars on the highways leading to the fair. The Camden, New Jersey, chapter of CORE sent a telegram to National CORE that "urgently requests that every effort be made . . . to settle the differences with the Brooklyn chapter so that national unity will be maintained." Even from the West Coast, a group called Seattle Friends of the Student Nonviolent Coordinating Committee declared its "heartiest support" for Brooklyn CORE, "for your plans at the World's Fair. Your courageous action is a fine example to others across the country. You do not stand alone."[48] Indeed, Brooklyn CORE did not stand alone, especially on its home turf. Some municipal labor organizations even went against city officials and supported the stall-in. John J. Delury, president of the Sanitation Men's Local 831, said that all 10,000 of his men would stay home on April 22 if they were asked to tow cars. "We're not going to scab on anyone fighting for freedom or civil rights," he said.[49]

Brooklyn CORE's members remained focused on their objective. Arnold Goldwag reminded critics that Brooklyn CORE had an "ultimate responsibility to the people of this community who look to us for leadership and for solutions to the long-standing problem of discrimination and exploitation." Oliver Leeds emphasized the role Brooklyn's black citizens would play in the stall-in: "It's not so much that CORE is planning [the stall-in] but that the man in the street is going to do it. From what I've heard in Bedford-Stuyvesant, neither CORE nor anyone else is going to be able to stop him. That's the beauty of this whole operation." Brunson summarized the need for the radical nature of the stall-in in his responses to people who had written to the Brooklyn office:

> As you are obviously aware, we have up until this very day used every means at our disposal to awaken the City Fathers of New York to the crying needs of their city. We have picketed, boycotted, sat-in, lied-in, etc. All of our efforts have been in vain.
>
> The time has come. The Power structure of this city, state, and country must be made to realize that we will accept palliation no longer. Empty promises, investigative committees, and such have done nothing to alleviate the problems that exist.
>
> We have, therefore, been forced into the position of using the only path left open to us. Our demands are simple. They can

be instituted immediately, and do not necessitate the passage of any new laws. Rather, all we are actually asking is that all existing laws are enforced.

Enforcing antidiscrimination laws and creating an open, democratic society, Brooklyn CORE learned over the years, did not come easily for elected officials, power brokers, and even ordinary citizens. Brooklyn CORE's "simple" demands were, even for liberals and "friends" of the civil rights movement, not at all simple. A glaring irony of the entire stall-in scare was that, as noted earlier, in the words of Craig Wilder, "the entire authority of the state could be marshaled so easily and effectively to stop a protest of racial inequalities, but was not available to prevent those injustices." Ordinary citizens and power brokers were quick to suggest multiple, inventive, expensive solutions for thwarting the stall-in, but when it came to redressing racial discrimination in schools, housing, and jobs, many people's response was to continue to blame black people for their own poverty, congested neighborhoods, and underresourced schools. Preventing civil rights activism and punishing audacious activists seemed to be a bigger priority for city officials and everyday citizens than addressing the types of inequality Brooklyn CORE's stall-in highlighted.[50]

The Most Successful Protest That Never Happened

Fear, along with an unseasonably chilly drizzle, dampened the mood in Flushing Meadows Park on April 22, 1964. Only 49,642 people attended the first day of the World's Fair, a number far short of the quarter million expected by the World's Fair's president, Robert Moses. City officials said the threat of the stall-in, combined with the cold weather, kept people away. Robert Caro writes that Moses ascribed the low attendance to "overdramatization" of the stall-in "and to chilly, drizzly weather. But attendance the next day, clear and warm, was 88,130. On the first weekend there were crowds each day of 170,000. But during the following week, the fatal figures read: 45,000; 53,000; 38,000."[51] Many who attended the opening day of the World's Fair opted to take public transportation, so there were few cars on the roads. The one thousand patrolmen working that day probably did not see much traffic.[52] Police arrested twenty-three protestors for lying down on subway tracks at the 74th Street IRT station in Queens and delaying a train bound for the World's Fair. Transit Authority and city police inflicted severe head injuries on five subway demonstrators by beating them with nightsticks. Though the stall-in disrupted the opening day of the World's Fair by generating high levels of fear and anxiety, there were no paralyzing traffic jams. Gilbert Banks was reportedly the only person who disrupted traffic with a stalled car that day.[53] The organizers seemed far better at publicizing this action than at coordinating it.

The guerrilla theater and media storm that led up to the fair's opening day constituted the protest action, not Brooklyn CORE's ability to orchestrate massive, citywide traffic jams. Former Brooklyn CORE members speculated about different reasons the chapter did not stall cars on the roads that morning. According to Frances Phipps Crayton, the chapter's vice chairwoman during the stall-in, one major reason Brooklyn CORE did not mobilize a significant number of automobiles for the stall-in was that organizers feared the police had infiltrated the chapter and could use a list of specific names of persons who volunteered to stall their cars on the highways to thwart the entire campaign. Brooklyn CORE did not organize a specific roster of participants out of fear of government retaliation against stall-in volunteers. Those who would stall their cars would do so on their own, at random, and in such a way as to have no clear connection to the planned protest. In the end, few decided to participate in the stall-in. Perhaps Crayton and other Young Turks framed these rationales as a way to cover up their poor logistical planning of the protest. But in some ways they did not even have to follow through with their plan because, as numerous former Brooklyn CORE members remembered, there were few cars traveling to the World's Fair, or anywhere in New York City, on the advertised day of the stall-in. Almost 50,000 people attended the fair's opening day, and they could not all have taken public transportation. Brooklyn CORE members overstated the effectiveness of the stall-in media campaign, but even without the massive stall-in, the weeks of media coverage leading up to the opening day and the spectacle of a demonstration that descended on the fair during its first weeks touched a nerve with many citizens, who began their own backlash protest.[54]

The Payton family canceled its trip from Ohio to New York City after reading in local newspapers about the civil rights demonstrators who targeted the World's Fair. Referring to the "degrading spectacle" of picket lines outside the World's Fair construction sites, Joseph Payton told the World's Fair Corporation that he and his wife did "not wish to subject our children to such inhuman actions." Edward Meadows of Fort Wayne, Indiana, remarked that "disgraceful demonstrations by CORE" caused his family to cancel their trip to New York City to visit the World's Fair. "It seems a shame to miss out on seeing something as wonderful as the World's Fair," Meadows complained, but protest was the only fit way for him to respond to what he saw as Democratic pandering to special interest. "As long as the politicians are greedy enough to sell the country down the river for the sake of the Negro vote," Meadows concluded, "decent citizens will miss out on many things," including the privilege of enjoying the World's Fair's celebration of national "progress" without having to consider the lack of progress black New Yorkers experienced after decades of living in the city. After witnessing on the news the large numbers of nonviolent civil rights demonstrations that targeted World's Fair pavilions on the opening day, many of them organized by National CORE as its way of opposing Brooklyn CORE's stall-in, Walter Wasser of Los Angeles said the only way he'd attend the fair would be if New York State "guaranteed free hospitalization should I run across some of those hoodlums in the daylight," or if the state would allow him to carry his .38-caliber Smith and Wesson in public for protection. Jack Pinkston of Silver Spring, Maryland, seethed when he learned the World's Fair and New York State liberalism permitted "certain fanatical Negroes and other subversive groups to harass, intimidate, and even endanger the lives, persons and property of white American citizens in New York City and the World's Fair." He simply canceled the vacation his family of six had planned to spend in New York. W. C. Kottemann of Metairie, Louisiana, was more direct in his opposition to "how much mixing of niggers and whites was permitted" at the fair. But one New Yorker decided to boycott the fair precisely because its administration and the city had taken such a hard stance against protestors. Sylvia Tatz of Levittown, Long Island, was "shocked" to learn that four women "who had been picketing peacefully" at the fair were arrested. "We are supposed to be setting an example to the Southern states of our democracy and liberality, and pickets are arrested like criminals."[55]

But the entire purpose of the stall-in was to highlight the ways New York City's democracy and liberality were just as destructive to black citizenship as the South's system of Jim Crow segregation. Indeed, the historical significance of the stall-in lies in the grassroots organizers' refusal to work within a system they felt gave them nothing for their efforts. As activists engaged the city's reform mechanism on its own terms, real change for poor citizens of color remained an illusion. Thus, Brooklyn CORE decided that it had to go outside the tactical rules of engagement. When Congress passed civil rights legislation in June 1964, for example, little actually changed in the streets of Bedford-Stuyvesant and Harlem. One Harlem resident remarked that the Civil Rights Bill was "still a piece of paper. Let's wait until the letter of the law is carried out."[56] Brooklyn CORE's threat to create havoc throughout the city on the opening day of the World's Fair spoke directly to these issues and signaled a new direction in the local and national movement. If the laws could not improve the lives of struggling citizens, community activists would employ more antagonistic and radical measures to exert power over their lives, and thus change the focuses, tactics, and language of their political activism.

Brooklyn CORE's stall-in demonstrated how local movements had the ability to spread and inspire other activists' protest tactics and ideas about effective ways to bring about social change. Ivory Perry, of St. Louis CORE, responded to National CORE's request that members come to New York City and help with the picket lines that Farmer would lead outside the fairgrounds. While in New York, Perry came in contact with members of the Brooklyn chapter and learned about their stall-in. He supported the tactic because he "felt that the life-and-death issues facing black people, and their exclusion from access to political power, justified obstructive actions like the stall-in." Eleven months after Brooklyn CORE's stall-in, Perry brought the tactic to St. Louis in order to focus attention on the recent string of violent attacks against blacks and movement workers in Selma, Alabama. On March 15, 1965, along with Ernest Gilkey, another of St. Louis's "local people," Perry stalled a truck at a busy exit ramp off Highway 40 in St. Louis's Central West End. His intent was to create a massive traffic tie-up that would paralyze the city.[57]

The activist comedian Dick Gregory elicited laughs from audiences around the country when he joked about the stall-in in his 1964 stand-up performance, "So You See . . . We All Have Problems." He told a Midwestern audience: "I was in New York City for the stall-in. Got there early that morning, was walking through Harlem, and right next to a filling station, a cat walked up to me and said, 'Hey, baby, can you loan me three pennies? I want to buy some gas. I'm driving to the World's Fair.' One cat pulled into the filling station, looked at the attendant and said, 'Empty me up!'" The crowd responded with vociferous laughter and applause. Gregory even commented on the conclusion that the stall-in and other demonstrations were total failures, a position that failed to see how the stall-in effectively prevented the city and fair organizers from profiting from discriminatory practices. "And at the fair, you know the attendance was down so low on opening day of the fair," Gregory said. "They had big signs out in front of the World's Fair that said, 'Welcome picketers.'" In an interview with *Playboy*, Dick Gregory accentuated the contradictions in people's quick condemnation of the stall-in and uncritical support for legislative processes as a means of ending racism in America. To the question "Do you feel that such extreme tactics are either wise or justified?" Gregory said, "Yes. If the duly elected senior citizens of this country, the United States Senators, can hold a stall-in in the sacred halls of Congress, a second-class citizen ought to be able to hold one on a bloody American highway."[58]

Though we can and should debate the effectiveness of the stall-in and of similar disruptive tactics in social movements that seek to challenge status quo power dynamics in society, those who dismiss them outright as immature and foolhardy miss the ways that such antagonistic measures are meant to create disturbances that force *all* citizens to consider how racial discrimination shapes many patterns of privilege and privation in society. The history of the stall-in demonstrates the ways that public discourses shape "acceptable" forms of social protest, which, in effect, puts limits on activists' abilities to illuminate social problems and patterns of systemic inequality. Labeling the stall-in as inherently "violent" automatically placed it outside conventional methods of direct-action protest, which allowed citizens, politicians, and editorialists to ignore Brooklyn CORE's call to end practices of racial discrimination in various facets of social, economic, and political life in New York City.

Indeed, by 1964 members of Brooklyn CORE felt that something as antagonistic and provocative as the stall-in was the only tactic that would make citizens and politicians listen to the chapter's demands for a more egalitarian and democratic city. The large amount of media attention generated by the tactic gave Brooklyn CORE's message a platform, and for one last time the chapter was able to powerfully insert into public political discourse a conversation about systematic forms of racial discrimination in New York City and a debate about the best ways for citizens to try to eliminate those practices from their social lives. But like its past campaigns, the stall-in resulted in few, if any, concrete changes. In fact, Brooklyn CORE's more focused campaigns from 1960 to 1964 at least forced power brokers to negotiate with the chapter's leaders and make promises to change aspects of their discriminatory policies or, in some cases, such as Operation Clean Sweep, to ameliorate the situations Brooklyn CORE revealed with improved services. But, for the most part, many promises went unfulfilled. Brooklyn CORE's use of dramatic direct-action protest had established it as a forceful, dynamic, and creative organization that landlords, politicians, and corporate leaders were forced to reckon with, but its victories were often piecemeal and incomplete.

The stall-in may have been the chapter's most symbolic victory of all, since that tactic did not actually have to happen to produce at least one of its desired effects: lessening the number of people who attended the fair's opening day. Brooklyn CORE can take some credit for the World's Fair's dismal attendance that day, and even for the rest of the first week, but for the most part the campaign's demands fell on deaf ears. Chapter leaders never even won an audience with the governor or the mayor, and the demands that Brooklyn CORE raised during the stall-in—for better schools in poor black neighborhoods; for decent, affordable housing; for an end to racial discrimination in government funded projects; and for an end of police brutality against blacks—continued to be items on Brooklyn's political agenda into the late 1960s and later. But some activists during the latter half of the decade picked up where Brooklyn CORE's stall-in had left off. Heightened militancy and calls for greater local control over political and economic resources in Brooklyn's predominantly black sections shaped activism and politics during the mid- to late 1960s and altered the face of power in the city for the remainder of the century. And if the stall-in was not a clear enough barometer of the escalating tensions percolating within Brooklyn's protest movement, Bedford-Stuyvesant, along with Harlem, became a site of some of the first waves of urban violence that rocked the nation in the late 1960s. Demands for greater civic power were always a part of the northern civil rights movement, but nothing made clearer the failures of urban liberalism to those who chose to ignore activists like the ones in Brooklyn CORE than the explosion of the simmering social pressure cooker that had lain hidden in north-central Brooklyn.

Brooklyn CORE's interracial, nonviolent, direct-action protest movement may have ended in the mid-1960s, but other social movements would form in its wake. People in Brooklyn—black, white, Latino, and others—would develop many different ways to protest the racial discrimination that shaped their social worlds. They would also develop new organizations and political agendas, and some of them, like early 1960s Brooklyn CORE's, were firmly committed to remaking Brooklyn into the just, democratic society that many of its residents believed their borough could become.

Conclusion

"BROOKLYN STANDS WITH SELMA"

Things are moving, but the whites have got to understand that we are flesh and blood, and we want our rights now, and through protest is the only way we are going to get it.
                    —Bedford-Stuyvesant resident, July 1964

After the stall-in, Brooklyn CORE members struggled to find an action campaign. The Young Turks faded away from power. Isaiah Brunson disappeared from the organization. Oliver Leeds remembered that Brunson was so disturbed by the logistical failures of the stall-in that he never recognized its success in keeping people off the roads that day. The rest of his cohort stepped aside and let more moderate leaders come to the fore, although Arnold Goldwag remained as the public relations chairman.[1]

Many of the same people who had been members of Brooklyn CORE since 1960 remained involved to some degree, albeit in lesser roles. Although no longer chairman, Oliver Leeds continued to advise the chapter's leadership cadre and participate in meetings. Marjorie Leeds and Mary Ellen Phifer divided their time between Brooklyn CORE and the Parents' Workshop, which had organized the massive one-day school boycott in February 1964 and continued its grassroots efforts to gather community support for widespread reform of the school system. But since Brooklyn CORE had slowly moved away from the types of community-organizing efforts it experimented with during Operation Clean Sweep and the Bibuld campaign, Marjorie Leeds and Phifer no longer felt it was the type of organization in which they, as individuals, could have the most influence. Others, like Elaine Bibuld, felt tired and frustrated after the stall-in and turned their attention toward their home lives. She spoke for others of her cohort who "felt that our time had gone and it was about time for us to get out of it. And our children were becoming teenagers and needed us at home and things like that."[2]

Maurice Fredericks continued to attend meetings, and he began bringing younger blacks from the neighborhood as his guests. Sonny Carson, who had gravitated toward Brooklyn CORE during the Downstate campaign, was a frequent visitor to Brooklyn CORE meetings in late 1964 and throughout 1965. Fredericks remained committed to his friends in Brooklyn CORE, but he also gravitated toward local activists who were more aligned with black nationalism than the African Americans still in the chapter.[3]

Rioghan Kirchner remained a member of Brooklyn CORE's Housing Committee, but she also formed an interracial housing advocacy group in a small, predominantly white old fishing community in Brooklyn called Sheepshead Bay. She and some of her black and white friends from the neighborhood's public housing projects, which were the most integrated residential areas of the community, called their group Freedom Organizations Coordinated for Unity in Shorefronts (FOCUS) and modeled it after Brooklyn CORE as an action-oriented, interracial organization.[4]

But the political and social winds in Brooklyn, and indeed in many other cities with large, racially segregated, poor black populations, had started to change direction as early as the summer of 1964. During the hot weeks of July, the failure of the city to address many of the problems with housing, schools, and jobs that civil rights activists in Brooklyn CORE had brought to its attention boiled over into one of the nation's first urban "race riots" of the 1960s. As had been the case when riots broke out in New York City earlier in the twentieth century, the spark that ignited the summertime violence was an incident of police brutality. The murder of a fifteen-year-old African American boy by a white, off-duty police officer rubbed raw the deep wounds of social isolation, political frustration, and economic alienation that Brooklyn CORE had tried to correct through its numerous direct-action protest campaigns.[5]

When Lieutenant Thomas Gilligan shot and killed James Powell on the streets of the Upper East Side on the morning of July 16, 1964, he had no clue that his actions would be the touchstone for several days of violence in Harlem and Bedford-Stuyvesant. He probably thought he was coming to the aid of a white superintendent who, witnesses said, was attacked by black teenagers after he sprayed them with water, shouted racial epithets, and ordered them to move from the steps of one of his apartment buildings. The teens reacted by throwing bottles and garbage at the superintendent, and Powell was one of a few teens who chased him into an apartment building. When Powell exited the vestibule, Gilligan shot him three times. Powell was dead by the time ambulances arrived.[6]

Two days later Harlem erupted into violence that left one person dead, twelve policemen and nineteen civilians injured, thirty arrested, and twenty-two businesses looted. By July 20, when Harlem had cooled off, the violence continued in Bedford-Stuyvesant. Brooklyn CORE held a rally to protest Powell's murder and repeated a long-standing demand among New York City's civil rights activists for an independent civilian review board to hear and adjudicate police brutality cases. The rally attracted over one thousand people, and police officers drew their nightsticks and charged the crowd after participants threw bottles and smashed businesses' windows. More of the same continued the following night; CORE members worked with police to restore order. Oliver Leeds recalled that he and nearly one hundred other CORE supporters tried to instruct young people on the streets not to run. "If you come out of one of those stores," he remembered instructing people, "walk. Don't run. The minute you run, a policeman will assume that you are guilty of something and will shoot at you." The presence of so many civil rights activists may have had some positive effect because no one was killed that night. But the crowd was clearly not in a mood to cool off. Police officers mounted on horses stormed the area. Members of the mob attacked them with bottles and rocks. Civil rights activists who urged nonviolence were caught in the crossfire. Eighteen police officers were injured; those who tallied that number did not count the brutally bloodied citizens. Police arrested 302 people; 405 windows of clothing stores, groceries, check-cashing facilities, and liquor stores were broken. When sociologists surveyed residents of the neighborhood shortly after the riot and asked how they thought the trouble could have been avoided, the largest proportion of respondents blamed the riot on the failures of "the white establishment" to adequately address social problems in Bedford-Stuyvesant.[7]

Such violence and growing frustration with the piecemeal results of civil rights protest made Brooklyn CORE's earlier approaches to battling racial discrimination seem passé. What was the point of using nonviolent, direct-action protest to win access to jobs, housing, and quality public education if power brokers in government and unions turned a blind eye and a deaf ear to the demonstrations or blamed black people's culture and behavior for causing the very social and economic conditions civil rights activists sought to change? Brooklyn CORE tried to maintain its relevance during the months after the stall-in and the riots, but it never captured the public imagination or highlighted systematic racial discrimination through creative dramatic protests the same way that it had during the early 1960s.

After 1964 Major Owens, the librarian who spearheaded Brooklyn CORE's rent strike movement in 1963, stepped into the position of chairman. Owens was strongly committed to CORE's interracial philosophy. Initially, Owens seemed as though he would push the chapter toward community-organizing activities, in which Brooklyn CORE brought together ordinary citizens and worked with them to develop political solutions for their social and economic problems. Brooklyn CORE members placed a great deal of confidence in him to develop a more focused agenda for the chapter, and throughout the spring of 1964 the chapter continued organizing rent strikes. Brooklyn CORE's rent strikes might have generated more long-term success mobilizing black communities and building membership, but in 1965 Owens shifted the chapter's focus to voter registration drives. This effort did little to build a neighborhood-based social movement among poor black people in Brooklyn.

Brooklyn CORE's voter registration campaign was the interracial chapter's last effort at establishing a strong foothold in local activist politics. Owens modeled Brooklyn CORE's effort after the Mississippi Freedom Democratic Party (MFDP), which rose to national prominence during the summer of 1964 when its democratically elected, majority-black delegation attempted to unseat the all-white delegation that officially represented Mississippi at the Democratic National Convention in Atlantic City, New Jersey. Even though the MFDP received a great deal of press and was the culmination of a tremendous grassroots organizing campaign, it did not succeed in unseating the all-white delegation. Some of Mississippi's civil rights leaders became nationally known civil rights figures. Fannie Lou Hamer's speeches on the boardwalk, her televised testimony before the leaders of the Democratic Party, and her plaintive singing of freedom songs were inspirational and moving, but the MFDP's principled fight won only two at-large seats. Owens and members in Brooklyn CORE decided to try to build off the attention this stance brought to voting rights issues and initiate a similar effort with residents of Bedford-Stuyvesant.[8]

Brooklyn CORE attempted to arrange the Brooklyn Freedom Democratic Movement (BFDM) as a community-organizing effort to increase electoral participation in Bedford-Stuyvesant. The BFDM's main focus was to support Major Owens's candidacy for election to the City Council in the fall of 1965. Other members of Brooklyn CORE rejected this strategy and thought the chapter should return to its tactics of mobilizing dramatic actions and making large-scale demands on the city to improve employment, housing, and public education in Bedford-Stuyvesant. The BFDM certainly touched on a relevant issue in black Brooklynites' lives: voting districts in north-central Brooklyn were gerrymandered in ways that prevented black voters from banding together as a bloc to elect their own representative to Congress. Still, the type of grassroots organizing campaign against voter disenfranchisement that rallied people to action in the Magnolia State did not necessarily have the same effect in Kings County, New York. In the end, Brooklyn CORE floundered and lacked commitment to the BFDP initiative and its attempt to stage a dramatic mobilization campaign.[9]

Two mobilization actions that failed to bring Brooklyn CORE back to its roots of dramatic direct-action protests were the organization's 1964 "Boycott for Freedom," and the 1965 "Operation Beautify Bedford-Stuyvesant." The Boycott for Freedom encouraged local blacks to boycott sardines imported from Angola, which was a Portuguese colony, and products from South Africa. A flyer for the campaign read: "Every time you buy a can of Portuguese sardines you help pay for a bullet in a black man's back in Angola; a can of South African lobster tails buys two bullets for a Dutchman's gun. Don't buy bullets for your black brother's back!" The Operation Beautify Bedford-Stuyvesant plan listed twenty-eight items that the city needed to provide to improve the quality of life in the neighborhood. They ranged from a transfer of brutal police officers out of Bedford-Stuyvesant and into predominantly white areas to a rat-elimination program, more streetlights, and "a minimum requisite of a tree every fifty feet."[10]

Brooklyn CORE's leaders eventually ceased the boycott and criticized it as being too disconnected from the everyday needs of Bedford-Stuyvesant's residents. Though the Boycott for Freedom reflected a growing international consciousness among some civil rights activists, Brooklyn CORE leaders eventually realized that the campaign was too disconnected from CORE's central values: interracialism and nonviolent direct-action campaigns that targeted specific cases of racial discrimination. "Imported Portuguese sardines made with Angola slave labor and sold in Bedford-Stuyvesant is surely reprehensible," a Brooklyn CORE training program manual stated. "But this is hardly the best product to stage a boycott around." The manual went on to say, "Projects should be based on specific complaints coming from the black community. Or they should be based on known grievances of that area. . . . A good

CORE community project is one that is of close personal concern to the local citizen. Projects that lend themselves to this approach usually are housing complaints, consumer-merchant relations, poor city services, job discrimination, unemployment and segregated school problems."[11] Brooklyn CORE's manual also rejected Operation Beautify Bedford-Stuyvesant because it involved petitioning city hall and demanding government reform, which Brooklyn CORE members had learned was not the best way to organize people. "If a project has to be fought out at City Hall," they now argued, it would have less appeal to people "on the streets of the black community." Brooklyn CORE stressed that "an essential ingredient of a good CORE community project is that it personally affect people in the community."[12]

The BFDM did not seem to have a personal effect on local people, but Brooklyn CORE still invested most of 1965 in this community-organizing campaign, which became little more than an attempt to get Major Owens elected to the City Council. The BFDM was a clear indication that the chapter was struggling to find a purpose and a platform after the stall-in and the rent strikes.[13] The campaign ended in disaster. Major Owens, who was an outsider in Brooklyn Democratic politics, lost the election, and the BFDM did little to attract new members to Brooklyn CORE. Active members' interests in the chapter waned. Many had already moved on to other groups. Owens himself gradually faded away from Brooklyn CORE and became involved with a local community group in Brownsville.[14]

Almost immediately after the massive one-day public school boycott, the stall-in, and even the summertime riot, Brooklyn and New York City developed a severe case of amnesia with respect to the nonviolent, interracial civil rights movement that developed in the city. Jackie Robinson and Shirley Chisholm, the first black congressperson from Brooklyn, have always loomed large in the borough's narrative of civil right accomplishments, but just as soon as the interracial chapter of Brooklyn CORE began to fade from the headlines, there began a process of forgetting the types of nonviolent, direct-action protest that shaped activist politics during the early 1960s. The issues at the heart of the early 1960s civil rights movement had barely factored into Brooklynites' and New Yorkers' political consciousness when they imagined the nation's "race" problem, and nothing indicated this fact more than when power brokers held a major civil rights rally in the spring of 1965 to show the city's solidarity with people in Selma, Alabama. During this rally the speakers barely mentioned the civil rights activism, or the economic and social forms of racial discrimination, that shaped much of the everyday life in their own city. Indeed, on the very steps where Brooklyn CORE had dumped trash in protest against the city's discriminatory treatment of Bedford-Stuyvesant, Brooklyn and New York City officials held up the city's democracy as a shining example for the country to follow, almost as if Brooklyn's civil rights movement had never happened. When they did mention racism and activism in the city, they did so to highlight both the South's "exceptional" nature as a bastion of racism, and New York City's "exceptional" status as an exemplar of tolerance and democracy.

At 5:00 P.M. on Thursday, April 8, 1965, one month after the violent, chaotic standoff between peaceful activists and police officers at the Edmund Pettus Bridge in Selma, Alabama, political and religious leaders from throughout New York City held a rally in Brooklyn's downtown district to express their solidarity with southern civil rights activists, and to voice their outrage against the suppression of democracy in Alabama. One thousand people gathered in front of the steps of Brooklyn's Borough Hall. Brooklyn Borough President Abe Stark organized the "Brooklyn Stands with Selma, U.S.A." rally and sent special invitations to U.S. senators Jacob K. Javits and Robert Kennedy; all the members of the Kings County congressional delegation in Washington; the Brooklyn members of the State Legislature, City Council, and judges of the Brooklyn courts. Abe Stark even invited Martin Luther King Jr., but King's spokesman responded that, given the Southern Christian Leadership Conference president's pressing commitments in the South, his attendance was unlikely. Even without King present, the rally organizers were determined to put on a public spectacle that spoke to the nation and demonstrated New York City's disgust with southern violence and hope that the South would one day change its brutish ways. Stark told the city's African American weekly newspaper, the *New York Amsterdam News,* that he had prepared a formal proclamation that condemned "acts of brutality and terror perpetuated by racist elements of Alabama in their attempts to block Selma's citizens from gaining their civil rights." He made no comments, however, about condemning local acts of brutality and terror, which would have been relevant and timely. Instead, Stark announced to the crowd, "We are here to demonstrate our support of, and our spirit of solidarity with, the courageous Negro citizens of Selma, Alabama," and he declared that "Brooklyn would give to the nation and the world the example of harmonious relationship between people of all races."[15]

The gathering certainly seemed to confirm Stark's assessment of Brooklyn as an exemplary multiracial, multifaith, democratic society.

The *New York Amsterdam News* reported that people "of all races, creeds and standing in life" attended the rally, and the event became a mixture of interfaith prayer and political grandstanding. A Jewish rabbi and a Christian minister delivered convocations that made veiled references to local racial strife, but none of the opening prayers clearly connected the violence in Selma with the violence that had beset Brooklyn the previous summer. "Our brothers in Selma," the rabbi declared, "and in the tragically numerous Selmas in this land, have been enchained, brutally oppressed, and defiled." The Christian minister even issued a challenge to the audience "to examine our daily lives as we communicate, the one with the other—black and white, rich and poor, Roman Catholic and Protestant and Jew." Without reference to the actual strife and power imbalances that shaped social relations between those groups of New Yorkers, the words rang hollow.[16]

The rally's most personal denunciations of the violence in Selma, and southern racism in general, came from Mayor Robert F. Wagner Jr. Wagner's father, the New Deal–era senator from New York Robert F. Wagner Sr., had passed historic housing and labor legislation, and Mayor Wagner's words that spring evening were designed to confirm his own liberal credentials and to express his heartfelt commitment to civic equality. "Personally, the spectacle of Selma cut me as if it were a knife," the mayor declared. "I assure you that I would react the same way to police brutality wherever it might take place—whether on the highway between Selma and Montgomery, or in Fulton Street in Brooklyn."[17]

Mayor Wagner offered more than his personal sympathy and commitment that evening. He also shared with the crowd his analysis of how the civil rights movement existed beyond the South's borders. Indeed, Wagner pointed out that this struggle was connected to everyday life and politics in New York City. But in his condemnation of racism as a national problem, not merely a regional problem peculiar to the South, Wagner also took advantage of the opportunity to stress publicly that, although it was not perfect, New York City's government was exceptional, indeed more democratic and egalitarian than the southern municipal and state governments that sanctioned an atrocity like "Bloody Sunday." "The struggle for equal rights isn't just taking place in Alabama," Mayor Wagner reminded his audience in his concluding remarks.

> It is taking place in a far different form in New York City, too. The difference is that here in New York City, the government is for equal rights for everybody. Here, the government wants

everybody to vote. Here, the government wants to see every New Yorker regardless of color, race or origin to have an equal chance for a good education, for decent housing, for decent health and hospital care, for a decent job and a decent life. We haven't achieved our goal yet by a long way, but it is our official goal. To the extent that New York City becomes a safer and better place to live for all of us, Selma will be avenged, and the cause of justice will be served.[18]

As the history of Brooklyn CORE indicates, however, Wagner's record on local civil rights issues was at best mixed. His political influence on racial segregation in New York City neighborhoods and schools, tensions between African Americans and the New York City Police Department, and employment discrimination in private and public sectors did not always match his idealistic rhetoric or his personal sentiments. Though Wagner's personal dedication to civil rights policies, programs, and principles was genuine, his policy initiatives, by and large, did little to address entrenched patterns of racial inequality in housing, education, and employment. During Wagner's twelve years as mayor, the city had developed huge African American and Puerto Rican communities. But in 1965, his last year in office, New York City seemed more, not less, racially divided.[19]

Wagner had a chance at the "Brooklyn Stands with Selma" rally to speak about the ways racism affected social life in New York City, how it limited opportunities for some New Yorkers to exercise their full citizenship. He also had an opportunity to point out the local nonviolent activists, such as those in Brooklyn CORE, who were engaged in divisive struggles over the future of New York City schools and neighborhoods. Wagner chose instead to deliver platitudes that celebrated New York City's progressiveness and decried the South's backwardness. He said nothing about New York City's school integration battles, the fights to integrate the city's racially exclusive building trades industries, the rising rancor emanating from white neighborhoods, and the increasing militancy of black activists. Despite his claim that he would react strongly against local forms of police brutality, like Stark he failed to mention once that a police officer's murder of a black teenager the previous summer had sparked riots in the city's black neighborhoods. He also said nothing about his lack of support for a civilian board that would review misconduct by police. His speech that day, and many of his positions on racial issues during his three-term tenure as mayor, reflected Wagner's reluctance to implement decisive policy initiatives that might address the systematic ways racial discrimination shaped life and social power in New York City.

Perhaps, as Wagner stood in the shadow of Brooklyn's Borough Hall and spoke about New York City government's commitment to racial equality and civil rights, he had forgotten the city's recent tumult over public school integration and the riots that nearly nine months earlier had erupted in the city's two major black communities. Wagner certainly seemed to have forgotten all the civil rights activism that had occurred in Brooklyn and the rest of the city since 1960. He forgot the dramatic housing campaigns, the citywide protests against racial discrimination in the building trades industries, the civic calls for improved trash collection, the tumult that surrounded the opening day of the 1964–65 World's Fair, and the ongoing dissatisfaction that black and Puerto Rican parents expressed with the city's segregated public schools. But how could he forget such major moments that shaped the city he led, especially when they were connected to issues that had defined national policies ever since he took office in the mid-1950s?

It is more likely that Mayor Wagner had a clear eye on these social trends and activists' varied responses to them, but he could not recognize them as products of a social system shaped by racism. He had to have known that racism existed in New York City, and it was a powerful and destructive force in city life, but when he had a chance to illuminate the ways Brooklyn and Selma shared similar struggles with racism, his worldview of the South as "exceptionally" racist and New York City as "exceptionally" democratic only allowed him to laud New York City's progressiveness and condemn Selma's backwardness.[20] Such rhetoric continued to obscure the realities of racism in New York City, as well as the important work civil rights activists, like those in Brooklyn CORE, had done to try to create real opportunities for the city's black citizens in employment, public schools, housing, and municipal services. The political theater exhibited at the "Brooklyn Stands with Selma" rally showed that in the mid-1960s New York City's political elites and most of its citizens—blacks and whites—were more comfortable thinking about racism and civil rights activism as southern phenomena. They knew inequality existed in their own city, but they truly believed it was somehow less severe than the systematic, legalized racial discrimination that occurred in the Jim Crow South. Because Brooklynites did not publically display "whites only" signs, residents of Kings County believed that racism in their social order fundamentally differed in both degree (it was less frequent) and kind (it was less damaging) from racism in southern society.

Such beliefs, Jeanne Theoharis has summarized, "naturalize the Northern racial order as *not* a racial system like the South's but one operating on class and culture with racial discrimination as a byproduct."[21] The mechanisms and methods of Jim Crow racism in Brooklyn may have looked different when compared with those in the South—black people in Brooklyn were not turned away from the voting booth with the threat of deadly violence, for example—but in both regions the social effects of racist social systems that characterized America's Jim Crow era were largely the same. Black people in Brooklyn *and* black people in the South occupied a lower tier of citizenship and suffered from damaging racial ideologies that equated skin color with social undesirability; and local state officials in both regions proved incapable of counteracting such racism with solutions that were effective, tangible, and immediate.

Though racism certainly looked different in each region, one of the most significant contrasts was the way southern Jim Crow–era elected officials, police officers, realtors, bankers, store owners, and everyday citizens openly recognized and publically supported the racism in their societies. In such places as Brooklyn, Boston, Chicago, Detroit, Las Vegas, Milwaukee, Oakland, Pittsburgh, Philadelphia, and Saint Louis, almost everyone pretended that racism just *did not* exist; when power brokers in cities outside the South *did* acknowledge the ways their societies were plagued with racism, they usually delayed action, responded to civil rights activists' demands with piecemeal solutions, or blamed problems connected with the racialized ghetto directly on the racialized residents of the ghetto. Despite these tactics, or perhaps because of them, the urban crisis intensified. So did local activists' demands and tactics.[22]

Over time, other black activists filled the vacuum created by power brokers' inability to treat the results of Brooklyn's racially discriminatory history as serious social and political problems. The most prominent local leader to do this in Brooklyn was Sonny Carson, a black nationalist who recruited like-minded young black people to Brooklyn CORE's ranks and emerged as the chapter chairman around 1967.

Carson brought new ways of thinking about protest tactics and community involvement, some of which were in sync with a revived ethos of self-determination that emerged through the burgeoning national black power movement. He infused a new boldness and uncompromising posture into the chapter's leadership, and Brooklyn CORE once again became a vanguard chapter in CORE as the national organization embraced black nationalism and community-organizing projects. Much of what Carson did was to use his persona as a tough guy and street hustler to mix intimidating theatrics with strong-arm tactics and a rhetoric of community representation and protection. Carson replaced Brooklyn CORE's early 1960s action-oriented culture, which revolved around aggressive, nonviolent, direct-action protest, with a spirit more aligned with that of Carson's political hero, Malcolm X. An avowed and articulate black nationalist for most of his public life, Malcolm X often argued that black people needed to use "any means necessary" to secure their civil rights, which would come only when black people attained their own land and the political and economic autonomy that came with it.[23] Carson brought his own version of this philosophy to Brooklyn CORE. Sometimes through extortion and intimidation, sometimes through demonstration and community-organizing tactics, he attempted to revive Brooklyn CORE into a powerful vehicle of black protest that generated tangible results. Oliver Leeds remembered two stories that illustrate Carson's tendencies and Brooklyn CORE's new direction.

Leeds remained involved in Brooklyn CORE into the late 1960s. One day a black woman called CORE and complained that some furniture she had purchased from Mullin's Furniture Store on Myrtle Avenue in downtown Brooklyn had fallen apart by the time she brought it home. Carson told her not to worry; Brooklyn CORE would get her money back. Carson, Leeds, the woman, and two other men then drove to Mullin's Furniture, and Carson approached the manager with the woman's sales receipt for the broken furniture in hand. "The furniture fell apart. Give the woman back her money," Sonny ordered. When the manager protested, Carson bellowed, "Muthafucka, did you hear what I said? I said give the woman back her muthafucking money. Now!" After a few minutes of this exchange the lights in the store dimmed, Leeds heard the sound of fists striking the manager, then the cash register was opened and the exact amount on the woman's receipt was retrieved. "These are new CORE techniques," Leeds recalled. "That's the way they solved that problem."[24]

On another occasion Carson reasoned that, given the way white landlords and realtors had profited from redlining and blockbusting the neighborhood, Brooklyn CORE should not have to pay rent for office space in Bedford-Stuyvesant. They met with a man who was considered one of the biggest, richest real estate operators in north-central Brooklyn and demanded office space on Fulton Street, rent-free. "I got a hundred dudes that can tear up this town," Leeds remembered Carson telling the realtor. Leeds said that he had never seen a man so scared in his life. The realtor caved, and Carson's Brooklyn CORE "had that building for about two years, rent-free."[25] Carson also reflected on how these extortionist tactics served Bedford-Stuyvesant residents who dealt with slum-lords or landlords who refused to rent apartments to black people. "If a person went to a place and they couldn't get the apartment, we would go directly to the owners and ask them, what's going on? And if they didn't provide us with the right kind of answers, he may have a problem in the building," Carson recalled. His approach was decisively opposite what CORE had perfected with its white testers, direct-action protests, and appeals to the city:

> Asking in the manner that was once provided, no, we changed that philosophy. I remember this mother and her three, four kids, their housing was taken away from them and they were put out of their place, and I went up directly to the landlord and I said, you know what, if you don't give those people back their place in twenty-four hours I will come and run you out of business personally, physically. You understand that. I looked him right in his eye. I will run you out of business personally. And while I'm running you, I will break your legs.

Carson felt that black people in Bedford-Stuyvesant were entitled to compensatory treatment from landlords and merchants. He justified such tactics by asking rhetorically, "Why should I think about begging someone to do something that rightfully belongs to us anyway?" This philosophy won Carson many faithful admirers, as well as many fierce critics.[26]

Before Carson took over the chapter, Brooklyn CORE had become obscure and ineffective. Carson was able to infuse it with new vitality and to start it again on the road to prominence. Brooklyn CORE became a significant community group during an era shaped by social movements for community control of local public schools, government investment in antipoverty programs, and political fear of urban riots and unrest. Carson's brand of urban black nationalism never shied from controversy. Some of his flamboyant, provocative statements rankled white people and Jewish and Asian New Yorkers. Among those populations Carson developed a reputation as a bigot, an anti-Semite, and an antagonist against the Korean merchant community in Brooklyn. During the movement for community control of city public schools, in which Brooklyn's Ocean Hill–Brownsville neighborhood became a focal point, stories abounded of Carson intimidating white teachers, physically threatening teachers' union officials, and arriving at negotiation meetings armed. Typical of Carson's bellicose rhetoric was a warning he gave to white political science students who moved to Bedford-Stuyvesant in 1967 to study the neighborhood's impoverished conditions. Carson reportedly told them to "get the hell out of Bedford-Stuyvesant," and that Brooklyn CORE "did not want any white people in the community" because "it is our turf," and "whites are evil, all whites." He concluded by saying, "This community is going to be burned down, and you're going to be burned down with it if you don't get the hell out." In the 1980s, after a Korean merchant reportedly attacked a black woman, Carson was at the forefront of a boycott of Korean-owned grocery stores in north-central Brooklyn who black residents said consistently harassed them.[27]

It is difficult to separate fact from fiction when assessing Carson. How much of Carson's pugnacity and bigotry was exaggerated, both by Carson himself and by his detractors, for publicity purposes, and how much of it was part of his actual persona, his political philosophy, and his everyday community-organizing tactics? Among many black residents in Brooklyn, he became a folk hero. Carson's public personae combined an aura of criminality with his identity as a civic advocate for black people. He was acquitted of murder charges, but he spent fifteen months in prison for kidnapping and always claimed he was falsely accused of those charges. Throughout the late 1980s and early 1990s, Carson started a local movement to rid Bedford-Stuyvesant of crack houses, and he also participated in Pan-African nationalist movements that called for black people in American to receive reparations for slavery and land on which to establish an independent black state. In light of Carson's actions during the 1968 Ocean Hill–Brownsville standoff, many New Yorkers considered him an anti-Semitic demagogue. Oliver Leeds, on the other hand, spoke for many who saw Carson as a hero when he fondly recalled that Carson, even though he was a devoted black nationalist, was always kind and affectionate with his wife, Marjorie. Marjorie even predicted that "someday they'll name a street after him." Of course, when Carson posthumously entered public discourse in the early twenty-first century, and community-based efforts arose to have a street in Bedford-Stuyvesant named after the beloved local leader, the City Council and the mayor squelched the effort, citing Carson's history of "racism" against white people and Jews.[28]

The controversy over naming a street in Bedford-Stuyvesant after Carson was, like the "Brooklyn Stands with Selma" rally in 1965, largely an exercise in selective historical memory. Just as Mayor Wagner, Borough President Stark, and others had contrasted the South with Brooklyn's exceptionally liberal and progressive society and ignored the racism that shaped their own sociohistorical world, so too did many twenty-first-century New York power brokers emphasize Carson's bombastic, sensationalistic, and racially incendiary demagoguery while ignoring the ways he spoke to black Brooklynites' alienation and desire for cultural and political autonomy. Carson certainly relished his role as an agitator and provocateur; that personality gave him his public political cachet with the media and Bedford-Stuyvesant residents. But he also worked tirelessly in many different political and cultural community-organizing efforts that arose during the three and a half decades that followed the decline of Brooklyn's civil rights movement. He participated in and supported the East, a black cultural nationalist community center in Bedford-Stuyvesant, which became one of the city's most important centers of black arts and politics, and established an independent black school in the aftermath of the community-control movement. Carson served on the Board of Directors of the Bedford-Stuyvesant Restoration Corporation, the nation's first publicly-privately funded community development corporation designed to rehabilitate Brooklyn's north-central ghetto socially and economically with job-creation initiatives, medical centers, youth programs, and housing-restoration projects. Carson's politics were complicated and his personality was prickly, but multiple political movements were part of Carson's complex historical legacy. They also form the important, and still understudied, legacies of the black power movement in Brooklyn.[29]

Unfortunately, one depiction of Carson dominates many historical treatments of black activist politics in Brooklyn. A handful of historians who take a longer view of civil rights activism in the borough show that black political activism in Brooklyn predated the Ocean Hill–Brownsville controversies. They also show that Brooklyn's civil rights movement was much more multifaceted than either the accomplishments of individuals such as Jackie Robinson and Shirley Chisholm or the black nationalist identity politics associated with Carson reveal. Carson and the social movements he was a part of were certainly more complex than the one-dimensional brand of black nationalism and anti-Semitism people connect to him. Many factors contributed to Sonny Carson's rise as a prominent political and cultural figure; and Carson and the black nationalist movement in Brooklyn are certainly deserving of more serious scholarly treatment.[30]

But as this study of the early 1960s' rise and fall of Brooklyn CORE demonstrates, a significant reason that Carson rose to prominence was that figures like him filled in the leadership spaces created when an interracial, action-oriented protest group could not produce enough tangible results. Black nationalist movements that called for African Americans to repatriate Africa or form independent black communities in the United States and advocates of race pride and black economic empowerment have always been central aspects of African Americas' long freedom struggle. And these political and cultural philosophies existed side by side with calls for racial integration, assimilation, and expansion of African Americans' rights as U.S. citizens. Even if Brooklyn CORE and the northern interracial civil rights movement were not such powerful and dynamic political forces in postwar New York City, black nationalism would have inevitably been a part of African Americans' political and cultural movements during the mid- to late twentieth century.[31]

One consequence of New York City's failure to address effectively the problems that Brooklyn CORE raised was the ceding of local power and legitimacy to the strident rhetoric and demagoguery that were part of Carson's public persona and a central component of his approach to community organizing. A second failure occurs when historians use an oversimplified depiction of Carson and the black power movement of the late 1960s, or even Brooklyn CORE's stall-in, as the starting point for civil rights movement history in Brooklyn. This decision completely erases from the narrative and the analysis the hard-fought struggles for housing, jobs, desegregated schools, and improved city services waged by Brooklyn CORE, the Reverend Milton Galamison, and countless other everyday women and men. A certain brand of amnesia that overlooks the early history of Brooklyn CORE assumes that black nationalist–driven identity politics was always the form of black political activism that people in the North used to fight against racism and discrimination. Of course, the black power movement was, in many ways, bigger than Sonny Carson and the street-level politics he advocated. Carson represented only one dimension of the black power movement's cultural and community-based black nationalist politics. It would certainly be a mistake to reduce the black power movement—and even Carson himself—to static images of fiery black nationalism and antagonistic bigotry against whites. It would also be a mistake to overlook the history of an organization such as Brooklyn CORE in the early 1960s and the ways it fought, campaign after campaign, one demonstration at a time, for piecemeal victories. Brooklyn CORE gained some apartments for black people. It won a handful of jobs for black workers. It brought increased sanitation services to Bedford-Stuyvesant. And it helped one family, the Bibulds, fight against the unequal distribution of resources in the city's public schools, and, in doing so, it put a media spotlight on the ways racial discrimination shaped the nation's largest public education system. Those are the small victories—tangible and symbolic—that the early 1960s civil rights movement produced in Brooklyn. Those were also the types of achievements New York City's liberal power brokers were willing to grant civil rights activists who called attention to the systematic racism that shaped Brooklyn's neighborhoods, job markets, construction unions, trash collection, and public schools.

These achievements mattered a great deal to the citizens who benefitted from Brooklyn CORE's efforts, and to the women and men in Brooklyn CORE who tried to force citizens to see discriminatory practices many believed did not exist or were simply invisible. Far too often the history of early 1960s civil rights activism in a place like Brooklyn is overshadowed by the types of divisive politics and the worsening urban crisis that followed that period. We shortchange our own social and political development when we consciously oversimplify the complex struggles of Brooklyn's black power movements and when we ignore the borough's interracial civil rights movement that preceded them. When we forget, overlook, and distort the "freedom dreams" that activists in both movements envisioned, we substantially limit our own ability to learn from and, perhaps, build from those past movements.[32]

ACKNOWLEDGMENTS

I am very grateful for support from the following groups of people: participants in oral history interviews, which became the foundation for this book's research; the excellent teachers and mentors I had at Xavier High School, Fordham University's Departments of African and African American Studies, and History, and New York University's History Department; my colleagues in the Bowdoin College Africana Studies Program; the Bowdoin College Faculty Development Committee, for a generous grant that paid for the maps; my generous colleagues within and beyond the historical profession who shared with me primary sources and words of encouragement; the editors and the academic presses that published earlier versions of some of the chapters in this book; librarians and archivists who assisted me in my research, especially those at the Brooklyn Historical Society and the Brooklyn Public Library Central Branch's Brooklyn Collection; the New York State Historical Association and the Dixon Ryan Fox Manuscript Prize selection committee; staff members at the University Press of Kentucky; my handful of close, supportive friends; my loving parents, brother, extended family, and in-laws.

    I take full responsibility for this book's shortcomings, but whatever strengths it possesses would not have been possible without generous help from the following individuals: Kristin Anderson-Bricker, Adina Back, Elaine Bibuld, Martha Biondi, Mark Chapman, Geoffrey Cole, Maxine Leeds Craig, Angela Dillard, Anne Dean Dotson, David Goldberg, Arnie and Gilda Goldwag, Adam Green, Trevor Griffey, Joshua Guild, Martha Hodes, Joy Holland, Robin D. G. Kelley, Claire Jean Kim, Rioghan Kirchner, Mary Ellen Phifer Kirton, Matthew Klingle, Michael Latham, Steven F. Lawson, Natasha Lightfoot, Justin Lorts, Claude Mangum, Erik McDuffie, George Derek Musgrove, Mark Naison, Bill Nelson, Anna Nutter, Orlando Plaza, L. E. J. Rachell, Nick Salvatore, Jeffrey T. Sammons, Jennifer Scanlon, Jason Sokol, Thomas Sugrue, Joseph Sweeney, Clarence Taylor, Jeanne Theoharis, Ann Twombly, Chela Scott Weber, Jitu Weusi, Msemaji and Nandi Weusi, Komozi Woodard, and Craig Steven Wilder.

Finally, for their constant support, I give all my love and thanks to my wife, Leana Amaez, and our children: Isabella, Gabriel, Lillian, and Emilia.

Portions of chapter 5 previously appeared as "'Taxation without Sanitation Is Tyranny': Civil Rights Struggles over Garbage Collection in Brooklyn, New York, during the Fall of 1962," *Afro-Americans in New York Life and History* 31.2 (July 2007): 61–88, and was also reprinted in Clarence Taylor, editor, *Civil Rights in New York City: From World War II to the Giuliani Era* (New York: Fordham University Press, 2011), 52–76. An earlier version of chapter 7 previously appeared as "'Revolution Has Come to Brooklyn': The Campaign against Discrimination in the Construction Trades and Growing Militancy in the Northern Black Freedom Movement," in *Black Power at Work: Community Control, Affirmative Action, and the Construction Industry,* edited by David Goldberg and Trevor Griffey (Ithaca: Cornell University Press, 2010), 23–47. Portions of chapter 8 appeared previously as "'Drive Awhile for Freedom': Brooklyn CORE's 1964 Stall-In and Public Discourses on Protest Violence," in *Ground Work: Local Black Freedom Movements in America,* edited by Jeanne F. Theoharis and Komozi Woodard (New York: New York University Press, 2005), 45–75.

NOTES

Abbreviations Used in the Notes

AG-BCORE   Arnie Goldwag Brooklyn Congress of Racial Equality (CORE) Collection, ARC.002, Brooklyn Historical Society.

CORE   Congress of Racial Equality, *The Papers of the Congress of Racial Equality, 1941–1967* (Sanford, N.C.: Microfilming Corp. of America, 1980).

CRBC   Civil Rights in Brooklyn Collection, Series 1, Congress of Racial Equality (CORE) Documents, Brooklyn Collection, Brooklyn Public Library, Central Branch.

CRBC-OH   Civil Rights in Brooklyn Oral History Collection, Brooklyn Collection, Brooklyn Public Library, Central Branch. Unless otherwise indicated, all interviews in this collection were conducted by the author.

NYWF   New York World's Fair 1964–1965 Corporation Records, Manuscripts and Archives Division, box 85, folder A 4.0, "Discriminatory Practices Demonstrations 1964," New York Public Library, Astor, Lenox and Tilden Foundations.

NYW-OH   New Yorkers at Work, Oral History Collection, Wagner Labor Archives, Tamiment Library, New York University.

OH-AL   Oral History of the American Left, Oral History Collection, Wagner Labor Archives, Tamiment Library, New York University.

RMP   Robert Moses Papers, Humanities and Social Science Library, Rare Books and Manuscripts Division, box 126, folders 4/9/1964–4/16/1964 and 4/17/1964–4/24/1964, New York Public Library.

SHSW   Congress of Racial Equality (CORE), Brooklyn Chapter (N.Y.), Mss. 947, Archives Division, State Historical Society of Wisconsin, Madison.

1. Nostalgia, Narrative, and Northern Civil Rights Movement History

1. Clarence Taylor, *Knocking at Our Own Door: Milton A. Galamison*

and the Struggle to Integrate New York City Schools (Lanham, Md.: Lexington Books, 2001), 91–145; Clarence Taylor, *Civil Rights in New York City: From World War II to the Giuliani Era* (New York: Fordham University Press, 2011), 95–117; Daniel H. Perlstein, *Justice, Justice: School Politics and the Eclipse of Liberalism* (New York: P. Lang, 2004), 97–113; Diane Ravitch, *The Great School Wars: A History of the New York City Public Schools* (New York: Basic Books, 1988), 267–79; Craig Steven Wilder, *A Covenant with Color: Race and Social Power in Brooklyn* (New York: Columbia University Press, 2000), 220–22; Jerald E. Podair, *The Strike That Changed New York: Blacks, Whites, and the Ocean Hill–Brownsville Crisis* (New Haven: Yale University Press, 2002), 24–34; Sonia S. Lee and Ande Diaz, "'I Was the One Percenter': Manny Diaz and the Beginnings of a Black–Puerto Rican Coalition," *Journal of American Ethnic History* 26 (Spring 2007): 65–70; Adina Back, "Up South in New York: The 1950s School Desegregation Struggles" (Ph.D. diss., New York University, 1997), 402–31.

2. Charles M. Payne, *I've Got the Light of Freedom: The Organizing Tradition and the Mississippi Freedom Struggle,* 2nd ed. (Los Angeles: University of California Press, 2007), xiii–xxi; some aspects of the master narrative of civil rights movement history are evident in August Meier and Elliott Rudwick, *CORE: A Study in the Civil Rights Movement, 1942–1968* (New York: Oxford University Press, 1973); William Henry Chafe, *The Unfinished Journey: America since World War II* (New York: Oxford University Press, 1995), 146–76; Juan Williams, *Eyes on the Prize: America's Civil Rights Years, 1954–1965* (New York: Viking Penguin, 1987). Important historiographical essays on the civil rights and black power movements are Steven F. Lawson, "Freedom Then, Freedom Now: The Historiography of the Civil Rights Movement," *American Historical Review* 96.2 (1991): 456–71; Peniel Joseph, "The Black Power Movement: A State of the Field," *Journal of American History* 96.3 (2009): 751–76; and essays in Steven F. Lawson and Charles M. Payne, *Debating the Civil Rights Movement, 1945–1968,* 2nd ed. (Lanham, Md.: Rowman and Littlefield, 2006).

3. Representative works include Jeanne Theoharis and Komozi Woodard, *Freedom North: Black Freedom Struggles outside the South, 1940–1980* (New York: Palgrave Macmillan, 2003); James Ralph, *Northern Protest: Martin Luther King, Jr., Chicago, and the Civil Rights Movement* (Cambridge: Harvard University Press, 1993); Heather Ann Thompson, *Whose Detroit? Politics, Labor, and Race in a Modern American City* (Ithaca: Cornell University Press, 2001); Robert O. Self, *American Babylon: Race and the Struggle for Postwar Oakland* (Princeton: Princeton University Press, 2003); Martha Biondi, *To Stand and Fight: The Struggle for Civil Rights in Postwar New York City* (Cambridge: Harvard University Press, 2003); Matthew Countryman, *Up South: Civil Rights and Black Power in Philadelphia* (Philadelphia: University of Pennsylvania Press, 2006); Angela Dillard, *Faith in the City: Preaching Radical Social Change in Detroit* (Ann

Arbor: University of Michigan Press, 2007); Patrick Jones, *The Selma of the North: Civil Rights Insurgency in Milwaukee* (Cambridge: Harvard University Press, 2009); Clarence Lang, *Grassroots at the Gateway: Class Politics and Black Freedom Struggle in St. Louis, 1936–75* (Ann Arbor: University of Michigan Press, 2009); Donna Jean Murch, *Living for the City: Migration, Education, and the Rise of the Black Panther Party in Oakland, California* (Chapel Hill: University of North Carolina Press, 2010); See also Jeanne Theoharis, "Black Freedom Studies: Re-imagining and Redefining the Fundamentals," *History Compass* 4 (2006): 1–20, and Theoharis, "From the Stone the Builders Rejected: Towards a New Civil Rights Historiography," *Left History* 12.1 (2007): 103–10. The first narrative synthesis of this paradigm is Thomas Sugrue, *Sweet Land of Liberty: The Forgotten Struggle for Civil Rights in the North* (New York: Random House, 2008).

4. One of the first pieces of scholarship to articulate the "long civil rights movement" framework is Nikhil Pal Singh, *Black Is a Country: Race and the Unfinished Struggle for Democracy* (Cambridge: Harvard University Press, 2004), 1–14, esp. 5–6. See also the important essay by Jacquelyn Dowd Hall, "The Long Civil Rights Movement and the Political Uses of the Past," *Journal of American History* 91.4 (2005): 1233–63. Some studies engage multiple frameworks, such as Biondi, *To Stand and Fight*; Sugrue, *Sweet Land of Liberty*; Dillard, *Faith in the City*; and Lang, *Grassroots at the Gateway*. See also Tomiko Brown-Nagin, *Courage to Dissent: Atlanta and the Long History of the Civil Rights Movement* (New York: Oxford University Press, 2011), 2; Robert Korstad and Nelson Lichtenstein, "Opportunities Found and Lost: Labor, Radicals, and the Early Civil Rights Movement," *Journal of American History* 75.3 (1988): 786–811; Glenda Elizabeth Gilmore, *Defying Dixie: The Radical Roots of Civil Rights, 1919–1950* (New York: Norton, 2008); Clarence Taylor, *Reds at the Blackboard: Communism, Civil Rights, and the New York City Teachers Union* (New York: Columbia University Press, 2011); and Taylor, "Hurricane Katrina and the Myth of the Post–Civil Rights Era," *Journal of Urban History* 35.5 (2009): 640–55.

5. An excellent overview of this paradigm is Joseph, "The Black Power Movement"; see also Komozi Woodard, *A Nation within a Nation: Amiri Baraka (LeRoi Jones) and Black Power Politics* (Chapel Hill: University of North Carolina Press, 1999); Timothy Tyson, *Radio Free Dixie: Robert F. Williams and the Roots of Black Power* (Chapel Hill: University of North Carolina Press, 1999); Yohuru Williams, *Black Politics/White Power: Civil Rights, Black Power, and the Black Panthers in New Haven* (2000; repr., Malden, Mass.: Blackwell, 2008); Peniel Joseph, *Waiting 'til the Midnight Hour: A Narrative History of Black Power in America* (New York: Henry Holt, 2006); Joseph, *Neighborhood Rebels: Black Power at the Local Level* (New York: Palgrave Macmillan, 2010); Joseph, *The Black Power Movement: Rethinking the Civil Rights–Black Power Era* (New York: Routledge, 2006); Quito Swan, *Black Power in Bermuda: The Struggle for Decoloniza-*

tion (New York: Palgrave Macmillan, 2009); Hassan Kwame Jeffries, *Bloody Lowndes: Civil Rights and Black Power in Alabama's Black Belt* (New York: New York University Press, 2009); Kimberly Springer, *Living for the Revolution: Black Feminist Organizations, 1968–1980* (Durham: Duke University Press, 2005); James Smethurst, *The Black Arts Movement: Literary Nationalism in the 1960s and 1970s* (Chapel Hill: University of North Carolina Press, 2005); Daniel Widener, *Black Arts West: Culture and Struggle in Postwar Los Angeles* (Durham: Duke University Press, 2010); Ibram Rogers, *The Black Campus Movement: Black Students and the Racial Reconstitution of Higher Education, 1965–1972* (New York: Palgrave Macmillan, 2012); Martha Biondi, *The Black Revolution on Campus* (Berkeley: University of California Press, 2012).

6. On local studies see William Henry Chafe, *Civilities and Civil Rights: Greensboro, North Carolina, and the Black Struggle for Freedom* (Oxford: Oxford University Press, 1981); George Lipsitz, *A Life in the Struggle: Ivory Perry and the Culture of Opposition* (Philadelphia: Temple University Press, 1988); Payne, *I've Got the Light of Freedom;* John Dittmer, *Local People: The Struggle for Civil Rights in Mississippi* (Urbana: University of Illinois Press, 1994); Lawson and Payne, *Debating the Civil Rights Movement;* Emilye Crosby, *A Little Taste of Freedom: The Black Freedom Struggle in Claiborne County, Mississippi* (Chapel Hill: University of North Carolina Press, 2005), and Crosby, ed., *Civil Rights from the Ground Up: Local Struggles, a National Movement* (Athens: University of Georgia Press, 2011); Jeanne Theoharis and Komozi Woodard, *Groundwork: Local Black Freedom Movements in America* (New York: New York University Press, 2005). On welfare rights movements see Rhonda Williams, *The Politics of Public Housing: Black Women's Struggles against Urban Inequality* (New York: Oxford University Press, 2004); Annelise Orleck, *Storming Caesars Palace: How Black Mothers Fought Their Own War on Poverty* (Boston: Beacon Press, 2005); Felicia Ann Kornbluh, *The Battle for Welfare Rights: Politics and Poverty in Modern America* (Philadelphia: University of Pennsylvania Press, 2007). On black women in the civil rights and black power movements see Dayo Gore et al., eds., *Want to Start a Revolution? Radical Women in the Black Freedom Struggle* (New York: New York University Press, 2009); Barbara Ransby, *Ella Baker and the Black Freedom Movement: A Radical Democratic Vision* (Chapel Hill: University of North Carolina Press, 2003); Springer, *Living for the Revolution;* Katherine Mellen Charron, *Freedom's Teacher: The Life of Septima Clark* (Chapel Hill: University of North Carolina Press, 2009). On the Southwest see William Clayson, *Freedom Is Not Enough: The War on Poverty and the Civil Rights Movement in Texas* (Austin: University of Texas Press, 2010). On historical memory and the civil rights movement see Renee Christine Romano and Leigh Raiford, eds., *The Civil Rights Movement in American Memory* (Athens: University of Georgia Press, 2006). On multiethnic civil rights movement activism see Brian Behnken, *Fighting Their Own Battles: Mexican*

Americans, African Americans, and the Struggle for Civil Rights in Texas (Chapel Hill: University of North Carolina Press, 2010), and Behnken, *The Struggle in Black and Brown: African American and Mexican American Relations during the Civil Rights Era* (Lincoln: University of Nebraska Press, 2011); Scott Kurashige, *The Shifting Grounds of Race: Black and Japanese Americans in the Making of Multiethnic Los Angeles* (Princeton: Princeton University Press, 2008); Sonia S. Lee, "Between Boricua and Black: How the Civil Rights Struggle Shaped Puerto Rican Racial and Ethnic Identities in New York City, 1950s–70s" (Ph.D. diss., Harvard University, 2007).

7. Important critics include Charles Eagles, "Toward New Histories of the Civil Rights Era," *Journal of Southern History* 66.4 (2000): 815–48; Sundiata Cha-Jua and Clarence Lang, "The 'Long Movement' as Vampire: Temporal and Spatial Fallacies in Recent Black Freedom Studies," *Journal of African American History* 92.2 (2007): 265–88; Eric Arnesen, "Reconsidering the 'Long Civil Rights Movement,'" *Historically Speaking* 10.2 (2009): 31–34; Richard Kahlenberg, "Wrong on Race: Why Barack Obama Shouldn't Listen to Tom Sugrue," *Democracy: A Journal of Ideas* 12 (Spring 2009): 99–107. For a critical analysis of these revisionist contributions and the master narrative, see Steven Lawson, "Long Origins of the Short Civil Rights Movement, 1954–1968," in *Freedom Rights: New Perspectives on the Civil Rights Movement,* ed. Danielle McGuire and John Dittmer (Lexington: University Press of Kentucky, 2012), 9–38.

8. Lorrin Thomas, *Puerto Rican Citizen: History and Political Identity in Twentieth-Century New York City* (Chicago: University of Chicago Press, 2010); Carmen Teresa Whalen and Víctor Vázquez-Hernández, eds., *The Puerto Rican Diaspora: Historical Perspectives* (Philadelphia: Temple University Press, 2005); Monica Brown, *Gang Nation: Delinquent Citizens in Puerto Rican, Chicano, and Chicana Narratives* (Minneapolis: University of Minnesota Press, 2002), 1–35; Virginia Sánchez Korrol, *From Colonia to Community: The History of Puerto Ricans in New York City* (1983; repr., Berkeley: University of California Press, 1994); Clara E. Rodriguez, *Puerto Ricans: Born in the U.S.A.* (Boston: Unwin Hyman, 1989); Lee, "Between Boricua and Black."

9. James Baldwin is quoted in Back, "Up South in New York," 456; see also Matthew Lassiter and Joseph Crespino, "The End of Southern History," and Matthew Lassiter, "De Jure/De Facto Segregation: The Long Shadow of a National Myth," in *The Myth of Southern Exceptionalism,* ed. Matthew Lassiter and Joseph Crespino (New York: Oxford University Press, 2010), 3–22 and 25–48; Sugrue, *Sweet Land of Liberty,* xiii–xv.

10. James Wolfinger, *Philadelphia Divided: Race and Politics in the City of Brotherly Love* (Chapel Hill: University of North Carolina Press, 2007), 213. Myrdal is quoted in Sugrue, *Sweet Land of Liberty,* xiv–xv; Robert Self, "Matthew Countryman's *Up South* and Urban Political History," *Pennsylvania Magazine of History and Biography* 130.4 (2006): 394. See

also Jeanne Theoharis, "Hidden in Plain Sight: The Civil Rights Movement outside the South," in Lassiter and Crespino, *The Myth of Southern Exceptionalism,* 49–73.

11. On racial discrimination in the North see Sugrue, *Sweet Land of Liberty.*

12. Gates Avenue Association, Meeting Minutes, June 3, 1924; Oct. 29, 1924; Nov. 10, 1925; May 24, 1932; Nov. 20, 1935; Harold X. Connolly, *A Ghetto Grows in Brooklyn* (New York: New York University Press, 1977), 58–60, 68; Wilder, *A Covenant with Color,* 182.

13. Gates Avenue Association, Meeting Minutes, June 3 and 17, 1924.

14. Ibid., Oct. 29, 1924; Oct. 19, 1926; Nov. 10, 1926.

15. Ibid., Mar. 17, 1925; May 22, 1928; Connolly, *A Ghetto Grows in Brooklyn,* 59–60.

16. Gates Avenue Association, Meeting Minutes, Oct. 27, 1925; Nov. 10, 1925; Apr. 30, 1926; May 11, 1927; May 31, 1927; Connolly, *A Ghetto Grows in Brooklyn,* 67.

17. Wilder, *A Covenant with Color,* 181–97; Connolly, *A Ghetto Grows in Brooklyn,* 52–75. See also Wendell E. Pritchett, *Brownsville, Brooklyn: Blacks, Jews, and the Changing Face of the Ghetto* (Chicago: University of Chicago Press, 2002), 105–45; Walter Thabit, *How East New York Became a Ghetto* (New York: New York University Press, 2003), 37–55.

18. Wilder, *A Covenant with Color;* Biondi, *To Stand and Fight,* 113–21.

19. Wilder, *A Covenant with Color.*

20. On Brooklyn's nostalgia see Elliot Willensky, *When Brooklyn Was the World, 1920–1957* (New York: Harmony Books, 1986); Michael W. Robbins and Wendy Palitz, *Brooklyn: A State of Mind, 125 Stories from America's Most Colorful City* (New York: Workman, 2001); Andrea Wyatt Sexton and Alice L. Powers, eds., *The Brooklyn Reader: Thirty Writers Celebrate America's Favorite Borough* (New York: Three Rivers Press, 1994); Marc Eliot, *Song of Brooklyn: An Oral History of America's Favorite Borough* (New York: Broadway Books, 2008); Myrna Katz Frommer and Harvey Frommer, *It Happened in Brooklyn: An Oral History of Growing Up in the Borough in the 1940s, 1950s, and 1960s* (New York: Harcourt Brace, 1993); Peter Golenbock, *In the Country of Brooklyn: Inspiration to the World* (New York: HarperCollins, 2008). A very good analysis of nostalgia is Svetlana Boym, *The Future of Nostalgia* (New York: Basic Books, 2001).

21. Newfield quoted in Eliot, *Song of Brooklyn,* epigraph. Sleeper quoted in Frommer and Frommer, *It Happened in Brooklyn,* 237.

22. Frommer and Frommer, *It Happened in Brooklyn,* 14, 51.

23. Pete Hamill, "Willie Mays, the Say Hey Kid," *New York Times Book Review,* Feb. 28, 2010; Eliot, *Song of Brooklyn,* 81, 88.

24. Frommer and Frommer, *It Happened in Brooklyn,* 15, 169.

25. Ibid., 15, 38.

26. Robert Law interview, Apr. 14, 2004, CRBC-OH.

27. Ibid.

28. Ibid.

29. Ibid.

30. Brian Purnell, "Interview with John Hope Franklin," *Journal of African American History* 94.3 (2009): 413. See also John Hope Franklin, *Mirror to America: The Autobiography of John Hope Franklin* (New York: Farrar, Straus and Giroux, 2005), 176–79; Golenbock, *In the Country of Brooklyn,* 391–99.

31. Golenbock, *In the Country of Brooklyn,* 396.

32. Purnell, "Interview with John Hope Franklin," 413.

33. Eliot, *Song of Brooklyn,* 140–41, 142; Jerry Della Femina and Charles Sopkin, *An Italian Grows in Brooklyn* (Boston: Little, Brown, 1978), 161.

34. Paul and Rita Heinegg interview, Jan. 5, 2004, CRBC-OH.

35. Frommer and Frommer, *It Happened in Brooklyn,* 52, 167–68, 226.

36. On black violence against whites in Brooklyn see Norman Podhoretz, "My Negro Problem—and Ours," *Commentary* 35 (Feb. 1963): 93–101; on the "culture of poverty" see Oscar Lewis, *La Vida: A Puerto Rican Family in the Culture of Poverty—San Juan and New York* (New York: Random House, 1966); Jonathan Rieder, *Canarsie: The Jews and Italians of Brooklyn against Liberalism* (Cambridge: Harvard University Press, 1985).

37. Connolly, *A Ghetto Grows in Brooklyn,* 151; Clarence Taylor, *The Black Churches of Brooklyn* (New York: Columbia University Press, 1994), 141, and Taylor, *Knocking at Our Own Door,* 117–18, 127–28; Wilder, *A Covenant with Color,* 235–42.

2. "Pass Them By! Support Your Brothers and Sisters in the South!"

1. Meier and Rudwick, *CORE,* 3–39; Raymond Arsenault, *Freedom Riders: 1961 and the Struggle for Racial Justice* (Oxford: Oxford University Press, 2006), 11–55; Derek Catsam, *Freedom's Main Line: The Journey of Reconciliation and the Freedom Rides* (Lexington: University Press of Kentucky, 2009), 13–46.

2. Ibid., as well as passim in all three works.

3. Meier and Rudwick, *CORE,* 40–71.

4. CORE, series III, file 10, frame 683; Taylor, *Knocking at Our Own Door,* 47–90; Wilder, *A Covenant with Color,* 135–38, 152–74.

5. CORE, series III, file 10, frame 685–86.

6. Ibid., frame 690.

7. Meier and Rudwick, *CORE,* 40–71.

8. Ibid., 5, 72–98.

9. On student sit-ins, see Clayborne Carson, *In Struggle: SNCC and the Black Awakening of the 1960s* (Cambridge: Harvard University Press, 1981), 9–30; Williams, *Eyes on the Prize,* 122–40; Ransby, *Ella Baker and*

the Black Freedom Movement, 237–72; Martin Oppenheimer, *The Sit-in Movement of 1960* (Brooklyn, N.Y.: Carlson, 1989).

10. Meier and Rudwick, *CORE*, 102.

11. Ibid., 49, 77, 81, 102.

12. Williams, *Eyes on the Prize*, 129.

13. Ibid., 129, 132; Meier and Rudwick, *CORE*, 111.

14. Meier and Rudwick, *CORE*, 102–4.

15. Ibid., 103–6; quote on 106 (emphasis in original).

16. Ibid., 106–9; quotes on 109.

17. Ibid., 110.

18. Marjorie Leeds's FBI file, in Oliver and Marjorie Leeds personal papers, courtesy of Maxine Leeds Craig and in the author's possession; Maxine Leeds Craig interview, June 20, 2004, CRBC-OH; Edith Jefferson Diamond interview, July 20, 2004, CRBC-OH.

19. On the LYL see Gerald Horne, *Communist Front? The Civil Rights Congress, 1946–1956* (Rutherford, N.J.: Fairleigh Dickinson University Press, 1988), 63, 180. Information on Marjorie Leeds's early political activities is found in Marjorie Leeds's FBI file; Diamond interview.

20. On the YPA and the Popular Front, see Horne, *Communist Front?*; on the BSS in New York City, see Anthony Bouza, *Police Intelligence: The Operations of an Investigative Unit* (New York: AMS Press, 1976); and Joel Sucher and Stephen Fishler, *Red Squad* (New York: Pacific Street Films, 1972), documentary film.

21. Marjorie Leeds's FBI file; Diamond interview.

22. On the Unity Democratic Club, see Wayne Dawkins, *City Son: Andrew W. Cooper's Impact on Modern-Day Brooklyn* (Jackson: University Press of Mississippi, 2012), 32–47; Jeffrey Nathan Gerson, "Building the Brooklyn Machine: Irish, Jewish, and Black Political Succession in Central Brooklyn, 1919–1964" (Ph.D. diss., City University of New York, 1990). On Siloam Presbyterian Church, see Taylor, *The Black Churches of Brooklyn*, 11–13, 128–30, and Taylor, *Knocking at Our Own Door*, 31–35, 209–11.

23. On the BSNC see Brooklyn Public Library, Central Branch, Brooklyn Collection, vertical file, "Bedford Stuyvesant Neighborhood Council," n.d. For descriptions of Crown Heights see Community Council of Greater New York, *Brooklyn Communities: Population Characteristics and Neighborhood Social Resources*, 2 vols. (New York: Bureau of Community Statistical Services, 1959), 1:137–46.

24. Arnold Goldwag interview, Oct. 13, 2000, CRBC-OH; Taylor, *Civil Rights in New York City*, 52–76.

25. "Our Job," *New York Amsterdam News*, Jan. 9, 1960, 8.

26. "Bus, Subway Ills Mount," *New York Amsterdam News*, Jan. 23, 1960, 17–18.

27. Ibid.; "TA Orders 300 New Busses – 150 Slates for Use in Bedford-Stuyvesant," *New York Amsterdam News*, Apr. 9, 1960, 16.

28. "Crown Heights Doctor Makes Assembly Bid," *New York*

Amsterdam News, Jan. 16, 1960, 3; "Tom Jones, Lawyer-Candidate, Hits At 'Poor' School System," *New York Amsterdam News,* Mar. 19, 1960, 3. Connolly, *A Ghetto Grows in Brooklyn,* 162–83; Gerson, "Building the Brooklyn Machine," 153–330. See also Biondi, *To Stand and Fight.*

29. Meier and Rudwick, *CORE,* 83, 97.

30. Taylor, *Knocking at Our Own Door,* xvii–xxxvii.

31. CORE, series V, file 70, frame 768.

32. Ibid., frames 769–76.

33. Oliver Leeds, interview by Dianne Esses, Dec. 15, 1988, CRBC-OH.

34. Ibid.; Oliver Leeds's FBI File, Leeds personal papers. On the Scottsboro demonstrations in Harlem, see Mark Naison, *Communists in Harlem during the Depression* (Urbana: University of Illinois Press, 1983), 57–94. On demonstrations against police brutality, see Biondi, *To Stand and Fight,* 191–207. On police brutality in New York City, see Marilynn Johnson, *Street Justice: A History of Police Violence in New York City* (Boston: Beacon Press, 2003).

35. Craig interview; Nic Maclellan and Jean Chesneaux, *After Moruroa: France in the South Pacific* (Melbourne: Ocean Press, 1998), 46–49.

36. Craig interview; Oliver Leeds's service records, General Orders #1160, July 31, 1944, "Awards of the Soldier's Medal," and Oliver Leeds FBI file, both in Leeds personal papers.

37. Oliver Leeds's FBI file; Craig interview. On McCarthyism, see Ellen Schrecker, *Many Are the Crimes: McCarthyism in America* (Boston: Little, Brown, 1998); Biondi, *To Stand and Fight.*

38. Nick Salvatore interview, Jan. 6, 2003, CRBC-OH; Msemaji Weusi (Maurice Fredericks) and Nandi Weusi (Winnie Fredericks) interview, Mar. 9, 2001, CRBC-OH; Craig interview; Oliver Leeds's FBI file.

39. Oliver Leeds's FBI file. Marjorie Leeds and Oliver Leeds, interview by Clarence Taylor, Aug. 11, 1988, CRBC-OH. Oliver Leeds interview, Aug. 9, 1983, NYW-OH. So many of the oral history interviews with Oliver Leeds and other members of Brooklyn CORE emphasize his important role in the chapter's early development, but even he himself once told the historian Clarence Taylor that his wife "should be the one that should be interviewed. I get all the credit, but she was the one that started it."

40. Marjorie Leeds and Oliver Leeds interview by Taylor; Oliver Leeds interview by Esses.

41. Letters from National CORE, "No Service in the South No Purchase in the North," June 28, 1960, and "The Fight for Equal Rights Is Everyone's Fight," July 8, 1960, in SHSW, box 1, folder 10.

42. Oliver Leeds interview by Esses.

43. "CORE Leader Reports Woolworth Sales Drop," *New York Amsterdam News,* Apr. 23, 1960, 6.

44. Msemaji and Nandi Weusi interview. Throughout the 1960s, when they were members of Brooklyn CORE, Msemaji and Nandi Weusi were known as Maurice and Winnie Fredericks. I will refer to them by the latter names in the text.

45. Ibid.; Maurice Fredericks, interview by Clarence Taylor, May 9, 1990, CRBC-OH; Maurice Fredericks interview, Apr. 28, 1981, NYW-OH.

46. Maurice Fredericks interview, Apr. 28, 1981, NYW-OH.

47. Williams, *Eyes on the Prize,* 140; Oppenheimer, *The Sit-in Movement of 1960,* 177–84; Meier and Rudwick, *CORE,* 112.

48. Meier and Rudwick, *CORE,* 3–39. Goldwag interview; Kurt Flascher interview, May 23, 2011, CRBC-OH.

49. CORE, series V, file 70, frame 783.

3. Why Not Next Door?

1. For an overview of housing discrimination in the twentieth-century United States, see Stephen Grant Meyer, *As Long as They Don't Move Next Door: Segregation and Racial Conflict in American Neighborhoods* (Lanham, Md.: Rowman and Littlefield, 2000); Sugrue, *Sweet Land of Liberty,* 200–250; on New York City, see Biondi, *To Stand and Fight,* 112–36; Wilder, *A Covenant with Color,* 181–97; Rieder, *Canarsie,* 13–26, 57–94; Pritchett, *Brownsville, Brooklyn,* 105–74; Thabit, *How East New York Became a Ghetto;* Podair, *The Strike That Changed New York,* 48–70. On racially integrated housing in New York City during the 1960s, see Peter Eisenstadt, *Rochdale Village: Robert Moses, 6,000 Families, and New York City's Great Experiment in Integrated Housing* (Ithaca: Cornell University Press, 2010).

2. "'I Will Bar Negroes,'" *New York Amsterdam News,* Jan. 2, 1960, 1.

3. On restrictive covenants, see Thomas Sugrue, *The Origins of the Urban Crisis: Race and Inequality in Postwar Detroit* (Princeton: Princeton University Press, 1996), 44–46; Sugrue, *Sweet Land of Liberty,* 202–21, 244–48; Meyer, *As Long as They Don't Move Next Door,* 13–47; Arnold Hirsch, *Making the Second Ghetto: Race and Housing in Chicago, 1940–1960* (Cambridge: Cambridge University Press, 1983), 29–39, 145–56. On Local Law 80, see Biondi, *To Stand and Fight,* 233.

4. "'I Will Bar Negroes,'" *New York Amsterdam News,* Jan. 2, 1960, 1, 23.

5. Ibid.

6. "Tenants Howl: 'Rats as Big as Cats; Vermin Run Around Apartments,'" *New York Amsterdam News,* Aug. 20, 1960, 1.

7. Wilder, *A Covenant with Color,* 216.

8. "Housing Bias Victims Stage Realty Sit-in," *New York Amsterdam News,* Aug. 20, 1960, 1; Meier and Rudwick, *CORE,* 125.

9. "Housing Bias Victims Stage Realty Sit-in," *New York Amsterdam News.* Aug. 20, 1960, 1.

10. "Apartment Bias Smashed by CORE; First Case a Success for Brooklyn Office," *New York Amsterdam News,* Nov. 5, 1960, 21.

11. "Couple Lands Apartment with CORE, Amsterdam News Help," *New York Amsterdam News,* Nov. 19, 1960, 1. On July 1, 1955, the Council of the City of New York established the City Commission on Human Rights under Local Law 55. The Commission on Intergroup Relations (COIR) superseded the Mayor's Committee on Unity, a loosely arranged effort initiated by Mayor Fiorello H. LaGuardia on February 28, 1944, which lasted until 1954. The City Council empowered COIR to hold hearings, report its findings, and make recommendations to the mayor. The organization was renamed the Commission on Human Rights in March 1962. See "The City of New York Commission on Human Rights Historical Sketch," New York Municipal Archives Vertical File, N.Y.C. Human Rights Commission.

12. "'I Won't Move'; Mrs. Willins Says She's Not Afraid," *New York Amsterdam News,* Nov. 19, 1960, 1.

13. "KKK Strikes Again; The First and Only Negroes," *New York Amsterdam News,* Nov. 4, 1961, 1.

14. Douglass Bibuld interview, May 31, 2004, CRBC-OH.

15. Rioghan Kirchner interviews, Sept. 29 and Oct. 21, 2000, CRBC-OH; Rioghan Kirchner, "Why Not Next Door?" chap. 1, pp. 4–6, CRBC, box 3, folder 3.8.2. (*Note:* Since the publication of this book, the chapters of the unpublished manuscript "Why Not Next Door?" were filed separately in the CRBC according to the individual housing integration cases they describe. Citations here correspond to the manuscript as a single entity, which is how I first encountered the manuscript.)

16. Meier and Rudwick, *CORE,* 135–45. Kirchner interview, Sept. 29, 2000; Kirchner, "Why Not Next Door?" chap. 1, p. 5.

17. Kirchner interview, Sept. 29, 2000.

18. Kirchner, "Why Not Next Door?" chap. 1, pp. 8–9.

19. The following information on Eva McGuire's case comes from Rioghan Kirchner, "McGuire, Weiner Case," Feb. 4 (no year), in CORE, series V, file 70, frame 808; and Kirchner, "Why Not Next Door?" chap. 3, "A Bigot Sees the Light."

20. Kirchner, "Why Not Next Door?" chap. 3, p. 4.

21. Ibid.

22. Ibid., 7.

23. Ibid. There are many academic examinations of African American and Jewish political, cultural, and social relations. See Cheryl Lynn Greenberg, *Troubling the Waters: Black-Jewish Relations in the American Century* (Princeton: Princeton University Press, 2006); Jack Salzman et al., eds., *Bridges and Boundaries: African Americans and American Jews* (New York: George Braziller, 1992).

24. Kirchner interview, Sept. 29, 2000. On Margaret Chapman's case, see Kirchner, "Why Not Next Door?" chap. 1; "6 in CORE Stage Rental Office Sit-in," *New York World Telegram and Sun,* Oct. 5, 1961, n.p., in

clipping files, CRBC; "Sleep-ins Break Lily White House," *New York Amsterdam News,* Oct. 14, 1961, 21; "A New Twist," *New York Amsterdam News,* Oct. 21, 1961, 12; Meier and Rudick, *CORE,* 184.

25. "CORE Does It Again: Opens Lily-White House," *New York Amsterdam News,* Nov. 25, 1961, 19; "Lefrak Accused of Renting Bias in Federal Suit," *New York Times,* Aug. 7, 1970, 1; "U.S. Sues Lefrak Firm over Discrimination," *New York Post,* Aug. 16, 1970, 3, 62.

26. Kirchner, "Why Not Next Door?" chap. 4, p. 1; Oliver Leeds interview by Esses.

27. Miscellaneous apartment advertisements (clipping from unidentified newspaper), n.d., in CRBC, box 2, folder 4; Kirchner, "Why Not Next Door?" chap. 4, p. 1.

28. Kirchner, "Why Not Next Door?" chap. 4, pp. 2–5.

29. Ibid., chap. 4; "State and Federal Funds for Discrimination," CRBC, box 2, folder 2; CORE, series V, file 374, frame 458.

30. Kirchner, "Why Not Next Door?" chap. 4, pp. 7–9.

31. Ibid., 8–9.

32. Ibid., 10–11.

33. Ibid.

34. Ibid.

35. Marjorie and Oliver Leeds interview by Taylor.

36. CORE, series V, file 374, frame 535.

37. Kirchner, "Why Not Next Door?" chap. 4, p. 15.

38. Ibid.

39. Ibid., 16–17; "Signed Statement Dated November 16, 1961," and "Press Statement for Immediate Release," in CRBC, box 2, folder 2.

40. "CORE Does It Again: Opens Lily-White House," *New York Amsterdam News,* Nov. 25, 1961, 19.

41. "Queens Sit-in Wins Rental, CORE Reports," *New York Post,* Nov. 17, 1961, 41; Kirchner, "Why Not Next Door?" chap. 4, pp. 17–18. Photocopies of real estate advertisements for Lefrak buildings before and after the CORE sit-in are in CRBC, box 2, folder 2.

42. Kirchner, "Why Not Next Door?" chap. 4, p. 20.

43. Ibid., 22.

44. Ibid., 23.

45. Ibid.

46. Ibid.; "Why CORE Is Picketing Life Realty," press release, n.d., in CRBC, box 2, folder 4.

47. "U.S. Sues Lefrak Firm over Discrimination," *New York Post,* Aug. 16, 1970, 3, 62; "Lefrak Accused of Renting Bias in Federal Suit," *New York Times,* Aug. 7, 1970, 1.

48. "Lefrak Accused of Renting Bias in Federal Suit," *New York Times,* Aug. 7, 1970, 1.

49. "Major Builder Signs a Pact for Public Housing," *New York Times,* Jan. 28, 1971, 39; "Lefrak Settles U.S. Suit on Bias," *New York Times,* Jan. 29, 1971, 1.

50. Oliver Leeds interview by Esses.

51. Kirchner interview, Sept. 29, 2000; Elaine Bibuld, Mary Ellen Phifer Kirton, Rioghan Kirchner, Msemaji Weusi, and Nandi Weusi interview, Apr. 7, 2000, CRBC-OH; Marjorie and Oliver Leeds interview by Taylor.

52. Goldwag interview, CRBC-OH; Kirchner interview, Sept. 29, 2000.

53. Rioghan Kirchner, telephone conversation with the author, Aug. 2005.

54. Kirchner interview, Oct. 21, 2000.

55. Ibid.

56. Mary Ellen Phifer Kirton interview, Feb. 23, 2003, CRBC-OH; Bibuld, Kirton, Kirchner, Weusi, and Weusi interview.

57. Arnold Goldwag, interviews by Shelia Michaels, Apr. 23, 1999; May 5, 1999; Mar. 9, 2001, Nonviolent Oral History Project, Columbia University, Special Collections.

58. Kirchner interview, Oct. 21, 2000.

59. Ibid.; also see all Oliver Leeds interviews; Goldwag interview, CRBC-OH; and Elaine Bibuld interview, Feb. 18, 2001, CRBC-OH.

60. CORE, series V, file 70, frames 798, 801–2.

61. Oliver Leeds interview by Esses.

62. Ibid.

63. Robert Palmer to James Famer and Friends of Brooklyn CORE, CORE, series I, file 12, frame 854.

4. Operation Unemployment

1. Meier and Rudwick, *CORE*, 192–93.

2. Joshua Freeman, *Working-Class New York: Life and Labor since World War II* (New York: New Press, 2000), 3–22; Roger Waldinger, *Still the Promised City? African-Americans and New Immigrants in Postindustrial New York* (Cambridge: Harvard University Press, 1996), 106–18.

3. "Ebinger's Bakery Started in 1898, with German Pastry as a Specialty," *New York Times*, Nov. 10, 1961, 30; "If Only They'll Eat More Cake," *New York Times*, Mar. 26, 1972, 10; "F.Y.I.: The Ebinger Touch," *New York Times*, June 19, 2005, CY2.

4. "Brooklyn CORE's Report to the National Council on Projects," *Brooklyn CORE Newsletter*, March 1962, CORE, series V, file 70, frame 819; Dawkins, *City Son*, 31–32; Gerson, "Building the Brooklyn Machine," 310–12. On Operation Unemployment see "Operation Unemployment," *Unity Democrat*, April 1961, and Andrew Cooper, "Ebinger's Still Discriminates," *Unity Democrat*, Feb. 1962, in Thomas Russell Jones Papers, folder "Unity Democratic Club—Newsletters." On Jackie Robinson as an executive at Chock Full O'Nuts, see Mary Kay Linge, *Jackie Robinson: A Biography* (Westport, Conn.: Greenwood Press, 2007), 114.

5. On Operation Unemployment's assisting Brooklyn CORE in finding office space, see handwritten note at the bottom of Andrew Cooper to Operation Unemployment supporters, Mar. 12, 1962, SHSW, box 1, folder 2. On

Brooklyn CORE's early history in Bedford Stuyvesant, see Jitu Weusi interview, Mar. 21, 2000, CRBC-OH; on Brooklyn CORE's first office see Arnold Goldwag interview, CRBC-OH.

6. "Brooklyn CORE's Report to the National Council on Projects," *Brooklyn CORE Newsletter,* March 1962, CORE, series V, file 70, frame 819.

7. CORE, series V, file 70, frame 813; Eleanor Stein interview, Mar. 23, 2005, CRBC-OH; John Akula interview, Apr. 25, 2005, CRBC-OH; Meier and Rudwick, *CORE,* 141, 152, 169.

8. Akula interview; Stein interview.

9. CORE, series V, file 70, frame 813.

10. Ibid.

11. CORE, series V, file 70, frame 822.

12. Goldwag interview, CRBC-OH.

13. CORE, series V, file 70, frame 804.

14. Ibid., frame 846.

15. Goldwag interview, CRBC-OH; minutes, Brooklyn CORE meeting, May 21, 1962, SHSW, box 1, folder 1.

16. Minutes, Brooklyn CORE meeting, May 21, 1962.

17. "Statement of Understandings between Ebinger Baking Company, Brooklyn CORE and Ministers Movement of Bedford-Stuyvesant regarding the Employment Practices of the Ebinger Baking Company," SHSW, box 1, folder 6.

18. Ibid.

19. Notes from Executive Committee meeting, May 30, 1962, and minutes of meeting of membership of Brooklyn CORE held on June 4, 1962, both in SHSW, box 1, folder 1.

20. *Brooklyn CORE Newsletter,* no. 4, June 1962, SHSW, box 1, folder 1.

21. "A Call to Action," SHSW, box 1, folder 6.

22. Maurice Fredericks to Fredricka Teer, July 29, 1962, CORE, series V, file 70, frames 841–42.

23. Anonymous to Brooklyn CORE, Aug. 4, 1962, SHSW, box 1, folder 2.

24. Linda Marks to Brooklyn CORE, Aug. 1962, SHSW, box 1, folder 6.

25. Ibid.; Michael B. Katz, ed., *The "Underclass" Debate: Views from History* (Princeton: Princeton University Press, 1993), 3–23, and other essays in that collection. See also William Julius Wilson, *The Truly Disadvantaged: The Inner City, the Underclass, and Public Policy* (Chicago: University of Chicago Press, 1987).

26. St. Clair Drake and Horace Cayton, *Black Metropolis: A Study of Negro Life in a Northern City,* rev. ed. (Chicago: University of Chicago Press, 1993), 495–754; Joe W. Trotter, *Black Milwaukee: The Making of an Industrial Proletariat, 1915–45,* 2nd ed. (Urbana: University of Illinois Press, 2007), 80–114; Gilbert Osofsky, *Harlem: the Making of a Ghetto: Negro New York, 1890–1930* (New York: Harper and Row, 1966), 53–67.

27. E. J. Stelzer to Brooklyn CORE, Aug. 4, 1962; "Ebinger Campaign Memo" and sample pledge card, SHSW, box 1, folder 6.

28. "Equal Employment Opportunity vs. Ebinger Baking Company," Brooklyn CORE flyer, SHSW, box 1, folder 6.

29. Goldwag interview by the author.

30. Stein interview.

31. David L. Lewis, "Parallels and Divergences: Assimilationist Strategies of Afro-American and Jewish Elites from 1910 to the early 1930s," in Salzman et al., *Bridges and Boundaries*, 17–69.

32. Mark Naison, *White Boy: A Memoir* (Philadelphia: Temple University Press, 2002), 28–29. *Schvartze* was the Yiddish term for *black*. Depending on context and usage, it could be a racial epithet or simply mean "black person."

33. Overviews of Puerto Ricans in New York City can be found in Thomas, *Puerto Rican Citizen;* Joseph Fitzpatrick, *Puerto Rican Americans: The Meaning of Migration to the Mainland* (Englewood Cliffs, N.J.: Prentice-Hall, 1971), and Fitzpatrick, *The Stranger Is Our Own: Reflections on the Journey of Puerto Rican Migrants* (Kansas City, Mo.: Sheed and Ward, 1996); Rodriguez, *Puerto Ricans: Born in the U.S.A.* Nathan Glazer and Daniel Moynihan, *Beyond the Melting Pot: The Negroes, Puerto Ricans, Jews, Italians, and Irish of New York City* (Cambridge: MIT Press, 1963); Sánchez Korrol, *From Colonia to Community;* Lee, "Between Boricua and Black."

34. CORE, series V, file 70, frames 804, 847.

35. "Brooklyn CORE Membership Meeting, Aug. 6, 1962," SHSW, box 1, folder 1.

36. Ibid.

37. Ibid.

38. Ibid.

39. Ibid.

40. Ibid.

41. Ibid.

42. Kirchner interviews.

43. Petition to Remove Kurt Flascher, Aug. 6, 1962, SHSW, box 1, folder 2.

44. Flascher interview.

45. Ibid.

46. Ibid.; Petition to Remove Kurt Flascher.

47. Petition to Remove Kurt Flascher; "Brooklyn CORE Membership Meeting, Aug. 6, 1962."

48. CORE minutes, Aug. 13, 1962, SHSW, box 1, folder 1.

49. Ibid.

50. CORE, series V, file 70, frames 844–45.

51. Ibid., frame 804; "Civil Rights Battle: Northern Style," *Ebony*, Mar. 1963, 96–102.

52. CORE, series V, file 70, frame 804; Oliver Leeds interview by Esses; Martin Oppenheimer and George Lakey, *A Manual for Direct Action* (Chicago: Quadrangle Books, 1965), 106–7, 112; Meier and Rudwick, *CORE*, 192–93.

53. Joseph Eckhaus to Carl Rachlin, Esq. (cc: Benjamin Brown), Aug. 27, 1962, SHSW, box 1, folder 2.

54. "If Only They'll Eat More Cake," *New York Times,* Mar. 26, 1972, 10; "F.Y.I.: The Ebinger Touch," *New York Times,* June 19, 2005, CY2.

55. Meier and Rudwick, *CORE,* 201–2.

56. On Brooklyn CORE's other jobs campaigns see Meier and Rudwick, *CORE,* 187, 191–92; Stacy Kinlock Sewell, "The 'Not-Buying Power' of the Black Community: Urban Boycotts and Equal Employment Opportunity, 1960–1964," *Journal of African American History* 89.2 (2004): 141.

5. Operation Clean Sweep

1. Joseph, *Waiting 'til the Midnight Hour;* Murch, *Living for the City.*

2. *Stuyford Leader* 1.5 (Dec. 1950), SHSW, box 1, folder 5.

3. Goldwag interview, CRBC-OH.

4. "Brooklyn Sanitation Problem," SHSW, box 1, folder 5.

5. Goldwag, CRBC-OH.

6. Oliver Leeds interview by Ennes.

7. Marjorie and Oliver Leeds to Hortense Gable, assistant to the mayor, Rent and Rehabilitation Administration, Apr. 9, 1962, SHSW, box 1, folder 2.

8. Ibid.

9. Jacqueline Young interview, CRBC-OH. Vincent Young file, Bureau of Special Services, Vincent Young personal papers, in the author's possession, courtesy of Jacqueline Young.

10. Paul Robeson Jr., "A Tribute to Vincent Young," *New York Amsterdam News,* Dec. 10, 1988, 15; Young interview.

11. Law interview, Apr. 14, 2004.

12. Marjorie Leeds's handwritten notes, Aug. 24, 1962, SHSW, box 1, folder 5.

13. "Memo to Kings County and New York City Authorities Regarding the unsanitary and dilapidated condition of the sidewalks, building, and garbage collection on Gates Avenue, between Broadway and Bedford Avenues in the borough of Brooklyn," SHSW, box 1, folder 5.

14. Marjorie Leeds's handwritten notes, Aug. 24, 1962.

15. Ibid.

16. *North Star* (Sept. 1962), AG-BCORE, box 4, folder 9. On fear of informants, see Law interview, Apr. 14, 2004.

17. Oliver Leeds to Abe Stark, Sept. 7, 1962, SHSW, box, 1, folder 2.

18. Dawkins, *City Son,* chaps. 3–4; Gerson, "Building the Brooklyn Machine," 153–329; Connolly, *A Ghetto Grows in Brooklyn,* 162–80.

19. Henry Liebman to Brooklyn CORE, Sept. 13, 1962, SHSW, box 1, folder 2.

20. Gilbert Banks interview, Apr. 1–2, 2000, CRBC-OH; Kirton interview; Msemaji and Nandi Weusi interview.

21. Ibid.

22. "Plan Garbage Dump at Official's Door" (clipping from unidentified newspaper), Sept. 15, 1962, CRBC, box 1, folder 6.

23. Msemaji and Nandi Weusi interview; Oliver Leeds interview by Esses; Law interview, Apr. 14, 2004.

24. Msemaji and Nandi Weusi interview; Law interview, Apr. 14, 2004; "Brooklyn Group Flaunts Debris," *New York Times,* Sept. 16, 1962.

25. Oliver Leeds interview by Esses; "B'klyn Rebels Slop Boro Hall with Garbage" (clipping from unidentified newspaper), Sept. 16, 1962, CRBC, box 1, folder 6; summons #K295101, Leeds personal papers.

26. *North Star* (Oct. 1962): 1, AG-BCORE, box 4, folder 9. Law interview, Apr. 14, 2004; Oliver Leeds interview by Esses; Dave Snitkin, "Neighborhood Action Report" (clipping from unidentified newspaper), n.d., CRBC, box 1, folder 6; "Stark to Seek End to Garbage Mess," *New York World Telegram,* Sept. 18, 1962; Robert Brookins Gore (assistant community relations director for National CORE) to William Fetherston, SHSW, box 1, folder 5.

27. "Stark to Seek End to Garbage Mess," *New York World Telegram,* Sept. 18, 1962; "Stark Asks Daily Garbage Pickup"; "Stark to Take Birns on Tour of Housing"; "'Jail All Slumlords; They Don't Mind Paying $$': Abe Stark Appeals to Courts" (clippings from unidentified newspaper), all in CRBC, box 1, folder 6.

28. "CORE Gets 2 Promises on Garbage: Summonses Sure; 5 Day Pickup Depends on Budget" (clipping from unidentified newspaper), CRBC, box 1, folder 6.

29. "Five Day Pick-up Achieved," *North Star* (Oct. 1962): 1; Frank J. Lucia to Oliver Leeds, Dec. 3, 1962, SHSW, box 1, folder 5.

30. Lucia to Oliver Leeds, Dec. 3, 1962.

31. Ibid.; Oliver Leeds and Bob Law to Mayor Wagner, Jan. 20, 1963; and Oliver Leeds and Bob Law to Frank J. Lucia, Jan. 20, 1963, SHSW, box 1, folder 5.

32. Thomas Jones to Oliver Leeds, Jan. 22, 1963, Frank Lucia to Oliver Leeds, Jan. 24, 1963, and Henry Liebman to Oliver Leeds, Feb. 1, 1963, all in SHSW, box 1, folder 5; Gerson, "Building the Brooklyn Machine," 288–98.

33. Bernice Fisher to Oliver Leeds, Feb. 5, 1963, Bernice Fisher to Marjorie Leeds, Mar. 21, 1963, Central Brooklyn Coordinating Council, "Statement of the Executive Committee re: Garbage Collection in Bedford-Stuyvesant," May 2, 1963, all in SHSW, box 1, folder 5.

34. Bernice Fisher to Oliver Leeds, Feb. 5, 1963; Bernice Fisher to Marjorie Leeds, Mar. 21, 1963.

35. Central Brooklyn Coordinating Council, "Statement of the Executive Committee, re: Garbage Collection in Bedford-Stuyvesant."

36. "Moms Block Street for Traffic Light," *Brooklyn Eagle,* Jan. 18, 1963, 1; "Parent Rally Blocks Cars to Demand Traffic Light," *Worker,* Jan. 27, 1963, 12; "Brooklyn Parents Win Traffic Lights Pledge," *Worker,* Jan.

29, 1963, 3; "Will Your Child Be Next?" flyer, Jan. 16, 1963, and "Give Us Our Traffic Lights," flyer, n.d., AG-BCORE, box 1, folder 6.

37. "Brooklyn Parents Win Traffic Lights Pledge," *Worker,* Jan. 29, 1963; "Help Save a Child's Life," flyer, Feb. 18, 1963, AG-BCORE, box 1, folder 6.

38. Brooklyn community leaders to Oliver and Marjorie Leeds, Aug. 29, 1963, AG-BCORE, box 1, folder 6.

39. "Its War on Slum Profits," *New York Herald Tribune,* July 16, 1963; "Promise Cleanup of Bedford Section" *New York World Telegram and Sun,* July 16, 1963, clippings in AG-BCORE, box 1, folder 5.

40. *North Star* (Oct. 1962): 1; Robert Law, "The Take-Charge Negro," ibid., 3–4.

41. James Steward, "A Black Man Looks at the Fight for Freedom," ibid., 5.

42. Ibid.

43. For comments on Brooklyn CORE as a "ghetto chapter," see Oliver Leeds interview by Esses; Oliver Leeds, interview by August Meier, Apr. 28, 1971, August Meier Papers, Schomburg Center for Research in Black Culture.

44. Arnold Goldwag, "On Being White," *North Star* (Oct. 1962): 4–5; James Steward, "Why You Should Join CORE," *North Star* (Nov. 1962): 2, AG-BCORE, box 4, folder 9.

45. Maurice Fredericks to the editor, *North Star* (Nov. 1962): 5.

46. Meier and Rudwick, *CORE,* 205–6.

47. Frances Phipps Crayton interview, Nov. 28, 2003, CRBC-OH.

48. Bibuld, Kirton, Kirchner, Weusi, and Weusi interview; Craig interview; Kirchner interviews.

49. Kirton interview.

6. "A War for the Minds and Futures of Our Negro and Puerto Rican Children"

1. Ravitch, *The Great School Wars;* Taylor, *Knocking at Our Own Door;* Podair, *The Strike That Changed New York;* Back, "Up South in New York"; Heather Lewis, "Protest, Place, and Pedagogy: New York City's Community Control Movement and Its Aftermath" (Ph.D. diss., New York University, 2006).

2. Douglass Bibuld interview; Elaine Bibuld interview, Feb. 18, 2001, CRBC-OH; Jerome Bibuld interview, Jan. 2, 2003, CRBC-OH.

3. Jack Dougherty, *More Than One Struggle: The Evolution of Black School Reform in Milwaukee* (Chapel Hill: University of North Carolina Press, 2004), 3; Paul Zuber, "The 'De Facto Segregation' Hoax," *Liberator* 3.8 (Aug. 1963): 7; Theoharis and Woodard, *Freedom North,* 65–91; Back, "Up South in New York"; Adina Back, "Blacks, Jews and the Struggle to Integrate Brooklyn's Junior High School 258," *Journal of American Ethnic History* 20.2 (Winter 2001): 38–69; Taylor, *Knocking at Our Own Door.*

Taylor, *Reds at the Blackboard,* reveals how a retreat from desegregation of New York City public schools, and from structural critiques of education inequality, became more acute when Communists and leftists were purged from the city teachers' union. Some texts that also explore the "culture of poverty" argument and public education in the city are Harold Saltzman, *Race War in High School: The Ten-Year Destruction of Franklin K. Lane High School in Brooklyn* (New Rochelle, N.Y.: Arlington House, 1972); Mwlina Imiri Abubadika, *The Education of Sonny Carson* (New York: Norton, 1972); Vincent Cannato, *The Ungovernable City: John Lindsay and His Struggle to Save New York* (New York: Basic Books, 2001), 267–351. Brooklyn CORE's argument about racial segregation and public education mirrored Craig Wilder's summary: "Ghettoization meant that the school system had to compensate for the economic and political vulnerabilities of the black community; or, as white Brooklynites long demanded, social equality could only come if African Americans overachieved." See Wilder, *A Covenant with Color,* 224.

4. Douglass Bibuld interview; Community Council of Greater New York, *Brooklyn Communities,* 1:138–40.

5. Jerome Bibuld interview.

6. Elaine Bibuld, interview by Sheila Michaels, May 23, 2000, Nonviolent Oral History Project, Columbia University, Special Collections.

7. Ibid.; Jerome Bibuld interview; Elaine Bibuld interview, CRBC-OH; Douglass Bibuld interview.

8. Community Council of Greater New York, *Brooklyn Communities,* 1:142. Puerto Rican children were a clear minority and made up only 5 percent of the student population, whereas African Americans constituted 44 percent.

9. Elaine Bibuld interview by Michaels; Douglass Bibuld interview.

10. "The Bibuld Case—Fact Sheet," SHSW, box 2, folder 5; Community Council of Greater New York, *Brooklyn Communities,* 2:24.

11. Douglass Bibuld interview; Community Council of Greater New York, *Brooklyn Communities,* 2:26–27, 30.

12. "The Bibuld Case—Fact Sheet": "For Release to the *North Star*" (n.d.), SHSW, box 2, folder 5; "First Sit-in in N.Y.C. History," *Newsletter of the Parents' Workshop for Equality in N.Y.C. Schools* (Dec. 1962): 6, Elaine Bibuld personal papers; "Principal Raps CORE and Press on School," *Brooklyn Eagle,* Dec. 4, 1962, 1.

13. Elaine Bibuld interview, CRBC-OH; Douglass Bibuld interview. The story of the spelling test and math homework was told many times in subsequent newspaper articles and Brooklyn CORE's flyers: "First Sit-in in N.Y.C. History," "Sit-in for Equality," n.d., in SHSW, box 2, folder 5; "Parents Face Jail/Padres Riesgan Cárcel," in Elaine Bibuld personal papers (English-Spanish flyer; copy in author's possession), n.d.

14. Douglass Bibuld interview.

15. Elaine Bibuld interview, CRBC-OH; Jerome Bibuld interview.

16. For an overview of history of New York City public schools, see Ravitch, *The Great School Wars*. On racial segregation and northern schools, see Davison Douglas, *Jim Crow Moves North: The Battle over Northern School Segregation, 1865–1954* (New York: Cambridge University Press, 2005); Dougherty, *More Than One Struggle*; Theoharis and Woodard, *Groundwork*, 17–44.

17. "The Bibuld Case—Fact Sheet."

18. Douglass Bibuld interview; Jerome Bibuld interview; "Mom Called to Court in School Fight," *New York World Telegram and Sun* (Brooklyn section), Nov. 28, 1962, 1.

19. See all Elaine Bibuld interviews.

20. Kirton interview, CRBC-OH.

21. "Parents Win Wide Support in School Boycott," *New York Amsterdam News*, Nov. 17, 1962, 23.

22. "The Bibuld Case—Fact Sheet."

23. Elaine Bibuld interview, CRBC-OH; Elaine Bibuld interview by Michaels; "Unequal Education = Unequally Qualified" (flyer), n.d., CRBC, box 1, folder 9.

24. "Sit-in for Equality." Statistics on P.S. 200's student body are from "In Brooklyn, a 1-Boy School Sit-in," *New York Post*, Nov. 27, 1962; "Threaten B'klyn Negro Pupils," *New York Post*, Dec. 3, 1962; "Negro Lad Tries to Crash 'White' School," *New York Daily News*, Nov. 28, 1962, 72; "Defy School Board: Long Armed Law," *New York Amsterdam News*, Dec. 8, 1962, 25.

25. On the early history of public schools and racial and ethnic minorities, see Ravitch, *The Great School Wars*.

26. "Brooklyn CORE Fights School Segregation," *North Star* (Nov. 1962), AG-BCORE, box 4, folder 9.

27. Douglass Bibuld interview; Elaine Bibuld interview, CRBC-OH; Elaine Bibuld interview by Michaels.

28. Ibid.

29. Douglass Bibuld interview.

30. "In Brooklyn, a 1-Boy School Sit-in," *New York Post*, Nov. 27, 1962; "Seeking School Change," *Brooklyn Eagle*, Nov. 28, 1962, 1; "Sit-in for Equality in P.S. 200" (flyer), n.d., SHSW, box 2, folder 5; placard slogans listed in AG-BCORE, box 2, folder 4.

31. "In Brooklyn, a 1-Boy School Sit-in," *New York Post*, Nov. 27, 1962; "Seeking School Change," *Brooklyn Eagle*, Nov. 28, 1962; "Negro Lad Tries to Crash 'White' School," *New York Daily News*, Nov. 28, 1962; "Mom Called to Court in School Fight," *New York World Telegram and Sun*, Nov. 28, 1962.

32. "Parents Face Jail/Padres Riesgan Cárcel."

33. Thomas, *Puerto Rican Citizen*; Whalen and Vázquez-Hernández, *The Puerto Rican Diaspora*.

34. Jerome Bibuld interview; Douglass Bibuld interview; Elaine Bibuld

interview, CRBC-OH; Elaine Bibuld interview by Michaels; "School Is Defied by Negro Parents," *New York Times,* Dec. 15, 1962.

35. A. Shapiro to Elaine Bibuld, postmarked Nov. 28, 1962, and anonymous letter writer to Elaine Bibuld, n.d., both in AG-BCORE, box 2, folder 5. Mention of the threatening note also appears in "Gifted Child Continues School Sit-in Despite Threats," press release, CORE, series V, file 374, frame 484. On whites' attitudes toward blacks in Brooklyn see Rieder, *Canarsie;* Podair, *The Strike That Changed New York,* 9–20, 48–70.

36. Unidentified letter writer to Brooklyn CORE, n.d., in Elaine Bibuld's personal papers (copy in author's possession).

37. "Bibulds Find School O.K.," *New York Amsterdam News,* Feb. 16, 1963, 1. This newspaper article included a photo of the Bibulds holding placards that described the lack of resources at P.S. 282, which is also featured later in this chapter.

38. "Gifted Child Continues School Sit-in Despite Threats"; "Flyers, Bibuld Campaign," CRBC, box 1, folder 9.

39. "Threaten B'klyn Negro Pupils," *New York Post,* Dec. 3, 1962; "3 Negro Students Get Police Escort," *New York Times,* Dec. 4, 1962, 34; "Principal Raps CORE and Press on School," *Brooklyn Eagle,* Dec. 4, 1962, 1; "Defy School Board: Long Armed Law," *New York Amsterdam News,* Dec. 8, 1962, 1; "School Is Defied by Negro Parents," *New York Times,* Dec. 15, 1962.

40. Williams, *Eyes on the Prize,* 213–18.

41. "Acting Superintendent of Schools Bernard E. Donovan Flouts the Law of the Land" (flyer), n.d., SHSW, box 2, folder 5; *Liberator* (Feb. 1963), 21.

42. Elaine Bibuld interview, CRBC-OH; Elaine Bibuld interview by Michaels; handwritten notes with the heading "phone call," in CRBC, box 1, folder 9.

43. "Guard 3 Negro Pupils," *New York Journal-American,* Dec. 3, 1962, 3; "Threaten B'klyn Negro Pupils," *New York Post,* Dec. 3, 1962; "3 Negro Students Get Police Escort," *New York Times,* Dec. 4, 1962, 34; "Principal Raps CORE and Press on School," *Brooklyn Eagle,* Dec. 4, 1962, 1; "Defy School Board: Long Armed Law," *New York Amsterdam News,* Dec. 8, 1962, 1; "School Is Defied by Negro Parents," *New York Times,* Dec. 15, 1962.

44. Elaine Bibuld interview by Michaels; Douglass Bibuld interview; "Parents Willing to Risk Jail in Brooklyn School Case; Due in Court Dec. 17," *New York Courier,* Dec. 15, 1962; "Defy School Board: Long Armed Law," *New York Amsterdam News,* Dec. 8, 1962, 1.

45. "School Is Defied by Negro Parents," *New York Times,* Dec. 15, 1962; handwritten note by Oliver Leeds, n.d., SHSW, box 2, folder 5; "Defy School Board: Long Armed Law," *New York Amsterdam News,* Dec. 8, 1962; "Parents Willing to Risk Jail in Brooklyn School Case; Due in Court Dec. 17," *New York Courier,* Dec. 15, 1962; Elaine Bibuld interview, CRBC-OH; Douglass Bibuld interview.

46. "For Immediate Release," press release, Jan. 7, 1963, in SHSW, box 2, folder 5; "Couple Kept Kids Out of School to Be Sentenced Jan. 28th," *Brooklyn Daily,* Jan. 3, 1963, 3; "Convict Negro Couple Fighting School Bias," *Worker,* Jan. 8, 1963, 1.

47. "For Immediate Release," Jan. 7, 1963.

48. "Picket Schools to Protest Negro Parents' Conviction," *Worker,* Jan. 15, 1963, 8.

49. Taylor, *The Black Churches of Brooklyn,* 49–50, 93–94, 135.

50. "Mother Is Defiant in School Fight," *Brooklyn Eagle,* Jan. 14, 1963; "Picket Schools to Protest Negro Parents' Conviction," *Worker,* Jan. 15, 1963.

51. CORE, series V, file 374, frame 490; *Worker,* Jan. 22, 1963, AG-BCORE, box 2, folder 4; Gilbert Banks to Abe Stark, n.d., SHSW, box 2, folder 5.

52. "Bibulds Take Case to Human Rights Body," *Worker,* Jan. 29, 1963, 5; complaint filed by Bibulds, Jan. 24, 1963 (photocopy), and commission's response mentioned in "For Immediate Release," press release, Jan. 26, 1963, Elaine Bibuld personal papers, box 1, folder 9.

53. "Bibulds Take Case to Human Rights Body," *Worker,* Jan. 29, 1963, 5; "Jim Crow's Funeral," *Jet,* Feb. 21, 1963, 10; placard slogans listed in AG-BCORE, box 2, folder 4.

54. "Bibulds Take Case to Human Rights Body," *Worker,* Jan. 29, 1963, 5; *North Star* (Feb. 1963), AG-BCORE, box 5, folder 9.

55. "Bibulds Take Case to Human Rights Body," *Worker,* Jan. 29, 1963, 1; "Start Board Sit-in over School Shift," *Brooklyn Eagle,* Jan. 29, 1963; "Bd. of Ed. Hit on Race Bias," *Brooklyn Eagle,* Jan. 30, 1963, 23; "N.Y. School Bias Continues," *Newark News,* Jan. 29, 1963; "Sitting It Out," *Newark News,* Jan. 30, 1963; "CORE Keeps Up Protest Sit-in," *Jersey Journal* (Jersey City, N.J.), Jan. 31, 1963.

56. Jerome Bibuld to Congressman Adam Clayton Powell Jr. and Senator Jacob Javits, Jan. 30, 1963 (emphasis in original); "Racial Question—Figures in the News," *Metropolitan Daily*, Jan. 31, 1963, AG-BCORE, box 2, folder 5.

57. Odell Clark to the Board of Education, Jan. 31, 1963, CRBC, box 1, folder 9.

58. "Bureaucratic Mixup," *Brooklyn Eagle,* Jan. 31, 1963, 12.

59. See Ravitch, *Great School Wars;* Douglas, *Jim Crow Moves North;* Dougherty, *More Than One Struggle.*

60. Paul Kirchner, "Letter from a TV Fan," CRBC, box 1, folder 8; "Brooklyn CORE Group Sits-in at Board of Education," *Brooklyn Daily,* Jan. 29, 1963, 5.

61. Paul Kirchner, "Letter from a TV Fan."

62. "Bibuld Sit-in in 4th Day, CORE in Finish Fight," *Brooklyn Eagle,* Feb. 1, 1963, 1; "CORE Aids Sit-in," *New York Amsterdam News,* Feb. 2, 1963, 1.

63. *North Star* (Feb. 1963); "Turning Point Today on Bibuld School Sit-in," *Brooklyn Eagle,* Feb. 4, 1963, 1; "Bibulds Enroll, Sit-in Ended," *Brooklyn Eagle,* Feb. 5, 1963, 1; "CORE Halts Sit-in as N.Y. Transfers Pupils," *Chicago Daily Defender,* Feb. 5, 1963; "CORE Ends Sit-in at School Board," *Jersey Journal* (Jersey City, N.J.), Feb. 5, 1963; "Sit-in Brings Change in School," *Christian Science Monitor,* Feb. 6, 1963; "Victorious Sit-in at New York's Board of Education," *National Guardian,* Feb. 7, 1963, 3; "Board of Ed. Yields to Sit-in Pressure," *New York Courier,* Feb. 6, 1963.

64. "Judge Dismisses Charges against Family," *Brooklyn Daily,* Feb. 14, 1963; "Bibulds Find School O.K.," *New York Amsterdam News,* Feb. 16, 1963; *North Star* (Feb. 1963).

65. *North Star* (Feb. 1963); Jerome Bibuld interview.

66. On decentralization and the Ocean Hill–Brownsville experimental community control district see, Podair, *The Strike That Changed New York;* Perlstein, *Justice, Justice;* Jane Anna Gordon, *Why They Couldn't Wait: A Critique of the Black-Jewish Conflict over Community Control in Ocean Hill–Brownsville, 1967–1971* (New York: RoutledgeFalmer, 2001); Taylor, *Knocking at Our Own Door;* Lewis, "Protest, Place, and Pedagogy."

67. On the social and economic crises that beset New York City during and after the 1960s, see T. J. English, *The Savage City: Race, Murder, and a Generation on the Edge* (New York: William Morrow, 2011); Cannato, *The Ungovernable City;* Barry Gottehrer, ed., *New York City in Crisis: A Study in Depth of Urban Sickness* (New York: D. McKay, 1965); Sam Roberts, ed., *America's Mayor: John V. Lindsay and the Reinvention of New York* (New York: Museum of the City of New York, 2010); Frederick F. Siegel, *The Future Once Happened Here: New York, D.C., L.A., and the Fate of America's Big Cities* (New York: Free Press, 1997).

68. Back, "Up South in New York"; Taylor, *Knocking at Our Own Door.* On New York City's knowledge-based economy, see Freeman, *Working-Class New York.*

7. "We Had Struggled in Vain"

1. Thomas Sugrue, "Affirmative Action from Below: Civil Rights, the Building Trades, and the Politics of Racial Equality in the Urban North, 1945–1969," *Journal of American History* 91 (2004): 145. Sugrue mentions similar demonstrations in Newark and Trenton, New Jersey; Cleveland, Ohio; and the ones in Harlem and Brooklyn that are discussed below. Thomas Sugrue, *Sweet Land of Liberty,* 276–78, 291–303, 362–64; Nancy MacLean, *Freedom Is Not Enough: The Opening of the American Workplace* (New York: Russell Sage, 2006), 90–103; Paul Moreno, *From Direct Action to Affirmative Action: Fair Employment Law and Policy in America, 1933–1972* (Baton Rouge: Louisiana State University Press, 1997), 135–61; Clarence Taylor, "'Whatever the Cost, We Will Set the Nation Straight': The

Ministers' Committee and the Downstate Center Campaign," *Long Island Historical Journal* 1.2 (1989): 136–46.

2. Biondi, *To Stand and Fight,* 17–37; Sugrue, *Sweet Land of Liberty;* David Goldberg and Trevor Griffey, *Black Power at Work: Community Control, Affirmative Action, and the Construction Industry* (Ithaca: Cornell University Press, 2010), 1–22; Nancy Banks, "'The Last Bastion of Discrimination': The New York City Building Trades and the Struggle over Affirmative Action, 1961–1976" (Ph.D. diss., Columbia University, 2006).

3. "State University Sets Vast Growth," *New York Times,* Jan. 8, 1960, 1.

4. Oliver Leeds interview by Esses; Oliver Leeds, and Maurice Fredericks interviews, NYW-OH; Gilbert Banks interview, Oct. 22, 1980, NYW-OH; Kirton interview; Elaine Bibuld interview, CRBC-OH.

5. Taylor, "'Whatever the Cost, We Will Set the Nation Straight,'" and *The Black Churches of Brooklyn,* are two important studies of the Downstate demonstration. Taylor focuses on the leadership of the ministers. I analyze Brooklyn CORE and argue that it was more influential than the ministers in the protest's on-the-ground developments. The ministers, however, had more influence on negotiations with power brokers.

6. "State's Construction Outlays to Rise to Record 345 Million," *New York Times,* Feb. 2, 1961, 20. F. Ray Marshall and Vernon M. Briggs, *The Negro and Apprenticeship* (Baltimore: Johns Hopkins Press, 1967), 47, 50; and F. Ray Marshall, *The Negro and Organized Labor* (New York: Wiley, 1965), 123; Roger Waldinger and Thomas Bailey, "The Continuing Significance of Race: Racial Conflict and Racial Discrimination in Construction," *Politics & Society* 19.3 (1991): 291–323.

7. Waldinger, *Still the Promised City?* 178–82.

8. Ibid. On sheet metal unions, see Moreno, *From Direct Action to Affirmative Action,* 150–53.

9. Banks interview, CRBC-OH; Banks interview, NYW-OH.

10. "Wagner Directs Agencies to Push Minority Rights," *New York Times,* June 5, 1963, 1, 31; "Building Unions Pledge Bias Fight," *New York Times,* June 7, 1963, 1, 15; "Mayor Moves on Bias," *New York Amsterdam News,* June 8, 1963, 1–2.

11. Williams, *Eyes on the Prize,* 179–95, quote on 188.

12. Hill quoted in "Promise Mass Action on Building Trade Unions," *New York Amsterdam News,* June 8, 1963."Race Relations in Crisis," on *The Open Mind,* aired June 12, 1963; transcript courtesy of Richard Heffner (in author's possession).

13. "Promise Mass Action on Building Trade Unions," *New York Amsterdam News,* June 8, 1963; "Unions Here Get Warning on Bias," *New York Times,* June 13, 1963, 1; "300 Cops Present: Pickets Clash at Hospital Site," *New York Amsterdam News,* June 15, 1963, 1–2; "City Halts Work at Site in Harlem," *New York Times,* June 14, 1963, 1, 32.

14. "City Halts Work at Site in Harlem," *New York Times,* June 14, 1963, 32; "The Time Is Now," *New York Amsterdam News,* June 29, 1963, 10.

15. Marilyn Rubin to the editor, *New York Times*, June 20, 1963.

16. Oliver Leeds interview, NYW-OH; Oliver and Marjorie Leeds interview by Taylor; Oliver Leeds interview by Esses.

17. Oliver Leeds interview by Esses.

18. Taylor, *Black Churches of Brooklyn*, 143; Oliver Leeds interview by Esses.

19. Taylor, *Black Churches of Brooklyn*, 118, 144–46.

20. Oliver and Marjorie Leeds interview by Taylor.

21. Ibid.

22. Some of the other members of the Ministers' Committee were Walter G. Henson Jacobs, pastor of St. Augustine Episcopal Church; Carl McCall from the New York Mission Society; Richard Saunders, pastor of Stuyvesant Heights Christian Church; Benjamin Lowery of Zion Baptist Church; George Lawrence of Antioch Baptist Church; William A. Jones of Bethany Baptist Church; and A. W. Wilson of Morningstar Baptist Church. Except for Carl McCall, all the ministers had churches in Bedford-Stuyvesant and led churches with over one thousand members each. See Taylor, *Black Churches of Brooklyn*, 144, 146–47.

23. "Governor's Office Here Is Besieged as Sit-ins Spread," *New York Times*, July 11, 1963, 1; "Sit-ins Hit Mayor, Governor," *New York Amsterdam News*, July 13, 1963, 1.

24. Elaine Bibuld, Kirton, Kirchner, Weusi, and Weusi interview; Elaine Bibuld interview, CRBC-OH; Jerome Bibuld interview; Elaine Bibuld interview by Michaels.

25. Elaine Bibuld interview by Michaels.

26. Elaine Bibuld interview, CRBC-OH.

27. Taylor, *Black Churches of Brooklyn*, 151; Aldon Morris, *The Origins of the Civil Rights Movement: Black Communities Organizing for Change* (New York: Free Press, 1984), 284.

28. Oliver and Marjorie Leeds interview by Taylor; Oliver Leeds interview, NYW-OH; Oliver Leeds interview by Esses.

29. Banks, "The Last Bastion of Discrimination"; Oliver Leeds interview, NYW-OH. On Birmingham see Williams, *Eyes on the Prize*, 181–95.

30. Oliver and Marjorie Leeds interview by Taylor; italics indicate Leeds's changing intonation.

31. Oliver and Marjorie Leeds interview by Taylor; Oliver Leeds interview by Esses.

32. "42 Rights Pickets Arrested by City," *New York Times*, July 16, 1963, 1, 15.

33. Ibid.

34. Ibid.

35. Oliver and Marjorie Leeds interview by Taylor.

36. Ibid.

37. A. H. Rivera to the editor, *New York Daily News*, July 17, 1963, 31;

Howard Bell to the editor, "Don't Need Help," *New York Amsterdam News,* Aug. 3, 1963, 10.

38. Fitzpatrick, *Puerto Rican Americans;* Rodriguez, *Puerto Ricans;* Sánchez Korrol, *From Colonia to Community;* Lee, "Between Boricua and Black"; Thomas, *Puerto Rican Citizen.*

39. Taylor, *Black Churches of Brooklyn,* 150–52.

40. "Wagner to Help Negroes Get More Building Jobs," *New York Times,* July 22, 1963, 1, 9; "Agency Proposed to Bar Union Bias," *New York Times,* July 23, 1963, 57.

41. "Builders Try New Tactics to Get through Pickets," *New York Times,* July 24, 1963, 18; "Police Cut Chains to Seize Pickets," *New York Times,* July 26, 1963, 13; "18 Children among 49 Pickets Seized in Brooklyn," *New York Times,* July 31, 1963, 14.

42. "27 Pickets Seized with 17 Children in Street Blockade," *New York Times,* July 20, 1963, 1, 10; "18 Children among 49 Pickets Seized in Brooklyn," *New York Times,* July 31, 1963.

43. "Rockefeller Bars Negro Job Quota; Hails Union Plan," *New York Times,* July 26, 1963, 1; "Wagner Extends Civil Rights Talks on Job Practices," *New York Times,* July 31, 1963, 1, 14; Shelly Spector Ipiotis, e-mail to the author, Mar. 24, 2005, CRBC-OH; Maurice Fredericks interview, Apr. 28, 1981, NYW-OH.

44. Oliver and Marjorie Leeds interview by Taylor; Elaine Bibuld, Kirton, Kirchner, Weusi, and Weusi interview, CRBC-OH.

45. Maurice Fredericks interview, NYW-OH; Elaine Bibuld, Kirton, Kirchner, Weusi, and Weusi interview, CRBC-OH.

46. Elaine Bibuld, Kirton, Kirchner, Weusi, and Weusi interview, CRBC-OH.

47. Robert "Sonny" Carson, interview, Nov. 13, 2000, CRBC-OH.

48. Ibid.

49. Taylor, *Black Churches of Brooklyn,* 151.

50. Goldwag interview, CRBC-OH; Diane Fujino, *Heartbeat of Struggle: The Revolutionary Life of Yuri Kochiyama* (Minneapolis: University of Minnesota Press, 2005), 116, 119–20.

51. Fujino, *Heartbeat of Struggle,* 120.

52. Crayton interview.

53. Ibid.

54. Taylor, *Black Churches of Brooklyn,* 153–55.

55. "Information Available on Group Known as 'Procepts,'" Bureau Special Services File, Vincent Young personal papers. See also "[Police Reports] Procept," AG-BCORE, box 8, folder 4.

56. "Investigation of Activities of Procept Members in Connection with Brooklyn Chapter of Congress of Racial Equality," Aug. 14, 1963, Bureau Special Services File, #334-M, Vincent Young personal papers.

57. "Near-Riot Flares in Race Protest at Project Here," *New York Times,* Aug. 1, 1963, 1, 12; Taylor, *Black Churches of Brooklyn,* 155.

58. Oliver Leeds interview, NYW-OH.

59. "Information Available on Group Known as 'Procepts.'"

60. Ibid.; Oliver Leeds interview by Esses; Oliver and Marjorie Leeds interview by Taylor; Oliver Leeds interview, NYW-OH.

61. Taylor, *Black Churches of Brooklyn,* 155. Moreno, *From Direct Action to Affirmative Action,* 150–53.

62. Oliver Leeds interview by Esses; Oliver and Marjorie Leeds interview by Taylor; Oliver Leeds interview, NYW-OH.

63. Oliver and Marjorie Leeds interview by Taylor.

64. Oliver and Marjorie Leeds interview by Taylor; Taylor, *Black Churches of Brooklyn,* 156.

65. Banks interview, CRBC-OH; New York City Commission on Human Rights and New York City Office of Labor Services, *Public Hearing on the Construction Industries in New York* (New York: City Hall Library, 1990).

66. Elaine Bibuld interview, CRBC-OH.

8. "A Gun at the Heart of the City"

1. Wilder, *A Covenant with Color,* 235–42; see also Lawrence Samuel, *The End of the Innocence: The 1964–1965 New York World's Fair* (Syracuse, N.Y.: Syracuse University Press, 2007); Tamar Jacoby, *Someone Else's House: America's Unfinished Struggle for Integration* (New York: Free Press, 1998), 15–32.

2. On the 1964 school boycott, see Taylor, *Knocking at Our Own Door;* Podair, *The Strike That Changed New York;* Back, "Up South in New York;" Lee and Diaz, "'I Was the One Percenter.'"

3. Wilder, *A Covenant with Color,* 237; Mary Caraballo to Robert Moses, Apr. 14, 1964, RMP.

4. Ronald Lawson, ed., *The Tenant Movement in New York City, 1904–1984* (New Brunswick, N.J.: Rutgers University Press, 1986), 23, 24, 175–77.

5. Major Owens interview, Dec. 12, 2003, CRBC-OH.

6. "Rent Strike in Brooklyn," press release, Oct. 3, 1963, AG-BCORE, box 1, folder 4; "CORE Rally Set to Spur Rent Strike," *New York World Telegram and Sun,* Oct. 19, 1963, B-1.

7. Payne, *I've Got the Light of Freedom,* 236–64.

8. Stanley Brezenoff interview, July 1, 2004, CRBC-OH; Paul and Rita Heinegg interview; "Slum Drive Funds 3000 Violations," *New York World Telegram and Sun,* Aug. 1, 1963; "Picket Landlord's Home on LI," *Long Island Press,* Nov. 4, 1963; Brooklyn CORE Rent-Strike Committee, Major Owens, chairman, "Progress Report," Jan. 18, 1964, in AG-BCORE, box 1, folder 4. For information on Brooklyn CORE's rent strikes, see clippings, flyers, and documents in AG-BCORE, box 1, folders 3, 4; box 8, folder 6.

9. Edwin Lewinson interview, Nov. 20, 2003, CRBC-OH.

10. Robert Caro, *The Power Broker: Robert Moses and the Fall of New York* (New York: Knopf, 1974), 1082–116; "New York World Telegram

Souvenir Guide," *New York World Telegram and Sun,* Apr. 20, 1964, 38; "Questions about the Fair? . . . The Answers," *New York Journal-American,* Apr. 22, 1964, 28.

11. Caro, *The Power Broker,* 1087.

12. Brooklyn CORE to Governor Nelson Rockefeller and Mayor Robert F. Wagner, Apr. 9, 1964 (telegram), AG-BCORE, box 3, folder 7.

13. "Barnes Says CORE's Fair Tie-up Can Paralyze the City," *New York Post,* Apr. 10, 1964, 3.

14. "What Sort of Man Is Activist Who Threatens Fair Stall-in?" *Baltimore Afro-American,* Apr. 25, 1964, 17.

15. Oliver Leeds interview, NYW-OH; Oliver and Marjorie Leeds interview by Taylor; Oliver Leeds interview by Esses.

16. "Queens Traffic Jam Threatened in Racial Protest," *New York Journal-American,* July 11, 1963, 1.

17. "Going Too Far," *New York Journal-American,* July 12, 1963.

18. "Muddy Thinking," *New York Journal-American,* Apr. 10, 1964.

19. "Real Issues vs. Organized Chaos: James Farmer Takes His Stand," *New York Post,* Apr. 12, 1964, 28.

20. WMCA, "Radio Editorials," Apr. 14, 15, 1964, AG-BCORE, box 4, folder 10.

21. WLIB, "What Is the Purpose?" Apr. 18, 19, 1964, AG-BCORE, box 4, folder 10.

22. Clayborne Carson et al., eds., *The Eyes on the Prize: Civil Rights Reader: Documents, Speeches, and Firsthand Accounts from the Black Freedom Struggle, 1954–1990* (New York: Penguin Books, 1991), 163–65.

23. Theoharis and Woodard, *Freedom North,* ix–xiii.

24. Craig Turnbull, "'Please Make No Demonstrations Tomorrow': The Brooklyn Congress of Racial Equality and Symbolic Protest at the 1964–65 World's Fair," *Australasian Journal of American Studies* 17.1 (1998): 23–24; "Statement of Demands," n.d., AG-BCORE, box 3, folder 7.

25. "Press Release from Bronx CORE & Brooklyn CORE to the Officials of New York City and the General Public," Apr. 4, 1964, AG-BCORE, box 3, folder 7.

26. CORE, series I, file 12, frames 907–8.

27. Ed Miller, e-mail to the author, Mar. 3, 2001, CRBC-OH.

28. "CORE Threatens to Waste Water," *New York Times,* Apr. 14, 1964, 1; "CORE Unit Plans to Hit Water Supply—Would Let Faucets Flow in City Homes," *New York Newsday,* Apr. 13, 1964, 1, 3.

29. "Mayor Warns Fair Stallers: 'The Law Will be Enforced,'" *New York Daily News,* Apr. 21, 1964, 1, 3.

30. Mary R. MacArthur to Arnold Goldwag, Apr. 14, 1964, AG-BCORE, box 10, folder 9.

31. John Keating to Isaiah Brunson, Apr. 20, 1964 (postcard), AG-BCORE box 3, folder 7.

32. Myra Zuckerman to Brooklyn CORE office, Apr. 13, 1964, AG-BCORE, box 3, folder 7; Mary Caraballo to Robert Moses, Apr. 14, 1964.

33. Robert Moses to F. M. Flynn, Apr. 14, 1964, RMP.

34. Anne McHenry to Robert Moses, Apr. 11, 1964, and Robert Nehring to Robert Moses, Apr. 19, 1964 (telegram), RMP. William Sunners to Robert Moses, Apr. 15, 1964; Hans Poll to Mayor Wagner, Apr. 17, 1964; Edward A. Burns to Robert Moses, Apr. 18, 1964 (telegram); Louis Cook to Robert Moses, Apr. 20, 1964 (telegram), NYWF. Wilder, *A Covenant with Color,* 236–38.

35. Anonymous writer to Arnold Goldwag, Apr. 15, 1964, AG-BCORE box 10, folder 9.

36. Margaret V. Martyn to Brooklyn CORE office, Apr. 17, 1964; and anonymous writer to Brooklyn CORE office (postcard), Apr. 17, 1964, AG-BCORE, box 3, folder 7.

37. Jerry H. Gumpert to the editor, *New York Post,* Apr. 21, 1964.

38. "A. White" to the editor, *New York Daily News,* Apr. 26, 1964.

39. Mrs. L. W. to the editor, *New York World Telegram and Sun,* Apr. 21, 1964.

40. Charles T. Jackson to the editor, "Better Than a Stall-in," *New York Herald Tribune,* Apr. 19, 1964, 22.

41. On the civil rights movement and the Cold War context, see Mary Dudziak, *Cold War Civil Rights: Race and the Image of American Democracy* (Princeton: Princeton University Press, 2000); on the press and the civil rights movement, see Gene Roberts and Hank Klibanoff, *The Race Beat: The Press, the Civil Rights Struggle, and the Awakening of a Nation* (New York: Knopf, 2006).

42. Frederick Lydecker to the editor, *New York Post,* Apr. 17, 1964; Mrs. Freeman to Brooklyn CORE office, Apr. 16, 1964, AG-BCORE, box 3, folder 7.

43. "CORE Suspends Brooklyn Wing for Urging Traffic Jam at Fair," *New York Times,* Apr. 11, 1964, 1, 8.

44. James Farmer to Isaiah Brunson (telegram), Apr. 9, 1964, CORE, series I, file 12, frame 879.

45. "Barnes Says CORE's Fair Tie-up Can Paralyze the City," *New York Post,* Apr. 10, 1964, 1, 3.

46. "2 Rights Bill Sponsors Assail Negro 'Ultras,'" *New York Herald Tribune,* Apr. 16, 1964, 1, 10.

47. Banks interview, CRBC-OH.

48. Camden, N.J., CORE to National CORE (telegram), Apr. 29, 1964, CORE, series I, file 12, frame 909; Seattle Friends of the Student Non-Violent Coordinating Committee to Brooklyn CORE (telegram), Apr. 22, 1964, AG-BCORE, box 3, folder 7.

49. "Sanitation Union Backs 'Stall-in,' Won't Tow Cars," *New York Times,* Apr. 15, 1964, 1, 20.

50. Leeds quoted in "Barnes Says CORE's Fair Tie-up Can Paralyze the

City," *New York Post,* Apr. 10, 1964, 1, 3; Isaiah Brunson to Mr. and Mrs. Thurow, Apr. 19, 1964, AG-BCORE, box 3, folder 7; Wilder, *A Covenant with Color,* 238.

51. Caro, *The Power Broker,* 1102.

52. Craig Turnbull, "'Please Make No Demonstrations Tomorrow,'" 31.

53. "Seize Scores at Fair Racial Flare Up; Subway Blocked," *New York Journal-American,* Apr. 22, 1964, 1, 2, 3.

54. Crayton interview.

55. Joseph Payton to World's Fair Commission, Apr. 8, 1964; Edward Meadows to World's Fair Commission, Apr. 24, 1964; Mr. and Mrs. Walter Wasser to World's Fair Commission, Apr. 27, 1964; Jack Pinkston to World's Fair Commission, Apr. 28, 1964; W. C. Kottemann to World's Fair Commission, Apr. 23, 1964; Sylvia Tatz to World's Fair Commission, Apr. 29, 1964, NYWF.

56. "Tie-up on Subway Planned to Back Stall-in at Fair," *New York Times,* Apr. 20, 1964.

57. Lipsitz, *A Life in the Struggle,* 81–83, 87–89.

58. Dick Gregory, "The Stall-in—Rockefeller," on *So You See . . . We All Have Problems* (New York: Colpix Records, 1964); Dick Gregory interview, *Playboy,* Aug. 1964, 42.

Conclusion

1. Oliver and Marjorie Leeds interview by Taylor; Oliver Leeds interview, NYW-OH; Oliver Leeds interview by Esses.

2. Oliver and Marjorie Leeds interview by Taylor; Kirton interview, Elaine Bibuld interview, CRBC-OH

3. Msemaji and Nandi Weusi interview, CRBC-OH.

4. An extensive collection of documents on FOCUS, including newsletters, newspaper articles, and the FOCUS housing testing handbook, is in CRBC, series 2, box 4, folders 1–12.

5. On other twentieth-century race riots in New York City, see Gilbert Osofsky, "Race Riot, 1900: A Study of Ethnic Violence," *Journal of Negro Education* 32, no. 1 (Winter 1963): 16–24. Dominic J. Capeci Jr., *The Harlem Riot of 1943* (Philadelphia: Temple University Press, 1977); Cheryl Lynn Greenberg, *"Or Does It Explode?" Black Harlem in the Great Depression* (New York: Oxford University Press, 1991), 3–6, 136–37, 193, 211–14, 219–21; Biondi, *To Stand and Fight,* 60–78, 191–207; M. Johnson, *Street Justice.*

6. Janet Abu-Lughod, *Race, Space, and Riots in Chicago, New York, and Los Angeles* (New York: Oxford University Press, 2007), 171–72.

7. Ibid., 173–78; Oliver Leeds interview by Esses; Joe R. Feagin and Paul B. Sheatsley, "Ghetto Resident Appraisals of a Riot," *Public Opinion Quarterly* 32.3 (1968): 360. After years of activists denouncing police corruption and officers' use of excessive force, city hall created a civilian complaint review board (CCRB) in 1953. Staffed with three police officers who

reported directly to the police commissioner, this early CCRB developed an administrative process through which citizens could lodge complaints. But the board was ineffective because it did little to stop police brutality and lacked actual civilian oversight. The police were left to monitor themselves. Civil rights activists demanded reform well into the 1990s, and finally, in 1993, the CCRB's staff expanded to include independent citizen administrators and investigators. See Cannato, *The Ungovernable City,* 155–88; Johnson, *Street Justice,* 227–49; Biondi, *To Stand and Fight,* 70, 75, 277–78.

8. On the MFDP see, Chana Kai Lee, *For Freedom's Sake: The Life of Fannie Lou Hamer* (Urbana: University of Illinois Press, 1999), 85–102; Juan Williams, *Eyes on the Prize,* 207–50.

9. On north-central Brooklyn activists' fight for a congressional district, see Dawkins, *City Son.* See also Cooper v. Power, 260 F.Supp.207 (1966), available at www.leagle.com/xmlResult.aspx?xmldoc=1966467260FSupp 207_1439.xml&docbase=CSLWAR1-1950-1985 (accessed November 26, 2012). This struggle culminated in the redrawing of the district lines of the twelfth congressional district and the election in 1968 of Shirley Chisholm, the first African American woman to serve in Congress and Brooklyn's first black congressional representative. Chisholm held the seat until she retired in 1982. Major Owens won the 1982 election. On Chisholm see Dayo Gore et al., *Want to Start a Revolution?* 248–70; Julie Gallagher, "Waging 'The Good Fight': The Political Life of Shirley Chisholm, 1953–1982," *Journal of African American History* 92 (Summer 2007): 393–416.

10. "Boycott for Freedom," n.d., and "Operation Beautify Bedford-Stuyvesant—Community Improvement Plan," n.d., AB-CORE, box 1, folder 7.

11. Oliver Leeds, "Developing Good Community Projects," pamphlet, n.d., SHSW, box 1, folder 1.

12. Ibid.

13. "A List of Dos and Don'ts for Brooklyn CORE Task Force Workers," n.d., SHSW, box 1, folder 1.

14. On Major Owens's work in Brownsville, see Pritchett, *Brownsville, Brooklyn,* 193–255.

15. "Montgomery Marchers Speaking in Brooklyn," *New York Amsterdam News,* Apr. 10, 1965, 27; quotes from "Stand with Selma," *New York Amsterdam News,* Apr. 17, 1965, 30. On the "Brooklyn Stands with Selma, U.S.A." rally see "Civil Rights Rally Held in Brooklyn," *New York Times,* Apr. 9, 1965, 38; John Rudolph, *New York in Black and White* (radio documentary, WNYC, 2000; CD copy and transcript in author's possession). Rudolph's documentary contains clips of sound recordings of speeches delivered at the rally, which come from the WNYC radio archives.

16. "Stand with Selma," *New York Amsterdam News,* Apr. 17, 1965, 30. Rabbi and minister quoted in Rudolph, *New York in Black and White.*

17. "Civil Rights Rally Held in Brooklyn," *New York Times,* Apr. 9, 1965, 38. On Wagner see "Robert Wagner, 80, Pivotal New York Mayor Dies," *New York Times,* Feb. 13, 1991; Siegel, *The Future Once Happened*

Here, 24, 33–35, 56; Charles Morris, *The Cost of Good Intentions: New York City and the Liberal Experiment, 1960–1975* (New York: Norton, 1980), 15–24.

18. Rudolph, *New York in Black and White*, 8:20–9:20.

19. Morris, *The Cost of Good Intentions*, 20; Roberts, *America's Mayor*, 4–18.

20. On Wagner, see Roberts, *America's Mayor*, 12, 15.

21. Theoharis and Woodard, *Freedom North*, 3.

22. Excellent discussions of racism in cities outside the South can be found in Biondi, *To Stand and Fight*; Countryman, *Up South*; Hirsch, *Making the Second Ghetto*; Jones, *The Selma of the North*; Lang, *Grassroots at the Gateway*; Lipsitz, *A Life in the Struggle*; Murch, *Living for the City*; Ralph, *Northern Protest*; Self, *American Babylon*; Sugrue, *Origins of the Urban Crisis* and *Sweet Land of Liberty*; Taylor, *Civil Rights in New York City* and *Knocking at Our Own Door*; Theoharis and Woodard, *Freedom North* and *Groundwork*; Thompson, *Whose Detroit?*; Trotter, *Black Milwaukee*; Wilder, *A Covenant with Color*; Wolfinger, *Philadelphia Divided*; and Woodard, *A Nation within a Nation*. See also Jason Sokol's *The Northern Mystique: Race and Politics from Brooklyn to Boston* (forthcoming, Beacon Press); and "Northeast Politics Once a Tangled Web for Black Candidates," an interview with Jason Sokol by Michel Martin, Feb. 10, 2010, available at www.npr.org/templates/story/story.php?storyId=124081751.

23. Scholarship on Malcolm X is extensive. Perhaps the best places to view his thoughts are his speeches. See Malcolm X, *By Any Means Necessary: The Trials and Tribulations of the Making of Malcolm X*, 2nd ed. (New York: Pathfinder, 1992); Malcolm X, *Malcolm X: The Last Speeches*, ed. Bruce Perry (New York: Pathfinder, 1989).

24. Oliver Leeds interview by Esses; Oliver and Marjorie Leeds interview by Taylor.

25. Oliver and Marjorie Leeds interview by Taylor.

26. Carson interview, CRBC-OH.

27. Carson quoted by Cannato, *The Ungovernable City*, 136. On Carson and the movement for the community control of public schools, see Podair, *The Strike That Changed New York*; Marjorie Murphy, *Blackboard Unions: The AFT and the NEA, 1900–1980* (Ithaca: Cornell University Press, 1992); and Murphy, "From New York City to Memphis: Teacher Unions and Politics," lecture delivered at Swarthmore College, available at http://media.swarthmore.edu/faculty_lectures/?p=82. Tamar Jacoby, "Sonny Carson and the Politics of Protest," *City Journal* (Summer 1991), www.city-journal.org/html/issue1_4.html. On the Korean grocery boycott see Claire Jean Kim, *Bitter Fruit: The Politics of Black-Korean Conflict in New York City* (New Haven: Yale University Press, 2000); and Sonny Carson, interview by Claire Kim, Nov. 12, 1995, CRBC-OH. See Carson's autobiography, Abubadika, *The Education of Sonny Carson*.

28. Oliver and Marjorie Leeds interview by Taylor; for criticisms of

Carson, see John Derbyshire, "Burn in Hell, Sonny Carson," *National Review Online*, Dec. 27, 2002, www.nationalreview.com/corner/58297/burn-hell-sonny-carson/john-derbyshire#; "The Real Sonny Carson," *New York Post*, Dec. 26, 2002, 30; Edward S. Shapiro, *Crown Heights: Blacks, Jews, and the 1991 Brooklyn Riot* (Waltham, Mass.: Brandeis University Press, 2006), 16; Cannato, *The Ungovernable City*; Murphy, "From New York City to Memphis: Teacher Unions and Politics"; Jacoby, "Sonny Carson and the Politics of Protest"; Jacoby, *Someone Else's House*, 190–226. One reviewer of this book noted that Jacoby depicted Carson as a "psycho terrorist"; see Alan Wolfe, "Enough Blame to Go Around," *New York Times*, June 21, 1998. Carson was most famously quoted as saying that he was not anti-Semitic but was anti-white; see Carson interview, CRBC-OH; Carson interview with Kim, CRBC-OH; "Ex-Dinkins Worker Says He Used Campaign Money in Vote Effort," *New York Times*, Oct. 20, 1989, B2; "Ex-Dinkins Organizer Boasts He's 'Anti-White,'" *New York Post*, Dec. 21, 1989, 3. On Carson's activism in New York City, see "Limelight Shines Again on Sonny Carson," *New York Times*, July 6, 1987, 33, 35; "Anti-Crack Group Anniversary," *New York Amsterdam News*, Feb. 21, 1987, 5; "Drug Fighters Mark First Year Tomorrow," *New York Daily News*, February 19, 1987, K3.1; "Malcolm Legacy Is Remembered," *New York Amsterdam News*, May 28, 1988, 9. On the December 12 Movement see Kim, *Bitter Fruit*, 63–88, 120–38; "Pan-Africanism, African Liberation Convention at CCNY in Harlem," *New York Amsterdam News*, Dec. 14, 1991, 4; "Black Nationalist Group Holds Convention at City College," *New York Amsterdam News*, Dec. 21, 1991, 5; "Sonny Carson, 66, Figure in 60's Battle for Schools, Dies," *New York Times*, Dec. 23, 2002, B7; "Sonny Carson Dies: Legendary Black Nationalist Figure in Bedford-Stuyvesant," *Village Voice*, Dec. 31, 2002; Herb Boyd, "Warrior Passes On," *New York Amsterdam News*, Dec. 26, 2002, 1. On the New York City Council decision to reject the call to name street after Carson, see "Council Rejects Street Name for Black Activist," *New York Times*, May 31, 2007.

29. On the East, see Kwasi Konadu, *A View from the East: Black Cultural Nationalism and Education in New York City* (Syracuse, N.Y.: Syracuse University Press, 2009); see also the issues of *Black News* from 1969 to 1984 in CRBC, series IV, boxes 7–11. On the Bedford-Stuyvesant Restoration Corporation, see Kimberley Johnson, "Community Development Corporations, Participation, and Accountability: The Harlem Urban Development Corporation and the Bedford-Stuyvesant Restoration Corporation," *Annals of the American Academy of Political and Social Science*, 594.1 (2004): 109–24; on the Republic for a New Africa, see Robin Kelley, *Freedom Dreams: The Black Radical Imagination* (Boston: Beacon Press, 2002), 124–29.

30. On the longer view of civil rights activism in Brooklyn, see Biondi, *To Stand and Fight*; Freeman, *Working-Class New York*; Pritchett, *Browns-*

ville, Brooklyn; Taylor, *Civil Rights in New York City;* and Wilder, *A Covenant with Color.*

31. On the long black power movement see Woodard, *A Nation within a Nation;* Joseph, *Waiting 'til the Midnight Hour.*

32. Kelley, *Freedom Dreams.*

BIBLIOGRAPHY

Interviews

Akula, John. Apr. 25, 2005. Civil Rights in Brooklyn Oral History Collection, Brooklyn Collection, Brooklyn Public Library.

Banks, Gilbert. Oct. 22, 1980. New Yorkers at Work Oral History Collection, Wagner Labor Archives, Tamiment Library, New York University.

Banks, Gilbert. Apr. 1–2, 2000. Civil Rights in Brooklyn Oral History Collection, Brooklyn Collection, Brooklyn Public Library.

Bibuld, Douglass. May 31, 2004. Civil Rights in Brooklyn Oral History Collection, Brooklyn Collection, Brooklyn Public Library.

Bibuld, Elaine. Feb. 18, 2001. Civil Rights in Brooklyn Oral History Collection, Brooklyn Collection, Brooklyn Public Library.

Bibuld, Elaine. Interview by Shelia Michaels, May 23, 2000. Nonviolent Oral History Project, Special Collections, Columbia University.

Bibuld, Elaine, Mary Ellen Phifer Kirton, Rioghan Kirchner, Msemaji Weusi (Maurice Fredericks), and Nandi Weusi (Winnie Fredericks). Apr. 7, 2000. Civil Rights in Brooklyn Oral History Collection, Brooklyn Collection, Brooklyn Public Library.

Bibuld, Jerome. Jan. 2, 2003. Civil Rights in Brooklyn Oral History Collection, Brooklyn Collection, Brooklyn Public Library.

Brezenoff, Stanley. July 1, 2004. Civil Rights in Brooklyn Oral History Collection, Brooklyn Collection, Brooklyn Public Library.

Carson, Robert "Sonny." Nov. 13, 2000. Civil Rights in Brooklyn Oral History Collection, Brooklyn Collection, Brooklyn Public Library.

Carson, Robert "Sonny." Interview by Claire Jean Kim, Nov. 12, 1995. Civil Rights in Brooklyn Oral History Collection, Brooklyn Collection, Brooklyn Public Library.

Craig, Maxine Leeds. Jun. 20, 2004. Civil Rights in Brooklyn Oral History Collection, Brooklyn Collection, Brooklyn Public Library.

Crayton, Frances Phipps. Nov. 28, 2003. Civil Rights in Brooklyn Oral History Collection, Brooklyn Collection, Brooklyn Public Library.

Diamond, Edith Jefferson. July 20, 2004. Civil Rights in Brooklyn Oral History Collection, Brooklyn Collection, Brooklyn Public Library.

Flascher, Kurt. May 23, 2011. Civil Rights in Brooklyn Oral History Collection, Brooklyn Collection, Brooklyn Public Library.

Fredericks, Maurice (Msemaji Weusi). Interview by Clarence Taylor, May 9,

1990. Civil Rights in Brooklyn Oral History Collection, Brooklyn Collection, Brooklyn Public Library.

Fredericks, Maurice (Msemaji Weusi). Apr. 28, 1981. New Yorkers at Work Oral History Collection, Wagner Labor Archives, Tamiment Library, New York University.

Goldwag, Arnold. Oct. 13, 2000. Civil Rights in Brooklyn Oral History Collection, Brooklyn Collection, Brooklyn Public Library.

Goldwag, Arnold. Interview by Shelia Michaels, Apr. 23, 1999; May 5, 1999; Mar. 9, 2001. Nonviolent Oral History Project, Special Collections, Columbia University.

Gregory, Dick. *Playboy,* Aug. 1964, 39–48.

Heinegg, Paul, and Rita Heinegg. Jan. 5, 2004. Civil Rights in Brooklyn Oral History Collection, Brooklyn Collection, Brooklyn Public Library.

Ipiotis, Shelly Spector. E-mail to the author, Mar. 24, 2005. Civil Rights in Brooklyn Oral History Collection, Brooklyn Collection, Brooklyn Public Library.

Kirchner, Rioghan. Sept. 29, 2000; Oct. 21, 2000; telephone conversation, Aug. 2005. Civil Rights in Brooklyn Oral History Collection, Brooklyn Collection, Brooklyn Public Library.

Kirton, Mary Ellen Phifer. Feb. 23, 2003. Civil Rights in Brooklyn Oral History Collection, Brooklyn Collection, Brooklyn Public Library.

Law, Robert. Apr. 14, 2004; Mar. 29, 2005. Civil Rights in Brooklyn Oral History Collection, Brooklyn Collection, Brooklyn Public Library.

Leeds, Oliver. Interview by August Meier, Apr. 28, 1971. August Meier Papers, Schomburg Center for Research in Black Culture, New York Public Library.

Leeds, Oliver. Aug. 9, 1983. New Yorkers at Work Oral History Collection, Wagner Labor Archives, Tamiment Library, New York University.

Leeds, Oliver. Interview by Dianne Esses, Dec. 15, 1988. Civil Rights in Brooklyn Oral History Collection, Brooklyn Collection, Brooklyn Public Library.

Leeds, Oliver, and Marjorie Leeds. Interview by Clarence Taylor, Aug. 11, 1988. Civil Rights in Brooklyn Oral History Collection, Brooklyn Collection, Brooklyn Public Library.

Lewinson, Edwin. Nov. 20, 2003. Civil Rights in Brooklyn Oral History Collection, Brooklyn Collection, Brooklyn Public Library.

Miller, Ed. E-mail to the author, Mar. 3, 2001. Civil Rights in Brooklyn Oral History Collection, Brooklyn Collection, Brooklyn Public Library.

Owens, Major. Dec. 12, 2003. Civil Rights in Brooklyn Oral History Collection, Brooklyn Collection, Brooklyn Public Library.

Rich, Marvin. Mar. 22, 2005. Civil Rights in Brooklyn Oral History Collection, Brooklyn Collection, Brooklyn Public Library.

Salvatore, Nick. Jan. 6, 2003. Civil Rights in Brooklyn Oral History Collection, Brooklyn Collection, Brooklyn Public Library.

Stein, Eleanor. Mar. 23, 2005. Civil Rights in Brooklyn Oral History Collection, Brooklyn Collection, Brooklyn Public Library.

Weusi, Jitu (Leslie Campbell). Mar. 21, 2000. Civil Rights in Brooklyn Oral History Collection, Brooklyn Collection, Brooklyn Public Library.

Weusi, Msemaji (Maurice Fredericks), and Nandi Weusi (Winnie Fredericks). Mar. 9, 2001. Civil Rights in Brooklyn Oral History Collection, Brooklyn Collection, Brooklyn Public Library.

Young, Jacqueline. Dec. 3, 2003. Civil Rights in Brooklyn Oral History Collection, Brooklyn Collection, Brooklyn Public Library.

Young, Vincent. Aug. 4, 1983. Oral History of the American Left, Wagner Labor Archives, Tamiment Library, New York University.

Articles, Books, Dissertations, Manuscript Collections

Abubadika, Mwlina Imiri. *The Education of Sonny Carson.* New York: Norton, 1972.

Abu-Lughod, Janet L. *Race, Space, and Riots in Chicago, New York, and Los Angeles.* New York: Oxford University Press, 2007.

Arnesen, Eric. "Reconsidering the 'Long Civil Rights Movement.'" *Historically Speaking* 10.2 (2009): 31–34.

Arnie Goldwag Brooklyn Congress of Racial Equality (CORE) Collection, ARC.002, Brooklyn Historical Society.

Arsenault, Raymond. *Freedom Riders: 1961 and the Struggle for Racial Justice.* Oxford: Oxford University Press, 2006.

Back, Adina. "Blacks, Jews and the Struggle to Integrate Brooklyn's Junior High School 258: A Cold War Story." *Journal of American Ethnic History* 20.2 (Winter 2001): 38–69.

———. "Up South in New York: The 1950s School Desegregation Struggles." Ph.D. diss., New York University, 1997.

Banks, Nancy. "'The Last Bastion of Discrimination': The New York City Building Trades and the Struggle over Affirmative Action, 1961–1976." Ph.D. diss., Columbia University, 2006.

Behnken, Brian. *Fighting Their Own Battles: Mexican Americans, African Americans, and the Struggle for Civil Rights in Texas.* Chapel Hill: University of North Carolina Press, 2010.

———. *The Struggle in Black and Brown: African American and Mexican American Relations during the Civil Rights Era.* Lincoln: University of Nebraska Press, 2011.

Biondi, Martha. *The Black Revolution on Campus.* Berkeley: University of California Press, 2012.

———. *To Stand and Fight: The Struggle for Civil Rights in Postwar New York City.* Cambridge: Harvard University Press, 2003.

Bouza, Anthony V. *Police Intelligence: The Operations of an Investigative Unit.* New York: AMS Press, 1976.

Boym, Svetlana. *The Future of Nostalgia.* New York: Basic Books, 2001.

Brown, Monica. *Gang Nation: Delinquent Citizens in Puerto Rican, Chi-*

cano, and Chicana Narratives. Minneapolis: University of Minnesota Press, 2002.

Brown-Nagin, Tomiko. Courage to Dissent: Atlanta and the Long History of the Civil Rights Movement. New York: Oxford University Press, 2011.

Cannato, Vincent J. The Ungovernable City: John Lindsay and His Struggle to Save New York. New York: Basic Books, 2001.

Capeci, Dominic J., Jr. The Harlem Riot of 1943. Philadelphia: Temple University Press, 1977.

Caro, Robert A. The Power Broker: Robert Moses and the Fall of New York. New York: Knopf, 1974.

Carson, Clayborne. In Struggle: SNCC and the Black Awakening of the 1960s. Cambridge: Harvard University Press, 1981.

Carson, Clayborne, et al., eds. The Eyes on the Prize: Civil Rights Reader: Documents, Speeches, and Firsthand Accounts from the Black Freedom Struggle, 1954–1990. New York: Viking, 1991.

Catsam, Derek. Freedom's Main Line: The Journey of Reconciliation and the Freedom Rides. Lexington: University Press of Kentucky, 2009.

Chafe, William Henry. Civilities and Civil Rights: Greensboro, North Carolina, and the Black Struggle for Freedom. New York: Oxford University Press, 1980.

———. The Unfinished Journey: America since World War II. New York: Oxford University Press, 1995.

Cha-Jua, Sundiata, and Clarence Lang. "The 'Long Movement' as Vampire: Temporal and Spatial Fallacies in Recent Black Freedom Studies." Journal of African American History 92.2 (2007): 265–88.

Charron, Katherine Mellen. Freedom's Teacher: The Life of Septima Clark. Chapel Hill: University of North Carolina Press, 2009.

"Civil Rights Battle: Northern Style." Ebony, Mar. 1963, 96–102.

Civil Rights in Brooklyn Collection, Brooklyn Collection, Brooklyn Public Library, Central Branch.

Clayson, William S. Freedom Is Not Enough: The War on Poverty and the Civil Rights Movement in Texas. Austin: University of Texas Press, 2010.

Community Council of Greater New York. Brooklyn Communities: Population Characteristics and Neighborhood Social Resources. 2 vols. New York: Bureau of Community Statistical Services, Research Department, 1959.

Congress of Racial Equality. The Papers of the Congress of Racial Equality, 1941–1967. Sanford, N.C.: Microfilming Corp. of America, 1980.

Congress of Racial Equality (CORE), Brooklyn Chapter (N.Y.) Records. 1959–1978. Mss. 947, State Historical Society of Wisconsin, Archives Division.

Connolly, Harold X. A Ghetto Grows in Brooklyn. New York: New York University Press, 1977.

Countryman, Matthew. *Up South: Civil Rights and Black Power in Philadelphia*. Philadelphia: University of Pennsylvania Press, 2006.

Crosby, Emilye. *A Little Taste of Freedom: The Black Freedom Struggle in Claiborne County, Mississippi*. Chapel Hill: University of North Carolina Press, 2005.

———, ed. *Civil Rights History from the Ground Up: Local Struggles, a National Movement*. Athens: University of Georgia Press, 2011.

Dawkins, Wayne. *City Son: Andrew W. Cooper's Impact on Modern-Day Brooklyn*. Jackson: University Press of Mississippi, 2012.

Della Femina, Jerry, and Charles Sopkin. *An Italian Grows in Brooklyn*. Boston: Little, Brown, 1978.

Department of Sanitation, City of New York. *Annual Reports*. Municipal Archives, City Hall Library, New York.

Dillard, Angela D. *Faith in the City: Preaching Radical Social Change in Detroit*. Ann Arbor: University of Michigan Press, 2007.

Dittmer, John. *Local People: The Struggle for Civil Rights in Mississippi*. Urbana: University of Illinois Press, 1994.

Dougherty, Jack. *More Than One Struggle: The Evolution of Black School Reform in Milwaukee*. Chapel Hill: University of North Carolina Press, 2004.

Douglas, Davison M. *Jim Crow Moves North: The Battle over Northern School Segregation, 1865–1954*. New York: Cambridge University Press, 2005.

Drake, St. Clair, and Horace Cayton. *Black Metropolis: A Study of Negro Life in a Northern City*. Rev. ed. Chicago: University of Chicago Press, 1993.

Dudziak, Mary. *Cold War Civil Rights: Race and the Image of American Democracy*. Princeton: Princeton University Press, 2000.

Eagles, Charles W. "Toward New Histories of the Civil Rights Era." *Journal of Southern History* 66.4 (2000): 815–48.

Eisenstadt, Peter. *Rochdale Village: Robert Moses, 6,000 Families, and New York's Great Experiment in Integrated Housing*. Ithaca: Cornell University Press, 2010.

Eliot, Marc. *Song of Brooklyn: An Oral History of America's Favorite Borough*. New York: Broadway Books, 2008.

English, T. J. *The Savage City: Race, Murder, and a Generation on the Edge*. New York: William Morrow, 2011.

Feagin, Joe R., and Paul B. Sheatsley. "Ghetto Resident Appraisals of a Riot." *Public Opinion Quarterly* 32.3 (1968): 352–62.

Fitzpatrick, Joseph P. *Puerto Rican Americans: The Meaning of Migration to the Mainland*. Englewood Cliffs, N.J.: Prentice-Hall, 1971.

———. *The Stranger Is Our Own: Reflections on the Journey of Puerto Rican Migrants*. Kansas City, Mo.: Sheed and Ward, 1996.

Franklin, John Hope. *Mirror to America: The Autobiography of John Hope Franklin*. New York: Farrar, Straus and Giroux, 2005.

Freeman, Joshua B. *Working-Class New York: Life and Labor since World War II*. New York: New Press, 2000.

Frommer, Myrna Katz, and Harvey Frommer. *It Happened in Brooklyn: An Oral History of Growing Up in the Borough in the 1940s, 1950s, and 1960s*. New York: Harcourt Brace, 1993.

Fujino, Diane C. *Heartbeat of Struggle: The Revolutionary Life of Yuri Kochiyama*. Minneapolis: University of Minnesota Press, 2005.

Gallagher, Julie A. "Waging 'The Good Fight': The Political Life of Shirley Chisholm, 1953–1982." *Journal of African American History* 92 (Summer 2007): 393–416.

Gates Avenue Association (Brooklyn, N.Y.). Meeting Minutes, 1922–1944. MS 1977. 1777 S-36, Brooklyn Historical Society.

Gerson, Jeffrey Nathan. "Building the Brooklyn Machine: Irish, Jewish, and Black Political Succession in Central Brooklyn, 1919–1964." Ph.D. diss., City University of New York, 1990.

Gilmore, Glenda Elizabeth. *Defying Dixie: The Radical Roots of Civil Rights, 1919–1950*. New York: Norton, 2008.

Glazer, Nathan, and Daniel P. Moynihan. *Beyond the Melting Pot: The Negroes, Puerto Ricans, Jews, Italians, and Irish of New York City*. Cambridge: MIT Press, 1963.

Goldberg, David, and Trevor Griffey. *Black Power at Work: Community Control, Affirmative Action, and the Construction Industry*. Ithaca: Cornell University Press, 2010.

Golenbock, Peter. *In the Country of Brooklyn: Inspiration to the World*. New York: HarperCollins, 2008.

Gordon, Jane Anna. *Why They Couldn't Wait: A Critique of the Black-Jewish Conflict over Community Control in Ocean Hill–Brownsville, 1967–1971*. New York: RoutledgeFalmer, 2001.

Gore, Dayo F., Jeanne Theoharis, and Komozi Woodard, eds. *Want to Start a Revolution? Radical Women in the Black Freedom Struggle*. New York: New York University Press, 2009.

Gottehrer, Barry, ed. *New York City in Crisis: A Study in Depth of Urban Sickness*. New York: D. McKay, 1965.

Greenberg, Cheryl Lynn. *"Or Does It Explode?" Black Harlem in the Great Depression*. New York: Oxford University Press, 1991.

———. *Troubling the Waters: Black-Jewish Relations in the American Century*. Princeton: Princeton University Press, 2006.

Hall, Jacquelyn Dowd. "The Long Civil Rights Movement and the Political Uses of the Past." *Journal of American History* 91.4 (2005): 1233–63.

Hirsch, Arnold. *Making the Second Ghetto: Race and Housing in Chicago, 1940–1960*. Cambridge: Cambridge University Press, 1983.

Horne, Gerald. *Communist Front? The Civil Rights Congress, 1946–1956*. Rutherford, N.J.: Fairleigh Dickinson University Press, 1988.

Jacoby, Tamar. *Someone Else's House: America's Unfinished Struggle for Integration*. New York: Free Press, 1998.

———. "Sonny Carson and the Politics of Protest." *City Journal* (Summer 1991), www.city-journal.org/html/issue1_4.html.

Jeffries, Hasan Kwame. *Bloody Lowndes: Civil Rights and Black Power in Alabama's Black Belt.* New York: New York University Press, 2009.

Johnson, Kimberley. "Community Development Corporations, Participation, and Accountability: The Harlem Urban Development Corporation and the Bedford-Stuyvesant Restoration Corporation." *Annals of the American Academy of Political and Social Science* 594.1 (2004): 109–24.

Johnson, Marilynn. *Street Justice: A History of Police Violence in New York City.* Boston: Beacon Press, 2003.

Jones, Patrick D. *The Selma of the North: Civil Rights Insurgency in Milwaukee.* Cambridge: Harvard University Press, 2009.

Joseph, Peniel. "The Black Power Movement: A State of the Field." *Journal of American History* 96.3 (December 2009): 751–76.

———. *The Black Power Movement: Rethinking the Civil Rights–Black Power Era.* New York: Routledge, 2006.

———. *Neighborhood Rebels: Black Power at the Local Level.* New York: Palgrave Macmillan, 2010.

———. *Waiting 'til the Midnight Hour: A Narrative History of Black Power in America.* New York: Henry Holt, 2006.

Kahlenberg, Richard. "Wrong on Race: Why Barack Obama Shouldn't Listen to Tom Sugrue." *Democracy: A Journal of Ideas* 12 (Spring 2009): 99–107.

Katz, Michael B., ed. *The "Underclass" Debate: Views from History.* Princeton: Princeton University Press, 1993.

Kelley, Robin D. G. *Freedom Dreams: The Black Radical Imagination.* Boston: Beacon Press, 2002.

Kim, Claire Jean. *Bitter Fruit: The Politics of Black-Korean Conflict in New York City.* New Haven: Yale University Press, 2000.

Kirchner, Rioghan. "Why Not Next Door?" CRBC, box 5.

Konadu, Kwasi. *A View from the East: Black Cultural Nationalism and Education in New York City.* Syracuse, N.Y.: Syracuse University Press, 2009.

Kornbluh, Felicia Ann. *The Battle for Welfare Rights: Politics and Poverty in Modern America.* Philadelphia: University of Pennsylvania Press, 2007.

Korstad, Robert, and Nelson Lichtenstein. "Opportunities Found and Lost: Labor, Radicals, and the Early Civil Rights Movement." *Journal of American History* 75.3 (1988): 786–811.

Kurashige, Scott. *The Shifting Grounds of Race: Black and Japanese Americans in the Making of Multiethnic Los Angeles.* Princeton: Princeton University Press, 2008.

Lang, Clarence. *Grassroots at the Gateway: Class Politics and Black Freedom Struggle in St. Louis, 1936–75.* Ann Arbor: University of Michigan Press, 2009.

Lassiter, Matthew, and Joseph Crespino, eds. *The Myth of Southern Exceptionalism*. New York: Oxford University Press, 2010.

Lawson, Ronald, ed. *The Tenant Movement in New York City, 1904–1984*. New Brunswick, N.J.: Rutgers University Press, 1986.

Lawson, Steven F. "Freedom Then, Freedom Now: The Historiography of the Civil Rights Movement." *American Historical Review* 96.2 (1991): 456–71.

Lawson, Steven F., and Charles M. Payne. *Debating the Civil Rights Movement, 1945–1968*. 2nd ed. Lanham, Md.: Rowman and Littlefield, 2006.

Lee, Chana Kai. *For Freedom's Sake: The Life of Fannie Lou Hamer*. Urbana: University of Illinois Press, 1999.

Lee, Sonia S. "Between Boricua and Black: How the Civil Rights Struggle Shaped Puerto Rican Racial and Ethnic Identities in New York City, 1950s–70s." Ph.D. diss., Harvard University, 2007.

Lee, Sonia S., and Ande Diaz. "'I Was the One Percenter': Manny Diaz and the Beginnings of a Black–Puerto Rican Coalition." *Journal of American Ethnic History* 26 (Spring 2007): 52–80.

Lewis, Heather. "Protest, Place, and Pedagogy: New York City's Community Control Movement and Its Aftermath." Ph.D. diss., New York University, 2006.

Lewis, Oscar. *La Vida: A Puerto Rican Family in the Culture of Poverty—San Juan and New York*. New York: Random House, 1966.

Linge, Mary Kay. *Jackie Robinson: A Biography*. Westport, Conn.: Greenwood Press, 2007.

Lipsitz, George. *A Life in the Struggle: Ivory Perry and the Culture of Opposition*. Philadelphia: Temple University Press, 1988.

MacLean, Nancy. *Freedom Is Not Enough: The Opening of the American Work Place*. New York: Russell Sage, 2006.

Maclellan, Nic, and Jean Chesneaux. *After Moruroa: France in the South Pacific*. Melbourne: Ocean Press, 1998.

Marshall, F. Ray. *The Negro and Organized Labor*. New York: Wiley, 1965.

Marshall, F. Ray, and Vernon M. Briggs. *The Negro and Apprenticeship*. Baltimore: Johns Hopkins Press, 1967.

McGuire, Danielle L., and John Dittmer, eds. *Freedom Rights: New Perspectives on the Civil Rights Movement*. Lexington: University Press of Kentucky, 2012.

Meier, August, and Elliott Rudwick. *CORE: A Study in the Civil Rights Movement, 1942–1968*. New York: Oxford University Press, 1973.

Meyer, Stephen Grant. *As Long as They Don't Move Next Door: Segregation and Racial Conflict in American Neighborhoods*. Lanham, Md.: Rowman and Littlefield, 2000.

Moreno, Paul D. *From Direct Action to Affirmative Action: Fair Employment Law and Policy in America, 1933–1972*. Baton Rouge: Louisiana State University Press, 1997.

Morris, Aldon D. *The Origins of the Civil Rights Movement: Black Communities Organizing for Change.* New York: Free Press, 1984.

Morris, Charles R. *The Cost of Good Intentions: New York City and the Liberal Experiment, 1960–1975.* New York: Norton, 1980.

Murch, Donna Jean. *Living for the City: Migration, Education, and the Rise of the Black Panther Party in Oakland, California.* Chapel Hill: University of North Carolina Press, 2010.

Murphy, Marjorie. *Blackboard Unions: The AFT and the NEA, 1900–1980.* Ithaca: Cornell University Press, 1992.

Naison, Mark. *Communists in Harlem during the Depression.* Urbana: University of Illinois Press, 1983.

———. *White Boy: A Memoir.* Philadelphia: Temple University Press, 2002.

New York City Commission on Human Rights. "The City of New York Commission on Human Rights Historical Sketch." New York Municipal Archives, New York, Vertical File.

New York City Commission on Human Rights and New York City Office of Labor Services. *Public Hearing on the Construction Industry in New York City,* Mar. 12, 1990, and Apr. 24, 1990. New York: City Hall Library.

New York World's Fair 1964–1965 Corporation Records. Manuscripts and Archives Division. New York Public Library, Astor, Lenox and Tilden Foundations.

Oppenheimer, Martin. *The Sit-in Movement of 1960.* Brooklyn: Carlson, 1989.

Oppenheimer, Martin, and George Lakey. *A Manual for Direct Action.* Chicago: Quadrangle Books, 1965.

Orleck, Annelise. *Storming Caesars Palace: How Black Mothers Fought Their Own War on Poverty.* Boston: Beacon Press, 2005.

Osofsky, Gilbert. *Harlem: The Making of a Ghetto: Negro New York, 1890–1930.* New York: Harper and Row, 1966.

———. "Race Riot, 1900: A Study of Ethnic Violence." *Journal of Negro Education* 32.1 (Winter 1963): 16–24.

Payne, Charles M. *I've Got the Light of Freedom: The Organizing Tradition and the Mississippi Freedom Struggle.* 2nd ed. Berkeley: University of California Press, 2007.

Perlstein, Daniel H. *Justice, Justice: School Politics and the Eclipse of Liberalism.* New York: P. Lang, 2004.

Podair, Jerald E. *The Strike That Changed New York: Blacks, Whites, and the Ocean Hill–Brownsville Crisis.* New Haven: Yale University Press, 2002.

Podhoretz, Norman. "My Negro Problem—and Ours." *Commentary* 35 (Feb. 1963): 93–101.

Pritchett, Wendell E. *Brownsville, Brooklyn: Blacks, Jews, and the Changing Face of the Ghetto.* Chicago: University of Chicago Press, 2002.

Purnell, Brian. "Interview with John Hope Franklin." *Journal of African American History* 94.3 (2009): 407–21.

Ralph, James R. *Northern Protest: Martin Luther King, Jr., Chicago, and the Civil Rights Movement.* Cambridge: Harvard University Press, 1993.

Ransby, Barbara. *Ella Baker and the Black Freedom Movement: A Radical Democratic Vision.* Chapel Hill: University of North Carolina Press, 2003.

Ravitch, Diane. *The Great School Wars: A History of the New York City Public Schools.* New York: Basic Books, 1988.

Rieder, Jonathan. *Canarsie: The Jews and Italians of Brooklyn against Liberalism.* Cambridge: Harvard University Press, 1985.

Robbins, Michael W., and Wendy Palitz. *Brooklyn: A State of Mind, 125 Stories from America's Most Colorful City.* New York: Workman, 2001.

Robert Moses Papers. Manuscripts and Archives Division, New York Public Library, Astor, Lenox and, Tilden Foundations.

Roberts, Gene, and Hank Klibanoff. *The Race Beat: The Press, the Civil Rights Struggle, and the Awakening of a Nation.* New York: Knopf, 2006.

Roberts, Sam, ed. *America's Mayor: John V. Lindsay and the Reinvention of New York.* New York: Museum of the City of New York, 2010.

Robeson, Paul, Jr. "A Tribute to Vincent Young." *New York Amsterdam News,* Dec. 10, 1988, 15.

Rodriguez, Clara E. *Puerto Ricans: Born in the U.S.A.* Boston: Unwin Hyman, 1989.

Rogers, Ibram. *The Black Campus Movement: Black Students and the Racial Reconstruction of Higher Education, 1965–1972.* New York: Palgrave Macmillan, 2012.

Romano, Renee Christine, and Leigh Raiford, eds. *The Civil Rights Movement in American Memory.* Athens: University of Georgia Press, 2006.

Saltzman, Harold. *Race War in High School: The Ten-Year Destruction of Franklin K. Lane High School in Brooklyn.* New Rochelle, N.Y.: Arlington House, 1972.

Salzman, Jack, Adina Back, and Gretchen Sullivan Sorin, eds. *Bridges and Boundaries: African Americans and American Jews.* New York: George Braziller, 1992.

Samuel, Lawrence R. *The End of the Innocence: The 1964–1965 New York World's Fair.* Syracuse, N.Y.: Syracuse University Press, 2007.

Sánchez Korrol, Virginia. *From Colonia to Community: The History of Puerto Ricans in New York City.* 1983. Reprint, Berkeley: University of California Press, 1994.

Schrecker, Ellen. *Many Are the Crimes: McCarthyism in America.* Boston: Little, Brown, 1998.

Self, Robert O. *American Babylon: Race and the Struggle for Postwar Oakland.* Princeton: Princeton University Press, 2003.

———. "Matthew Countryman's *Up South* and Urban Political History." *Pennsylvania Magazine of History and Biography* 130.4 (2006): 393–98.

Sewell, Stacy Kinlock. "The 'Not-Buying Power' of the Black Community: Urban Boycotts and Equal Employment Opportunity, 1960–1964." *Journal of African American History* 89.2 (2004): 135–51.

Sexton, Andrea Wyatt, and Alice L. Powers, eds. *The Brooklyn Reader: Thirty Writers Celebrate America's Favorite Borough.* New York: Three Rivers Press, 1994.

Shapiro, Edward S. *Crown Heights: Blacks, Jews, and the 1991 Brooklyn Riot.* Waltham, Mass.: Brandeis University Press, 2006.

Siegel, Frederick F. *The Future Once Happened Here: New York, D.C., L.A., and the Fate of America's Big Cities.* New York: Free Press, 1997.

Singh, Nikhil Pal. *Black Is a Country: Race and the Unfinished Struggle for Democracy.* Cambridge: Harvard University Press, 2004.

Smethurst, James Edward. *The Black Arts Movement: Literary Nationalism in the 1960s and 1970s.* Chapel Hill: University of North Carolina Press, 2005.

Springer, Kimberly. *Living for the Revolution: Black Feminist Organizations, 1968–1980.* Durham: Duke University Press, 2005.

Sugrue, Thomas. "Affirmative Action from Below: Civil Rights, the Building Trades, and the Politics of Racial Equality in the Urban North, 1945–1969." *Journal of American History* 91 (2004): 145–73.

———. *The Origins of the Urban Crisis: Race and Inequality in Postwar Detroit.* Princeton: Princeton University Press, 1996.

———. *Sweet Land of Liberty: The Forgotten Struggle for Civil Rights in the North.* New York: Random House, 2008.

Swan, Quito. *Black Power in Bermuda: The Struggle for Decolonization.* New York: Palgrave Macmillan, 2009.

Taylor, Clarence. *The Black Churches of Brooklyn.* New York: Columbia University Press, 1994.

———. "Hurricane Katrina and the Myth of the Post–Civil Rights Era." *Journal of Urban History* 35.5 (2009): 640–55.

———. *Knocking at Our Own Door: Milton A. Galamison and the Struggle to Integrate New York City Schools.* Lanham, Md.: Lexington Books, 2001.

———. *Reds at the Blackboard: Communism, Civil Rights, and the New York City Teachers Union.* New York: Columbia University Press, 2011.

———. "'Whatever the Cost, We Will Set the Nation Straight': The Ministers' Committee and the Downstate Center Campaign." *Long Island Historical Journal* 1.2 (1989): 136–46.

———, ed. *Civil Rights in New York City: From World War II to the Giuliani Era.* New York: Fordham University Press, 2011.

Thabit, Walter. *How East New York Became a Ghetto.* New York: New York University Press, 2003.

Theoharis, Jeanne. "Black Freedom Studies: Re-imagining and Redefining the Fundamentals." *History Compass* 4 (2006): 1–20.

———. "From the Stone the Builders Rejected: Towards a New Civil Rights Historiography." *Left History* 12.1 (2007): 103–10.

Theoharis, Jeanne, and Komozi Woodard, eds. *Freedom North: Black Freedom Struggles outside the South, 1940–1980.* New York: Palgrave Macmillan, 2003.

———. *Groundwork: Local Black Freedom Movements in America.* New York: New York University Press, 2005.

Thomas, Lorrin. *Puerto Rican Citizen: History and Political Identity in Twentieth-Century New York City.* Chicago: University of Chicago Press, 2010.

Thomas Russell Jones Papers, Schomburg Center for Research in Black Culture, New York Public Library (at the time of publication this collection had not been arranged and described).

Thompson, Heather Ann. *Whose Detroit? Politics, Labor, and Race in a Modern American City.* Ithaca: Cornell University Press, 2001.

Trotter, Joe W. *Black Milwaukee: The Making of an Industrial Proletariat, 1915–45.* 2nd ed. Urbana: University of Illinois Press, 2007.

Turnbull, Craig. "'Please Make No Demonstrations Tomorrow': The Brooklyn Congress of Racial Equality and Symbolic Protest at the 1964–65 World's Fair." *Australasian Journal of American Studies* 17.1 (1998): 22–42.

Tyson, Timothy B. *Radio Free Dixie: Robert F. Williams and the Roots of Black Power.* Chapel Hill: University of North Carolina Press, 1999.

Waldinger, Roger. *Still the Promised City? African-Americans and New Immigrants in Postindustrial New York.* Cambridge: Harvard University Press, 1996.

Waldinger, Roger, and Thomas Bailey. "The Continuing Significance of Race: Racial Conflict and Racial Discrimination in Construction." *Politics and Society* 19.3 (1991): 291–323.

Weld, Ralph Foster. *Brooklyn Is America.* New York: Columbia University Press, 1950.

Whalen, Carmen Teresa, and Víctor Vázquez-Hernández, eds. *The Puerto Rican Diaspora: Historical Perspectives.* Philadelphia: Temple University Press, 2005.

Widener, Daniel. *Black Arts West: Culture and Struggle in Postwar Los Angeles.* Durham: Duke University Press, 2010.

Wilder, Craig Steven. *A Covenant with Color: Race and Social Power in Brooklyn.* New York: Columbia University Press, 2000.

Willensky, Elliot. *When Brooklyn Was the World, 1920–1957.* New York: Harmony Books, 1986.

Williams, Juan. *Eyes on the Prize: America's Civil Rights Years, 1954–1965.* New York: Viking Penguin, 1987.

Williams, Rhonda Y. *The Politics of Public Housing: Black Women's Struggles against Urban Inequality.* New York: Oxford University Press, 2004.

Williams, Yohuru. *Black Politics/White Power: Civil Rights, Black Power, and the Black Panthers in New Haven.* 2000. Reprint, Malden, Mass.: Blackwell, 2008.

Wilson, William Julius. *The Truly Disadvantaged: The Inner City, the Underclass, and Public Policy.* Chicago: University of Chicago Press, 1987.

Wolfinger, James. *Philadelphia Divided: Race and Politics in the City of Brotherly Love.* Chapel Hill: University of North Carolina Press, 2007.

Woodard, Komozi. *A Nation within a Nation: Amiri Baraka (LeRoi Jones) and Black Power Politics.* Chapel Hill: University of North Carolina Press, 1999.

X, Malcolm. *By Any Means Necessary: The Trials and Tribulations of the Making of Malcolm X.* 2nd ed. New York: Pathfinder, 1992.

———. *Malcolm X: The Last Speeches.* Edited by Bruce Perry. New York: Pathfinder, 1989.

Miscellaneous Sources

Elaine Bibuld personal papers. In author's possession (courtesy of Elaine Bibuld).

Gregory, Dick. *So You See . . . We All Have Problems.* New York: Colpix Records, 1964.

Murphy, Marjorie. "From New York City to Memphis." Lecture delivered at Swarthmore College, available at http://media.swarthmore.edu/faculty_lectures/?p=82.

Oliver and Marjorie Leeds personal papers. In author's possession (courtesy of Maxine Leeds Craig).

"Race Relations in Crisis." From television series, *The Open Mind.* Episode aired June 12, 1963. Transcript courtesy of Richard Heffner (in author's possession).

Rudolph, John. *New York in Black and White.* Radio documentary, WNYC, 2000. CD copy and transcript in author's possession.

Sokol, Jason. "Northeast Politics Once a Tangled Web for Black Candidates." Interview on National Public Radio, Feb. 25, 2010, www.npr.org/templates/story/story.php?storyId=124081751.

Sucher, Joel, and Stephen Fishler. *Red Squad.* Documentary film. New York: Pacific Street Films, 1972.

Vincent Young personal papers. In author's possession (courtesy Jacqueline Young).

INDEX

Civil Rights and the Struggle for
Black Equality in the Twentieth Century

Series Editors
Steven F. Lawson, Rutgers University
Cynthia Griggs Fleming, University of Tennessee

Freedom's Main Line: The Journey of Reconciliation and the Freedom Rides
Derek Charles Catsam

Subversive Southerner: Anne Braden and the Struggle for Racial Justice in the Cold War South
Catherine Fosl

Constructing Affirmative Action: The Struggle for Equal Employment Opportunity
David Hamilton Golland

River of Hope: Black Politics and the Memphis Freedom Movement, 1865–1954
Elizabeth Gritter

Sidelined: How American Sports Challenged the Black Freedom Struggle
Simon Henderson

Becoming King: Martin Luther King Jr. and the Making of a National Leader
Troy Jackson

Civil Rights in the Gateway to the South: Louisville, Kentucky, 1945–1980
Tracy E. K'Meyer

In Peace and Freedom: My Journey in Selma
Bernard LaFayette Jr. and Kathryn Lee Johnson

Democracy Rising: South Carolina and the Fight for Black Equality since 1865
Peter F. Lau

Civil Rights Crossroads: Nation, Community, and the Black Freedom Struggle
Steven F. Lawson

Selma to Saigon: The Civil Rights Movement and the Vietnam War
Daniel S. Lucks

In Remembrance of Emmett Till: Regional Stories and Media Responses to the Black Freedom Struggle
Darryl Mace

Freedom Rights: New Perspectives on the Civil Rights Movement
edited by Danielle L. McGuire and John Dittmer

This Little Light of Mine: The Life of Fannie Lou Hamer
Kay Mills

After the Dream: Black and White Southerners since 1965
Timothy J. Minchin and John A. Salmond

Fighting Jim Crow in the County of Kings: The Congress of Racial Equality in Brooklyn
Brian Purnell

Roy Wilkins: The Quiet Revolutionary and the NAACP
Yvonne Ryan

Thunder of Freedom: Black Leadership and the Transformation of 1960s Mississippi
Sue [Lorenzi] Sojourner with Cheryl Reitan

For a Voice and the Vote: My Journey with the Mississippi Freedom Democratic Party
Lisa Anderson Todd

Art for Equality: The NAACP's Cultural Campaign for Civil Rights
Jenny Woodley

For Jobs and Freedom: Race and Labor in America since 1865
Robert H. Zieger

20

CPSIA information can be obtained at www.ICGtesting.com
Printed in the USA
BVOW08s1639030515

398356BV00001B/1/P